Aberdeen FC

Who's Who

Every Red Ever

Aberdeen FC

Who's Who

Every Red Ever

Paul Smith

pitch

Pitch Publishing Ltd
A2 Yeoman Gate
Yeoman Way
Durrington
BN13 3QZ

Email: info@pitchpublishing.co.uk
Web: www.pitchpublishing.co.uk

Published by Pitch Publishing 2012

A CIP catalogue record for this book is available from the British Library.

13-digit ISBN: 978-190805-111-0

Cover design by Bill Swallow.

Images by Eric McCowat, SNS and Dod Dow.

Typesetting and origination by Pitch Publishing.

Printed in Malta.
Manufacturing managed by Jellyfish Solutions.

INTRODUCTION

Reasons to be cheerful are not always plentiful in the world of football, a world in which the game itself has at times appeared to play second fiddle to finance and administrative detail.

But pull up a seat, sit back and take the time to concentrate on what's important and suddenly the gloom lifts and the sunny outlook returns.

It is footballers, not accountants, who made the beautiful game and that applies whether it is the samba kings of Brazil you follow or the Dandy Dons.

The Pittodrie faithful have been more fortunate than most, having been treated to starring shows from some of the most celebrated and talented individuals ever to grace the Scottish stage.

The pages which follow join that celebration, paying tribute to the legends who have treated generations of supporters to glorious moments of triumph. From the heroes of the early days to the championship winners of the 1950s and European kings of the 80s, every era is covered.

But this is a book about far more than simply marking the achievements of the chosen few to have scaled the highest heights.

It is a project that pieces together every piece of the club's rich history, right through to those who played the smallest cameo role in Aberdeen colours.

Every man who has ever pulled on his boots and run out to play for the Dons has made a contribution to the cause, whether over the course of 15 minutes or 15 years.

There's everything from the weird to the wonderful, charting momentous highs alongside intriguing pieces of trivia sure to make fans of every age raise an eyebrow.

At the time of writing Scottish football was in a state of flux, in a period of transition that posed many questions. The answers will become clear in the years ahead, but through it all Aberdeen Football Club remained rock solid and striving to play a central role.

The Dons themselves face changing times, with the prospect of the curtain falling on football at Pittodrie and a new dawn at a new home. The prospect of that new chapter naturally leads to pining for the past.

Aberdeen Who's Who is about indulging in that nostalgia for the many wonderful characters who have thrilled generations – and looking forward to a bright new period with the current crop of young stars.

ACKNOWLEDGEMENTS

A project of this scale is impossible to tackle single handed and owes much to many people I have never even had the pleasure of meeting – the many men who have worn the Aberdeen shirt with distinction for more than a century and, just as importantly, the army of journalists and historians who recorded their contributions and preserved their legacy in print. Without their efforts, the wonderful stories of the past simply could not be brought to a modern audience. On a personal level, my thanks go to Paul and Jane at Pitch Publishing for their support and to Graham Hales for his tenacious efforts in piecing the design jigsaw together. Eric McCowat played a huge role in sourcing the bulk of the images used so well in the pages that follow while Dod Dow's artistic contribution is also hugely appreciated. Colin Macleod, with his eagle eye, was a great ally once again at the proof reading stage while Team Smith – Coral, Finlay, Mia and Zara – with their love and laughs made the work feel like a breeze.

DEDICATION

To Coral, Finlay, Mia and Zara

Derek Adams

Debut: League, 7 August 2004 v Rangers (h) drew 0-0
Appearances: League 19, Scottish Cup 2, League Cup 2
Goals: League 4, League Cup 1
Also played for: Burnley, Ross County, Motherwell, Livingston
Managed: Ross County

Derek Adams holds the dubious distinction of never kicking a ball in anger for the manager who recruited him for the Pittodrie cause. It was Steve Paterson who signed the Aberdonian from Motherwell in May 2004 but within weeks of clinching that close-season deal he had been dismissed from his post and replaced by Jimmy Calderwood. Adams, who had been born in the city due to his father George's own playing career taking him to the north-east to play for the Dons in the late 1960s, proved to be a reliable performer in midfield and attack for the new boss in the 2004/05 season but was allowed to move on to join Livingston at the end of that single campaign in the red shirt of his home town.

He had arrived in Aberdeen having been released by the club as a youngster. He went on to play for Burnley and Ross County before winding up at Motherwell in 1998 to begin a six year association which saw him take on the captaincy at Fir Park. He spent a season with Livingston after leaving Aberdeen for a second time before signing as a player with Ross County and rising to become manager of the Dingwall side, leading his men to the Scottish Cup final in 2010 and suffering the pain of Hampden defeat against Dundee United. Months after the cup run he was tempted south to become Colin Calderwood's assistant at Hibs, but returned to take the helm once again at the Highland club and lead them to the SPL in 2012.

George Adams

Debut: League Cup, 24 September 1969 v Celtic (a) lost 2-1
Appearances: League 1, League Cup 1
Also played for: Partick Thistle, East Stirling, Buckie Thistle

George Adams is renowned as one of Scottish footall's foremost talent spotters and youth gurus. He has served both halves of the Old Firm in that role as well as working as director of football at Motherwell and, most recently, with Ross County.

However, playing was Adams' first love and it was Aberdeen who gave him his big break when he was signed from junior side Petershill in 1969 as a teenager. He made only a handful of appearances before a knee injury forced his retirement. Adams, a tall and direct forward, made a comeback with Partick Thistle and also turned out for Alex Ferguson's East Stirlingshire before moving back to the north-east to play for Buckie Thistle. In 1980 he was handed his first managerial role by Fraserburgh. Two years later he was reunited with Ferguson when he joined the Aberdeen staff as a youth coach.

He combined his role with his television repair business in the city and returned to the Highland League with Keith in 1990, departing in the same year to take the helm at Peterhead for a two year stint.

Adams was appointed by Celtic in 1994 to lead the club's north-east scouting and coaching network and that led to his high profile roles heading up the youth development departments for both the Hoops and Rangers prior to his service with Motherwell, where son Derek was on the playing staff. The father and son team were reunited at Ross County, with George as director of football and Derek as manager for the run to the Scottish Cup final in 2010 and beyond.

Dave Aitken

Debut: League, 31 October 1953 v Clyde (a) won 4-2
Appearances: League 2
Also played for: Arbroath, Huntly

Left back Dave Aitken joined as a full-time player from Banks o' Dee juniors in 1950. The energetic and wholehearted defender struggled to win a first team place despite captaining the reserves and moved on to Arbroath in 1954. He retired to concentrate on business commitments in the bakery trade before making a comeback with Highland League side Huntly in 1956.

Roy Aitken

Debut: League, 1 August 1992 v Hibs (h) won 3-0
Appearances: League 29, Scottish Cup 4, League Cup 5, Europe 1
Goals: League 2
Also played for: Celtic, Newcastle United, St Mirren
Managed: Aberdeen

With a combined haul of 122 Scotland caps between them, the management pairing of Willie Miller and his new assistant Roy Aitken looked to be a dream team when it was finalised in time for the 1992/93 season. The Ayrshire-born veteran, with 57 of those international appearances to his credit, was hired as much for his influence off the pitch as his contribution on the park – but still went on to make more than 39 appearances in Dons colours.

The former Celtic and Scotland captain, who won six league titles with the Hoops in the 1970s and 80s as well as the Scottish Cup five times and the League Cup, arrived at Pittodrie after a stint with St Mirren. His career had taken him through the youth ranks at Parkhead and led to 15 glittering years in the first team before he was tempted to try English football with Newcastle United in 1990.

He was approaching his 34th birthday when he checked in with Aberdeen in 1992 but was fit enough to provide a steadying influence at the heart of the team for Miller's first season in charge.

He was given the chance to succeed Miller as manager in 1995 and led his team to League Cup success against Dundee in the Hampden final in his first year in charge, Aberdeen's last major honour. Silverware was not enough to prevent Aitken from being dismissed in 1997 but he bounced back with key coaching roles with Scotland, Aston Villa, Birmingham City and then Al Ahli in Dubai. He served as David O'Leary's assistant with Al Ahli until the pair's dismissal in May 2011.

John Allan

Debut: League, 24 December 1955 v Airdrie (h) won 7-2
Appearances: League 21, Scottish Cup 1
Goals: League 15
Also played for: Dunfermline, Bradford City, Halifax Town, Brechin City, Fraserburgh, Peterhead

An impressive scoring ratio was not enough to protect John Allan's long term future at Pittodrie. Signed from Dunfermline by David Halliday in 1953, the forward was promoted to the first team in 1955/56 and scored 11 league goals in just 17 outings – including a hat-trick against Falkirk and four against Stirling Albion. Just months into the following term he was transferred to Third Lanark and commuted from his home on Aberdeen's King Street to Glasgow to turn out for the west coast side for three years before joining Bradford City. Allan also represented Halifax Town south of the border but returned to Scottish football with Brechin City in 1962, then to the Highland League with Fraserburgh the following year and also with Peterhead.

Willie Allan

Debut: League, 28 October 1961 v Motherwell (h) won 3-0
Appearances: League 35, Scottish Cup 3, League Cup 4
Goals: League 1
Also played for: St Mirren, Falkirk, Morton, Alloa, Cowdenbeath

Inside forward Willie Allan was a fixture in Tommy Pearson's side in the 1962/63 season. He made more than 30 appearances and strong early form put Aberdeen in title contention before dropping out of the race. Allan had been recruited from junior outfit Bo'ness in 1961 as an 18-year-old and spent almost three years in the top team squad before joining St Mirren as part of the swap deal which took Don Kerrigan north. A stint with Falkirk and then working in South Africa followed before he joined Morton in 1967. Alloa and Cowdenbeath were the other playing credits on Allan's cv before his retirement in the early 1970s.

Sone Aluko

Debut: Uefa Cup, 27 October 2007 v Panathanaikos (a) lost 3-0
Appearances: League 92, Scottish CPanathinaikosCup 4, Europe 6
Goals: League 10, Scottish Cup 2, Europe 1
Also played for: Nigeria, Birmingham City, Blackpool (on loan))

When on-loan Birmingham City teenager Sone Aluko stepped onto the Pittodrie turf it appeared a new hero had been born. With electrifying pace, dazzling ball control and a killer instinct that drew him towards goal there was at last a player to behold who could draw supporters to their feet.

The Birmingham-born starlet was just 18 when he was brought north by Jimmy Calderwood and displayed the type of fearlessness that only youth can bring with his daring displays on the wing and as a central striker.

He spent the whole of the 2007/08 season at Pittodrie and, while the form of his early matches could not be maintained week in and week out, became and important part of Calderwood's attacking game plan when fit and available.

Aluko, who had made a single appearance for Birmingham as a substitute in the Carling Cup before being farmed out to the Dons, returned to his club in the summer of 2008.

Opportunities at Birmingham continued to be limited and he and was sent out on loan to Blackpool briefly at the start of the new season before the Dons returned with a bid which made him an Aberdeen player on a permanent contract.

Capped by Nigeria in May 2009 after switching allegiance from England, the young player rejected the opportunity to remain a Red and opted to join Rangers in the 2011/12 season. He moved to Hull City the following term.

Jack Allister

Debut: League, 11 October 1952 v Third Lanark (h) won 4-3
Appearances: League 117, Scottish Cup 21, League Cup 25
Goals: League 18, Scottish Cup 4, League Cup 2
Also played for: Chelsea, Chesterfield, Elgin City, Deveronvale

Jack Allister, a key player from the legendary class of 55 in this collection of greats, died in 1999 but his part in the club's first ever title success will survive for as long as football records are preserved.

He and his team-mates earned legendary status as part of Dave Halliday's dominant Dons team and demonstrated their manager's talent for piecing together a winning side.

Allister was recruited by Halliday in 1952 for the not inconsequential fee of £6,000 having taken his first steps in football with Chelsea. He had made just four appearances for the Stamford Bridge side, having moved south from Tranent Juniors in 1949, but Halliday was convinced he was the man to make the No.6 shirt his own and thrust the new half-back straight into his side following his arrival six games into the 1952/53 campaign.

His relationship with the Pittodrie fans was not always smooth, with his strong tackling and competitive spirit failing to win over some sections of the crowd.

That all changed within two seasons of his arrival when he formed the formidable half-back line of Allister, Young and Glen as Aberdeen marched triumphantly to the 1955 championship.

Allister played in 21 of the 30 league games that term, weighing in with four goals in the top division, as the Dons beat Celtic by three points to lift the prize.

Not surprisingly it proved to be the highlight of Allister's career, although he came close to adding to his collection of honours in two major finals prior to that.

The first was the Scottish Cup final of 1953, when Rangers were taken to a replay before the Ibrox men ran out 1-0 winners.

The second came the following year in the same competition when the Dons were beaten 2-1 by Celtic in the Hampden showdown. Allister had been among the goalscorers when Rangers were dumped 6-0 in the semi-final.

In 1955 he came within an ace of earning full Scotland recognition, turning out for the B team but just failing to win promotion to the senior side.

Having requested a transfer the same year, Allister changed his mind and opted to stay.

Two years later, at the end of the 1957/58 season in which he made just 11 appearances, he again looked for an escape route and found it in the form of a switch to Chesterfield.

Allister tried Canadian football briefly in 1958 after failing to settle back in England but returned to the north-east of Scotland just months later to join Elgin City.

He went on to add Deveronvale to his Highland League credits as he combined his playing commitments with a career as a plumber in Aberdeen.

In 1961 he moved into coaching, appointed trainer at Stirling Albion, but it was after emigrating to Australia he found the opportunity to get his teeth into that role.

TEN: Players who slipped through the net

1 Shaun Maloney: A product of the Albion Boys Club in Bridge of Don, former Cults Academy pupil Shaun Maloney was recruited by Celtic as a teenager and went on to become a star for club and country as well as sampling English top flight football with Aston Villa and then Wigan Athletic.

2 Barry Robson: Inverurie lad Barry Robson starred for home town side Colony Park in the juvenile leagues before joining Deeside Boys Club in Aberdeen and being snapped up by Rangers. It took a move to Caley Thistle to ignite his senior career and he went on to star for Dundee United, Celtic, Scotland and Middlesbrough.

3 Ron Yeats: Aberdeen Lads' Club product Ron Yeats was working as a slaughterman in Aberdeen when he was given his big break by Dundee United. The imposing defender, who went on to be capped by Scotland, became pivotal for the Tannadice side before being recruited by Liverpool and skippering the English side to glory in the league and FA Cup in the 1960s on his way to becoming a club legend.

4 Denis Law: The most famous of Aberdeen's sporting sons, Denis Law rose to prominence in the city's school football scene and with Aberdeen Lads' Club. Initially lured south by Huddersfield Town, Law, who also turned out for Torino and Manchester City, will forever be remembered as one of Manchester United and Scotland's greatest forwards.

5 Gavin Rae: It was Dundee who were first to pick up on the potential of young Glentanar Boys Club player Gavin Rae. After serving his apprenticeship with the Dens side, Rae was given an opportunity to shine by Rangers and went on to captain the Ibrox side before moving south to join Cardiff City. Capped by Scotland, Rae eventually joined the Dons in the 2011/12 season after a spell with Dundee.

6 John Sjoberg: Classy defender John Sjoberg was part of the Banks o' Dee set-up before Leicester City added him to their growing Scottish contingent in the late 1950s. He went on to be a mainstay of the Foxes rearguard for a decade and a half, winning the League Cup with the Midlands side in the 1963/64 campaign after playing on the losing side in the FA Cup final the previous term.

7 Colin Jackson: Scotland defender Colin Jackson was born in London but raised in Aberdeen, playing juvenile football for Sunnybank before being tempted to Glasgow by Rangers. Jackson became a mainstay for Rangers, agonisingly missing out on the 1972 European Cup Winners' Cup triumph through injury but savouring the domestic dominance of the late 1970s.

8 John Fitzpatrick: Part of Manchester United's squad for the European Cup win in 1968, John Fitzpatrick is another of the Aberdeen Lads' Club old boys to have made it big in England. He made close to 150 appearances for the Old Trafford side after joining in the early 1960s but was forced to retire early from football due to knee problems.

9 Doug Cowie: It was with Dundee that Aberdonian star Doug Cowie made his name, earning 20 caps for Scotland in the 1950s on the back of his displays with the Dens side. A two-time League Cup winner with Dundee, where he served with distinction as captain, Cowie also turned out for Morton and managed Raith Rovers during a long and illustrious career.

10 Ian Wilson: When midfielder Ian Wilson made his Scotland debut in 1987, he became the latest in a select band of Aberdonians to represent his country. Initially given a chance to shine by Elgin City in the Highland League, Wilson starred for Leicester City and Everton before carving out a coaching career in Japan and Turkey prior to a stint in charge of Peterhead. He now runs a successful coaching school in his home city.

Russell Anderson

Debut: League, 4 January 1997 v Dunfermline (h) lost 2-0
Appearances: League 284 (up to the end of 2011/12), Scottish Cup 24, League Cup 20, Europe 4
Goals: League 18, Scottish Cup 1
Also played for: Scotland (11 caps up to end of 2010/11), Sunderland, Burnley, Plymouth Argyle, Derby County

Through one of the most turbulent periods in Aberdeen's history, Russell Anderson was the one constant. At the age of 27, in 2006, he was honoured with a testimonial match against Everton in recognition of the influential Dons captain's contribution to the club. Well before his 30th birthday the Aberdonian had amassed enough experience to be classed as a veteran and had become one of the few modern day players to achieve legendary status in the eyes of the supporters.

After making his debut as an 18-year-old under Roy Aitken in January, 1997, he went on to become a first choice selection for a further five managers. Alex Miller, Paul Hegarty, Ebbe Skovdahl and Steve Paterson had all been and gone during Anderson's first tenure in the top team. When the reliable stopper left, it was the job of Jimmy Calderwood to fill the void.

More than 10,000 fans turned out to voice their approval of Anderson's contribution to the cause when he ran out for his testimonial game, a humbling experience for a local boy turned Dons star.

He said after the match: "I felt honoured to be given a testimonial by the club. Some really great players received them before me - I don't think I'm at the same level, but it was a delight to be honoured. The supporters have always been good to me. Through all the time I have been here, I've realised they appreciate those who put in the effort. The least you can give the fans is full effort."

Under Paterson he was installed as captain and retained the armband when Calderwood took over as manager in 2004. A player who started life as a right back has become established as one of Scotland's leading central defenders. He made his international debut as a late substitute in a 2-0 win over Iceland in Reykjavik in 2002, earning the bizarre distinction of having to wait for his second cap, three days later against Canada on home soil, to win his first touch of the ball. The fact that he was starring for a Dons team that, for the vast majority of his time in the top team, was toiling at the wrong end of the SPL table undoubtedly hindered Anderson's international ambitions. The nagging suspicion among the Aberdeen fans who sang his praises week in and week out

was that he would have been a regular in the dark blue of his country if he had been playing for either one of the Old Firm sides.

Domestic honours proved elusive while wearing the red of his home town club, with appearances in two national finals serving only to whet his appetite for the big stage. On both occasions the showpiece game ended in defeat. In March, 2000, the Dons fell 2-0 to Celtic in the final of the League Cup. Just two months later Rangers were the conquerors in the Scottish Cup final, winning 4-0 against an Aberdeen side featuring striker Robbie Winters as a makeshift goalkeeper after an early injury to Jim Leighton.

The disappointment of those defeats has only strengthened Anderson's resolve to savour victory. His determination has seen him overcome potentially career threatening injuries along the way. During pre-season in 2000/2001 he suffered a cruciate ligament injury which kept him out for the entire campaign. He did not return to first team action until November, 2001, after a 16-month absence. In 2004 the same knee was damaged in a Scottish Cup tie against Livingston, leading to another five months of recovery work.

Each time Anderson came back stronger and became firmly established as mentor to Aberdeen's next generation of emerging stars. His one piece of advice to those around him was to make the best of the chance they have with the Dons.

He said: "The years have gone really quickly and I think that intensifies more as you get older. People talk about the benefits of experience in the game and I'm not sure you fully understand that when you are younger. Over the years you realise how important it is to savour every good experience as well as trying to learn from every circumstance and experience you face. Trying to take it all in and appreciate the opportunities you have is important."

The biggest opportunity of all arose in the summer of 2007 when Roy Keane, then in charge at Sunderland, weighed in with an offer in the region of £1million for the Dons skipper. It was too good for the club to refuse and understandably a challenge Anderson was keen to embrace, making the move to the English top flight at a time when he was at the peak of his powers. It was financially rewarding, but more importantly it presented a playing platform at the very highest level under a manager with a huge profile south of the border. Keane had seen Anderson at close quarters during his playing stint with Celtic and had been hugely impressed by the efficient and composed Aberdeen centre-half.

The move to the Black Cats turned out to be a massive anti-climax, with Anderson suffering an injury after just a single substitute appearance for his new club. He went out on loan to Plymouth and then Burnley but suffered a cruciate ligament injury to add to his woes. Once again the plucky Aberdonian battled back to full fitness and joined Derby County at the start of 2010 after being released by Sunderland. Now entering the veteran stage of his career, the stopper is hoping his bad run of luck is behind him and he can make up for lost time after returning to the Dons in January 2012.

Bobby Ancell

Debut: League, 8 January 1949 v Third Lanark (h) drew 2-2
Appearances: League 15, Scottish Cup 1
Also played for: Scotland (2 caps), Dundee, Berwick Rangers
Managed: Berwick Rangers, Dunfermline, Motherwell, Dundee

Two Scotland caps in the 1930s hinted at full-back Bobby Ancell's ability as a player. The resilient defender turned out for St Mirren and Newcastle before the war stopped his career in its tracks. He went on to guest for Aberdeen during wartime and returned in 1948/49 to spend a season at Pittodrie, turning out at left-back for Dave Halliday in his single campaign as a Dons player. The veteran went on to play for Dundee and also served as player-manager of Berwick Rangers. He also took charge of Dunfermline, Motherwell and Dundee.

Jim Anderson

Debut: League, 27 April 1963 v Kilmarnock (a) drew 2-2
Appearances: League 4, League Cup 1

The formidable obstacle of Doug Coutts stood in the way of Jim Anderson and a place in the Aberdeen team. Anderson deputised on a smattering of occasions after rejecting overtures from Manchester United and Dundee United to sign for the Dons from Banks o' Dee A in 1960. The reserve captain, who served as a policeman in Aberden, had a break from football after leaving Pittodrie but returned with junior side Rosemount in 1970.

Myles Anderson

Debut: League, 19 February 2011 v Kilmarnock (h) won 5-0
Appearances: League 1
Also played for: Leyton Orient, Blackburn Rovers

Young defender Myles Anderson became the latest in a succession of promising English players to be snared by Aberdeen. The Leyton Orient player, who had attracted interest from Blackburn Rovers, was recruited by Craig Brown in January 2011.

The left-sided player had earlier impressed while on trial with Brown and Archie Knox at Motherwell but disappointed during his time with the Dons. He went on to join Blackburn.

Chris Anderson

Debut: League, 1 January 1949 v Dundee (h) lost 3-1
Appearances: League 71, Scottish Cup 13, League Cup 19
Goals: League 1, Scottish Cup 1, League Cup 1
Also played for: Arbroath

Chris Anderson served as a player, director and ambassador for Aberdeen Football Club. Renowned as a visionary and inspiration during his time on the board at Pittodrie, Anderson's contribution on the pitch is all too easy to overlook but should not be ignored.

He had been an outstanding centre-half with Sunnybank school and the Aberdeen select during the 1930s, going on to win Scotland schoolboy international honours before progressing from juvenile football to the junior game with Mugiemoss. He signed for the Dons in 1944 amid a flurry of interest from clubs on both sides of the border and, despite national service taking a chunk out of his time with the club, recorded more than a century of appearances in club colours up to his farewell appearance in the closing weeks of 1952. He was released to join Arbroath in 1953 and spent three seasons with the Gayfield side before retiring due to burgeoning work commitments as he embarked on a long career with the Robert Gordon Institute of Technology. Anderson continued to serve as a scout and coach with the Angus side but returned to Pittodrie in 1967 when he was appointed to the Aberdeen board, rising to become vice-chairman. His achievements as a director included acting as a leading light in the creation of the Premier Division in the mid-1970s and his role in the redevelopment of the ground to create a modern stadium that was the envy of many larger clubs. Anderson, who had a prominent role in the Scottish Sports Council and served on a variety of league and SFA committees, died in 1986 at the age of 60 after suffering from motor neurone disease.

Ian Angus

Debut: League, 6 December 1980 v Morton (a) lost 1-0
Appearances: League 84+21, Scottish Cup 15+3, League Cup 10+4, Europe 11+6
Goals: League 9, Scottish Cup 2, Europe 1
Also played for: Dundee, Motherwell, Clyde, Albion Rovers, Stirling Albion

Ian Angus did not play as many games as many Aberdeen stars, he did not earn the same plaudits as many Aberdeen stars and he did not earn international recognition. What he did walk out of the Pittodrie main entrance with when he moved to Dundee in 1986 was a Premier Division winner's medal and that is something many, many players past and present would walk over hot coals to emulate. The Glaswegian, a product of Eastercraigs Boys Club, enjoyed his most productive season in a red jersey in the 1984/85 campaign. He was still only 24 when he helped the Dons to sweep to the league title by a margin of seven points but already had four seasons under his belt before that championship winning term even began.

Up to that point he had been a valuable squad man for Alex Ferguson but far from a first team regular. After breaking into the team just a fortnight after his 19th birthday, Angus quickly forced his way into Ferguson's starting 11 and spent the remainder of his rookie season vying for the No.10 jersey with Drew Jarvie and Andy Harrow.

Injury stalled his progress and after a frustrating second term, in which he made just a single appearance, he had to be patient in his quest for regular football at Pittodrie.

In the famous 1982/83 season he was again restricted to a bit-part role, his starts in the final three league games the only time he made it into the starting 11 in the Premier Division and bringing a haul of three goals. Angus made a cameo appearance in the run to the European Cup Winners' Cup trophy, coming on as a substitute in the semi-final second leg against Waterschei and on the bench for the final.

He enjoyed his first taste of success as a professional when he helped the Dons to the championship in 1984, with nine starts and three substitute appearances.

In 1985 he stepped up to take a central role in the successful defence of the Premier Division prize, in the first team a total of 21 times and used from the bench in seven other games.

In the summer of 1986 he moved down the A90 to join Dundee as part of the deal that took Robert Connor in the opposite direction and helped the Dens Park side maintain mid-table security in the top flight for three seasons until their relegation in 1990.

Motherwell stepped in with a £40,000 bid to offer Angus a Premier Division lifeline and he grabbed it with both hands, going on to score the third goal for the Steelmen in the pulsating 4-3 Scottish Cup final victory against Dundee United in 1991 to cap his first season in Lanarkshire in style.

Angus made more than 100 appearances for Well over four years before winding down his senior career with Clyde and Albion Rovers.

Steve Archibald

Debut: League, 7 January 1978 v Ayr United (a) drew 0-0.
Appearances: League 76+2, Scottish Cup 10, League Cup 18, Europe 6
Goals: League 29, Scottish Cup 11, League Cup 6
Also played for: Scotland (27 Caps), Clyde, Tottenham Hotspur, Barcelona, Espanyol, Hibs, St Mirren.
Managed: East Fife, Airdrie.

Enigmatic, charismatic ... infuriating, frustrating. Everyone has their own opinion on Steve Archibald and his colourful career in football. The Glaswegian was recruited by Billy McNeill in January, 1978, as a raw 21-year-old midfielder from Clyde.

From First Division midfielder he was converted to Premier League striker with the Dons. He made his debut for McNeill's side in the red No.8 jersey in a 1-1 draw with Ayr United at Somerset Park on January 7, 1978. His first goals came in the shape of a double in a 3-0 win over Rangers at Ibrox. Joe Harper, who became his strike partner in a formidable pairing, was the other scorer.

The Pittodrie side were runners-up to the Gers in the Premier League in Archibald's first season.

Alex Ferguson was the new man at the helm by the time the 1978-79 campaign kicked-off and Archibald had a taste of things to come when he and his team-mates marched to the final of the League Cup.

His first taste of the big occasion ended in bitter disappointment, Rangers winning 2-1, but the following term provided sweet success. Archibald was the key man as the Dons swept aside all challengers to win the Premier League title by a single point from Celtic.

It was the Pittodrie swansong for Archibald, who made his final appearance for the Reds in the 1-1 draw with Partick on the final day of the 1979/80 season to complete a 15 game unbeaten run. His relationship with Ferguson was stormy. Legend has it that the manager named a chair in his office after his bolshy striker, such was the frequency of his visits to see the top man.

In May, 1980, the divorce was completed when Spurs weighed in with an offer Aberdeen could not refuse. A fee of £800,000 took him to White Hart Lane. He was England's leading scorer in his first season with Tottenham and won the FA Cup in 1981 when he played in the 3-2 win over Manchester City at Wembley.

By that time he was also a fully fledged international, making his debut in dark blue on May 19, 1980, against Northern Ireland. His confidence extended to the international arena, scoring within 20 minutes of his introduction as a substitute for Kenny Dalglish as Scotland won 2-0. In all he made 27 appearances for his country, including at the 1986 World Cup finals in Mexico.

With Spurs he won another FA Cup winner's medal in 1982 and the Uefa Cup in 1984, scoring in the 4-3 penalty shoot-out victory over Anderlecht. That propelled him to a global audience and a £1.15million switch to Barcelona, coached by Terry Venables, followed in August, 1984. He won the Spanish title in his first campaign.

Spells as a player with Espanyol, Hibs and St Mirren followed before Archibald's first venture into management with East Fife, steering them to the First Division. He added club chairman to his portfolio in 2000 when he took control of struggling Airdrie while the club was in the hands of administrators. Archibald left in 2001 and the club folded. He returned to Spain to concentrate on business commitments.

Matt Armstrong

Debut: League, 21 November 1931 v Falkirk (a) lost 3-0
Appearances: League 191, Scottish Cup 24
Goals: League 136, Scottish Cup 19
Also played for: Scotland (3 caps), Port Glasgow juniors, Elgin City.

The statistics say it all when it comes to Matt Armstrong's career with Aberdeen: 215 games, 155 goals. It puts him second in the club's all time scoring record, behind Joe Harper with 200 goals in 308 games and guarantees legendary status.

Successive modern managers have searched for a striker who could consistently pass the magical 20 goal a season mark. Armstrong, who died in Aberdeen in 1995, beat 30 in four consecutive seasons in the 1930s.

He had been signed on a provisional form with Celtic, having starred with Port Glasgow in the junior ranks, but Aberdeen manager Pat Travers took advantage of a lapse in the paperwork to nip in and recruit the 19 year-old. Opportunities were limited after his 1931 debut and it was in the 1933/34 season that Armstrong began to make his mark – scoring five in the first game of the season as the home crowd was treated to an 8-0 win against Ayr United. That helped take his tally to fourteen goals in just thirteen games and convinced Travers his rising striker could be depended on to wear the No.9 shirt week in and week out.

The following season was the most prolific in his Aberdeen career with the staggering return of 39 goals in 43 games to finish leading scorer at the club, a place he retained for the next three years thanks to hauls of 31, 30 and 22 goals. His ability to hit the target at club level brought three caps for Scotland to join the junior international cap he had won as a teenager. He was never on the losing side for the national team, playing in a 1-1 draw against Wales on his debut in 1935 as well as a 2-1 win over Northern Ireland later that year and a 2-0 win over Germany in 1936.

Honours proved agonizingly elusive for one of the finest attacking talents Aberdeen has ever had. In 1936/37 he came closest, scoring in the Scottish Cup final against Celtic in front of 146,433 as his side fell to a 2-1 defeat. In the league it was Rangers who stood between the Dons and the league title, winning the title by seven points.

The war interrupted Armstrong's career when he was in full flight but, at the age of 34, he returned in 1945/46 to ease the club back into competitive action and still knew the way to goal, netting eight goals in just 13 appearances.

Armstrong, born in Newton Stewart, remained in the north and continued playing well into his 40s with Elgin City where he remained a potent striker. He later acted as a scout for Falkirk, among other clubs.

Post-football Armstrong worked in the motor trade in Aberdeen, combining work with his love of golf, a member of Murcar Golf Club who played off a handicap of two at his prime, before returning to Aberdeen FC as manager of the Pittodrie Development Association. He retired in 1976 after a 45 year association with the Dons.

TEN: Sponsors who saw their name in lights

1 Hydrasun: Years before the Aberdeen playing strip boasted its first sponsor, local firm Hydrasun, suppliers primarily to the oil and gas industry, got in on the act when it secured the rights to have its logo on the tracksuits of the squad during the glorious European Cup Winners' Cup run of 1983.

2 JVC: If it was good enough for Arsenal, it was good enough for Aberdeen. In 1987 the Japanese electronics firm JVC, already well established in British football through their link with the Gunners, became the first company to have their name emblazoned on the famous red shirt of the Dons.

3 Abtrust: After the international brand came the local influence as financial firm Abtrust took over as shirt sponsor in 1990. The west end company, in the lucrative unit trust management sector, had their name in pride of place for three seasons on the last of the traditional looking Umbro kits worn by the Dons.

4 A-Fab: After Abtrust came another city outfit in the shape of A-Fab. Specialising in steel and pipe work for the offshore industry, the firm was sponsor for the 1993/94 season before returning to the fold between 2001 and 2004 to become the only company to date to serve as kit sponsor twice.

5 Northsound: The arrival of North-east radio station Northsound as main sponsor in 1994 coincided with a break with the norm as the Reds were hit by a touch of the blues – the navy blues, to be precise. Umbro introduced a patterned print to the strip and it proved to be a lucky touch as it was sported for the 1995 League Cup triumph.

6 Living Design: The design was tempered when the kit was reworked by Umbro in 1996, but the navy blue detailing remained as home improvements firm Living Design took over as sponsor. Puma became the manufacturer for the company's second season with their name on the shirt and normal service was resumed as the all-red tradition returned.

7 Atlantic Telecom: Spearheaded by businessman Graham Duncan, Atlantic Telecom was a boom business in a boom industry when it took over as shirt sponsor in 1998. At one stage valued at £1billion, the company's name remained in pride of place until 2001 – the year the firm collapsed under the weight of crippling debts.

8 ADT: It was a double whammy in time for the start of the 2004/05 campaign as the club announced a double deal that saw Nike strips introduced for the first time and fire and security outfit ADT installed as sponsor for a two year partnership with the Dons.

9 Apex Tubulars: It was a return to the oil and gas services industry in 2006 when Apex Tubulars became the latest name to adorn the red shirt of Aberdeen. Apex managing director Jim Geddie, a lifelong Pittodrie fan, said it was a "dream come true" to have his company's logo emblazoned on the kit.

10 Team Recruitment: Initially tied to a two year contract, the relationship with Team Recruitment was extended beyond the original agreement to make the Aberdeen enterprise the club's longest serving kit sponsor, remaining onboard long enough to see the club switch from Nike to Adidas kit in time for the 2011/12 season.

Kari Arnason

Debut: League, 23 July 2011 v St Johnstone (h) drew 0-0
Appearances: League 33, Scottish Cup 5, League Cup 2
Goals: League 3
Also played for: Iceland, Hafnarfjordur (Iceland), Aarhus (Denmark), Plymouth Argyle

Icelandic international Kari Arnason's impressive displays early in his Aberdeen career made his recruitment on a free transfer look an inspired piece of business. The midfielder, who chipped in with some excellent goals, quickly emerged as a player Craig Brown wanted for the long haul but his wage demands proved impossible to meet and he left after a single season, in which his form dipped as the campaign progressed.

Armour Ashe

Debut: League, 17 September 1949 v Clyde (h) drew 1-1
Appearances: League 1
Also played for: Stockport County, Accrington Stanley, Gateshead, Southport

Paisley-born defender Armour Ashe's debut in a 1-1 home draw against Clyde in the second league game of the 1949/50 season proved to be his one and only Aberdeen appearance. Having joined from junior side Dalry Thistle he revived his senior career with a move to Stockport County in 1953 and went on to establish himself as a stalwart with Accrington Stanley. He also had spells with Gateshead and Southport in the late 1950s.

Eric Baikie

Debut: League, 17 December 1949 v Motherwell (h) won 5-0
Appearances: League 3, League Cup 1
Also played for: Dunfermline, St Johnstone

Eric Baikie served as deputy to reliable wing-half Tony Harris for two seasons. Recruited from Edinburgh side Hutchison Vale, Baikie made his debut midway through the 1949/50 season and his two appearances that term were matched by two in the following campaign. A move to Dunfermline Athletic in 1951 gave Baikie the regular first team football he craved, making more than a century of appearances for the Pars before joining St Johnstone five years later.

Hugh Baird

Debut: League, 11 October 1958 v Stirling Albion (a) lost 3-2
Appearances: League 66, Scottish Cup 8, League Cup 12
Goals: League 21, Scottish Cup 2, League Cup 2
Also played for: Airdrie, Leeds United, Brechin City

It was a mark of Aberdeen's ambition that they were willing to shatter the Pittodrie transfer record to clinch the signing of Hugh Baird in October 1958. Manager Dave Shaw was desperate to return the Dons to the top of the tree after the championsip success three years previously and paid £11,500 for the Scotland international striker.

Baird had spent just over a year at Leeds United – but it was with Airdrie that he made his mark. Over the course of three glorious seasons he bagged 117 goals for the Diamonds and emerged as one of the most potent strikers in the domestic game. His phenomenal return included 53 in the Second Division title win in 1955 and he settled into life in the top flight with ease after that promotion.

It paved the way for a £12,000 switch to Elland Road but Shaw moved swiftly to bring him back north of the border to join the Aberdeen cause. Baird drew a blank in his first two games but broke his duck in spectacular style with a four goal blast in a 5-0 win against Falkirk.

The goals did not flow thick and fast though, with the marksman transformed into a utility player who turned out in every position except full-back and on the left wing. In one game he even served as an emergency goalkeeper after No.1 Fred Martin had suffered an injury.

Baird spent four years with the Dons before moving on to Brechin in 1962. The Bellshill-born star, who earned one cap for his country, died in 2006.

Rachid Belabed

Debut: League, 27 November 1999 v Hibs (a) lost 2-0
Appearances: League 37, Scottish Cup 10, League Cup 4, Europe 2
Goals: League 1
Also played for: RWD Molenbeek (Belgium), La Louviere (Belgium)

Fiery midfielder Rachid Belabed arrived at Aberdeen as a raw 18-year-old in October 1999. Although born in Brussels, he was a Moroccan national. Belabed made his debut for the first team soon after landing on Scottish soil but grew frustrated with the lack of guaranteed action and left for Belgian outfit La Louviere in June 2002. He courted controversy during his time with the Dons, and continued that trend back in Belgium when he disappeared without trace for a six week period and then was dismissed by his club for allegedly assaulting a journalist following a debate on terror and Islam.

Dave Bennett

Debut: League Cup, 27 August 1960 v Ayr United (a) drew 1-1
Appearances: League 111, Scottish Cup 12, League Cup 16
Also played for: Inverness Caledonian

Educated at the rugby playing Aberdeen Grammar, he continued to get his football fix by turning out for his Boys' Brigade side and Kaimhill, winning a break with Sunnybank juniors as a 17-year-old. After three years with Bank Bennett was promoted to the senior game by Tommy Pearson, who recruited him in 1960. Two games for the reserves was all it took for the manager to be persuaded his new boy had star quality and he was promoted to the first team early in the 1960/61 campaign to fill the right-back berth.

Bennett was a studious character and graduated with an MSc while still in the midst of his playing career, although that commitment to education cost him his place with the Dons after six impressive years in the red shirt. His refusal to give up the part-time status that enabled him to combine university studies with training was frowned upon by new manager Eddie Turnbull and in 1966 he was allowed to join Inverness Caledonian.

Bennett later took up a science post in London before returning to Aberdeen to become a teacher in 1969. Bennett died following a heart attack, aged just 49.

Dougie Bell

Debut: League, 11 August 1979 v Partick Thistle (a) lost 1-0
Appearances: League 109+22, Scottish Cup 22+11, League Cup 28+5, Europe 25+5
Goals: League 6, League Cup 7, Europe 1
Also played for: St Mirren, Rangers, Hibs, Shrewsbury, Hull, Birmingham, Partick, Portadown, Clyde, Elgin City, Alloa, Albion Rovers.

Dougie Bell could not have picked a better season to walk through the front door at Pittodrie for the first time. The Paisley-born player was signed by Alex Ferguson from St Mirren on a free transfer and made his debut in the opening game of the 1979/80 season.

Few who played a part in the 1-0 defeat at the hands of Partick Thistle at Firhill could have predicted what the campaign would yield, except perhaps the manager with the midas touch.

Bell was a substitute in that game and proved a reliable squad man as the Dons pipped Celtic to the Premier Division title by a single point.

The classy midfielder made 10 appearances in that league winning run, his first start in a 4-0 win at Dundee on September 29, 1979. After contributing to league success in 1980, Bell's second experience of that winning feeling came in the 1982 Scottish Cup final when he came on from the bench to help the Dons to a 4-1 extra-time win over Rangers.

He missed the rematch with the Ibrox side in the final the following year, which the Dons won 1-0, but had established himself as a regular by then. He wore the No.8 jersey in each of the four rounds leading to that final but was sidelined by injury for the Hampden showdown with the Gers.

The same injury forced him to miss out on the club's finest hour in Gothenburg having started eight of the 11 European Cup Winners' Cup ties in that legendary tournament, scoring the only goal of the game in the second round second leg tie against Lech Poznan to give the Dons a 3-0 aggregate win. Bell did add a European winner's medal to his collection when he played a key role in the 1983 Super Cup win over SV Hamburg, a main man as Aberdeen won 2-0 over two legs to confirm their place among Europe's elite.

The 1983/84 season also brought further Premier Division success and Bell was a mainstay, making 23 appearances in the league as the Dons beat Celtic by seven points to take the crown.

He came on from the bench in the tense 2-1 extra-time win over Celtic in the Scottish Cup final and also played in every tie as the Dons came agonizingly close to earning a shot at a third European title, beaten 2-0 on aggregate by Porto in the semi-final of that season's European Cup Winners' Cup.

His final winner's medal in the red shirt of Aberdeen came in 1985 as he helped the club claim a second consecutive Premier Division title, this time clocking up 22 appearances in the dominant Dons side of the day to take his total to 227 games and 14 goals.

Bell was snapped up by Rangers for £160,000 that summer and stayed at Ibrox for two seasons before heading across the country to Hibs in 1986. He went on to play in England with Shrewsbury, Hull and Birmingham and added Northern Ireland to his playing CV when he joined Portadown in 1992 after a stint with Partick Thistle. Bell played out his career with Clyde, Elgin in the Highland League, Alloa and Albion Rovers.

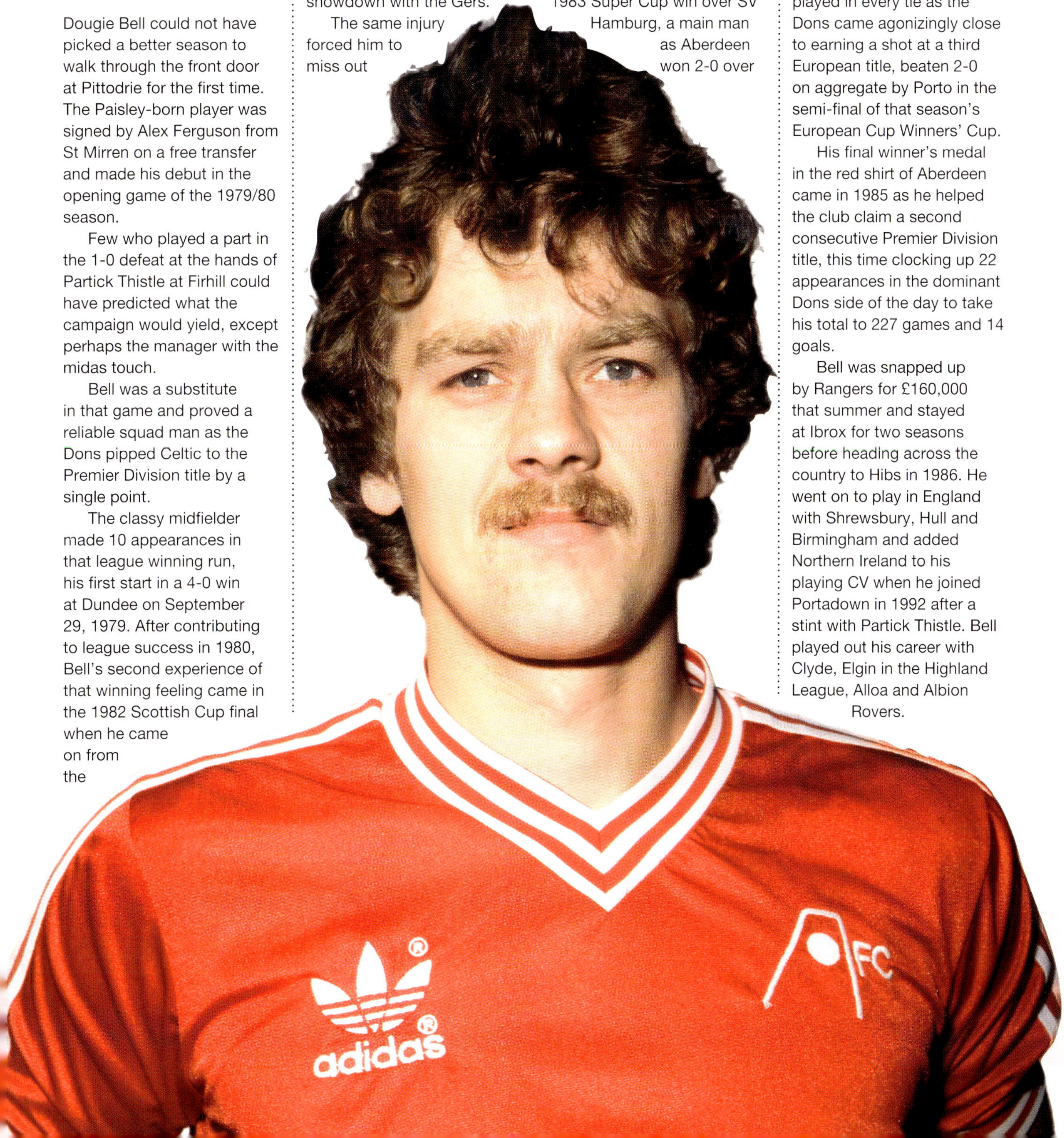

Archie Baird

Debut: League, 11 August 1945 v Third Lanark (h) won 3-0
Appearances: League 104, Scottish Cup 17, League Cup 23
Goals: League 26, Scottish Cup 2, League Cup 9
Also played for: Scotland (1 cap), St Johnstone

Aberdeen supporters waited 43 years to savour the taste of success. From the first baby steps of the club at the turn of the 20th century it took a combination of inspiration, determination and dedication to take the vision of the city's founding football fathers and turn it into the reality of a trophy winning club. It took men of character and of strength to make it happen and in Archie Baird the Dons found one of those valuable individuals.

It was in 1946 that the leap from potential to substance was made as Aberdeen secured the Southern League Cup for the Pittodrie trophy cabinet, the forerunner to the League Cup.

For Archie Baird, the cup victory was sweeter than it was for most. He wore the No.10 shirt with pride as the Dons defeated Rangers 3-2 in front of 135,000 fans at Hampden to lift the club's first major piece of silverware. To launch a memorable day, the cultured attacker notched the opener after just 90 seconds and was joined on the scoresheet by George Taylor and Stan Williams.

The Glaswegian signed for the Pittodrie side in 1938 on a £4-per-week contract after making his breakthrough with Strathclyde Juniors in his home city as a stylish inside forward, although the outbreak of war meant it was not until 1945 that he made his debut for the club.

Not that he spent the years in between living the quiet life. In fact, his military service took him to the deserts of North Africa and, after being captured by a squadron of German tanks, a prisoner of war camp in Italy.

In 1943 Baird made a break from the camp in Rimini, through a gap in a wire fence, and found refuge with an Italian family for nine months. When the Germans eventually pulled out of Italy, he was free to return to Scotland and live out his football dream. He had put his renowned intellect to good use during his time in hiding, learning the local language, and when he returned to British soil went on to gain degrees in Italian and English through University of London correspondence courses.

While education and learning was a passion, football was his great love. Baird's first competitive action for Aberdeen came on August 11, 1945, against the famous old name of Third Lanark at Pittodrie. His side won 3-0, competing in the Scottish Southern A League.

He waited just another month to open his goalscoring account, on the scoresheet in a 4-1 win over Motherwell early that season. The club went on to finish third in the league, behind champions Rangers and runners-up Hibs, as the progress on the Pittodrie pitch continued at great pace.

His first season would prove to be his most prolific as an Aberdeen player, bringing 17 goals in total. Nine came in the league, two in the Scottish Cup and, most crucially, six were bagged in the Southern League Cup campaign.

In addition to his vital strike in the final, Baird scored in the semi-final against Airdrie to earn a 2-2 draw and was on target again in the replay of that tie, which the Dons won 5-3 after extra-time, to help his side to the final. Rangers awaited at Hampden but the Ibrox stars held no fears for Baird and his colleagues as they stormed to victory in a pulsating 3-2 win.

The Southern League Cup success in 1946 was followed the next season by a 3-2 victory over Hibs in the Scottish Cup final, with Baird again resplendent in the red No.10 shirt.

The Scottish Cup win was a momentous moment for the club, a fact demonstrated by the 15,000 strong welcome committee which greeted the team when it pulled in at Aberdeen's Joint Station to parade the famous trophy on home soil. Two seasons and two cups gave the city and its football supporters a sense of belonging, an appreciation that their fledgling club had arrived as a serious force in the Scottish game with a chance to win prizes on a regular basis.

It was a glorious period for the player, who made his debut for Scotland in 1946 against Belgium. The solitary appearance in Dark Blue was in a 2-2 draw at Hampden.

Baird underwent three cartilage operations and also recovered from a fractured leg during his time in the game, with none of those injury lay-offs denting his great enthusiasm for the sport that made him a household name. He was a creative force for the Dons in the 1940s and 50s, driving the club forward at a crucial time, but never lost sight of his humbling experiences during the war.

After an association stretching back 15 years, he waved farewell to his Pittodrie terracing backers in January, 1953. His final appearance came in a 2-2 league draw against Dundee. Each of his 144 appearances came under the stewardship of manager Dave Halliday, who himself departed three years later.

His spirit and skill led St Johnstone to tempt him to Muirton Park when his Dons career ended after 37 goals for the Pittodrie side. He spent three seasons with the Perth men before retiring and concentrating on his many and varied interests in and around Aberdeen.

Baird served as a sports journalist and teacher, rising to become assistant head of Hilton Academy prior to his retirement from full-time employment in 1979. He continued to work as a columnist with *The Leopard* magazine, taught night classes and also penned his autobiography *Family of Four* in 1989. He died in November 2009 at the age of 90.

Baldur Bett

Debut: League, 21 November 1998 v St Johnstone (h) lost 1-0
Appearances: League 2
Also played for: Peterhead

Baldur Bett became the first of Jim Bett's two sons to follow in their famous father's football footsteps and pull on the Aberdeen jersey. Baldur was 18 when Alex Miller handed him his debut in 1998. He played just once more for the Dons before being released in 2000. Bett turned out for Peterhead briefly before moving to Iceland, the country of his birth, to continue his professional career.

Calum Bett

Debut: League, 21 April 2001 v Dunfermline (h) won 1-0
Appearances: League 5
Also played for: Forfar Athletic

The youngest member of the Bett sporting dynasty was 19 when he made his Dons breakthrough under Ebbe Skovdahl in 2001. He was on the fringes of the Dane's first team for two terms before being loaned to Forfar and then released in 2002. The Icelandic under-19 international followed his brother's lead and opted to continue his professional career in Iceland.

Patrizio Billio

Debut: League, 11 September 2002 v Dundee United (h) lost 2-1
Appearances: League 10, Scottish Cup 1, League Cup 1
Goals: League 1
Also played for: AC Milan, Crystal Palace (on loan), Dundee, Livorno

Italian midfielder Patrizio Billio was a headline maker in Scotland due to his lengthy dispute with Dundee during his time on the Dens Park books. It began when he was frozen out of the first team along with compatriot Marco de Marchi and rumbled on for months, bringing police involvement at one stage. He split from the Tayside club in August 2002 and joined Aberdeen on a short term deal under Ebbe Skovdahl, adding depth to the midfield options until his release by Steve Paterson after five months at Pittodrie. The former AC Milan trainee had first sampled British football while on loan at Crystal Palace but returned to more familiar surroundings with Livorno in Italy after leaving the Dons.

Michael Bird

Debut: League, 30 August 2003 v Hibs (a) drew 1-1
Appearances: League 2, League Cup 1
Also played for: Bolton Wanderers, Glenavon

Bolton Wanderers youth academy product Michael Bird was signed as a 19-year-old by Steve Paterson in 2003. The tall young striker, first spotted by coach Oshor Williams, made two appearances from the bench but failed to make the transition to first team football and left to join Irish outfit Glenavon less than a year later. He went on to play non-league football in England.

Roberto Bisconti

Debut: League, 27 August 2001 v Rangers (h) Lost 3-0
Appearances: League 42, Scottish Cup 3, League Cup 3, Europe 4
Goals: League 1
Also played for: Monza (Italy), Charleroi (Belgium), Rapid Bucharest (Romania), Nice (France), Guingamp (France), Standard Liege ,Vise (Belgium)

Ebbe Skovdahl's reign as Aberdeen manager was peppered with some eccentric signings, littered with some disappointing signings and punctuated by the occasional smash hit. In some respects the recruitment of Roberto Bisconti could be considered to fall into all three categories.

The out of contract Belgian midfielder arrived on a free transfer from Charleroi in his homeland in the summer of 2001. His eccentricities mainly related to discipline, on and off the park, and could perhaps be traced back to the Latin temperament inherited from his Italian parents. With dual nationality, he had crossed from Belgium to Italy to play for Monza earlier in his career.

On the pitch his robust and commanding displays at the heart of Skovdahl's team added a steel that had been absent from the Dons side for years. The shaven-headed combatant instantly won admirers among the Red Army, picking up a clutch of player of the year awards from fans during his first campaign.

Unfortunately the continental star proved to be a one hit wonder. He and his young family struggled to settle in Scotland and when Steve Paterson took over from Skovdahl as boss the relationship between club and player broke down completely. His contract was terminated in January 2003 and Bisconti set off on a club hopping adventure which took him to Romania with Rapid Bucharest, back to Belgium with Standard Liege then on to France with Nice. He briefly turned out for French side Guingamp before linking up with CS Vise in Belgium in 2008.

Nick Blackman

Debut: League, 22 January 2011 v Celtic (a) lost 1-0
Appearances: League 15, Scottish Cup 3
Goals: League 2
Also played for: Macclesfield, Blackburn Rovers, Blackpool (on loan), Oldham (on loan), Motherwell (on loan)

Ten goals in just 17 starts while on loan at Motherwell proved that Nick Blackman had the credentials to be a productive SPL striker. He had been taken north on loan from Blackburn Rovers by Craig Brown during his tenure at Fir Park, taking him in for the start of the 2010/11 season. When the manager moved to Pittodrie midway through that campaign he went back to Blackburn to sign Blackman on loan for a second spell in Scotland but he struggled to rediscover his form. The 6ft 2in tall former Macclesfield trainee has also been farmed out by Rovers to Blackpool and Oldham while waiting for his break at Ewood Park.

Lubomir Blaha

Debut: League, 2 April 2005 v Caley Thistle (a) won 1-0
Appearances: League 8
Also played for: Sparta Prague (Czech Republic), Slovan Liberec (Czech Republic)

Lubomir Blaha was one of the overseas imports that failed to pay dividends for Aberdeen. Jimmy Calderwood gambled on the former Czech Republic under-21 international in the closing months of the 2004/05 season but in eight outings, mainly from the bench, he failed to find the net and returned home without a long term deal in the summer of 2006. Blaha, who had first been targeted by Calderwood in 2005, had arrived after turning out for Slovan Liberec in his home country. Sparta Prague were among the other clubs on Blaha's cv and he also boasted Champions League experience from his time in the Czech game.

Tommy Bogan

Debut: Scottish Cup, 10 March 1951 v Celtic (a) lost 3-0
Appearances: League 4, Scottish Cup 1, League Cup 4
Goals: League 1
Also played for: Celtic, Manchester United, Southampton, Blackburn Rovers

Forward Tommy Bogan made his debut against his old club Celtic in front of more than 75,000 spectators at Parkhead in 1950/51 and spent a further season with the Dons before switching to Southampton. He also played for Blackburn Rovers after leaving Pittodrie, having moved to the Dons from Manchester United.

Bertrand Bossu

Debut: League Cup, 27 August 2008 v Ayr United (a) won 1-0
Appearances: League 2
Also played for: Lens, Barnet, Gillingham, Darlington, Walsall, Crewe

At 6ft 7in there were raw ingredients for goalkeeping coach Jim Leighton to work with when French shot stopper Bertrand Bossu was signed by Jimmy Calderwood from Walsall in 2008. He made two starts, the last of which was a chaotic 4-2 League Cup defeat at Kilmarnock, and joined Crewe in 2009.

Ray Botha

Debut: Scottish Cup, 25 January 1947 v Partick Thistle (h) won 2-1
Appearances: League 1, Scottish Cup 2, League Cup 1
Goals: Scottish Cup 1

South African winger Ray Botha played professional cricket and football during his time in the Granite City, turning out for Gordonians as well as the Dons.

Botha made three appearances in 1946/47, his single season in the Aberdeen first team, before returning to live in his homeland with his Aberdonian wife.

Paul Bernard

Debut: League, 30 September 1995 v Raith Rovers (h) won 3-0
Appearances: League 91+9, Scottish Cup 11, League Cup 12, Europe 1
Goals: League 6, Scottish Cup 2
Also played for: Scotland (2 caps), Oldham Athletic, Barnsley, Plymouth, St Johnstone

As football clubs count the cost of past extravagance and budgets creak and groan under the strain of historic debts it is difficult to envisage a day when Paul Bernard will be dislodged from his unique place in the history of Aberdeen.

Bernard became the club's record signing in September, 1995, when Oldham Athletic pocketed a fee in the region of £1million, in the form of £850,000 up front and additional payments as the contract progressed.

The deal eclisped the £800,000 it took to take Billy Dodds to Pittodrie, the £750,000 paid to Hull for Dean Windass or the £500,000 paid to recruit Robbie Winters from Dundee United, although the Winters deal does not factor in the worth of Dodds when he moved in the opposite direction as part of the package.

In cash terms at least Bernard is the costliest player ever to cross the threshold at Pittodrie after chairman Ian Donald backed manager Roy Aitken's judgement to the hilt. The big question is whether he provided value for money and the majority of Dons fans would argue that he did not.

The hefty price tag saddled Bernard with a weight of expectation. While he sparkled at times, looking every ounce a £1million player, he struggled to produce his best form consistently as a series of injuries restricted him to 115 starts in six years, bringing just eight goals.

He was a player who undoubtedly had talent, a modern midfield player with the ability to break up play and start attacks with precise passing and an unflappable attitude. Unfortunately those qualities were displayed only in flashes during his time at Pittodrie, a frustrating period in his career.

Bernard's time at the club started on a high as within two months of his arrival he got his hands on a League Cup winner's medal following the 2-0 win over Dundee.

With one prize in the bag and two Scottish caps already nestling at home, courtesy of appearances in the Kirin Cup in May, 1995, the stock of the young midfielder was at an all time high. Those Scotland games, as a substitute in a 0-0 draw with Japan and 90 minutes in a 2-1 win against Ecuador, proved to be his last.

Bernard was still only 22 when he achieved those milestones, having burst onto the English scene as a teenager with Oldham as they battled for Premiership survival in 1992. He played two seasons in the top flight before the Latics dropped down to the First Division for the 1994/95 season. The following term, after the club's failure to regain their seat at the top table, the Dons made their move.

Bernard, complete with Ferrari, rolled into the Pittodrie car park for the first time a month after the start of the season in 1995, making his debut from the bench in a 3-0 win at home to Raith Rovers on September 30. The League Cup final followed on November 26, by which time he had been eased into Aitken's starting 11.

He appeared in all but five of the Premier Division fixtures as the Dons finished third behind Rangers and Celtic, having arrived after the first four, on his way to 36 appearances in all competitions. It proved to be a rare full campaign for the midfielder.

An ankle injury, first feared to be a broken leg, sidelined the record buy for a month in the first half of the 1996/97 season and a groin injury struck at the turn of the year. All in all he made just 15 appearances.

The stop-start introduction meant Bernard never truly won over the Aberdeen supporters, even though he was more consistently available for selection in 1997/98 as the club switched manager from Aitken to Alex Miller.

He did enough to persuade the new manager to extend his contract but it proved to be a false dawn for the former Oldham star, who made just eight appearances the following season due to injury.

He returned to full fitness in Ebbe Skovdahl's debut campaign, sitting out just eight league games and playing in every one of the seven Scottish Cup ties which culminated in the 4-0 defeat in the 2000 final against Rangers following an early injury to goalkeeper Jim Leighton. Bernard had also played in the 2-0 defeat in the final of the League Cup against Celtic earlier that season.

Just as he had established himself as a mainstay the old injury problems returned, with just three appearances in the Millennium season as his contract was allowed to run down by the club. Short spells with Barnsley and Plymouth Argyle followed before Bernard returned to Scotland with St Johnstone in 2003 and later wound down his career in Ireland with Drogheda. He is now back in England and carving out a new niche in the house building industry as a property developer, speculating to accumulate in the way Roy Aitken and Ian Donald did all those years ago when they signed the cheque to take the midfielder north.

Will we ever see his likes again? A £1million man in Aberdeen colours. No doubt it will happen, inflation will see to that, but it will be years, if not decades, until that daunting figure is matched. Until then, Paul Bernard will keep his place among legendary names in the history of the Dons as the most expensive player ever to grace the home dressing room at Pittodrie.

McEWAN'S
LAGER

Jim Bett

Debut: League, 10 August 1985 v Hibs (h) won 3-0
Appearances: League 256+2, Scottish Cup 27, League Cup 31+1, Europe 21
Goals: League 33, Scottish Cup 2, League Cup 10, Europe 2
Also played for: Scotland (26 caps), Airdrie, Rangers, Lockeren, Hearts, Dundee United.

Dougie Bell's departure coincided with the arrival of Jim Bett, recruited by Alex Ferguson in a £300,000 deal in the summer of 1985. That fee, paid to Belgian side Lokeren, represented a record for the Dons at the time but proved to be money very well spent.

At the time, Ferguson said: "Jim will give us quality. He'll give us stature. He will give us stability and his European experience will be invaluable. He's a player of the same class as Gordon Strachan. In short, Jim is an outstanding player."

High praise indeed from the highest source of all at Pittodrie for a man who had starred in Belgian football and had also made an impression in the Icelandic league.

The cultured midfielder started on the long and winding road to stardom with Airdrie before heading for the continent. In those pre-Bosman days it was virtually unheard of for a young Scot to venture onto foreign shores and it showed courage and intelligence on Bett's part to make an unpredictable yet hugely beneficial switch at such an early stage in his career.

He went on to make more than 100 appearances for Rangers between 1980 and 83, a rare bright spot in a miserable period for the Ibrox team. He began his career in Light Blue under John Greig as he struggled to replicate the success the club had enjoyed in he 1970s, living in the shade of the Dons and the emerging Dundee United side managed by Jim McLean.

Bett did not let the team's struggles hamper his personal progress and he continued to perform well before returning to Lockeren for a second spell with the club in 1983 and when it was time to return to Scotland two years later there was no shortage of offers, including from Rangers.

Instead he chose Aberdeen and made the perfect start to his Dons career, scoring in a 3-0 debut win over Hibs on August 10, 1985. He was the creative force as the team stormed to a cup double that season, with his fluid style and creativity in dead ball situations proving to be crowd pleasing and effective in equal measure.

Bett did not play in the League Cup final due to an ankle injury but wore his familiar No.10 jersey for the Scottish Cup win against Hearts, helping his side to a 3-0 win over the Edinburgh side who just the week before had blown their Premier Division title hopes in the final league game of the season. The Dons and Bett, not surprisingly, were in no mood to be sympathetic.

The Glaswegian was a loyal servant in a transitional period for the club, at the heart of the team under first Ferguson, then his successor Ian Porterfield and, more successfully, Alex Smith and his co-manager Jocky Scott.

Smith and Scott's spell at the helm brought the Dons fans and players the silverware they had taken for granted

under Ferguson and Bett was there to enjoy it as his side claimed a dramatic and nerve shredding 9-8 penalty shoot-out win over Celtic in the 1990 Scottish Cup final after the match had ended without a goal.

To cap a memorable campaign he was voted Scotland's player of the year by his fellow professionals. Team-mate Alex McLeish won the Scottish Football Writers' Asssociation and Tartan Special player of the year awards to make it a Dons hat-trick that year.

Bett was an ever present in the Premier Division campaign in 1990/91 when Aberdeen came within 90 minutes of winning another league title. His prompting from midfield could not unlock a resolute Rangers defence as the Light Blues ran out 2-0 winners in the infamous final day decider at Ibrox to win the championship by just two points ... the value of a single win in those days.

The Glaswegian was part of the Scotland set-up throughout his time at Pittodrie, amassing 26 caps in a career spanning from 1982 to his final appearance as an Aberdeen player in 1990.

His international career took in the World Cup finals in Italy in 1990, where he made his final appearance in dark blue in the 1-0 defeat against Costa Rica. He was also a squad member at the 1986 World Cup finals in Mexico having featured in every qualifying game. His single international goal came against Iceland, the homeland of his wife, in a 1-0 win in 1985.

Bett eventually left Pittodrie in the summer of 1994, by which time former team-mate Willie Miller was the man steering the ship. His final appearance came in a 4-0 league win over Raith Rovers at Pittodrie on February 12 that year to take his tally to 338 games and 47 goals.

He went on to turn out for Hearts and Dundee United over the following two seasons, making more than 20 appearances for each, before retiring. His career had taken him to many countries and many clubs, but it is with Aberdeen that the crafty midfielder formed the strongest bond on and off the park as the Granite City tempted him to put an end to his nomadic existence and settle for the longest period in his life.

Bett's association with Aberdeen did not end when he called time on his own playing career, with sons Baldur and Calum both turning out for the club under Ebbe Skovdahl. Baldur made his first appearance in 1998 and Calum followed in his boot-steps in 2001.

Bett, who continued to live in the Aberdeen area at the end of his playing career, served as a youth coach with both Dundee United and Celtic in the north-east before upping sticks once again to return to Iceland and join the coaching staff at his former club Valur.

Eric Black

Debut: League, 31 October 1981 v Dundee United (h) drew 1-1
Appearances: League 115+19, Scottish Cup 25+3, League Cup 18+4, Europe 22+4
Goals: League 45, Scottish Cup 5, League Cup 12, Europe 7
Also played for: Scotland (2 caps), Metz
Managed: Motherwell, Coventry City

The Gothenburg triumph in 1983 not only produced a team of legends, it created a legacy. Whether it was the inspiration of savouring European success or the indelible mark left by Sir Alex Ferguson, a disproportionate number from that European Cup Winners' Cup side have gone on to make their mark in coaching.

Black is no exception, most recently serving as assistant to boss Steve Bruce in the Premiership with Sunderland. Black led Motherwell and Coventry City in his own right, having cut his teeth on the coaching staff at Celtic. He also came very close to taking over the Pittodrie manager's office following the departure of Alex Miller in the 1990s and tantalisingly to this day refuses to rule out the possibility of a Dons homecoming in the future.

His playing career with the club began in 1980 when he was taken south as a teenager straight from Alness Academy in the Highlands by Alex Ferguson and his far reaching scouting network.

He introduced himself to the fans with a goal on his debut in a 1-1 home draw against Dundee United in the Premier Division on October 31, 1981.

Black was eased into life with the club, starting 10 top flight games that term, and came on from the bench in the 4-1 extra-time triumph over Rangers in the final of the Scottish Cup to cap his introductory campaign with a medal.

By the time the memorable 1982/83 season started Black was still short of his 20th birthday but was one of the first names on Ferguson's team-sheet. He was integral to the double success the year brought.

Against Real Madrid in *that* final he scored the opener in the 2-1 European Cup Winners' Cup final win to earn himself a permanent place in the hearts of the Dons faithful. Black was a thorn in Madrid's side throughout the game, hitting the crossbar in the opening minutes before tucking home his goal after just six minutes when he met an Alex McLeish knock-down inside the box. He continued to force saves from the Real keeper before limping out injured to make way for the other goalscoring hero, John Hewitt, in the second half.

Ten days later, on the home soil of Hampden Park, Black again showed his aptitude for the big occasion when his solitary goal gave the Dons victory over Rangers in the Scottish Cup final. Black had arrived, in style.

Rangers were not alone in suffering at his hands, with Black's first Dons hat-trick destroying Celtic in the league earlier that season as they were beaten 3-1. He went one better in the following season's League Cup, bagging four in a 9-0 romp against Raith Rovers.

The league medal was added in the 1983/84 campaign and a third consecutive Scottish Cup winner's prize joined it on the mantelpiece, Black again on target as the Dons claimed a 2-1 win over Celtic in a tense final that went to extra-time. By that time, he had already helped the side to success in the European Super Cup against SV Hamburg.

In the summer of 1984 Aberdeen lost the services of Mark McGhee, leading scorer for the previous two terms. Would it prove terminal to Ferguson's hopes of dominating

domestically? The answer was a resounding no.

Frank McDougall took over the mantle as the ultimate danger man but Black stepped up his contribution and, in what proved to be his penultimate campaign in red, made the most prolific contribution of his Dons career with 20 goals in all competitions in 1984/85.

The Dons retained the Premier Division trophy and Black's 17 goals in the league, including the mandatory hat-trick, this time in a 5-0 success over Hibs, were vital to that success.

It proved to be the final medal for Black, who missed the 1986 Scottish Cup final after scoring in the 3-0 semi-final win over Hibs. He was dropped for announcing, before the campaign had ended, that he would be leaving for new pastures. Not common in those pre-Bosman ruling days.

In the summer of that year he moved on, broadening his horizons with a switch to Metz in France when his Dons contract expired. While on the continent he became a Scotland international, capped twice in 1987 in a 2-0 win over Hungary and 0-0 draw against Luxembourg during Andy Roxburgh's tenure as national coach.

In France, at the age of 28, a back injury cut short his playing career and hastened his entry to the coaching ranks. Black's decision to turn his back on the Dons after 210 appearances and 69 goals in 1986 angered Alex Ferguson, who made no secret of his displeasure at the time.

But, more than a decade later, the Manchester United coach was the first to send a congratulatory card to his former player on his

appointment at Motherwell in 2001. The message simply read: "Welcome to the rat's world". And so the Ferguson legacy continued.

Black spent less than a year in charge at Fir Park before moving to England as assistant to Gary McAllister at Coventry City in 2002. When McAllister stepped down for personal reasons, his fellow Scot was promoted to the top job. Black spent just four months in charge at the Midlands side but was soon back on the training pitch after Steve Bruce appointed the former Dons forward as first team coach at Birmingham in the summer of 2004.

It has proved to be a relationship that has stood the test of time. Black was promoted to assistant manager and followed Bruce from St Andrews to Wigan and then on to Sunderland as the duo proved adept at working on tight budgets in the engine room of the Premier League, two one-time Sir Alex Ferguson protégés linking with great aplomb.

Craig Brewster

Debut: League, 2 January 2007 v Hibs (a) drew 0-0
Appearances: League 15, Scottish Cup 1
Goals: League 3, Scottish Cup 1
Also played for: Forfar Athletic, Raith Rovers, Dundee United, Ionikos, Hibs, Dunfermline, Caley Thistle
Managed: Caley Thistle, Dundee United

When 40-year-old Craig Brewster penned a Pittodrie contract in January 2007 it was not with the long haul in mind. Manager Jimmy Calderwood, who had worked with the veteran striker at Dunfermline, moved quickly to snap up the wily Dundonian after he had been sacked from his post as manager of Dundee United and got a good return for his short term investment. Despite suffering a dislocated shoulder soon after joining, the powerful forward proved a useful attacking weapon as well as a steadying influence on those around him.

Brewster, best known for his Scottish Cup winning goal against Rangers for the Arabs in the 1994 final at Hampden, remained at his temporary north-east staging post until the end of the 2006/07 season. It was the latest stop on a football odyssey which had taken him from the backwaters of Forfar in the late 1980s to Raith Rovers and then Dundee United before a Greek adventure with Ionikos. He returned from the continent to serve with Hibs and the Pars before moving into management with Inverness.

His successful spell in charge between 2004 and 2006 led to his appointment to the top job at United. It was after leaving the Tannadice side that he hooked up with Aberdeen before being spirited north once again by the lure of Caley Thistle. The Highland return lasted until he was dismissed in January 2009 and took up a coaching role with Ross County under Derek Adams, assisting the young boss as he led the Dingwall side to the Scottish Cup final in 2010. Brewster left County when Willie McStay took over as manager later that year.

Alan Boyd

Debut: League Cup, 12 August 1950 v Clyde (h) won 4-3
Appearances: League 69, Scottish Cup 4, League Cup 16
Goals: League 21, Scottish Cup 1, League Cup 2
Also played for: Queen's Park, East Fife

Winger Alan Boyd boasts a unique claim to fame at Pittodrie. As a youngster on the Dons books he penned the winning design to adorn the 1955 championship flag, an indication of the artistic talent which led to a career in architecture.

Boyd was a star of Glasgow schools football and was snapped up by Aberdeen after a spell with Queen's Park as he combined his playing career with studies at Gray's School of Art. Boyd, a member of Britain's 1948 Olympic football team, proved to be a reliable goal scoring winger over the course of nine years. He was released in May 1959 and recruited by East Fife.

Jason Brown

Debut: League Cup, 23 August 2011 v Dundee (h) won 1-0
Appearances (up to the end of 2011/12): League 20, Scottish Cup 5, League Cup 1
Also played for: Wales, Gillingham, Blackburn Rovers

Welsh international Jason Brown made his way to the head of the queue for the goalkeeper's berth during his first season at Pittodrie, having initially been behind David Gonzalez in the line. When Gonzalez departed, the path was open for Brown to stake his claim with some assured displays as he aimed to cement regular first team football after being sent out on loan by Blackburn to Leeds United, Leyton Orient and Cardiff City.

Jimmy Brown

Debut: League Cup, 8 August 1953 v Celtic (a) won 1-0
Appearances: League 3, League Cup 4
Goals: League 1, League Cup 1
Also played for: Falkirk

Right place, wrong time. Those four words sum up Jimmy Brown's career with Aberdeen as the right winger arrived from Falkirk in 1953 just as Graham Leggat began to emerge as a rising star in his position. After finding opportunities limited he was released to return to the central belt in 1955. Brown later coached Whitburn juniors.

John Brown

Debut: League, 23 January 1954 v Airdrie (a) won 3-1
Appearances: League 5
Goals: League 1
Also played for: Arbroath, East Fife, Fraserburgh, Peterhead

Sunnybank juniors product John Brown was snapped up by Aberdeen in 1952. He deputised for Graham Leggat in three games during the championship winning season in 1954/55, scoring once that term. Brown left to join Arbroath in 1957 and skippered the Gayfield men before spells with East Fife, Fraserburgh and Peterhead in the 1960s.

Ken Brownlee

Debut: League, 28 January 1956 v Queen of the South (a) drew 2-2
Appearances: League 132, Scottish Cup 10, League Cup 25
Goals: League 28, Scottish Cup 5, League Cup 6
Also played for: Newtongrange Star, Third Lanark, St Johnstone, Airdrie, Boksburg (South Africa)

An eye catching display in a trial match against a Celtic reserve side at Pittodrie in the autumn of 1955 was the match that turned Ken Brownlee's life around. Aged 20, he was a Newtongrange Star junior player who by day was a stock keeper for an Edinburgh firm one moment and a full-time member of the reigning league champions' squad the next.

Brownlee did have pedigree, having previously gone on trial with St Johnstone, and had rejected advances from Sunderland just weeks before the Dons made their move. It was Davie Shaw who recruited the powerfully built wing-half and the club got good service from him over the course of eight years on the books, playing in half a dozen different positions and earning plaudits for his enthusiastic approach to the game.

A product of Newtongrange Victoria Star amateurs, Brownlee rose to the top in the game through hard work and dedication as he progressed to the junior and then senior ranks. With his 6ft frame, there was no chance of him hiding in the shadows and he gained a reputation as a solid professional who could be relied upon to do an honest shift wherever he was deployed.

In 1963 Brownlee moved south to join Third Lanark, where he went on to become captain.

He also had stints with St Johnstone and Airdrie before venturing to South Africa to represent Boksburg in Johannesburg.

Johnny Bruce

Debut: League, 14 April 1950 v East Fife (a) lost 3-1
Appearances: League 3
Also played for: Dundee

Wing-half Johnny Bruce learnt his trade with junior side Dundee Violet before turning senior with Dundee in the post-war years. He moved north to Aberdeen for the 1949/50 season and made three appearances over two seasons as he waited patiently behind Chris Anderson in the queue for the No.4 jersey. Bruce was released in 1951.

Willie Bruce

Debut: League, 13 August 1947 v Hibs (h) lost 2-0
Appearances: League 1
Also played for: Raith Rovers, Peterhead, Inverness Caledonian, Keith

Aberdonian goalkeeper Willie Bruce had to travel to Fife to get his senior break after starring for Torry FPs, turning out for Raith Rovers in the post war years before being signed by the Dons in 1947. He stood in for George Johnstone in a single game against Hibs before becoming a popular figure on the Highland League scene with Peterhead, Inverness Caledonian and then Keith.

Henning Boel

Debut: League, 4 January 1969 v Dundee United (a) won 4-1
Appearances: League 105+1, Scottish Cup 16, League Cup 22, Europe 6
Goals: League 2, Scottish Cup 1, League Cup 1
Also played for: Denmark (15 caps), Ikast, Boston Beacons, Washington Whips, New England Revolution

Aberdeen has welcomed its share of continental imports but very few have left the shores of the north-east with a precious souvenir from their time at Pittodrie. Henning Boel earned his memento in the 1970 Scottish Cup final, when Celtic were humbled by the Dons as they ran out 3-1 winners to lift the old trophy for the first time since 1947. Boel played an important role, thwarting the attacking threats of John Hughes and Jimmy Johnstone during that pulsating final.

It was the undoubted high spot for the Danish stopper, who had been taken to the club by Eddie Turnbull mid-way through the 1968/69 season having first been spotted while the Dons toured America.

The Dons finished the campaign 15th, just two places clear of relegation, and Boel's addition to the squad was an attempt by Turnbull to close the door on the dreaded possibility of dropping out of the elite. The defender proved a popular addition, among players and supporters, and stayed longer than many imports. In 2006 he was voted by fans as one of the top five foreign imports ever brought to Scotland by the Dons.

He had arrived as the fourth member of a Scandinavian quartet, which had begun to fall into place under Tommy Pearson in 1965 with the recruitment of Leif Mortensen, Joergen Louis Ravn and Jens Petersen. While Ravn and Mortensen fell by the wayside less than a year and a half after arriving, Petersen went on to captain the Dons and successfully blazed a trail.

Having begun his career with Ikast in his homeland, Boel also featured for the Boston Beacons in their one and only season in the North American Soccer League and the Washington Whips. By coincidence, the Dons had adopted the Washington Whips moniker during their tour of America in 1967, with a clutch of top class teams from Britain and beyond each being assigned a local name in an attempt to sell the game to a still sceptical US public.

When the NASL folded, for the first but not last time, in 1968 he returned to Denmark in search of alternative employment and it was Turnbull who came up with the best offer.

He was only 23 when he arrived in Aberdeen for a trial period in November 1968 but had good pedigree, with 13 consecutive appearances for Denmark up to the point

of turning professional with Boston in 1968. By accepting the lucre of the paid game, Boel had crossed the divide as far as the Danish football federation were concerned. By opting to pursue a pay packet he immediately barred himself from representing his country, although he did return briefly to add a further two caps once the anti-pro rule had been abolished in 1971.

After Boel's debut in a 4-1 win over Dundee United at Tannadice on January 4, 1969, he established himself as a regular in Turnbull's rearguard and played every game in the run-in to the end of the season. By the time his first full season began he had been shifted from the centre of the defence to the right side, although he continued to deputise at centre-half when called upon, and the Dons enjoyed a more fruitful period. They shrugged off the relegation fears of the previous season to finish in the comfort of eighth and clinched the cup.

In the 1970/71 season Boel played a major part in a British club record run of 12 consecutive games without conceding a goal. He also chipped in with four goals, breaking his Dons duck when he netted in a 4-0 win at Kilmarnock early in the season.

Aberdeen went on to miss out on the Premier Division title by just two points, with Celtic taking the honours. Boel, an ever present in the league, could take a share in the small consolation that his side's defensive record could not be bettered, with a miserly 18 goals conceded by a steely unit over 34 games. Not even the champions could match that.

The foundations began to crumble the following season, with manager Turnbull departing for Hibernian and captain Martin Buchan, another vital cog in the defensive machine, moving south in a dream move to Manchester United.

Boel, who had vied with George Murray for the No.2 jersey under new boss Jimmy Bonthrone, played out the season for the club as they again finished runners-up to the Hoops, this time by a margin of 10 points.

The Dane, who made 15 appearances for his country, was still on the books as the 1972/73 campaign burst into life but made only 13 further appearances.

A broken ankle suffered in the 1972 Uefa Cup tie against Borussia Monchengladbach pushed him out of the frame at Pittodrie.

The Danish international did make a comeback after that, returning to football in America with New England Revolution in the NASL's era of Pele and George Best, but never hit the same heights.

He went on to play alongside Eusebio for Boston but the club folded, as so many American franchises did. Aberdeen's adopted son remained in the states, going on to play for and manage the New England Tea Men before returning to Denmark to wind down back where it started with Ikast.

Boel, who appeared 150 times for the Dons, worked as a sales representative for sports firms Nike and Hummel in his homeland before moving into the oil sector and then in the travel industry as a tour guide in Scotland for Danish visitors.

Scott Booth

Debut: League, 28 April 1990 v St Mirren (h) won 2-0
Appearances: League 170+15, Scottish Cup 6+1, League Cup 6, Europe 4+3
Goals: League 51, Scottish Cup 3, League Cup 1
Also played for: Scotland (22 caps), Borussia Dortmund, Utrecht, Twente Enschede

Scottish club football may not have seen the last of one of Aberdeen's best homegrown players. Alongside a certain Alan Shearer on the list of budding young coaches to have passed the SFA's A-licence in the summer of 2006 was a Mr S. Booth. Like Shearer, Booth starred for his home town club. Like Shearer, he hung up his boots when it appeared to most he could have played on.

In 2004 Booth, then aged 32 and in his second spell at Pittodrie, was told by new manager Jimmy Calderwood that he would not be retained.

There were other options on the table in Scotland but Booth instead signed for Setanta - not an exotic far-flung club but the Irish satellite broadcaster. Booth took to his new role as a television presenter, reporting on Scottish Premier League football week in and week out before stepping up to become the station's co-commentator, with the same type of ease as he played the game. When Setanta was placed in administration in 2009 there were 200 job losses and Booth was among them, with fame no shield against the downturn gripping Europe. Like he had to do so often during his playing days, the Aberdonian dusted himself down and regrouped to fight another day. He was soon back in broadcasting as a radio analyst with BBC Scotland's Sportsound team and added another string to his bow as his media career continues apace.

However, the fact he has passed his coaching qualifications hinted that he could return to the other side of the lens and in 2012 he was appointed to the SFA staff to work with the nation's young stars.

Putting Booth through his coaching paces in 2006 on behalf of the SFA was Alex Smith, the manager who 16 years earlier, in 1990, had given a teenage striker his big break for Aberdeen. Smith, the godfather of Scottish coaching, has an impressive track record of recognizing young talent and he was convinced that in Booth he had one of the finest players of his generation.

The rookie made his entrance on April 28 in a 2-0 win at home to St Mirren as a substitute. He waited just a week for his first start, entrusted with the No.9 jersey for a 3-1 win over Celtic at Parkhead.

The first goals came on February 2, 1991, with a double in a 5-0 win at home to Hearts. His return in the league, as the Dons missed out on the title on the final day of the season at the hands of Rangers, was six goals in just eight starts.

Booth, along with sidekick Eoin Jess, went from strength to strength under Smith's considered tutelage. His successor Willie Miller also put his faith in the confident and cultured youngster.

Miller's side, sent on their way by a Booth hat-trick in the 4-1 first round win over Hamilton, his first senior treble, ran to the final of the 1993 Scottish Cup but tasted defeat when Rangers won 2-1 and also finished second to the Ibrox side in the league.

The Light Blues again stood in the way of Booth and the Premier Division winner's medal he craved in 1993/94.

His solitary reward for his endeavours at Pittodrie should have come in the League Cup of 1995, by which time Roy Aitken was in charge. Booth was joint top scorer in that 1995/96 campaign, tied with Billy Dodds on 12, and scored three in the League Cup before agonisingly missing out on the final triumph over Dundee due to injury on the eve of the game. His replacement for the match was Duncan Shearer, an indication of the wealth of attacking options possessed by Aberdeen during a period in which the team carried a threat from every area of the pitch.

The pain of that cup final disappointment was eased by international recognition, Booth making his Scotland debut against Germany in a 1-0 defeat when he was selected by Andy Roxburgh. He went on to appear in Dark Blue 22 times, including at Euro 96 and the World Cup finals in France in 1998, scoring six goals in the process and looking comfortable among the best in the business.

Having come through the ranks alongside Jess and Stephen Wright, both sold in seven-figure deals in 1996, it was perhaps no surprise Booth himself opted to test the water away from his boyhood team. His path was not a well trodden one, stunning the Dons fans in 1997 when he clinched a move to German giants Borussia Dortmund having fallen out of contract at Pittodrie. It was a dream transfer and a life changing moment for a young man who had his football education on his doorstep, taking him to a different professional culture and allowing him to work alongside legends of the European game.

He stayed on the continent, with spells at FC Utrecht and Twente Enschede in Holland, for six years before returning to Scotland and Aberdeen in 2003 to play for Steve Paterson. Like so many who ventured abroad, the FP returned with fresh wind in his sails. His game looked to have been enhanced by his experiences in Germany and Holland and age had given him a new maturity. The coaching staff raved about the new-look Booth, following his studies in the leagues of Europe, but his return did not bring an upturn in fortunes for the club as they struggled in the top flight.

Booth, brought up on a diet of European football and championship challenges in his early days with the Dons, was in a very different era but at least ended his career with the merit of only ever playing for one Scottish side. In two spells he turned out 228 times and hit the back of the net on 70 occasions, remembered fondly as one of the most naturally gifted attacking players to pull on the red shirt of his home city's team.

Martin Buchan

Debut: League, 8 October 1966 v Dunfermline (a) drew 1-1
Appearances: League 133+3, Scottish Cup 20, League Cup 23, Europe 12+1
Goals: League 9, League Cup 1, Europe 1
Also played for: Scotland (34 caps), Manchester United, Oldham Athletic.
Managed: Burnley.

In November, 2006, Martin Buchan was named as one of only three football players among 21 stars from all genres to earn a place in the newly created Aberdeen sporting hall of fame. The trio was completed by Denis Law and another former Dons player featured later in the pages of this book, inducted alongside Olympic medal winning heroes and champions from the upper echelons of golf and rugby.

The Dons have been blessed with a string of home grown talents throughout the decades but Buchan is regarded by fans of his home town club as one of the finest Pittodrie products.

Unlike Law he launched his career at home, signing for Aberdeen straight from school having grown up playing school and boys' brigade football. It was Eddie Turnbull who recruited the 16 year-old, a pupil at Robert Gordon's College in the city, in 1965. The following year, on October 8, 1966, he made his debut wearing No.6 in a 1-1 draw against Dunfermline at East End Park.

It was a transitional period for the club under Turnbull, who made sweeping changes to the playing squad as he built a side around his new found defensive rock.

Buchan went on to become Turnbull's captain and his crowning glory in the red of Aberdeen came at Hampden in May, 1970 when, at the age of just 21, he held aloft the Scottish Cup in front of 108,324 supporters at the national stadium. The Dons defeated Celtic 3-1 with a double from Derek McKay and a Joe Harper goal.

It ended a 23 year famine in the national cup competition for the Dons and Buchan's place as a hero for the Pittodrie faithful was assured.

His standing in the Scottish game was also being elevated to new levels and in 1971 he was named as the Scottish Football Writers' Player of the year, becoming the first Aberdonian ever to win the honour. He would be followed by another north-east player the following year, another man featured in the pages which follow.

Buchan followed Old Firm captains John Greig and Billy McNeill in winning the award and 36 years on remains crystal clear about the reasons for his recognition.

Now based in the north-west of England, Buchan said: "It was a reflection that Aberdeen as a club was rising to prominence under Eddie Turnbull and it's often the captains who receive the individual recognition for a team's achievements.

"The trophy I received for the player of the year award was a cigarette box in the shape of a football, which

seems a bit ironic now for a sports award. I was only 21 at the time and I remember the biggest thing for me was having to go down to Glasgow and stand up to make an acceptance speech, hoping I could remember everyone I wanted to thank.

"It isn't until later in life that you realise how many people make sacrifices to help every player in their career. Thinking back to my own primary school days at Cummings Park, we had four teachers with an interest in football who gave up their evenings and weekends to help with the teams. Running any team is a major commitment, you have to give up nine months of your year, and anyone who does that at any level deserves appreciation."

Buchan was growing accustomed to getting his hands on prized football mementoes but admits the moment he collected the Scottish Cup passed in a blur.

He said: "I remember a picture of myself and Billy McNeill shaking hands before the cup final in 1970. It looked like a big man with a wee laddie. We rose to the occasion as a team - Aberdeen were seen as underdogs but didn't feel that way. We had beaten Celtic at Parkhead in the league in the weeks leading up to the final. They only needed a point to win the title - there were crates of champagne stacked up outside the home dressing room and that made Eddie Turnbull's team talk easy. Eddie simply said to us: 'Do you think they are going to celebrate tonight at our expense?'

"We won the league game 2-1 and before the cup final George Murray stopped Eddie to asked him for the same words again and the manager obliged. It obviously worked. It was a big occasion but I don't remember too much about collecting the cup - I remember more about lifting the FA Cup for Manchester United six years later. In saying that, the memories of the parade down Union Street are more vivid. It was fantastic."

Buchan also won the first of 34 Scotland caps while with the Pittodrie side. He was selected by Tommy Docherty and made his debut in a 1-0 win against Belgium in Aberdeen courtesy of a John O'Hare strike.

The promise of the budding international defender was reaching a wider audience and early in 1972 a clutch of English clubs moved in on Scottish football's hot property.

Leeds United and Liverpool were keen but it was Manchester United who won the chase, shelling out £125,000 to take Buchan to Old Trafford.

Buchan, who scored 11 times, played 192 games for Aberdeen over the course of five years and four months. Many have served the club for longer but nobody on the Pittodrie terraces grudged their local hero the chance to test himself in the English league.

Frank O'Farrell was the manager who did the deal for Manchester United but within months he was replaced by Docherty and Buchan was given another big break, appointed captain of the Red Devils to follow Bobby Charlton. As he had done with the Dons he led United to cup glory, lifting the FA Cup at Wembley after a 2-1 win over Liverpool at Wembley in 1977. While with the English giants he featured in both the 1974 and 1978 World Cup finals tournaments with Scotland.

Buchan, who captained Scotland twice, remained at Old Trafford for 11 years before joining Oldham Athletic in 1983. He also had a brief spell as a manager with Burnley before moving into the sportswear industry with Puma. He remains based in Manchester and now works with the Professional Footballers' Association.

George Buchan

Debut: League, 24 March 1969 v Dunfermline (h) drew 2-2
Appearances: League 35, Scottish Cup 4, League Cup 13, Europe 5
Goals: League 2, League Cup 1
Also played for: Manchester United, Bury

The Scottish Cup final victory against Celtic in 1970 was a family affair for the Buchans. While Martin took the limelight as skipper for the memorable win, his younger brother George was also part of the triumphant squad as an unused substitute in Eddie Turnbull's side. The former Banks o' Dee A player had come on from the bench in the semi-final win against Kilmarnock to play his part in the cup run. Buchan was released in 1973 and the speedy forward won a dream move to join his elder brother at Manchester United. He went on to play for Bury before playing non-league football as he combined playing commitments with a new career as a PE teacher in the Manchester area.

Jamie Buchan

Debut: League, 2 March 1996 v Kilmarnock (h) won 3-0
Appearances: League 58, Scottish Cup 1, League Cup 3, Europe 1
Goals: League 4
Also played for: Stockport County, Dundee United, Partick Thistle, Peterhead, Montrose, Cove Rangers

When Jamie Buchan made his breakthrough with Aberdeen he was entering a team on a real high. Just three months earlier his new colleagues had lifted the League Cup and in the Premier Division they were well on their way to a top three finish under the steady hand of manager Roy Aitken in the 1995/96 season.

It was the perfect scenario for a young player to be introduced to the fray and Aitken was careful in his handling of the 18-year-old defender, giving him three tastes of top flight football from the bench before promoting him to the starting line-up for the final game of the campaign.

His progress was measured and steady, helped by the careful handling of the coaching staff, and continued at that pace for a further two seasons before Buchan became a regular fixture in the team under Alex Miller and then Paul Hegarty in the turbulent 1998/99 term. He had grown into the team under close scrutiny thanks to the media and public attention generated by his famous father, Dons legend and former Pittodrie captain Martin Buchan.

Like his dad he was a defender who was comfortable with the ball at his feet. While he served primarily as a full-back with Aberdeen, Buchan proved adept at playing as a centre-half later in his career and also proved to be comfortable in midfield.

He moved on from Pittodrie in 2000 and played for Dundee United, Partick Thistle, Peterhead and Montrose through to 2009. He went on to turn out for Cove Rangers in the Highland League.

Eddie Buchanan

Debut: League, 23 December 1967 v Airdrie (a) lost 1-0
Appearances: League 5, Scottish Cup 1
Goals: League 1
Also played for: Berwick Rangers

Eddie Turnbull brought the junior half-back to Aberdeen from Shettleston in his native Glasgow in 1966. The promising and intelligent youngster broke into the Dons side within a year, but after just a clutch of appearances was released to allow him to return to live on the west coast. Buchanan was picked up by Berwick Rangers in 1969 and spent a season at Shielfield.

Richie Buckley

Debut: League, 27 March 2004 v Kilmarnock (a) lost 3-1
Appearances: League 8
Also played for: East Fife, Albion Rovers

Defender Richie Buckley made his first team breakthrough under Steve Paterson and played in the shock 2-1 win at Celtic in 2004, he was farmed out to Ayr United by Jimmy Calderwood in the 2004/05 season and then joined the Honest Men permanently. Spells with East Fife and Albion Rovers followed as well as service in the junior ranks with Cumnock, Troon and Bellshill.

John Burridge

Debut: League, 2 April 1994 v Rangers (a) drew 1-1
Appearances: League 3, Scottish Cup 1
Also played for: Workington, Blackpool, Aston Villa, Crystal Palace, QPR, Wolves, Sheffield United, Southampton, Newcastle United, Hibs, Scarborough, Lincoln, Dumbarton, Falkirk, Manchester City, Notts County, Darlington, Grimsby, Queen of the South

It takes a special character to be able to make their Aberdeen debut against Rangers at Ibrox and not feel intimidated. John Burridge was one of those individuals. The eccentric

English goalkeeper was targeted as an understudy for Theo Snelders in the 1993/94 season and made his first appearance in a 1-1 draw against the Light Blues. It was the first of four appearances following his switch from Lincoln City, with draws against Partick, Dundee United and Celtic following before he moved on to Dumbarton. The Dons were one of more than 20 senior clubs the shot stopper featured for during a career spanning the 1970s, 80s and 90s.

Ian Burns

Debut: League Cup, 10 August 1957 v Queen of the South (h) won 5-1
Appearances: League 142, Scottish Cup 16, League Cup 34
Goals: League 2, League Cup 4
Also played for: Brechin City, Deveronvale

Rugged, hard in the tackle, decisive and powerfully-built. Just some of the words used to describe this midfielder when he was at his peak as a pocket dynamo at the heart of the Dons team in the early 1960s.

His all action style of play led to brushes with the disciplinary chiefs but, off the park at least, Burns was credited as being the perfect gentleman.

He was a product of the Banks o' Dee A conveyor belt of talent in the 1950s and gained two youth international caps before joining the Dons. He made his Aberdeen debut early in the 1957/58 season, displaying confidence with the ball at his feet and precise passing, before quickly moving up the pecking order to earn the captaincy. Even national service could not keep Burns at bay, with duty with the Gordon Highlanders at Bridge of Don Barracks enabling him to continue playing for the club.

The 5ft 8in star, capped at under-23 level and picked for the Scottish League select, was hit by a ligament injury in his second campaign and required surgery in 1962 when knee trouble continued to pose problems.

At the end of the 1965/66 season Burns was given a free transfer and joined Brechin City for a four year stint. After a season as player coach with Deveronvale he hung up his boots in 1971.

Dave Bus

Debut: League Cup, 5 February 2008 v Dundee United (a) lost 4-1
Appearances: League 6, League Cup 1
Also played for: De Graafschap, Go Ahead Eagles

Aberdeen's Dutch network was extended in January 2008 when defender Dave Bus joined former team-mate Jeffrey De Visscher on the Pittodrie staff. Bus was signed on loan from De Graafschap having fallen out of favour at the top flight side. He was a tall and imposing stopper but never looked entirely comfortable in the SPL and, even when he was freed by his club in the Netherlands during his time in Scotland, there was no offer of an extended contract by Jimmy Calderwood. He returned to his home country and found a new lease of life with Go Ahead Eagles, captaining the side after joining them in the summer of 2008.

Andy Cadenhead

Debut: League, 19 September 1959 v Partick Thistle (h) won 5-2
Appearances: League 39, Scottish Cup 3, League Cup 6
Also played for: St Johnstone, Nairn County

Right-back Andy Cadenhead was 20-years-old when he swapped life with junior cracks Sunnybank to try his hand in the senior game with Aberdeen in 1957. He was promoted to the first team two years later, playing in both full-back positions. A brief stop with St Johnstone in the 1963/64 season was a precursor to an eight-year tour of duty at the heart of Highland League side Nairn County's back line. Cadenhead combined his playing duties with his career as a scientist at the Rowett Institute.

Willie Callaghan

Debut: League, 7 September 1961 v St Mirren (a) lost 3-2
Appearances: League 24, Scottish Cup 1, League Cup 1
Goals: League 8, Scottish Cup 3
Also played for: East Stirling, Dumbarton

Right winger Willie Callaghan had a spell with Arsenal as a teenager, but was recruited by Aberdeen in 1961 after making a name for himself with East Stirling. He rattled in a hat-trick against Airdrie in a 5-2 Scottish Cup win at Pittodrie. That was the highlight of Callaghan's time with the Dons, with the flanker released in the summer of 1963. He had a stint with Barnsley as well as a second spell with East Stirling and also featured for Stranraer and Albion Rovers.

Richie Byrne

Debut: Scottish Cup, 5 February 2005 v Caley Thistle (h) won 2-1
Appearances: League 50, Scottish Cup 4, League Cup 3, Europe 2
Goals: League 1, Scottish Cup 1
Also played for: Shamrock Rovers, Dunfermline Athletic, Oldham Athletic, Caley Thistle

Manager Jimmy Calderwood made no secret of his penchant for signing players on the strength of what they offered off the pitch as much as they contributed on the park. Calderwood was often heard to muse that certain players were 'good to have about the place' and Irishman Richie Byrne certainly fell into that camp. The laid-back Dubliner was a popular figure at Pittodrie during his three and a half years on the payroll – even if not every supporter shared the enthusiasm of his colleagues at the club. What he lacked in touch and passing ability he made up for with heart on sleeve passion and an infectious enthusiasm for the game.

Byrne was one of a string of players Calderwood recruited from his former club Dunfermline. He was big, strong, fast and physical. Those attributes made him a decent defender but also brought their own problems as Byrne was struck by injuries which restricted his contribution to 59 games spanning the four seasons he featured in for the Dons.

Byrne had a short spell with Oldham after being released by Aberdeen in the summer of 2008. He was brought back over the border in January 2009 when Craig Brewster snapped him up for Caley Thistle. After a year in Inverness the Irish stopper was sent out on loan to St Johnstone and later moved on to spend a period with Darlington towards the end of the 2009/10 season.

Paddy Buckley

Debut: League Cup, 9 August 1952 v Motherwell (a) lost 5-2
Appearances: League 106, Scottish Cup 20, League Cup 26
Goals: League 58, Scottish Cup 16, League Cup 18
Also played for: Scotland (3 caps), Bo'ness United, St Johnstone

In 1955 Aberdeen were crowned champions of Scotland for the first time since the club's formation in 1903 and it is safe to say that success would not have been possible without the goals of one man. His name was Paddy Buckley and his prolific form as the feared No.9 of the championship winning Dons team was a key factor in the title success savoured by the Pittodrie faithful.

Buckley smashed home seventeen goals in that Division A campaign as his side pipped Celtic by just three points to lift the trophy. The speedy Leith-born forward missed just two of the 30 league games that term and consistently provided a match-winning contribution. As the title race went to the wire, he crashed home a hat-trick in a 4-0 win over Rangers as the season entered its final month and a double in a 3-2 win over Raith Rovers on the final day of the season.

Aberdeen's class of 55 were living the dream the club's supporters had been harbouring for more than half a century when the Scottish league crown was claimed. For the proud provincial team far from football's traditional heartland in the central belt, it was a truly momentous achievement. The might of the Old Firm and the lofty ambitions of the two Edinburgh sides had been pushed to one side by the young upstarts from the north-east corner of the country. It was time for the establishment to move over, there were new kids in town.

At the pinnacle of that team was the forward who struck fear into the hearts of the Old Firm. The 1954/55 season was Buckley's most profitable as a Dons player. He netted six goals in six games in the League Cup and five in six games in the Scottish Cup for a return of 28 in just 40 appearances to secure his place as leading scorer at the club. It was a strike ratio worth millions in the modern game, the type of player that in the present day would be far out of reach.

Buckley was no stranger to celebrating before that glorious season, on target 27 times the previous term. That form propelled him onto the international stage and he made his debut for Scotland in a 1-0 win over Norway in May, 1954, to become one of the early Dons in dark blue. Two further caps followed all in the same year, the highlight coming when he scored the winner in a 1-0 win over Wales in Cardiff.

Buckley faced fierce competition from Hibs legend Lawrie Reilly in the fight for Scotland places but at club level he could not be budged from the Aberdeen team.

He cut his teeth with Bo'ness United before switching to the senior game at the age of 23 in 1948 with St Johnstone, although Celtic had also been on the trail of one of the stars of the junior game. After four years in Perth it cost Aberdeen manager Dave Halliday the considerable sum of £7,500 to tempt Saints to part with their striker, now in his prime.

In fact, in the week leading up to his switch to the north-east he scored an incredible eight goals in seven days. He hit four against East Fife for St Johnstone at the start of the week, added a midweek hat-trick against Breadalbane in the Dewar Shield and then signed off with his final goal for the Muirton men against Clyde in the Supplementary Cup. Not bad form. Not surprisingly he found himself in demand from bigger clubs and, having started in his native Edinburgh, his football path continued north as his brightest years loomed.

Dons manager Halliday had a growing reputation as a talent spotter and was quietly but efficiently piecing together a team that would soon be challenging the big guns for major honours. With his raid on St Johnstone, the manager had secured the man who would provide an attacking spark and ruthless streak to his side just in time for the big league push.

Buckley's first appearance in red came in a 5-2 League Cup defeat at the hands of Motherwell on August 9, 1952. It was a miserable game but Buckley's goal on his debut at least gave a glimmer of hope for the Dons fans in the crowd at Fir Park. The hope turned to tangible success as the goals flew in thick and fast and the championship flag followed with them as he settled quickly and found his stride.

Buckley remained at Pittodrie until 1957, when a serious knee injury brought the curtain down on a glittering career. He was short of his century of goals but still had an impressive ratio during his relatively short spell on the staff.

He remains one of the leading fifty strikers at the top level in the post-war Scottish game, with the record of 198 goals at club and international level putting him on par with Andy Penman of Dundee and Rangers. For the Dons he grabbed 92 goals in the space of 152 games and remains one of the most potent forwards ever to star for Aberdeen. For those who watched him star at Pittodrie he is also one of the most fondly remembered, thanks to his willingness to play the game with a smile on his face and savour the good times he enjoyed. Despite his diminutive stature, he was a giant in the Scottish game and a giant for the club he served so well during the glory days and champagne celebrations of the 1950s.

THE MANAGERS: PART ONE

JIMMY PHILIP

Job security is a part of football management that appears to live in the past and the first incumbent of the Aberdeen manager's office must be the envy of every modern coach. Jimmy Philip took charge of the club's first ever competitive match in 1903 and remained in post until 1924, during an era in which the role was very much centred on administration. Philip's background was as a prominent referee in Aberdeen footballing circles but he proved himself as a shrewd manager and skilled organiser before stepping down to take a place on the board of directors at Pittodrie.

PAT TRAVERS

After a playing career that took in Aberdeen as well as clubs including Celtic, Clyde and Barnsley there was no shortage of experience on Pat Travers' cv when he took charge in 1924. He had been coaching at Pittodrie for two years by that stage, having performed a similar role in Norwegian football, and went on to spend 13 as manager as he began to build for the future by blooding a clutch of new players. He left in 1937 when he was lured back to Clyde to take charge of the Bully Wee after impressing as Dons boss.

DAVE HALLIDAY

Close to 100 men applied for the manager's job when the vacancy arose in 1937. After a five-week selection process, it was former Dundee, Sunderland, Arsenal and Manchester City striker Dave Halliday who won the day. After a career interrupted by the war, Halliday went on to establish the Dons as a major force as his rebuilt side swept to victory in the Southern League Cup in 1946, the Scottish Cup the following year and then the league championship in 1955. Halliday, with his stock at an all-time high, was tempted back to England with Leicester City after landing the title.

DAVE SHAW

Dave Shaw, the brother of Rangers and Scotland star Jock 'Tiger' Shaw, served as player, captain, trainer and then manager within five years of joining the club from Hibs in 1950. Shaw served in the top job from 1955 to 1959 and was a figure hugely respected by the players who served under him, not least because of his success in leading them to the League Cup in his first season in charge. Shaw stepped down in the winter of 1959 after a run of poor form but remained on the staff as trainer under Tommy Pearson and Eddie Turnbull.

TOMMY PEARSON

Tommy Pearson was a phenomenon during his halcyon days patrolling the Pittodrie turf. The Pearson double shuffle was a thing of football legend, a crowd thrilling manoeuvre that tied a succession of bemused defenders in knots. With fleet of foot, intelligence and deceptive pace he was a star man for the Dons in the post-war years.

He was already 34 when he signed for the club – but age was no barrier. He went on to put in five years of impeccable service, drawing crowds through the gates even when he was featuring in reserve matches and becoming an idol to a generation of impressionable youngsters wowed by his trickery and ability on the ball. His skills were no accident, with Pearson spending hours honing the double shuffle before unleashing it on unsuspecting defenders.

Pearson worked in the bacteriology department of the public health department before turning to full-time football when he was spotted playing amateur football in Edinburgh by Newcastle United.

He had failed to impress Hearts during trial spells in Gorgie but made up for lost time when he made the short hop down the east coast and over the border. He made his Magpies debut as a 19-year-old and stayed for fifteen years, making more than 200 appearances in black and white and establishing himself as a firm favourite at St James' Park.

Despite playing for big clubs on both sides of Hadrian's Wall, Pearson won just a single medal in more than a quarter of a century playing the game - that came as a 16 year-old, when he helped Murrayfield to the Scottish Amateur Cup. Still, he did make an impression that has stood the test of time. His legacy proved to be memories rather than trophies and medals.

Although he ended his playing days at Pittodrie empty handed, he was handed a second bite at the cherry by the club's directors. As one of the game's great thinkers, he was appointed manager in 1959 in succession to Dave Shaw and great things were expected of the former wing wizard.

He spent five years in the manager's chair but it was a difficult time for the team and the coach as results failed to live up to expectations. He was eventually replaced by Eddie Turnbull.

After severing his ties with the game, Pearson moved into journalism with the *Daily Mail* and also became a published author.

EDDIE TURNBULL

The legendary Eddie Turnbull was brought in to restore pride at Pittodrie and set about his task with the type of determination never before seen. A renowned disciplinarian and tactician, he ripped the Dons squad apart and started from scratch as he pulled together a nucleus of players who went on to serve with distinction long after his departure for Hibs in 1971 as well as blooding a clutch of talented young players. In his six years at the helm he claimed the Scottish Cup in 1970 to confirm his place among the greatest managers ever to serve the club.

JIMMY BONTHRONE

There was no questioning Jimmy Bonthrone's coaching credentials. He had managed East Fife, a team he served as a player, and worked on the Scotland staff under Bobby Brown prior to linking up with Eddie Turnbull at Pittodrie. When Turnbull departed, the Dons board turned to Bonthrone to fill the void. He had to watch as star men Martin Buchan and Joe Harper left for English football and subsequently saw his side's fortunes slide, leading to his departure in 1975 as the club struggled at the wrong end of the Premier Division in the first season of the competition's existence.

Robert Connor

Debut: League, 16 August 1986 v Hamilton (h) won 2-0
Appearances: League 197+9, Scottish Cup 17, League Cup 21+1, Europe 16+1
Goals: League 17, Scottish Cup 2, League Cup 3
Also played for: Scotland (4 caps), Ayr United, Dundee, Kilmarnock, Partick Thistle, Queen of the South.
Managed: Ayr United.

Robert Connor's time in Aberdeen provided him with the best of times and the worst of times. The dark day, without question, came on 11 May 1990. The Dons, under Alex Smith, travelled to Ibrox needing a point against Rangers to win the Premier Division title. The home side won 2-0, the trophy stayed in Glasgow and Connor and his team-mates returned north with only thoughts of what could have been.

That low was countered by a succession of highs for Connor, who played for the Dons at a time when they ran Graeme Souness and his Rangers side to the wire in every competition in a gallant attempt to counter the impact of David Murray's open cheque book policy at Ibrox.

A native of Kilmarnock, he launched his career with Ayr United in 1977 before moving on to Dundee seven years later in a £50,000 deal. By that time he had collected eight caps for Scotland's under-21 team and was emerging as one of the country's finest young talents, possessing a sophisticated left foot, that rarest of commodities, and ensured his value was rising. The price tag did not deter Dundee and finance proved no barrier when the west coast man made his next, and most important, move up the football ladder.

Dens Park was a temporary staging post, with Pittodrie boss Alex Ferguson parting with £275,000 in cash and £75,000 rated Ian Angus in exchange for the versatile star in the summer of 1986. It was Ferguson's penultimate signing before his departure for Old Trafford, but having the Fergie seal of approval was a useful addition to any player's cv. His legendary eye for talent proved to be 100 per cent accurate in the case of his midfield recruit, who would prove in the years ahead that he was a man who could handle the unique pressures of playing for a club still striving to build on the success achieved under the club's most famous manager. Connor had the strength of character and natural ability to thrive at Pittodrie.

After his brief spell under Ferguson's wing, the Ayrshireman went on to play under Ian Porterfield, Alex Smith and Willie Miller. He served all with distinction but it was Smith and co-manager Jocky Scott who got the best out of Connor, who was an ever present in the duo's first campaign as part of a midfield quartet completed by Jim Bett, Brian Grant and English winger Paul Mason. It was a group any Scottish club would have been happy to have had on their books.

With Charlie Nicholas, followed by Hans Gillhaus, in attack there was no doubt Aberdeen could mount a serious challenge in the league. The difficulty was turning that challege into success.

Between 1988 and 1994 he and his team finished runners-up in the top flight five times. His first taste of the winning feeling came in the League Cup in the 1989/90 season when Smith's men beat Rangers 2-1 to lift the trophy. It was a sweet occasion after losing to the Light Blues in the two previous finals. Connor played in that showpiece match and then helped the Dons complete the double with a penalty shoot-out victory over Celtic in the Scottish Cup to round off the season.

Connor also shone on the international stage and was an exemplary representative for both Dundee and Aberdeen, making his debut while still a Dens Park employee in a 0-0 friendly draw against Holland in Eindhoven in 1986. It was Alex Ferguson, in his role as national team boss, who gave him that precious first cap.

Three further international appearances followed for the cultured midfielder, with a record of one win and two draws against one defeat in Scotland colours. His first Scotland match as a Dons star was a 2-2 draw against Saudi Arabia in Riyadh in 1988, by which time Andy Roxburgh had taken control of international affairs. He played the following year in a 2-0 Auld Enemy defeat in front of a packed Hampden crowd before his final outing in 1990 when he helped Roxburgh's men to a 2-1 Euro Championship qualifying tie victory against Romania at the national stadium.

He also sampled European football regularly with the Dons, most notably in the double header against Italian giants Torino in the 1993/94 European Cup Winners' Cup when Aberdeen took the lead in both the home and away legs before losing 3-2 and 2-1 after pushing the Serie A side all the way. His passing ability and sweet left foot proved extremely valuable from free-kicks and corners.

After eight memorable years at Pittodrie, with 263 appearances and 22 goals under his belt, Connor was released by Willie Miller after a long battle against an Achilles tendon injury. It was a time when the old guard was rapidly being changed by a young manager desperate to make his mark, although replacing players of the calibre and consistency of Connor proved to be an impossible task.

The midfielder, who had also deputised as a full-back, returned west to hook up with Kilmarnock. He spent a further two years playing Premier Division football with his hometown team before winding down his playing days on a high with his first championship medal, at the age of 36, after helping Ayr United to the Second Division title in 1997. Partick and Queen of the South were his final staging posts after 19 years of plying his trade on Scotland's football pitches.

He went on to become a football writer and agent before returning to the staff at Ayr to start his coaching career where his playing days had begun in the 1970s. In 2005 he stepped up to become manager of the Somerset Park club, 28 years after first crossing the front door as a fresh faced teenage signing, and remained in charge until 2007.

TEN: Trips into the unknown

1 Moldova: When the Dons were paired with Moldovan outfit Nistru Otaci in the 2002/03 Uefa Cup there were stark warnings of heavily armed rebels controlling parts of the former Soviet state. Facilities were also a concern – with Aberdeen leaving nothing to chance, right down to taking their own food on the trip. Ebbe Skovdahl's side won 1-0 at Pittodrie and held out for a 0-0 draw overseas to progress.

2 Bulgaria: Iceland and Belgium had been the destinations during Aberdeen's maiden campaign in Europe in 1967/68. The following year the continental experience took an intriguing twist when Eddie Turnbull's men were sent to the east to tackle Slavia Sofia, a match that attracted 29,000 to the return leg at Pittodrie to witness a businesslike 2-0 win after a 0-0 draw abroad.

3 Lithuania: Roy Aitken's reward for steering Aberdeen back into Europe in the 1996/97 season was a potentially perilous trip to Lithuania to face Zalgiris Vilnius in the Uefa Cup. Any fears were swiftly dispelled as a four goal blast, courtesy of a Billy Dodds double and one apiece from Stephen Glass and Duncan Shearer, gave the Reds a 4-1 cushion after the away leg – although a 3-1 reverse at Pittodrie in the return fixture made for a nervy finish to the tie.

4 Albania: The road to Gothenburg in 1982/83 began with a double header against Dinamo Tirana. A 1-0 home win was the easy part – the away tie was far trickier. The Albanian authorities waited until just days before the fixture to grant visas for the Aberdeen players and staff, denying secretary Ian Taggart entry to the country. Searing heat only added to the challenge, although Alex Ferguson's team stuck to their task and played out a 0-0 draw to progress in the competition.

5 Ukraine: An adventure deep into former Soviet territory left Dons fans cold, with the club forced to abandon plans to charter a plane for supporters to travel to the away leg against Dnipro in the Uefa Cup in 2007/08 due to a lack of willing travellers. A 0-0 draw at Pittodrie set the stage for Darren Mackie to hog the limelight in the second match, scoring a memorable goal in a 1-1 draw to take his side through to the group stages thanks to the away goals rule.

6 Latvia: Skonto Riga – two words to send a shiver down the spine of Dons fans who lived through the rollercoaster ride of the 1990s. Willie Miller's team travelled to Latvia on Uefa Cup duty in 1994/95 and returned with a 0-0 draw after a match watched by just over 2,000 people. The plucky minnows hadn't read the script and took a 1-1 draw from the second leg at Pittodrie to dump Miller's men out of the competition and heap pressure on the manager.

7 Romania: The Romanian city of Pitesti was better known for its connections with the car manufacturer Dacia and its oil refinery than for football, but their team still gave Fergie's furies a run for their money in the 1981/82 Uefa Cup. After a 3-0 win on Scottish soil, the Dons travelled to play Arges Pitesti and held on for a 2-2 draw in front of a bumper crowd of almost 9,000 people.

8 Bulgaria: Bad refereeing and terrible weather were among the hurdles in the Bulgarian city of Stanke as Aberdeen fell to a 3-2 defeat in the first leg of the European Cup Winners' Cup in 1978/79. The Dons bounced back in style to win 3-0 at home and edge through to the second round, although a broken leg suffered by defender Willie Garner on the continent tempered the joy of the squad.

9 East Germany: The Dons had to go 'behind' the Berlin wall in 1984 to take on Dynamo in the European Cup first round. The two sides, locked at 3-3 after matching 2-1 wins in their home leg, were only separated by penalties as Willie Miller and Eric Black failed to convert as the opposition won 5-4.

10 Hungary: The Dons have mixed memories of Hungary, having been knocked out of the European Cup Winners' Cup in 1970/72 in Budapest by city side Honved after a 4-4 draw on aggregate. In 1983/84 it was Ujpest who took a turn to host Aberdeen, with Dozsa also providing sticky opposition in the ECWC and winning 3-0 in the game in Hungary before falling to a 3-0 defeat in Scotland and subsequently being edged out of the tournament by the Dons.

Dave Caldwell

Debut: League Cup, 22 August 1953 v Celtic (h) won 5-2
Appearances: League 132, Scottish Cup 16, League Cup 30
Also played for: Duntochter Hibs, Rotherham, Morton, Toronto City, Wick Academy, Forres Mechanics, Fraserburgh, Keith.
Managed: Sunnybank.

The Aberdeen team of the 1950s has gone down in history as one of the greatest in the history of the club. Attacking flair was mixed with defensive resilience and one of the key components was defender Dave Caldwell for the bulk of that decade.

Caldwell moved to Pittodrie from Duntocher Hibs, in Clydebank, in 1953 and was a mainstay for the Dons until his departure in 1960. He made his debut in a 5-2 League Cup win over Celtic on August 22, 1953, and the tenacious full-back made the No.3 jersey his own that term with 35 appearances, including in the 2-1 Scottish Cup final defeat at the hands of Celtic.

In the following season, the championship winning campaign, Caldwell was sidelined for most of the term. He returned for the final five league games to help the Dons clinch the title with four wins. If he had been a bit part player in the club's momentous triumph he was firmly in the limelight for the 1955/56 season's trophy success.

This time it was the League Cup which was taken back to the Granite City and Caldwell played in nine of the 10 games on that victorious run. St Mirren provided the opposition in the Hampden Final, which attracted a crowd of 44,000 people, and Caldwell played through the pain barrier to make sure he had a place on centre stage.

Manager Dave Shaw knew he wasn't fit but the pair agreed to take a gamble and it paid off. It was Shaw's first season in charge and it was capped with cup success thanks to a Jimmy Mallan own goal and Graham Leggat's deft chip.

Before departing for a brief stint at Rotherham in 1960 he racked up 178 appearances for Aberdeen. Caldwell, who never scored for the Dons, went from Rotherham to Toronto City the following season, making a short return to home soil with Morton in 1961, and stayed with the Canadian outfit for four years. He earned rave reviews in North America and played into his 30s with Toronto.

In 1965 Caldwell returned to Scotland and the Highland League, first with Wick Academy and in the following two years making appearances for Fraserburgh, Forres Mechanics and Keith.

Caldwell's experience as a league and cup winner with the Dons was tapped into by the city's junior giants Sunnybank when he was appointed coach in 1973, spending four years in charge of the Heathryfold side before resigning in 1977 in protest at the club committee's attempt to influence his team selection for an important league match.

Ian Cameron

Debut: League Cup, 16 August 1989 v Albion Rovers (a) won 2-0
Appearances: League 27, Scottish Cup 2, League Cup 6, Europe 2
Goals: League 1, League Cup 2
Also played for: St Mirren, Partick Thistle, Clydebank

Alex Smith returned to former club St Mirren in the summer of 1989 to sign winger Ian Cameron for £250,000. The pair had worked together at Love Street, where Cameron was a member of the 1987 Scottish Cup winning side. The Scotland youth and under-21 international went straight into the Dons team, viewed as the man to provide the ammunition for star striker Charlie Nicholas, and won admirers with his winning goal in the League Cup semi-final win against Celtic. The economics graduate missed the final after suffering concussion and suffered further bad luck with injuries before joining top flight newcomers Partick Thistle in a £75,000 deal in time for the 1992/93 campaign.

George Campbell

Debut: League Cup, 10 August 1974 v Hearts (h) lost 1-0
Appearances: League 12, League Cup 7
Also played for: Peterhead (on loan), Hellas (Australia)

Tricky winger George Campbell was just 14-years-old when he first travelled from Fort William and became

the youngest recruit in the club's history when he signed an S-Form in 1972. Campbell made his debut two years later after a loan spell with Peterhead. He was capped at youth level by Scotland but injuries hampered his progress and in 1978 the wide man was sold to Australian outfit Hellas for £10,000.

Mohamed Chalali

Debut: League Cup, 23 August 2011 v Dundee (h) won 1-0
Appearances: League 16, Scottish Cup 2, League Cup 2
Goals (up to the end of 2011/12): League 1, Scottish Cup 1
Also played for: Le Havre (France), Panionios (Greece)

Algerian under-23 captain Mohamed Chalali was expected to add a spark to the Dons team. Unfortunately his contribution turned out to be a damp squib, with the majority of his appearances coming from the bench as he attempted to find his feet in the frenetic surroundings of the SPL. He was released after a disappointing term in which he netted just twice.

Jimmy Chalmers

Debut: League, 17 September 1949 v Clyde (h) Drew 1-1
Appearances: League 2
Also Played for: Queen's Park

Banks o' Dee starlet Jimmy Chalmers made two appearances for the Dons in the 1949/50 season before turning his back on the professional game to carve out a career in the unpaid game with Queen's Park, where the defender won eight Scotland amateur caps while forging a career as a PE teacher. Chalmers went on to coach in non-league football in England before emigrating to New Zealand in the mid-1960s.

Kevin Christie

Debut: League Cup, 20 September 1995 v Motherwell (a) won 2-1 (after extra time)
Appearances: League 2, League Cup 1
Also played for: East Fife, Motherwell, Falkik, Airdrie United

Getting the seal of approval from Alex McLeish is every budding young Aberdeen defender's dream and that is exactly what Kevin Christie got, albeit after leaving Pittodrie. Christie made his Dons breakthrough in 1995/96 under Roy Aitken but, after three appearances from the bench, moved on to East Fife early in 1997. It was from the Fifers that McLeish, then in charge at Motherwell, snapped up the young defender for £10,000 and thrust him into top flight action. Christie, a versatile player capable of stepping forward into the midfield, spent two years with the Steelmen before spells as a key man with Falkirk and Airdrie United.

Chris Clark

Debut: Scottish Cup, 20 February 2000 v Caley Thistle (a) drew 1-1
Appearances (up to the end of 2011/12): League 222, Scottish Cup 22, League Cup 12, Europe 9
Goals: League 11, Scottish Cup 1
Also played for: Plymouth Argyle

Defender, winger or central midfielder? Pinpointing Chris Clark's best position proved to be a headache for Ebbe Skovdahl, Steve Paterson and Jimmy Calderwood. The Aberdeen-born player's versatility proved to be a huge advantage to his managers and his ability to slot effortlessly into any position across the back four or the midfield made him a vital player during almost eight years in the first team during his maiden spell with the club.

Clark was one of the unsung heroes throughout that time and his departure from Plymouth in the January transfer window of 2008 left a bigger void than many supporters would have anticipated. He was far from prolific, averaging little more than a goal a season, but did the simple things well and was comfortable in possession.

Having progressed through the Aberdeen youth system as a schoolboy, Clark was blooded by Skovdahl as the 1999/2000 season drew to a close. Between then and his departure he joined the exclusive 200 club as he raced past the double century of appearances for the Dons. He also pushed himself to the fringes of the Scotland squad, capped at B international level in 2006/07 as his stock within the game continued to rise.

During the 2007/08 season it became clear that Clark was not going to commit to another Aberdeen contract as his deal drew to a close. The Dons chose to cash in when they could and accepted a £200,000 bid from Paul Sturrock at Plymouth Argyle. He quickly settled into his stride with the south coast outfit and in the 2010/11 campaign celebrated his 100th appearance for the Pilgrims. He returned to Pittodrie under Craig Brown in 2011.

TEN: Club milestones

1 1903: Aberdeen Football Club bursts into life after the amalgamation of city sides Aberdeen, Orion and Victoria United. The idea had first been floated at the tail end of 1902 and it took four months, until April the following year, to complete the process and get the paperwork complete. AFC was born.

2 1903: After the administration was complete, attention turned to football. The newly formed Dons drew the club's first ever game 1-1 when Stenhousemuir travelled to the Granite City to take on the rookies. Captain Willie MacAulay was the man who claimed the honour of scoring Aberdeen's first goal.

3 1904: League entry is gained and a place in the Second Division awarded. The year also brought the first trophy to the club's cabinet as the Qualifying Cup was secured at Dens Park in Dundee, where the established side Renton were defeated 2-0 by the energetic new kids on the block.

4 1911: Aberdeen broadened their horizons and took the club name to a wider audience when they embarked on their first ever overseas tour. A four day trip took the Dons to Poland and Bohemia for fixtures against foreign opposition and reinforced the ambition and growing stature of the fledgling Scottish outfit.

5 1920: The final payments are made to complete the purchase of Pittodrie, prompting plans to further develop the ground. Building up the south embankment was top of the list of priorities, with home crowds regularly breaking through the 10,000 barrier as the Jimmy Philip led side captured the imagination of the North-east public.

6 1939: The black and gold colours adopted in Aberdeen's early years were replaced by the red and white that has become a trademark for generations of Dons teams. The Wasps would become a thing of the past. The initial designs featured white shorts and either red, black or white socks - with the first of the now familiar all red kits introduced in the 1960s.

7 1959: Lights, camera, action. The first game played under the new floodlights at Pittodrie heralded a new era of night-time football in the North-east. English side Luton Town were the visitors in the autumn of 1959 as the first game under the bulbs brought a 3-2 win for the hosts and sent the Pittodrie faithful home happy.

8 1967: Reinvented as the Washington Whips, Aberdeen competed in the burgeoning soccer scene in the USA and wowed the American crowds with some dashing displays. The Whips made it to the final of the President's Cup and were defeated only after over time in the showdown against the touring Wolves team, who ran out 6-5 winners.

9 1979: Pittodrie became the first all-seated football stadium in Britain when modernisation was completed at the ground. In 1971 there had been a major rebuild of the main South Stand after a fire caused major damage to the seating area as well as the club offices and changing rooms.

10 1992: The famous Beach End closed its gates for the last time. Just over a year later, the sparkling new Richard Donald Stand opened in its place as supporters got the chance to settle into the new £4.5million structure at the eastern tip of Pittodrie. Clydebank were defeated 5-0 in the League Cup in the first fixture in front of the new RDS, with Duncan Shearer bagging a hat-trick to mark the occasion in style.

Alex Cheyne

Debut: League, 2 January 1926 v Hibs (a) drew 0-0
Appearances: League 127, Scottish Cup 11
Goals: League 48, Scottish Cup 7
Also played for: Scotland (5 caps), Shettleston, Chelsea, Nimes
Managed: Chelmsford, Arbroath

Aberdeen Football Club has had its share of dark blue heroes and Alex Cheyne falls distinctly into that category. Cheyne was a star of the 1920s for his club and was one of the first Aberdeen players to be capped at international level, with the team still in its infancy.

He helped put the Dons on the British map in 1929 when he defeated England, stunning the 110,512 crowd at Hampden with a goal directly from a corner kick in the final minute of the match. His vicious swerving set piece gave Scotland the British International Championship bragging rights over the Auld Enemy and made Cheyne the pride of Pittodrie, coming on his first appearance for Scotland.

The Glaswegian inside forward arrived as a raw 18 year-old in 1925 from Shettleston Juniors, recruited by Pat Travers after Alex Jackson had been lost to Huddersfield.

Cheyne made his debut at Easter Road in a 0-0 draw against Hibs on January 2, 1926, but had to wait until the following season to bag the first of 55 career goals for the club in just 138 appearances. That strike came in a 6-1 win over Morton in Aberdeen. Pittodrie's new star No.8 had arrived.

Pittodrie was also the scene of arguably Cheyne's best performance for the club, netting a hat-trick in the space of just 10 minutes in a 4-2 win over Hibs in September, 1927.

Goalscoring heroics were not reserved for Aberdeen and he joined Scotland's own treble club in May, 1929, when he claimed a hat-trick in a 7-3 win over Norway in Bergen.

Despite his blistering start in international football, with those four goals coming inside his first three appearances, chances at the top level were few and far between.

Cheyne's Scotland career ended in 1930 but he could console himself with an unbeaten record in five appearances for his country, with wins against France and Holland and a draw against Germany adding to his experiences against England and Norway.

When Cheyne left Pittodrie for Chelsea in 1930 the Londoners had to pay £6,000 for his services, equalling the club's record sale at that time.

The talented Scot went on to star for French side Nimes before landing back on British soil for a second stint at Stamford Bridge. After retiring he turned to management with Chelmsford in 1937, coming back to his roots in Scotland when he took charge of Arbroath in the 1950s.

Cheyne wore the red of Aberdeen 138 times, scoring 55 goals, at a time when the club was not in a position to challenge the dominant Old Firm teams of the era but his goals helped propel the team from a mid-table outfit to genuine challengers.

Even without a medal to show for his Dons career, Cheyne left with five caps as his reward at a time when Aberdeen players barely registered on the radar of the national selectors.

Jim Clunie

Debut: League, 19 April 1954 v Hibs (a) lost 3-0
Appearances: League 104, Scottish Cup 16, League Cup 21
Goals: League 9
Also played for: Raith Rovers, St Mirren, Ballymena, Forfar, Irvine Meadow.
Managed: St Mirren, Kilmarnock

Jim Clunie, the imposing Fifer earns a place among Aberdeen's list of all time greats thanks to his role in securing the club's first League Cup triumph in 1955, anchoring the defence in the 3-1 win over St Mirren at Hampden. The club had won the Southern League Cup previously but the 1955 victory was the first time the League Cup had been taken back to the Pittodrie trophy cabinet since the competition's inception in 1946.

It coincided with Clunie establishing himself in the Aberdeen team, having made only four first team appearances before that 1955/56 campaign. The six-foot tall centre half was signed by David Halliday in 1953 for £7,000 and combined his playing commitments with his day job as an electrician in the mines. He was a schoolboy international who had attracted interest from Newcastle United but it was Halliday and the Dons who won the day.

He made his debut in the final game of the 1953/54 season on April 19, 1954. It was not a happy occasion, the Dons losing 3-0 against Hibs at Easter Road, but the new boy did enough to keep his place in the side for the next game – the Scottish Cup final against Celtic five days later.

Before even playing a game at Pittodrie he turned out in front of 130,000 fervent supporters at Hampden in the biggest game on the domestic calendar. The final ended 2-1 in favour of the Hoops but Clunie would enjoy his moment of cup glory just 18 months later in the League Cup.

It proved impossible for the young pretender to shift the defensive rock of Alec Young in the championship winning season and the following year a broken leg, the first of three he would suffer throughout a long playing career, stalled his attempts to establish himself.

There was no doubting his promise. After just 12 games for the Dons he was named in the Scottish League select to face England in 1955, his reputation as the country's most improved player cemented by his composed display in the League Cup final.

Clunie, a ball playing centre half who preferred to turn defence into attack with incisive passing rather than looking for a simple clearance, was used as a striker towards the end of his Dons career as a nod towards his attacking instincts.

He left the club in 1960 after 141 games and nine goals, to begin his association with St Mirren. He stayed for five years before moving south of the border with Bury in 1965. A year later he was back on the playing staff at Love Street before winding down his career with Ballymena in Ireland, Forfar and junior side Irvine Meadow.

In 1971 Clunie launched his coaching career when he joined Lawrie McMenemy on the Grimsby coaching staff and followed the Englishman to Southampton before being appointed manager in his own right at St Mirren in 1978, helping to foster the talents of a certain young striker by the name of Billy Stark. He was surprisingly sacked by the Paisley outfit just two years later but went on to have a stint in charge of Kilmarnock in 1981. Clunie, who died in 2003, spent four years at the Rugby Park helm.

Willie Clydesdale

Debut: League, 22 March 1958 v Raith Rovers (h) won 3-2
Appearances: League 27, Scottish Cup 4, League Cup 2
Goals: League 1
Also played for: Hartlepools United

Defender Willie Clydesdale was a miner in the central belt when he was spotted by Dons manager Davie Shaw and snapped up from juniors Petershill in 1955. Shaw had gone to watch a striker in action but instead had his attention drawn to the powerful young defender.

He served his time in the Pittodrie reserves before stepping up to make his first team debut in the 1957/58 season at left-back. He played regularly at right-back the following term but dropped out of the side before being sold to Hartlepools United, as the English side were then known, in 1960.

Juan Cobian

Debut: League, 6 November 1999 v Dundee (a) lost 3-1
Appearances: League 3, League Cup 1
Also played for: Boca Juniors, Sheffield Wednesday, Charlton Athletic, Swindon Town

He came, he saw, he went away again. Argentinian defender Juan Cobian played three games, one from the bench, after arriving via Sheffield Wednesday and Charlton Athletic in the winter of 1999. The former Boca Juniors defender failed to settle and moved on to Swindon eight months later.

Mike Coleman

Debut: League, 26 April 1947 v Queen's Park (a) drew 0-0
Appearances: League 1
Also played for: Alloa Athletic

Forward Mike Coleman was given just a single match to prove himself in a Dons shirt. He filled the considerable void left by George Hamilton's absence for a trip to Queen's Park at the tail end of the 1946/47 season. The game ended 0-0.

The Glaswegian, who joined from Mount Ellen in his home city, moved on to Alloa in 1948 to spend a season with the Wasps.

Andrew Considine

Debut: League, 15 April 2004 v Dundee (h) lost 2-1
Appearances (up to end of 2011/12): League 168, Scottish Cup 18, League Cup 12, Europe 9
Goals (up to end of 2011/12): League 8, Scottish Cup 3, League Cup 2

The Considines are not the first father and son partnership to have pulled on an Aberdeen shirt in competitive action but, to date, they are the most successful. Doug Considine was part of Alex Ferguson's successful squad of the early 1980s while his son Andrew has become firmly established as a first team regular and Scotland under-21 international.

By the time he celebrated his 24th birthday in 2011 the younger of the two defenders had already surpassed his father's appearance record by breaking through the 150 game barrier. It was a considerable achievement for a player who has shown resilience to bounce back from a clutch of troublesome injuries to add power to the Dons defence as a left-back or central defender. He also served as captain under Craig Brown.

The Banchory boy first appeared under Jimmy Calderwood in 2004 and worked hard to build his strength and stamina with extra gym sessions to ensure he was a match for anything the SPL could throw at him.

In addition to representing the national under-21 side he also appeared for the under-20 side at the Youth World Cup in 2007 as his stock continued to rise within the domestic game on the back of his regular displays for his home town club.

The European campaign of 2007/08 was one of the early highlights for the homegrown player as he featured in seven of the Uefa Cup ties and tested himself against some of the continent's best strikers during the run to the last 32 of the competition.

Donald Colman

Debut: League, 21 September 1907 v Dundee (a) lost 1-0
Appearances: League 324, Scottish Cup 23
Goals: League 1
Also played for: Scotland (4 caps), Maryhill, Motherwell, Dumbarton.

Player, captain and trainer. Donald Colman was a loyal servant to Aberdeen in the club's formative years and an innovator who ensured the Dons were at the forefront of the rapidly developing game.

Colman's influence extended beyond the field of play and to the infrastructure of the Pittodrie stadium he graced. As trainer, in the 1930s, the Dumbartonshire-born fans' favourite invented the dug-out to replace the traditional bench on the sidelines. He wanted shelter and a low point of view to observe the footwork of his players - the dug-out was the solution. Colman's love of football led him to explore the worlds of boxing and dancing for pointers on how his players could improve their groundwork.

Everton visited the north-east on friendly duty soon after Colman's blueprint became reality and took the idea south of the border to Liverpool. The rest, as they say, is history.

That well worn piece of trivia only scratches the surface of Colman's far more meaningful contribution to the club he grew to love. He grew up playing junior football on the west coast with leading Glasgow club Maryhill and became an international at that level before turning senior with Motherwell in 1905. Two years later, at the age of 27, he was released by the Steelmen but Aberdeen came to the rescue and took him north.

The relationship would be long and fruitful, replacing Alex Halkett as captain two years after his arrival as the Dons strived to establish themselves in the game. He made his debut on September 21, 1907, in a 1-0 away defeat at Dundee.

It was an exciting time under the stewardship of Jimmy Philip, with a new attendance record of 18,000 set at Pittodrie that season.

Over the course of the 1908/09 and 1909/10 seasons the defender did not miss a single league or cup match as he led by example on and off the pitch.

His club performances earned international recognition late in life, called up at the age of 33 in 1911. He played in all three internationals that season as Scotland drew against Wales and England either side of a 2-0 win against Northern Ireland. Colman won his fourth and final cap in 1913 when he captained the side to a 2-1 win over the Ulstermen at Dalymount Park.

At the end of the First World War, at the age of 42, Colman made a surprise comeback for an injury ravaged Aberdeen side in 1920 before leaving to play for Dumbarton in between summer stints coaching the game in Norway. The fact he continued playing for the Sons until after his 47th birthday was testimony to Colman's fitness and devotion to the game.

He arrived back at Pittodrie in 1931 as trainer under manager Pat Travers at the age of 53. Colman was in his element, implementing a philosophy ahead of its times and earning a reputation as one of the game's great thinkers before tuberculosis claimed his life in 1942.

TEN: International highlights

1 First of many: Willie Lennie won the distinction of being the first ever Dons player to pull on the dark blue jersey of his country when he played, and scored, in a 2-1 win against Wales at Dens Park in Dundee in 1908. It was the first of two caps for the Aberdeen star.

2 Auld Enemy antics: Alec Cheyne sent the Tartan Army into raptures with his cheeky winner against England at a packed Hampden Park in 1929. The Pittodrie wonder nicked a goal direct from a corner kick to give his country a 1-0 victory against the visitors from across the border.

3 Ally's Army: After his sterling efforts as boss in the Granite City, Dons boss Ally MacLeod was presented with the ultimate honour when he was entrusted with the Scotland manager's job in 1977. It came on the back of the charismatic coach winning the League Cup with the Dons.

4 Home comforts: Pittodrie was an international venue long before it had played host to league football at club level. Scotland travelled north early in 1900 to play at the stadium for the first time, beating Wales 5-2 in front of more than 11,000 supporters who had turned out to see the country's finest in action.

5 Safe hands: Jim Leighton claimed two records before bringing the curtain down on his Scotland career in 1998. With 91 caps to his credit, the Pittodrie legend has played more games for the national side than any other goalkeeper and he is also his club's most decorated star. Alex McLeish, with 77 caps, is next in line.

6 World Cup woe: Aberdeen goalkeepers have not always had it easy when playing for their country. At the 1954 World Cup finals it was Dons custodian Fred Martin who was between the sticks as Uruguay hit seven without reply. Martin won half a dozen caps over the course of 1954 and 1955.

7 Double vision: When keeper Ernie McGarr won his two caps in 1969 he joined his Pittodrie team-mate Bobby Clark in the reckoning for a Scotland place. Clark was briefly dislodged from the Scotland side by his Dons team-mate, but returned to round off his international career with 17 caps.

8 Captain fantastic: When the tank-like Jock Hutton ran out as Scotland captain in March 1924 he became the first Dons man to earn the honour. Hutton's one and only service as skipper brought a 2-0 victory in a match played at Celtic Park, with two late goals doing the damage for the home side.

9 Wonder goal: Stewart McKimmie shocked the world champions Argentina with his spectacular strike from distance against the South Americans in a friendly at Hampden in the build-up to the Italia 90 World Cup finals. It was the only goal of the game, coming in one of McKimmie's 40 appearances for Scotland, and the perfect preparation for Andy Roxburgh and his team.

10 Local heroes: When the SFA chose Pittodrie as the venue for the World Cup qualifier against Switzerland in 1993 it was a nod to the role Aberdeen played in supporting the national side. The club provided three of the starting 11 for that game in Brian Irvine, Stewart McKimmie and Scott Booth. Eoin Jess made it four Dons on the team list when he appeared as a substitute while Pittodrie youth product David Robertson, by then with Rangers, also started in the 1-1 draw.

Charlie Cooke

Debut: League Cup, 13 August 1960 v Ayr United (h) won 4-3
Appearances: League 125, Scottish Cup 14, League Cup 26
Goals: League 27, League Cup 3
Also played for: Scotland (16 caps), Port Glasgow, Renfrew, Dundee, Chelsea, Crystal Palace, LA Aztecs, Memphis Rogues, California Surf
Managed: Wichita

Charlie Cooke never won anything with Aberdeen. Charlie Cooke was never capped for Scotland when he was with Aberdeen. Yet he is the one name most fans of a certain vintage would place at the very top of their list of heroes. Cooke was an entertainer, nicknamed The Cavalier by appreciative Chelsea supporters in his post-Pittodrie days in tribute to his intricate runs and free-flowing attacking flair.

Despite being born in Fife, he was a Greenock boy and first came to the attention of the Dons while playing for Renfrew in the junior ranks. He signed provisionally for Aberdeen in 1959 and by the time he made his reserve team debut the following year it was clear the club had unearthed a gem.

With immaculate footwork and the ability to split a defence with an arrowed pass, he was soon catapulted into the first team. He made his debut in a League Cup win at home to Ayr United at the start of the 1960/61 season and within weeks words of his talents had spread south of the border. Newcastle United weighed in with an offer, Arsenal were on his trail and that was after just a single game.

He had landed in a team that was not challenging for honours, despite the championship success just half a decade earlier, but still managed to excel and put his distinctive mark on the team and the city. The swinging sixties had just begun and in the fast living Cooke there was a new pin-up boy to behold for the Pittodrie faithful.

Within months of his introduction to the Dons team he was in the thoughts of the SFA selectors, beig selected as a reserve for the Scotland under-23 squad at the start of 1961 before stepping up to become a key player for the young Scots in the months that followed.

His talents illuminated Pittodrie during a difficult spell for the club. Two sixth place finishes were the league highlights during Cooke's spell in the red of Aberdeen, during which time his esteemed talents on the ball were utilised both in the front line and, briefly, from deep as a right half. Wherever he was deployed, the rookie from Greenock had the knack for entertaining the masses in a way that few before or since have managed to do.

Frustrated by the failure to compete with the country's dominant clubs, Cooke asked for a transfer late in 1964 and before the year had ended his wish was granted.

Dundee, champions of Scotland two years previously, weighed in with a Scottish record fee of £44,000 to trump Coventry City and Wolves. It shattered Aberdeen's previous record haul, which was the £32,500 profit on George Kinnell's move to Stoke in 1963. Manager Tommy Pearson had stressed his desire to hold onto the player who had scored 32 goals in less than five full seasons and created many, many more. The offer from Dundee was simply too good to refuse and the windfall allowed other star players to be retained, a business model that would

prove successful throughout the 1960s and for decades after.

The young player was stung by the reaction to the move, with journalists rounding on him for daring to leave the club and directors fanning the flames of public fury by painting a picture of a star who was determined to leave by hook or by crook. Cooke is adamant the coverage of his transfer was unfair and the reaction was over the top, insisting the hefty fee Dundee paid for his services ensured it was Aberdeen who benefited most from the deal.

There were, naturally, advantages for the attacker himself. He was promoted to the Scotland senior team within a month of his move to Dens Park, eventually making his debut for his country in a 4-1 win against Wales in November 1965 under Jock Stein. He went on to win 16 caps in a nine year spell with the national team.

In the spring of 1966 Cooke collected the Dundee supporters' club player of the year award. The next morning he was gone, transferred to Chelsea in a £75,000 deal. It was a record for the Blues but a shrewd piece of business as their recruit went on to earn cult status.

It was at Stamford Bridge that Cooke's standing in the game was elevated to new levels, a masterful creative display in the London club's European Cup Winners' Cup victory over Real Madrid in 1971 having been a key player in the previous year's FA Cup win against Leeds United. His style on and off the pitch separated him from mere mortals, although in later years Cooke admitted his love of the good life had caught up with him on occasion. It was during his time in the US that he made the decision to steer clear of alcohol in a bid to give his career a second wind. Cooke had two spells with Chelsea, wrapped around a season with Crystal Palace in 1972/73, before leaving England behind for a new life in America in 1977.

As the hedonism of London was left behind, he starred in the US indoors and outdoors before moving into coaching with Wichita. The passion for coaching the arts which made him a darling of the terraces led Cooke to help with the creation of the Koerver Coaching empire, which became a global phenomenon in 1990 as countries across the world searched for a way of injecting the skills which made Cooke and his contemporaries household names.

The former Scotland star, who released his biography *The Bonnie Prince* in 2006, still remains based in the States.

Bobby Clark

Debut: League Cup, 28 August 1965 v Clyde (h) won 2-0
Appearances: League 425+1, Scottish Cup 49, League Cup 95, Europe 23
Also played for: Scotland (17 caps), Queen's Park
Managed: Highlanders (Zimbabwe), Dartmouth, Stanford, Notre Dame (all US)

In the list of great Aberdeen goalkeepers of all time, the name of Bobby Clark looms as large as the man himself. Throughout the 1960s, 1970s and 1980s managers came and went but Clark remained a rock solid constant at the spine of the team.

Significantly he was Eddie Turnbull's first signing, the boss determined to send out a message about the changing of the guard. Clark, at just 19, was young and determined to make a name for himself. He fitted the bill perfectly for Turnbull.

He arrived from amateurs Queen's Park in 1965, the club Turnbull had coached before he had taken up the challenge at Pittodrie.

Clark was thrust into the first team in a 2-0 win against Clyde on August 28, at the expense of Tubby Ogston, and never looked back. That debut win came against the club at which his father served as a director.

He was already well known to the Dons fans, having starred in two Scottish Cup ties for Queen's against Aberdeen the season prior to his transfer. It took extra-time in the replay to knock the plucky Glasgow side out.

In only his second season at the club he was an ever present and voted player of the year for the Dons. His performances earned a Scotland debut against Wales in 1967.

There was an incredible twist in Clark's career when he found himself out of the team in the 1968-69 team – and playing centre-half for the reserves. He even appeared as an outfield substitute in the second game of the following campaign in a 2-0 defeat against Rangers, replacing striker Jim Forrest.

He would soon return to the first team as first choice goalkeeper and did so in time for the last four games in the famous Scottish Cup run of 1970, culminating in the celebrated 3-1 win over Celtic which brought the keeper his first medal. He was again voted player of the year at Pittodrie.

His Dons comeback also put Clark back in the national reckoning and he established himself as Scotland's No.1 for a three year period from 1970, singled out by Portuguese star Eusebio after one tie in Lisbon. Clark won 17 caps, an Aberdeen record at the time.

He also set a record of 12 consecutive clean sheets in 1971.

Clark came close to leaving on several occasions, notably in 1970 when a switch to Rangers broke down when Bobby Watson refused to head in the opposite direction and two years later when a £100,000 move to Stoke fell through, but Clark's heart was at Pittodrie.

By 1974 he had 400 first team appearances to his credit and a year later he was appointed captain by Jimmy Bonthrone, who had succeeded Turnbull in 1971.

Bonthrone was soon replaced by Ally MacLeod but Clark still had an important part to play and battled through a hand injury to turn out in the League Cup final of 1976 when he was part of the Dons team which defeated Celtic 2-1 thanks to goals from Drew Jarvie and Davie Robb. Clark had chipped a bone in his thumb during a league match the previous week but that was not enough to prevent him picking up another winner's medal.

He retained his place as No.1 under Billy McNeill, who took Aberdeen to within two points of the league title

in the 1977/78 campaign, before Alex Ferguson's arrival the following term.

By that stage Clark was vying with up and coming youngster Jim Leighton for the Pittodrie gloves, holding off the challenge long enough to complete his set of domestic honours when he played in 34 of the Premier Division games on the way to Aberdeen's first championship success since 1955. The Dons beat Celtic to the prize by a single point and the miserly record of 18 goals against was a major factor.

A back injury kept Clark sidelined for two years. By the time he returned to full fitness he was 36 and Leighton was firmly established as Ferguson's main man.

After 570 games for Aberdeen he embarked on the first stop of a global coaching career when he left the north-east in 1983 to coach Highlanders in Zimbabwe. He moved on to the college scene in America and has become established as one of the leading coaches in the US after a succession of trophy wins with Dartmouth, Stanford and current institutition Notre Dame.

Preparing for the 2007/2008 season, Clark returned to Pittodrie to lure Aberdeen youth academy director Lenny Taylor to the States to lead a coaching seminar as he continues to draw on the experiences of his long and distinguished career with the Dons.

He said: "There were many highlights from my time with the club and I feel I was very fortunate to have worked under so many great coaches, starting with Eddie Turnbull and finishing with Alex Ferguson.

"I now realise that I got a great grounding in what turned out to be my profession. I think my final five years at Pittodrie, when Lenny Taylor and I ran the youth scheme at Pittodrie, were wonderful. It allowed me to get close to the mind of Alex Ferguson and also to be overseen by Teddy Scott. Both men passed on great knowledge. Alex showed me all about hard work and planning and Teddy gave wonderful examples of how to handle people on a daily basis. I look back to those five years and I'm proud to think of all the players who came through the youth scheme at that time - Neil Simpson, John Hewitt, Neale Cooper, Brian Mitchell, Andy Dornan and Willie Falconer are a few that instantly spring to mind."

For all the coaching highs Clark has experienced since leaving for foreign shores, the playing summits he scaled as a Dons star live strong in his memory.

Neale Cooper

Debut: League, 11 October 1980 v Kilmarnock (h) won 2-0
Appearances: League 133+16, Scottish Cup 27+2, League Cup 27+1, Europe 33+6
Goals: League 6, Scottish Cup 3, League Cup 1
Also played for: Aston Villa, Rangers, Reading, Dunfermline, Ross County.
Managed: Ross County, Hartlepool, Gillingham, Peterhead.

Neale Cooper was still more than a month short of his 17th birthday when he was thrust into Premier League action for Aberdeen by Alex Ferguson. It turned out Sir Alex knew a good young player when he saw one.

That first game in 1980, a 2-0 win at home to Kilmarnock on October 11, was the start of a special relationship with the Pittodrie crowd for a player born in India but an Aberdonian at heart. He grew up in the city, plucked from school football and juvenile club King Street by the Dons and rapidly promoted to first team duty.

He explained: "I was cleaning the manager's office as part of my duties around the club as one of the young players when Alex Ferguson came in and told me there was a problem with Alex McLeish and that I had to get myself home and prepare to play the next day.

"I think a mixture of panic and excitement set in. I'm sure my mum thought I was joking when I went home and told her. I was still a young boy - to have gone from growing up in Aberdeen and being a ball boy at Pittodrie to be playing in the first team was special.

"To be asked to step in for a player like Alex McLeish was daunting but once you get out on the pitch all of the nerves disappear. Being surrounded by so many good and experienced players helped and there was no way I wanted to let them down."

Cooper is of course one of the Gothenburg Greats, the 1983 European Cup Winners' Cup final against Real Madrid in the Swedish city a defining moment for one of the club's great characters.

He was a Scotland under-21 cap by the time he pulled on the red No.4 jersey in that landmark final against the Spanish giants, a dynamo in the Dons midfield. Cooper featured in nine of the 11 ties in that famous run, a

key component in the most famous side Aberdeen has ever produced.

That momentous triumph came when Cooper was still only 19, by which point he was already a regular in the Pittodrie first team and had a Scottish Cup medal safely tucked away.

The national cup win was in the 1982 final when Aberdeen sent out a message of intent to the Old Firm, hammering Rangers 4-1 and their emerging young midfielder was on the scoresheet. It was 3-1 when the opportunity presented itself, Gers keeper Jim Stewart's clearance bouncing off Cooper and leaving him with an open goal – he could have walked it home but chose to almost burst the net with a thunderous effort to cap a memorable day for the travelling Red Army. His forward roll and salute capped the occasion.

After European success in the 1982/83 season the following term added a Premier Division winner's medal to Cooper's rapidly expanding collection, Celtic beaten by seven points in the chase for the Scottish game's main prize. He also claimed a European Super Cup medal, having played in the first leg of Aberdeen's victory over SV Hamburg over two games in the same 1983/84 term that heralded a second Scottish Cup win. This time Celtic were beaten 2-1 in a final which went to extra-time.

Cooper made 20 appearances in the 1984/85 Premier Division as Aberdeen retained the title for the first time in the club's history and the following year played a key role in both the 3-0 League Cup final victory against Hibs and the Scottish Cup triumph against Hearts by the same margin.

That rout against the Jambos proved to be Cooper's final outing for the Dons. In the summer of 1986, just months before his manager headed south to Manchester United, he made the leap to English football with Aston Villa. A tribunal set a fee of £350,000 for a youth product who had played 220 games and scored 10 times.

Cooper spent two years at Villa, playing under Graham Turner and Billy McNeill before Graham Taylor allowed him to move back to Scotland as part of the Graeme Souness revolution at Rangers in 1988.

He was part of the Premier Division winning team at Ibrox in his first season, featuring in 14 games as he helped ensure the Dons had to settle for second place at the start of the Govan men's nine in a row run.

He was restricted to a handful of appearances under Souness the following term, returning to England for a short spell with Reading before finding a more permanent home with Dunfermline and smashing through the 100 game barrier with the Pars between 1991 and 1996. He called time on his spell in Fife when Ross County tempted him north to lead them as manager through the Scottish Football League, winning promotion from the Third Division and Second Division on his way to establishing the Dingwall side as an accomplished First Division outfit.

Cooper said: "I was 16 when I played my first game for Aberdeen, 17 when I scored in the Scottish Cup final win and 19 when we won in Europe. At the time I took it all in my stride but looking back now I appreciate most players will go through their whole career without those experiences.

"It meant a lot to me that someone like Alex Ferguson showed faith in me when I was starting out and I'll always be grateful for that. I took it into management with me - I've always believed in giving players a chance at 16 or 17 if they deserve it."

After resigning from his County post after six years at the helm, Cooper returned to management with Hartlepool in 2003 and led them to the League One play-offs in his first season. A stint in charge of Gillingham followed before Cooper came back to his roots in the north-east where his connection with football continued with his appointment as Steve Paterson's assistant at Peterhead. He succeeded Paterson as manager at the Blue Toon in 2008 to return to frontline duties after a spell in temporary charge, departing in 2011 with the club struggling at the foot of the Second Division. He was appointed by Hartlepool for a second time in the 2011/12 season.

TEN: Significant transfer deals

1 Jock Hutton: A giant of a man, Hutton commanded a hefty price when he was sold for a record breaking £5,000 in 1926. English side Blackburn Rovers were the club who stumped up the bumper fee for the talented and wholehearted Dons and Scotland defender and got good value from the star signing.

2 Bobby Clark: The goalkeeper was not a record breaker, but he was the first man recruited as Eddie Turnbull rebuilt the Pittodrie squad. The revolving door saw 17 players leave under the new manager and youngsters like Clark, who joined in 1965, recruited to fill the void and sow the seeds for a bright and exciting future.

3 Martin Buchan: The classy defender had been a shining light for Aberdeen supporters, the young and courageous captain who steered the team to the Scottish Cup in 1970. Then, in 1972, he was gone – in his place was a cheque from Manchester United for £125,000. It was a record sale for the Pittodrie board and a demonstration of Buchan's ability.

4 Joe Harper: The record breaking deal that took Martin Buchan south was usurped within the space of ten months as star striker Joe Harper was sold to Everton for £182,000 late in 1972. English scouts were beating a path to Scotland to look for top talent. Unlike Buchan, Harper would soon return to his old North-east stomping ground.

5 Peter Weir: The Scottish transfer record was shattered in the summer of 1981 when Alex Ferguson, not renowned for splashing the cash, spent £330,000 on Peter Weir. The St Mirren player proved to be a shrewd investment and he went on to play a huge role in the glory years under Ferguson.

6 Bobby Mimms: When Bobby Mimms answered an SOS call from Alex Smith in 1990, few Dons fans could have realised that the veteran goalkeeper was the shape of things to come. Loan deals were a rarity in the Scottish game at that stage, unheard of at Pittodrie, but have become a vital source of fresh blood.

7 Paul Bernard: Midfielder Paul Bernard became Aberdeen's first, and, to date, last £1million signing when he was recruited amid much fanfare from Oldham Athletic in 1995. An injury blighted spell in the north-east did not see the new recruit live up to his bumper price tag and his career fizzled out.

8 Gary Smith: The Bosman ruling changed the face of football and sent fear and alarm through boardrooms up and down the country. Aberdeen, a club built on the foundation of being able to rear and sell bright young players, had their first bitter taste of the new set-up when Gary Smith announced in 1996 that he would be leaving under the new found freedom of contract to join French side Rennes on a free transfer.

9 Eoin Jess: Many Dons youngsters have been linked with big money moves to England, few have made the leap. Eoin Jess was one of those who made the dream become reality and the £2million fee he commanded when he joined Coventry City in 1996 remains the biggest piece of business Aberdeen have ever been involved in.

10 Billy Dodds: The deal that saw Billy Dodds removed from the Pittodrie payroll remains a contender for the worst piece of business conducted by the club. Dodds left to join Dundee United in 1998, with Robbie Winters heading in the opposite direction. The fact Dons manager Alex Miller also sanctioned a £500,000 top up fee for United to smooth the deal ensured the Arabs got by far the better end of a deal that sparked outrage among the Pittodrie faithful.

Willie Cooper

Debut: League, 14 April 1928 v Cowdenbeath (h) won 3-0
Appearances: League 327, Scottish Cup 37, League Cup 9
Goals: League 2, Scottish Cup 1
Also played for: Mugiemoss, Forfar Athletic, Huntly
Also managed: Huntly

The Scottish Football Association is not known as a sympathetic organisation. The governing body bends its rules for no man, or at least for very few men. One exception was Aberdeen legend Willie Cooper. The cool and composed right-back played in every single game leading up to the 1947 Scottish Cup final before a pulled muscle in the semi-final forced him out of the showdown with Hibs.

The Dons, in Cooper's absence, defeated the Easter Road men 2-1 but the north-east fans who made the pilgrimage to Hampden to take their place in the 82,684 crowd were not happy. They, and the Dons team, refused to leave the turf of the national team until Cooper joined in the celebrations and took his bow.

Willie Waddell was the man taken into the Aberdeen team in Cooper's place but even he felt the injustice, insisting his winner's medal would be passed to the man he deputised for. In the end that gesture was not necessary, the the SFA made the unprecedented step of having an extra medal struck to ensure Cooper did not miss out.

He had got the cup run off and running with the winner in the first round against Partick Thistle, so it was only right he was there at the end to join the triumphant squad. By that time he already had a Southern League Cup win under his belt, part of the team that beat Rangers 3-2 in the 1946 final. That made up for the pain of defeat in the 1937 Scottish Cup final against Celtic, when a record 146,433 crammed inside Hampden and 20,000 were locked outside.

Cooper launched his career with Aberdeen junior side Mugiemoss, earning a trial for the Dons early in 1927 and signing in time for the start of the 1927/28 season at the tender age of 16. He was briefly farmed out on loan to Forfar Athletic before forcing his way into the first team and staying there for an incredible period of two decades.

Cooper made his first appearance in a 3-0 win at home to Cowdenbeath on April 14, 1928 and could not have predicted the way his career would unfold. His final game did not come until January 31, 1948, in a 3-1 defeat at Falkirk. Despite his heroics for the Pittodrie side, international recognition escaped Cooper. He could console himself with two caps for the Scottish League against England in 1936 and 1937.

His full-back partnership with Charlie McGill was legendary, with the pair clocking up 161 consecutive games together in the 1930s. Cooper went one further, clocking up a record 162 consecutive games between September, 1932 and October, 1936. Cooper played 373 games in an Aberdeen career spanning 21 years, his considerable tally of course limited by the outbreak of war.

After leaving Pittodrie in 1948, following 373 appearances and three goals, he spent two years as player coach of Huntly before retiring. Cooper died in 1994 at the age of 84.

Doug Considine

Debut: League, 11 November 1978 v Motherwell (a) drew 1-1
Appearances: League 41, Scottish Cup 5, League Cup 7, Europe 2
Also played for: Huntly, Dunfermline

The 1979/80 championship win was a tale of two Dougs for the Dons. It was Doug Considine who started the season in possession of the No.3 shirt but it was Doug Rougvie who ended the campaign in the left-back berth for Alex Ferguson. Considine played in 15 of the 36 league matches to play a key role in the title win. It was only his second season as a Dons player, having joined from Highland League side Huntly in April 1978 while Billy McNeill was in charge. The Banchory boy, a former junior player with Banks o' Dee, had rapidly progressed through the grades to earn full-time football and had been a target for Ayr United and Nottingham Forest before opting to accept Aberdeen's offer.

He was 21 when he signed at Pittodrie and was gently eased into the first team picture by McNeill in the 1978/79 term, establishing himself in time for the Premier Division triumph under Ferguson the following year.

After growing frustrated at a lack of first team football, in the face of competition from Rougvie, he joined Dunfermline in a £35,000 deal early in the 1981/82 season and was handed his favoured role in the centre of the Pars defence. He returned to home territory in the mid 1980s to settle back in Banchory and establish himself as a successful businessman on Deeside, maintaining his interest in football as a player and manager with Banchory St Ternan as the ambitious amateur side pushed for elevation to the junior ranks prior to his son Andrew's breakthrough as a Dons player.

Jim Cooper

Debut: League, 20 December 1958 v Rangers (h) lost 3-1
Appearances: League 1

A 3-1 defeat against Rangers at Pittodrie proved to be right winger Jim Cooper's solitary appearance for the Dons. That game in 1958 came just months after he had linked up with Aberdeen after being demobbed following national service in the Far East. The former Armadale Thistle player returned to the junior ranks with Coltness United in 1959.

Neil Cooper

Debut: League, 4 March 1975 v Airdrie (a) drew 2-2
Appearances: League 18, Scottish Cup 2, League Cup 5
Goals: League 1
Also played for: Barnsley, Grimsby, St Mirren, Hibs
Managed: Forfar Athletic

When Aberdeen's under-19 coach Neil Cooper addresses the Pittodrie youngsters he speaks with the authority of a man who has walked every step of the journey his charges are embarking upon. The Aberdonian was one of the Granite City's hottest football properties as a Hilton Academy pupil and rejected overtures from Aston Villa and Sunderland to commit to his home town team.

He had been a prolific goal scorer as a teenager but was switched to defence after joining the Pittodrie staff, making his debut in 1975 at the tender age of 16 when Jimmy Bonthrone pitched him into action.

Cooper spent six years on the fringes of the first team, with his path blocked by the blossoming partnership of Willie Miller and Alex McLeish, before moving to Barnsley in 1980. A stint at Grimsby followed before he returned to Scotland with St Mirren and played a starring role in the 1987 Scottish Cup final victory over Dundee United.

Cooper moved on to Hibs in 1989 and spent two years at Easter Road before receiving a surprise invitation to rejoin the Dons under Alex Smith, recruited to serve as a player-coach with the reserve side. He remained on the staff until being deemed surplus to requirements during Ebbe Skovdahl's term of office, branching out on his own to take charge of Forfar between 2001 and 2003. Cooper was tempted back to Aberdeen by Steve Paterson in his familiar youth role and has remained a major influence on a generation of Dons prospects while working under Jimmy Calderwood, Mark McGhee and Craig Brown.

Doug Coutts

Debut: League, 8 March 1960 v Clyde (h) lost 2-0
Appearances: League 99, Scottish Cup 10, League Cup 13
Goals: League 3, Scottish Cup 1
Also played for: Berwick Rangers, Wigan Athletic, Altrincham

Getting one over Rangers is an achievement always likely to curry favour with Aberdeen fans. Centre-half Doug Coutts had to wait until he had left Pittodrie to succeed in that goal – but when he did, he did it in style. When the Aberdonian was released by his home town club in 1965 he found a new football home with Berwick Rangers and skippered the Borderers when they shocked Rangers with a 1-0 win over their Ibrox namesakes in the Scottish Cup early in 1967.

That triumph came seven years after Coutts had stepped up from Banks o' Dee juniors and made his Dons debut. Despite interest from Blackburn Rovers, Partick Thistle and East Fife he had no hesitation in signing a Pittodrie contract and following Banks team-mates Bobby Turnbull and Lewis Thom to the club.

Coutts had been marked out to make an impact in the game from a young age, having skippered both the Aberdeen primary and secondary school select teams. As a primary school player at Kittybrewster he had played alongside Denis Law in the forward line and as a Grammar School pupil he was capped at schoolboy level.

After five years in the Dons team he joined Berwick in 1965 and spent four years at Shielfield before travelling further into England to link up with Wigan Athletic, who at that time were playing in the Northern Premier League. It allowed Coutts to combine football with a career in the civil service.

Andy Cowie

Debut: League, 10 December 1938 v Albion Rovers (h) won 2-1
Appearances: League 61, Scottish Cup 8, League Cup 14
Also played for: Swindon Town

Highlander Andy Cowie was one of a generation of players who had their football exploits interrupted by the more pressing matter of service during World War II. The Invernessian had arrived at Pittodrie via Dundee and made his debut in 1938 as a right-back. After the war he returned and remained a valuable squad man for Dave Halliday until he switched to Swindon Town in a swap deal which took Don Emery north in 1948. Cowie missed out on the Southern League Cup final victory in 1946 despite appearances in the early rounds of the competition.

John Craig

Debut: League Cup, 11 August 1973 v Motherwell (h) won 3-1
Appearances: League 20, League Cup 3
Also played for: Partick Thistle, Hearts, Keith

Midfielder John Craig continued family tradition when he followed in elder brother Tommy's footsteps and signed for Aberdeen in the opening weeks of 1970 after a spell on Chelsea's ground staff. Craig made his first team debut at the start of the 1973/74 campaign, his reward for being named Scotland's young player of the year on the back of impressive reserve displays the previous term. His slight build was cited as a reason for limited opportunities with the Dons and he joined Partick Thistle in the summer of 1973. After a spell with Hearts he returned to the North-east to turn out for Keith in the early 1980s.

Michael Craig

Debut: League, 4 May 1996 v Falkirk (a) won 2-1
Appearances: League 6, League Cup 2, Europe 1
Goals: League 1
Also played for: Celtic, Montrose, Huntly

Michael Craig is one of the few players to have made the jump from Celtic to Aberdeen in their prime. Craig, who grew up in the Granite City, was a highly rated teenager at Parkhead when he opted to accept the invitation to join the Dons and link up with his uncle Tommy Craig, who had switched from the Hoops coaching staff to the Pittodrie backroom team. The Scotland youth cap had already made his first team debut for Celtic, as a substitute in a Scottish Cup tie, but did not progress at the same rate after moving to Pittodrie. He made eight appearances over two seasons under Roy Aitken and was capped at under-21 level by Scotland before being released by Alex Miller. Craig went on to play for Montrose and Huntly as well as playing for a spell in Australia and in the junior ranks back in the north-east.

Steven Craig

Debut: League, 7 August 2004 v Rangers (h) drew 0-0
Appearances: League 17, Scottish Cup 1, League Cup 3
Goals: League 2, League Cup 1
Also played for: Falkirk, Motherwell, Dundee, Livingston, Ross County

Attacker Steven Craig was another player recruited by Steve Paterson who never played a single match under the manager. He was signed from Motherwell on a free transfer in the summer of 2004, just weeks before Paterson was sacked and replaced by Jimmy Calderwood. Craig, who had served with Falkirk before moving to Well in 2003, struggled to force his way into the new manager's plans and was not helped by a red card in one of his rare outings for the Dons. He was sent out on loan to Dundee in 2005/06 before a permanent move to Livingston in 2006. Two years with the Lions were followed by a move to Ross County in 2008.

Jonathan Crawford

Debut: League, 22 August 2009 v Hamilton (a) won 3-0
Appearances: League 2, League Cup 1
Also played for: Peterhead, Montrose

Defender Jonathan Crawford was pushed into the first team at the beginning of Mark McGhee's tenure. He made three appearances in the 2009/10 campaign before being loaned to Peterhead later that season. Crawford, who was part of Scotland's under-19 squad while at Pittodrie, was released in 2010 and established himself with Montrose in the Third Division, playing in defence and midfield for the Gable Endies.

Tommy Craig

Debut: League, 16 December 1967 v Stirling Albion (h) won 1-0
Appearances: League 47, Scottish Cup 9, League Cup 6, Europe 4
Goals: League 8, Scottish Cup 1, League Cup 1
Also Played for: Scotland (1 cap), Sheffield Wednesday, Newcastle United, Aston Villa, Swansea City, Carlisle United

Celtic, Liverpool, Leeds United and West Ham were just some of the clubs drawn towards prodigious striker Tommy Craig during his days as a schoolboy international star. In the end it was Aberdeen he chose to pledge his future to and Craig quickly established a reputation as one to watch as he cut his teeth with Banks o' Dee A after moving north from Drumchapel Amateurs in his native Glasgow in 1966.

At 5ft 7in he did not possess the stature of a bruiser but he was quick and tenacious, the ideal inside forward or winger. Eddie Turnbull blooded the golden boy on the left wing in 1967/68 and the following season he made the No.11 shirt his own.

He proved to be a one hit wonder, with sparkling form in his first full season leading to an irresistible £100,000 bid from Sheffield Wednesday in May 1969. Craig, capped by Scotland in 1976 also starred for Newcastle United, Aston Villa, Swansea and Carlisle before embarking on a long coaching career when he was appointed assistant manager to Alex Miller at Hibs in the early 1980s. He also served as No.2 to David Hay and Billy McNeill at Celtic as well as Scotland under-21 coach before returning to Aberdeen as assistant to Roy Aitken in 1995. He later coached Newcastle and assisted John Collins at Hibs and then Charleroi, stepping up to become manager of the Belgian side following the departure of Collins in 2009 for a five month stint.

Stevie Crawford

Debut: League, 10 September 2005 v Celtic (a) lost 2-0
Appearances: League 34, Scottish Cup 2, League Cup 3
Goals: League 8, Scottish Cup 2
Also played for: Scotland (25 caps), Raith Rovers, Millwall, Hibs, Dunfermline, Plymouth Argyle, Dundee United, East Fife, Cowdenbeath
Managed: East Fife

Experienced Scotland international striker Stevie Crawford should have been the answer to Aberdeen's goal scoring prayers when he checked in at Pittodrie in August 2005.

He had agreed a severance package at Dundee United to pave the way for a reunion with Jimmy Calderwood, the manager who had inspired him to produce some of the best form of his career while the pair worked together at Dunfermline.

The partnership did not work as effectively second time round, with Crawford never hitting top gear during his time in a red shirt and returning just 10 goals in 39 appearances. He had an impressive haul of 25 caps in his locker when he arrived but could not add to that tally while on the Dons books.

He was a veteran by that stage, having enjoyed his finest hour and a half while still a young player in the 1990s. Crawford, born in Dunfermline, was a member of the League Cup winning Raith Rovers side in 1993. He moved to Millwall three years later but returned to Scottish football with Hibs after a single season. Three years at Easter Road included two loan periods with Dunfermline before a permanent switch to the Pars led to a productive and consistent four year stay at East End Park.

In 2004 he packed his bags to head for Plymouth Argyle, staying one season on the south coast before half a season with Dundee United as the 2004/05 campaign drew to a close.

After leaving Aberdeen he returned to Dunfermline and went on to play for and manage East Fife. In January 2011 he linked up with former Pittodrie assistant manager Jimmy Nicholl at Cowdenbeath.

Ian Cumming

Debut: League, 16 March 1968 v Hibs (a) won 5-0
Appearances: League 7
Goals: League 1
Also played for: Inverness Thistle
Managed: Inverness Thistle, Elgin City

A string of senior clubs joined the chase for Scotland schoolboy international Ian Cumming as his time with Banks o' Dee A in youth football drew to a close in 1963. He opted to join his hometown team and eventually made his Aberdeen debut almost five years later, as deputy to Jimmy Smith in midfield. He was released to join Inverness Thistle in 1969 and was a stalwart for the Highland side as a player and manager. Cumming also had a spell in charge of Elgin City in the 1980s and led the Borough Briggs side to cup success in the north game.

Bobby Cummings

Debut: League, 1 March 1960 v Rangers (a) drew 2-2
Appearances: League 62, Scottish Cup 7, League Cup 17
Goals: League 33, Scottish Cup 11, League Cup 5
Also played for: Newcastle United, Ashington, Darlington, Hartlepool

Englishman Bobby Cummings was a character who knew all about hard work after linking up with the Dons during his days as a worker at a north-east colliery. A £2,000 transfer from Midland League side Ashington in February 1960 was his passport to full-time football and the 23-year-old forward grabbed the opportunity presented to him by manager Tommy Pearson.

He had been a reserve player for Newcastle United before dropping down to non-league football. The move to Scotland represented a second chance at the highest level.

He was a versatile attacker, having played as an inside forward and a central striker, and after moving north found himself posted on the right wing by Pearson. Wherever he played, Cummings had the ability to hit the back of the net and he underlined that in style at the end of the 1960/61 season when he bagged a hat-trick in the famous 6-1 demolition of champions elect Rangers at Pittodrie. A week earlier he had claimed a double against Dundee United and his purple patch continued with another strike against Partick in the following game. In 1962 he went two better when he notched five against Clyde in a 10-3 Scottish Cup victory at Pittodrie.

In 1963 Cummings' form brought a £6,000 move to Newcastle United, where he was restored to his previous berth as a centre forward. In 1965 he switched to Darlington and, after half a century of goals in just two seasons, also had a spell with Hartlepool before a stint in South African football brought his career to a close.

John Cummings

Debut: League, 6 March 1965 v Falkirk (a) won 1-0
Appearances: League 1
Goals: League 1
Also played for: Port Vale, Ayr United, Clydebank

Greenock-born striker John Cummings was given his debut by new manager Eddie Turnbull in the spring of 1965. Cummings, recruited from Port Glasgow juniors as a youngster, responded by scoring the only goal of the game as the Dons won at Falkirk. He joined Port Vale that summer. He returned to Scotland with Ayr United and also turned out for Clydebank.

John Curran

Debut: League, 23 October 1948 v Clyde (h) drew 4-4
Appearances: League 27, League Cup 6
Also played for: East Fife, Watford, Shrewsbury, Keith

Glaswegian goalkeeper John Curran vied for the No.1 jersey for four years in the late 1940s and early 50s. With opportunities limited he moved on to East Fife in 1952 and won the League Cup with his new club the following year.

Spells with Watford and Shrewsbury followed before he returned to the north-east with Keith, winning the Highland League in 1962.

Dyron Daal

Debut: League, 26 August 2006 v Dunfermline (h) won 1-0
Appearances: League 7
Goals: League 2
Also played for: Utrecht, Dundee (on loan), St Johnstone, Fuenlabrada (Spain), Ross County

Towering striker Dyron Daal checked in at Pittodrie in the summer of 2006. He had done enough during a trial spell eight months earlier to leave a lasting impression on Jimmy Calderwood. The former Utrecht youth product was an ungainly looking player but did show a nose for goal, scoring against Falkirk and Hearts during his handful of appearances, but found the SPL a bridge too far and was loaned out to Dundee. He hit a good run of scoring form for the Dens men and was signed permanently by St Johnstone after being released by the Dons in 2007. He left Perth to join Spanish side Fuenlabrada early in 2008 but returned to Scotland for the 2008/09 season with Ross County.

Eugene Dadi

Debut: League, 25 August 2001 v St Johnstone (a) drew 1-1
Appearances: League 28, Scottish Cup 3, League Cup 2
Goals: League 4, League Cup 1
Also played for: Toulouse, Livingston, Tranmere Rovers, Nottingham Forest, Notts County

Towering target man Eugene Dadi brought a breath of fresh air with him when he arrived at Pittodrie in search of a football home in August 2001. The 6ft 2in tall Frenchman had landed in Scotland on a short term contract. He quickly won an extension, with his winning goal against Motherwell in November that year proving the clincher. Dadi, who had starred for Toulouse in his homeland, led the line in his own distinctive style for a season. He left to accept a contract offer from Livingston in 2002 and has since featured for Tranmere, Nottingham Forest and Notts County.

Duncan Davidson

Debut: League, 8 April 1974 v Partick Thistle (a) lost 2-0
Appearances: League 105, Scottish Cup 23, League Cup 23, Europe 4
Goals: League 19, Scottish Cup 5, League Cup 4
Also played for: Tulsa Roughnecks, Toronto Blizzards, See Bee (Hong Kong), Manchester City

Duncan Davidson can boast of playing football in five countries and on three continents – but Pittodrie will always be where his heart lays. Now firmly ensconced in Granite City life, he is a driving force behind the Aberdeen Former Players' Association.

The Elgin-born lad moved to Aberdeen with his family as a 12-year-old, and his talent was spotted while playing for Lewis United juniors as a 16-year-old. Davie Robb, who took time out from his playing commitments with the Dons to train Lewis, picked up on Davidson's potential and, after earning Scotland junior caps and then impressing Teddy Scott during a match against the Pittodrie reserves, he was signed as a professional in 1972.

The youthful forward was handed his debut in the 1973/74 season and gradually edged his way into the side under Ally MacLeod and then Billy McNeill. He was still part of the squad when Alex Ferguson led the Dons to the league championship in 1978/80, playing a handful of games after scoring the first goal at Pittodrie during that victorious campaign when Hibs were defeated 3-0.

Davidson left in the summer of 1981 and moved to America with the Tulsa Roughnecks. During two seasons in North America he also represented the Toronto Blizzards before wanderlust took him to Asia with Hong Kong side See Bee. Billy McNeill, by then at Manchester City, took Davidson back to British football but a pelvic injury restricted the striker's appearances and ended his career at the age of 30. He returned to Aberdeen to embark on a successful career in the financial services sector.

Norrie Davidson

Debut: League, 15 October 1955 v St Mirren (a) won 3-0
Appearances: League 110, Scottish Cup 14, League Cup 23
Goals: League 55, Scottish Cup 13, League Cup 16
Also played for: Hearts, Dundee United, Partick Thistle, St Mirren, Barnsley, Ramsgate, Boksburg (South Africa)

A haul of 84 first team goals in less than five and a half years in the Aberdeen first team tells the story of striker Norrie Davidson's contribution to the cause. The Kintore boy joined as a teenager in 1955, having previously been on the books of Chelsea before returning to junior football with Inverurie Locos, and eased his way into the Dons fold.

He had failed to settle in London but rediscovered his goal touch after landing back on home soil, including during a guest spell in the Highland League with Keith during his prolific time in the Locos side. That tempted the Dons to make their move and they were rewarded with a healthy return.

By the 1957/58 campaign Davidson topped the Aberdeen scoring chart, netting 27 times in all competitions and scoring hat-tricks against Queen's Park and Motherwell, twice, along the way. He led the way again in 1959/60 with 17 goals to underline his importance to Dave Shaw's side.

It was after Tommy Pearson succeeded Shaw during that 1959/60 term that Davidson's career with the Dons drew to a close. Early in 1961 he was sold to Hearts in a £7,000 deal. Two and a half years later he was sold on to Dundee United for £6,000 for a short spell on Tayside, moving on to Partick Thistle in 1964 in a swap that took George Smith in the opposite direction. He turned out for St Mirren, Barnsley and Ramsgate before joining South African side Boksburg in Johannesburg in the closing weeks of 1966.

Marc De Clerck

Debut: League Cup, 30 August 1980 v Berwick Rangers (a) won 4-1
Appearances: League 1, League Cup 1
Goals: League Cup 1
Also played for: Go Ahead Eagles (Netherlands), Heracles (Netherlands)

Played two, scored one. That is the return goalkeeper Marc De Clerck provided during his time on the Pittodrie staff after his wind assisted strike in a 4-1 League Cup win at Berwick Rangers on his debut. The Belgian signed from Dutch side Go Ahead Eagles in 1980 and was released at the end of his first season to return to the continent with Heracles.

Jimmy Delaney

Debut: League, 18 November 1950 v Falkirk (h) won 5-1
Appearances: League 31, Scottish Cup 3, League Cup 5
Goals: League 8, Scottish Cup 1, League Cup 2
Also played for: Celtic, Manchester United, Falkirk, Derry City, Cork, Elgin City

Legendary Scotland international winger Jimmy Delaney was in the twilight of his career when he landed on the doorstep of Pittodrie Stadium in 1950. The fact he still commanded a £4,000 transfer fee told its own story about the new man recruited from Manchester United.

He had been an FA Cup winner with the Old Trafford side, to match the Scottish Cup winner's medal he collected with first club Celtic in 1937, in a career that spanned both sides of World War II. Delaney switched to England in 1946 and spent four years in Manchester before his surprise move to the Dons, where he replaced Alan Boyd on the right wing. With 20 caps collected between 1937 and 1948 he was a player with an impeccable track record and a big name signing for the Dons.

He spent a season and a half in Dave Halliday's side and then moved on to Falkirk in the closing weeks of 1951. Delaney sampled Irish football with Derry and Cork, completing a hat-trick of domestic trophy triumphs when he helped Derry City to the Irish Cup in 1954.

The Glaswegian made a comeback in Scottish football when he signed for Highland League challengers Elgin City while well into his 40s, eventually retiring at the tail end of the 1956/57 campaign at the end of a long and distinguished life in the game.

Eric Deloumeaux

Debut: League, 3 August 2002 v Hibs (a) won 2-1
Appearances: League 43, Scottish Cup 2, League Cup 5, Europe 4
Goals: League 4, League Cup 1
Also played for: Le Havre, Motherwell, Coventry City, Livingston

Cultured French defender Eric Deloumeaux was introduced to Scottish football by Dons legend Eric Black during his time in charge at Motherwell. His form with the Steelmen tempted Ebbe Skovdahl to make a £50,000 bid in the summer of 2002 and the former Le Havre player

made a promising start to his career with Aberdeen. Skovdahl's successor Steve Paterson had concerns about the continental player's work ethic and fitness and in January 2004 he was released early from his contract to be reunited with Black at Coventry City. He spent a year in the Midlands before returning north to join Livingston.

Gary Dempsey

Debut: League, 1 May 2005 v Rangers (h) lost 3-1
Appearances: League 54, Scottish Cup 3, League Cup 4
Goals: League 2
Also played for: Waterford (Ireland), Dunfermline Athletic, Yeovil, St Patrick's (Ireland), Darlington, Bray (Ireland)

Yeovil Town trumping Aberdeen in the transfer market. It sounds improbable, but that is exactly what happened when Irish midfielder Gary Dempsey's contract at Pittodrie expired in the summer of 2007 and he was persuaded to reject the opportunity to extend his stay in the north-east in favour of switching to the unfashionable English outfit with the lure of a bigger pay packet. Dempsey, another of the stream of players to follow Jimmy Calderwood from Dunfermline to the Dons, had proved a reliable utility player during the two previous seasons. The former Everton trainee's time at Yeovil was disappointing and he returned to Irish football with St Patrick's before reappearing in England with Darlington in 2010 for a brief stint. Bray, back in Ireland, was his next stop.

Jeffrey De Visscher

Debut: League, 4 August 2007 v Dundee United (a) lost 1-0
Appearances: League 32, Scottish Cup 4, League Cup 2, Europe 4
Goals: League 1, Scottish Cup 2
Also played for: FC Twente (Netherlands), De Graafschap (Netherlands), SC Cambuur Leeuwarden (Netherlands)

Wingers have long had the ability to set the Pittodrie crowd on the edge of their seats but have proved a rare breed in recent years. Dutchman Jeffrey De Visscher is one of the few wide men to have captured the imagination since the 1990s, although a lack of pace prevented the Jimmy Calderwood signing from putting his ability on the ball to its best use. He signed at Pittodrie in May 2007 after winning the Dutch Second Division title with De Graafschap. The former Netherlands under-21 international had previously played for FC Twente to underline his credentials. De Visscher left to join SC Cambuur Leeuwarden in January 2009 after growing frustrated at the lack of first team opportunities at Pittodrie.

Zander Diamond

Debut: League, 24 May 2003 v Dundee United (a) won 2-0
Appearances: League 205, Scottish Cup 23, League Cup 13, Europe 8
Goals: League 16, Scottish Cup 1, League Cup 1, Europe 1
Also played for: Hearts

During the 2010/11 season there was a landmark occasion for Zander Diamond. The Dons defender, second only to Darren Mackie in the long service stakes by that stage, celebrated his 25th birthday. Yes, 25. It may feel as though Diamond had been in with the bricks at Pittodrie but in fact he has yet to hit his peak years, with Oldham hoping to benefit after signing the stopper in the summer of 2011 under freedom of contract. Hitting the quarter century mark was a side issue during what proved to be a turbulent campaign, with Mark McGhee's tenure as manager lurching to an abrupt end. The manager was not the only individual to suffer, with Diamond himself enduring a torrid period as his decision to leave the club provoked the ire of the fans.

No longer a youngster with potential, Diamond had gone on to become one of the old heads in the side. That transition was not without its pitfalls, with the player finding that his position as a one-time fans' favourite did not make him immune from criticism when his form dipped and question marks over his place as the club's defensive pivot began to surface.

It was a far cry from the 2007/08 campaign, during which the club fought tooth and nail to retain Diamond's services when English clubs began to circle. Jimmy Calderwood managed to retain the star man with the help of a bumper contract, much to the delight of the support.

Diamond first hit the headlines in the 2003 Scottish Youth Cup final. The young Dons were beaten 3-1 by Celtic, but the gangly Scotland under-19 defender's performance was described as 'heroic' by the watching press.

He was raw and, on occasion, rash – but there was enough promise to suggest that the tall and rangy bundle of energy had a real chance of making an impact. His enthusiasm and passion for the game made him stand out from the crowd of young players aiming to make their mark and Diamond nudged his way to the front of the queue.

Steve Paterson gave him his first team break towards the end of the 2002/03 campaign as a substitute for Phil McGuire, with comparisons between Diamond and Alex McLeish quickly being made. Naturally he shied away from those daunting claims, but there was at least one common thread linking the two men – both owe much to the guiding hand of Billy McNeill. The Celtic legend gave McLeish his Aberdeen debut when he was in charge at Pittodrie and now, in his role as father to Diamond's agent, is on hand to offer advice and the benefit of his wisdom.

He has played through barren years at Pittodrie, with the highlight proving to be the 2007/08 campaign as the Dons returned to European competition with an almighty bang. For Diamond the Uefa Cup ties brought defiant performances against the might of Ukrainian big spenders Dnipro, not to mention the Bundesliga stars of Bayern Munich, and a goal scoring contribution against Lokomotiv Moscow. He rose to the big occasion in grand style.

Andy Dibble

Debut: League, 13 October 1990 v Motherwell (a) drew 0-0
Appearances: League 5
Also played for: Cardiff City, Luton Town, Manchester City, Rangers, Sheffield United, Middlesbrough, Altrincham, Hartlepool, Stockport County, Wrexham

When Theo Snelders suffered a sickening cheek injury when he clashed with Ally McCoist in October 1990 it left Alex Smith with a huge void to fill in his team. The experienced coach turned to England in his hour of need and recruited Andy Dibble as the man to fill the Dutchman's gloves. The Welshman had been at Manchester City for two years when he was allowed to answer the SOS and went on to play five games, keeping four clean sheets and never ending on the losing side as a Dons player. During nine years at Maine Road he was loaned to five clubs, eventually returning to Scotland for a brief stint with Rangers in 1997.

Laurent D'Jaffo

Debut: League, 10 August 2002 v Celtic (h) lost 4-0
Appearances: League 18, Scottish Cup 3, Europe 4
Goals: League 2, Europe 1
Also played for: Benin, Ayr United, Bury, Stockport County, Sheffield United, Mansfield

When Laurent D'Jaffo put pen to paper with Aberdeen in the summer of 2002 it ended a one year pursuit by Ebbe Skovdahl. The Danish coach was keen to land the tall and powerful French striker to add experience to his attack and the 31-year-old agreed a two year contract after spells with Bury, Stockport and Sheffield United in the English lower leagues.

He had first arrived in Britain to play for Ayr United in 1997. The 31-year-old Benin international could not find his goal touch with the Dons and was released early from his contract in January 2004, by which time Steve Paterson was in charge. He played for Mansfield before hanging up his boots to concentrate on a career as an agent.

Alex Di Rocco

Debut: League, 12 November 2000 v Rangers (h) lost 2-1
Appearances: League 10
Goals: League 3
Also played for: Sedan, St Etienne, Caen

A double in only his third game in Dons colours was French striker Alex Di Rocco's most notable contribution to the Pittodrie cause. That brace came in a 3-3 draw at home to Motherwell in November 2000, just a fortnight after he had arrived on trial from French side Sedan. Di Rocco was signed on loan by Ebbe Skovdahl and netted three times in ten appearances. At 6ft 2in the continental attacker added an extra dimension to the forward line but when his loan period expired at the end of the 2000/01 campaign he was one of a number of players who departed as the club tightened its purse strings.

John Docherty

Debut: League, 13 March 1976 v Dundee (h) lost 1-0
Appearances: League 1
Also played for: Falkirk, Inverness Thistle, Inverness Caley

John Docherty carved out a glowing reputation as coach to Caley Thistle's reserve team but it was with Aberdeen that he got his first break.

Docherty played a single match for the Dons in the 1975/76 campaign after the midfielder signed from junior side Benburb in 1973. Spells with Falkirk, Inverness Thistle and Inverness Caley followed before his move into coaching.

David Donald

Debut: League, 15 May 2004 v Dundee (h) lost 2-1
Appearances: League 2
Also played for: Peterhead, Montrose

Lifelong Dons fan David Donald became the youngest player to feature for the first team when he was handed his debut by Steve Paterson from the bench against Dundee at the end of the 2003/04 season at the age of 16 and a half.

Paterson's tenure was drawing to a close and Donald's progress was stalled as Jimmy Calderwood opted for experience over youth. The right-back made one further appearance under the new boss, against Celtic as a substitute in 2006, before joining Peterhead. He has clocked up more than a century of appearances for the Blue Toon and become one of the club's most consistent defenders.

Davie Dodds

Debut: League, 27 September 1986 v Rangers (a) lost 2-0
Appearances: League 72, Scottish Cup 12, League Cup 8, Europe 3
Goals: League 17, Scottish Cup 4, League Cup 5, Europe
Also played for: Scotland (2 caps), Dundee United, Arbroath (on loan), Neuchatel Xamax, Rangers

Strength on the ball, a fierce will to win and a happy habit of finding the back of the net were the qualities that attracted Alex Smith to Davie Dodds. It was Alex Ferguson who recruited the former Dundee United striker early in the 1986/87 season but it was his successors Ian Porterfield and Alex Smith who he primarily served under.

Dodds got off to a successful start, scoring a debut goal against Brechin, and proved to be a dependable squad man for the Dons during three years at Pittodrie. Had it not been for a series of niggling injuries the contribution would have been greater.

He left in 1989 and missed out on the chance to be part of Smith's cup winning sides, instead opting to join boyhood heroes Rangers when Graeme Souness came calling with a £125,000 offer for the 32-year-old.

He filled a similar support role at Ibrox as he had done at Pittodrie before joining the coaching staff in Govan. The high points of his career came much earlier while he was at Tannadice. Dodds was a key man in the 1982/83 Premier Division championship winning Arabs team. He was a League Cup winner in 1980 with his home town side and also earned two Scotland caps.

He left in 1986 to join Swiss outfit Neuchatel Xamax. It proved an unhappy chapter in the Scot's playing career and he was soon pining for a return. Rangers hoped to lure him to Glasgow but they were trumped by the Dons, as a £215,000 deal was agreed in September 1986.

Tommy Donaldson

Debut: League, 22 February 1964 v Falkirk (a) won 3-2
Appearances: League 2
Also played for: Montrose

Left winger Tommy Donaldson was introduced by Tommy Pearson during the 1963/64 season but the youngster, brought north from Edinburgh juvenile side Musselburgh Windsor, struggled to establish himself after first appearing as a 16-year-old. Donaldson turned to part-time football with Montrose after being released in 1965.

Andy Dornan

Debut: League, 1 November 1980 v Airdrie (h) won 4-1
Appearances: League 2
Also played for: Motherwell, Walsall
Managed: Montrose

Right back Andy Dornan lined up against the mighty Liverpool at Anfield in only his second appearance for the Dons in 1980. The European Cup tie ended in a 4-0 defeat and the youngster played just one more game for the club as Stuart Kennedy proved an immovable obstacle. Dornan, a former Rubislaw Academy pupil who had been capped by Scotland at youth level, moved to Motherwell in 1982 and had a successful spell with Walsall before injury forced his retirement. He went on to manage Montrose, leading the Gable Endies to promotion, and coach with Ross County under former Pittodrie colleague Neale Cooper in the 1990s. The pair were reunited when Dornan was appointed assistant manager to Cooper at Peterhead in 2008.

Andy Dow

Debut: League Cup, 8 August 1998 v Caley Thistle (a) won 3-0
Appearances: League 76, Scottish Cup 10, League Cup 6, Europe 2
Goals: League 6, Scottish Cup 1, League Cup 1
Also played for: Dundee, Chelsea, Bradford City (on loan), Hibs, Motherwell, St Mirren, Raith Rovers, Arbroath

The £80,000 paid for Andy Dow at the start of the 1998/99 season by Alex Miller proved to be a sound piece of business for the Dons. Recruited from Hibs, the Dundonian was comfortable playing on the left side of the defence or midfield and provided a genuine threat

with dangerous deliveries from set-pieces and a willingness to break forward at every opportunity.
For two years he solved what proved to be a recurring problem for a succession of Aberdeen managers by providing capable cover on the left flank until he fell out of favour under Ebbe Skovdahl in the 2000/01 campaign. The

Dane was prepared to swap Dow for St Johnstone full-back Gary Bollan that season but the player decided he wanted to stay and fight for his place at Pittodrie.
It was only a temporary reprieve and at the end of the term his contract was cut short to allow him to join Motherwell. It was the latest stop during a career which had taken him from Dundee to Chelsea and on to Bradford, on loan, before he landed at Hibs in 1996. His time at Well ended on a sour note when he became one of the group of players who lost their jobs when the club plunged into administration. Short spells with St Mirren, Raith and Arbroath followed before Dow dropped down into junior football in 2004 to represent Lochee, Dundee North End, Broughty Athletic and Blairgowrie.

Stuart Duff

Debut: League, 26 January 2008 v Hearts (h) lost 1-0
Appearances: League 47, Scottish Cup 3, Europe 2
Goals: League 1
Also played for: Dundee United, Caley Thistle

Aberdonian utility player Stuart Duff's football dream came true when he became a Dons player in January 2008. The former Pittodrie season ticket holder had to head south to launch his senior career, joining Dundee United while still a pupil at Aberdeen Grammar School, but made his way home eventually.

He made more than 150 appearances for the Arabs during sevens seasons in the Tannadice team and proved a reliable performer in defence and midfield, becoming a Scotland under-21 international in the process as well as going on to become the Tayside club's longest serving player.

Jimmy Calderwood moved quickly to add the versatile player to his squad when Duff became available after negotiating his release from United. Calderwood had been tracking Duff for several years and finally got his man at an ideal time as he looked for a replacement for the departing Chris Clark. His athleticism and aerial ability were two of the qualities cited by the Dons boss as he earmarked his new man for a midfield role.

Duff spent a season and a half with his boyhood heroes but found himself out of the first team picture during Mark McGhee's tenure and was ushered out of the exit door. Early in the 2010/11 season he was thrown a lifeline by Caley Thistle. He grasped the opportunity with both hands to cement a place in Terry Butcher's starting 11 during an impressive season for the Highlanders as they secured their status as an SPL side in their return to the top flight after promotion from the First Division.

Jack Dunbar

Debut: League Cup, 27 August 1952 v Hearts (a) drew 1-1
Appearances: League 4, League Cup 6
Also played for: Gloucester City

The Scottish Junior Cup winning side fielded by Kilbirnie Ladeside in 1952 featured imposing forward Jack Dunbar. At 6ft 1in tall he was a natural target man and featured for Dave Halliday's side at Aberdeen in 1952/53 after being recruited by the Dons. He returned to the side as a right winger the following term but departed at the end of that second season to join Gloucester City.

Frank Dunlop

Debut: League, 29 August 1936 v Falkirk (h) won 4-0
Appearances: League 112, Scottish Cup 20, League Cup 14
Also played for: Benburb

When Aberdeen clinched the Scottish Cup for the first time in 1947 with a hard fought 2-1 win over Hibs at Hampden Park there was no prouder man in the national stadium than Frank Dunlop. As captain he hoisted the famous trophy above his head in front of 82,140 and led the victorious team on their parade through the streets of the Granite City on their return. The win meant so much to the city, with 15,000 fans greeting their heroes when they returned by train.

Dunlop and goalkeeper George Johnstone had both been on the losing side 10 years earlier when the Dons fell at the final hurdle in the national cup competition against Celtic. In 1947 they made up for that pain when, despite losing a goal inside the first 30 seconds of the game, goals from George Hamilton and Stan Williams repaired the damage and saw the name of Aberdeen etched on the cup.

By that stage he already had a Southern League Cup medal safely in the vault, playing in the side which beat Rangers in the 1946 final. A crowd of 135,000 watched the Dons win that game 3-2 with goals from George Taylor, Stan Williams and Archie Baird and Dunlop was resplendent in the No.5 shirt which would prove to be his lucky charm in the Scottish Cup the following year.

Those senior prizes joined the Scottish Junior Cup winner's reward he secured with Benburb in 1936, the earliest sign that the Glaswegian had a fruitful career in the game ahead of him. Dunlop was snapped up by the Dons after the junior final and made his debut in a 4-0 win over Falkirk at Pittodrie on August 29, 1936.

War interrupted Dunlop's career but the defender's record of 146 hard fought games ensured legendary status. He played under Pat Travers and Dave Halliday and was an automatic pick for both managers. In the 1945-46 season he was the only man to play in each of the 45 games that term. A 4-2 Scottish Cup defeat against Hibs at Easter Road on February 21, 1948, spelled the end of a long and illustrious playing career. It was the same season in which Willie Cooper called time on his 20 year association with the club.

In 1949 Dunlop emigrated to Zimbabwe, then under the flag of Rhodesia, to concentrate on his professional life as a chiropodist but his football connection lived on as he went on to coach the national team in his adopted country.

He remained an avid Dons fan during his time in Africa, having local newspapers shipped out to his home to keep up to date with events at Pittodrie, and made annual return trips to the city. In the 1960s he even called upon Eddie Turnbull to pick up coaching tips to help him in his duties as chairman of selectors with the Bulawayo Callies club. Dunlop, who never recorded a senior goal for the Dons, came back 'home' to Aberdeen in 1979 and was a regular in the stands at Pittodrie until his death, at the age of 77, in 1991.

Billy Dodds

Debut: Uefa Cup, 9 August 1994 v Skonto Riga (a) drew 0-0
Appearances: League 132+8, Scottish Cup 4+3, League Cup 11+2, Europe 8
Goals: League 49, Scottish Cup 1, League Cup 14, Europe 4
Also played for: Dundee, St Johnstone, Dundee United, Rangers, Partick Thistle.

In September, 1998, Aberdeen Football Club and manager Alex Miller conducted a piece of business which baffled the Pittodrie faithful. Out went Billy Dodds, leading scorer in each of the four seasons he had spent at the club, to Dundee United along with £500,000 of Dons cash. In came Arabs striker Robbie Winters, a talented yet inconsistent young striker.

It would prove to be either a masterstroke by Miller or one of the biggest miscalculations in the history of the club. Most would argue the latter applied and United completed the steal of the century.

Winters proved to be a decent performer for the Dons but he could not match Dodds as an out and out goalscorer. Nor could he come close to trumping his predecessor when it came to spirit or

infectious enthusiasm. Miller was lambasted by furious supporters and lasted less than a year in the manager's chair.

The bubbly Glasgwegian was a hero in Aberdeen's most recent trophy success, the 1995 League Cup victory against Dundee. Dodds was on target along with Duncan Shearer in the 2-0 win. For the success starved Pittodrie regulars it was a moment to savour and one they hoped would herald a new era. It proved to be a false dawn and the chances were limited by the departure of Dodds, who had become a talisman in the eyes of everyone apart from Alex Miller.

As a player Willie Miller got to grips with a succession of top class strikers. As a manager he put that experience to good use when it came to identifying the man he wanted to spearhead his team, turning to St Johnstone's 25 year-old marksman.

Dodds had started out as a trainee with Chelsea and had a loan spell with Partick before carving out a reputation as a goalscorer with Dundee and Saints. He became a hero to the Dens faithful and became popular along the road at St Johnstone too, a mark not

just of his ability but also his personality. It cost Miller £800,000 to persuade the Perth side to part with their biggest asset but it proved to be a worthwhile investment and one of the greatest legacies of his spell in charge of the club.

Dodds made a low key debut on August 9, 1994, in the first leg of the disastrous Uefa Cup tie against Skonto Riga, which saw the Dons crash out against the unfancied Latvians, but was on target in his first league match against Hearts.

It was the first of 17 goals in the 1994/95 season for the struggling Dons. Miller departed and was replaced by assistant Roy Aitken as the club narrowly avoided relegation in a season which also saw them dumped out of the Scottish Cup by Stenhousemuir.

There was a marked improvement in the next term, when in addition to the League Cup triumph there was a third place finish in the Premier Division to hearten supporters. Dodds tied with Scott Booth on 12 goals at the head of the club's scoring chart.

The 1996/97 season was the diminutive striker's most prolific in a red shirt as he bagged a 26 goal haul which included hat-tricks against Raith and Morton.

That form brought the first of 26 Scotland caps, claiming seven goals in the process, when Craig Brown pitched him in against Latvia. Dodds spent five years on the international stage.

Twelve goals followed the next year but the 1998/99 term spelled the end of a fruitful relationship. A League Cup hat-trick against Caley Thistle in August was not enough to persuade Alex Miller of the merits of a forward who hit 68 goals in 162 games.

It proved to be costly as in 15 months Dodds scored 25 goals in 44 Premier League starts for United. It was arguably at Tannadice that he hit his most productive and consistent run of form, perhaps spurred on by his rejection at Pittodrie and with new fire in his belly as he set out to prove a point.

Inevitably for a player at his peak with a provincial club, the call of the Old Firm was not far away. Dodds was whisked away from Tayside by Rangers in a £1.3million deal in December, 1999. He proved a valuable squad man for the Ibrox side, netting 34 goals in just 46 starts and 38 appearances from the bench.

Dodds, now an established football pundit on television and radio, returned to Dundee United in 2003, serving as player coach for three years before a short spell on the Partick Thistle playing staff. He went on to combine his media commitments with a place on the Queen of the South staff, reunited with his former Tannadice gaffer Gordon Chisholm at Palmerston.

The duo established Queens as genuine challengers in the First Division and their efforts won them a dream return to Dundee, a club both had served with distinction as players. They arrived at Dens as replacements for Jocky Scott in 2010 with big promises from the club's board, but when the club slipped into administration later that year the duo found themselves out of work and left to ponder the vagries of life in the Scottish game. Dodds was able to return to his radio duties, although he has never hidden his desire to retun to coaching and test himself as a manager in his own right in the future. When Mark McGhee departed Pittodrie, Dodds made no secret of the fact he would jump at the opportunity to manage the Dons. It was Craig Brown who got the nod on that occasion but it would be foolish to bet against a man with the determination of Dodds from eventually realising his dream.

Keith Edwards

Debut: League, 3 October 1987 v Dunfermline (h) won 3-0
Appearances: League 9, Scottish Cup 1
Goals: League 2, Scottish Cup 1
Also played for: Sheffield United, Hull City, Leeds United, Stockport County, Huddersfield Town

When Ian Porterfield spent £60,000 on Leeds United striker Keith Edwards in 1987 he was investing in a player who boasted a better strike ratio in English league football than Geoff Hurst and Bobby Charlton. With more than 200 goals to his credit, he was expected to take Scottish football by storm. A goal on his debut against Dunfermline suggested a bright future but indifferent form and a knee injury hampered his efforts and, six months after arriving, he was sold to Hull City for a fee matching the one which had taken him to Pittodrie. Edwards returned to impressive form with the Humberside outfit.

Don Emery

Debut: League, 14 August 1948 v Third Lanark (a) lost 1-0
Appearances: League 89, Scottish Cup 11, League Cup 25
Goals: League 17, Scottish Cup 2, League Cup 6
Also played for: Swindon Town, East Fife, Fraserburgh

Size certainly did count when it came to Don Emery, the Welshman christened Two Ton Don by Aberdeen fans. He measured just under six-foot tall but weighed in at up to 17-stone during his playing career and used his strength to good effect with some thumping set-piece deliveries. When Emery hit the ball it stayed hit, with one of his trademark free-kicks even breaking the crossbar during one game against Partick Thistle in Glasgow. Emery, who died in 2003, became a regular goal scorer thanks to his role as penalty taker and free-kick master at Pittodrie. His other major contribution came at the other end of the park, where some meaty tackling gained him a reputation as a defender not to be messed with.

The Cardiff-born defender was a schoolboy international before being plucked away from his home town team to join Swindon before the outbreak of war. When peace resumed, he and his Aberdonian wife jumped at the opportunity to relocate to the north-east when a swap deal took Andy Cowie to Swindon in 1948. He spent four years with the Dons before joining East Fife, where he was part of the Bayview side's League Cup winning team in 1954 and won international honours with Wales.

In 1956, Emery was appointed player manager by Highland League side Fraserburgh and proved a smash hit. He scored 49 goals in a single season to announce his arrival in the north game.

The Welshman also served as a director at Fraserburgh and as president of Deveronvale in the 1980s.

Dickie Ewen

Debut: League, 2 November 1957 v Falkirk (a) drew 4-4
Appearances: League 82, Scottish Cup 13, League Cup 11
Goals: League 18, Scottish Cup 1, League Cup 5
Also played for: Forfar Athletic, Peterhead, Keith

Replacing local hero Graham Leggat was the task facing right winger Dickie Ewen when he made his breakthrough with Aberdeen. Like Leggat, he was a local lad who had first risen to prominence with Banks o' Dee A. Unlike Leggat, he had looked outside of the Granite City for his first break and featured for the Rangers reserve team in the mid-1950s. When he was released by the Ibrox side he returned to the north-east junior scene and from there was picked up by Aberdeen manager Davie Shaw – although not before he had helped Banks o' Dee lift the Scottish Junior Cup as part of the revered class of 1957.

Ewen made his senior debut in the 1958/59 season,

Ryan Esson

Debut: League, 14 May 2000 v Kilmarnock (h) won 5-1
Appearances: League 89, Scottish Cup 5, League Cup 4, Europe 2
Also played for: Rotherham (on loan), Shrewsbury Town, Hereford, Caley Thistle

It took Ryan Esson more than a decade to achieve his goal of establishing himself as a top flight goalkeeper in Scottish football. He had to travel far and wide to find his football home and for the Aberdonian shot stopper the winding road took him north to the Highlands, where in the 2010/11 season he was a key man as Inverness Caledonian Thistle re-established themselves as a force to be reckoned with in the SPL.

For Esson the journey began in his home city with the Dons. He had been a stand-out performer in Aberdeen's juvenile leagues when he was recruited by the Pittodrie talent spotters. He made his debut in 2000 and by 2000/01 was first choice for the gloves. The elevation proved temporary and Esson found himself back in a support role following the arrival of the experienced Peter Kjaer in the autumn of 2001. After five further frustrating years, briefly broken by a loan spell with Rotherham in 2002, the able keeper looked south and switched permanently to Shrewsbury Town in 2006.

Injury disrupted his time in England and, after a short stop with Hereford, he arrived back in Scotland to join Inverness in 2008. Once again Esson found himself as second choice goalkeeper but Michael Fraser's move to Motherwell for the start of the 2009/10 campaign paved the way for the Aberdonian to step up to the plate. Esson did not disappoint and was a mainstay of the First Division championship winning team, retaining his place for the return to the top flight the following term.

following Leggat's high profile move to Fulham, and was a key player in the run to the Scottish Cup final. Defeat against St Mirren at Hampden ensured the campaign did not end on a high, although the flanker could console himself with the fact he had pushed his way into the Scotland under-23 side.

The tricky winger continued to feature in the team following Tommy Pearson's appointment as manager, in the face of an unfortunate run of injuries and illness which included a broken leg, but was released to join Forfar in 1963. Ewen also featured for Peterhead and Keith in the Highland League before packing away his boots to concentrate on a career in teaching.

Ernie Ewen

Debut: League, 13 August 1952 v Hearts (h) lost 4-2
Appearances: League 1, League Cup 1
Goals: League Cup 1
Also played for: Dundee, St Johnstone, Rothes

A goal on his debut was not enough to prevent forward Ernie Ewen from ending that maiden match on the losing side as Hearts triumphed 4-2 at Pittodrie in a League Cup tie in 1952. Ewen, formerly of Dundee, made one further appearance before returning to Tayside with St Johnstone. He went on to play for Rothes in the Highland League.

Willie Falconer

Debut: European Cup Winners' Cup, 19 April 1983 v Waterschei (a) lost 1-0
Appearances: League 76, Scottish Cup 5, League Cup 9, Europe 9
Goals: League 14, Scottish Cup 1, League Cup 1, Europe 2
Also played for: Watford, Middlesbrough, Sheffield United, Celtic, Motherwell

Willie Falconer is one of the forgotten men of the run to glory in the 1983 European Cup Winners' Cup. He was a young man starting out in his profession when he was drafted in for his continental cameo, handed his debut by Alex Ferguson in the second leg of the semi-final against Waterschei in Belgium. A 1-0 defeat could not prevent the Dons from progressing and Falconer could celebrate as the mission was completed.

He had been capped at schoolboy level by Scotland and made rapid progress at Pittodrie to propel himself to the fringes of the dominant first team being carefully pieced together by Ferguson.

The Mastrick teenager, who had shot to prominence with Aberdeen Lads' Club and Lewis United, eventually became a regular in the 1987/88 campaign when he was converted from striker to defender by Ian Porterfield. He looked instantly at home in the back four and was given a second wind by the shift in position. In 1988 he was courted by Norwich City, Leicester City, Bradford and Aston Villa before agreeing to join Watford in a £300,000 transfer.

Spells with Middlesbrough and Sheffield United followed before he was tempted back across the border by Celtic in 1994. Falconer also represented Motherwell before hanging up his boots.

Nicolas Fabiano

Debut: League, 1 September 2002 v Partick Thistle (h) lost 1-0
Appearances: League 12, Scottish Cup 2, League Cup 1, Europe 2
Also played for: Paris Saint Germain (France), Istres (France, on loan), Swansea City, Racing Club (France), Red Star (France)

It took two attempts to land French midfielder Nicolas Fabiano. Ebbe Skovdahl first tried to sign the young player in March 2002 after an impressive trial spell but had to abandon those plans due to red tape. Fabiano, who had been on loan at Swansea and in France with Istres from Paris Saint Germain, eventually moved to Pittodrie five months later on a one year deal. He flitted in and out of the first team during his single season in Scottish football, returning to Paris and finding a new football home with Racing Club. He joined Red Star, another Paris outfit, in 2006.

Rory Fallon

Debut: League, 17 September 2011 v Kilmarnock (h) drew 2-2
Appearances (up to the end of 2011/12): League 22, Scottish Cup 5, League Cup 1
Goals (up to the end of 2011/12): League 2, Scottish Cup 4, League Cup 1
Also played for: New Zealand, Barnsley, Swindon, Swansea, Plymouth Argyle

The Pittodrie board pushed the boat out to allow Craig Brown to recruit Rory Fallon in the autumn of 2011, extending the manager's player budget. Fallon, who had been released by struggling Plymouth and had a short stint with Yeovil, was seen as the man to solve the goal scoring problems the Dons were suffering. With extensive experience of the English game, not to mention on the World Cup stage with New Zealand, he proved to be an able striker after signing his two-year deal.

Graeme Ferguson

Debut: League, 14 December 1991 v St Johnstone (h) won 4-1
Appearances: League 5
Also played for: Clydebank, Clyde, Forfar Athletic

Full-back Graeme Ferguson joined the Dons from school with an impressive pedigree as a Scotland schoolboy international. He went on to win youth international caps and was blooded in the Dons first team in the 1991/92 season but, after five appearances from the bench, was allowed to join Clydebank in a £15,000 deal in November 1993. He went on to feature for Clyde and Forfar.

Sandy Finnie

Debut: League, 2 October 1965 v St Mirren (h) won 4-1
Appearances: League 3
Goals: League 2
Also played for: Arbroath, Inverness Caledonian, Elgin City

Three games, two goals, two wins and a draw. Sandy Finnie's brief Dons record makes for impressive reading. His return in the 1965/66 season could not secure a long term future as a player with his home town club, having joined as a teenager from Banks o' Dee A two years earlier.

Finnie joined Arbroath on a free transfer in 1966 as he moved to combine playing with a career working for British Gas. He went on to star in the Highland League with Inverness Caledonian and Elgin City as his versatility, strength in the tackle and passing ability shone through. Finnie returned to Aberdeen in the 1990s in a community role and became a hugely popular figure at the club. He died in 2006 at the age of 79.

Ian Fleming

Debut: League, 7 February 1976 v Rangers (a) lost 2-1
Appearances: League 84, Scottish Cup 6, League Cup 22, Europe 4
Goals: League 12, Scottish Cup 4, League Cup 7
Also played for: Kilmarnock, Sheffield Wednesday, Dundee, Brechin City
Managed: Brechin City, Elgin City

When Ally MacLeod arrived from Ayr United to take charge of Aberdeen in 1975 it did not take him long to look west once again. Rather than his old club, it was Ayrshire rivals Kilmarnock that the new Dons boss raided for his first Pittodrie signing.

The top target was striker Ian Fleming and in December 1975 a £15,000 cheque changed hands as the transfer was pushed through. Fleming had spent five years with Killie and had been a key man in their promotion from the Second Division in 1974 before firing in 22 goals in the club's return to the top flight the following term.

Fleming failed to hit the heights he had scaled with his first club but became a useful squad man for the Dons over the course of three years in the north-east. The bustling forward, whose 5ft 8in frame belied his strength, served under MacLeod, Billy McNeill and Alex Ferguson before being sold to Jack Charlton at Sheffield Wednesday in February 1979 for £48,000.

He was back in Scottish football within a year, joining Dundee. When he was appointed player manager at Brechin City in October 1982 he became the youngest boss in Scotland as he took on the challenge at the age of 29.

The Maybole-born coach won the Second Division title with the Glebe Park side before parting company during the 1986/87 campaign. He went on to manage Elgin City in the Highland League in the 1990s after a spell as assistant to Jocky Scott at Arbroath.

Yoann Folly

Debut: League, 14 August 2010 v Hamilton (h) won 4-0
Appearances: League 18, League Cup 2
Goals: League 1
Also played for: Togo, St Etienne, Southampton, Nottingham Forest (on loan), Preston North End (on loan), Sheffield Wednesday, Plymouth Argyle, Dagenham and Redbridge (on loan)

Togo international midfielder Yoann Folly has an Aberdeen legend to thank for his break in British football. It was Gordon Strachan who took the former France youth international to the UK when he signed him for Southampton from St Etienne in 2003.

Spells with Nottingham Forest, Preston, Sheffield Wednesday, Plymouth and Dagenham and Redbridge followed before he was recruited by Mark McGhee for the Dons in 2010. Folly was released in 2012 after injury and illness.

Richard Foster

Debut: League, 10 May 2003 v Partick Thistle (h) won 2-1
Appearances: League 234, Scottish Cup 19, League Cup 21, Europe 9
Goals: League 8, Europe 1
Also played for: Rangers (on loan)

Rangers 1, Aberdeen 0. That was the result of one of the most baffling transfers of 2010 as the Ibrox club got one over on the Dons by swapping injury plagued striker Andrius Velicka. While Walter Smith benefited from Foster's energy and drive, Mark McGhee landed himself a striker who was not fit enough to be relied upon and made just one start and five appearances from the bench during an instantly forgettable time at Pittodrie in which a solitary goal against Caley Thistle was his only telling contribution.

Foster thrived at Ibrox during his season-long loan, excelling in Champions League appearances against Manchester United and Bursaspor as well as playing an important role in the challenge on all fronts in domestic competition during 2010/11. Meanwhile, his swap counterpart Velicka was quickly bombed out by Craig Brown following his appointment to the manager's chair.

Foster was another of the youngsters to have made their way through the Aberdeen system. The versatile and pacy player rose to prominence under Jimmy Calderwood and was used as a winger, full-back, central midfielder and in the heart of the defence. He proved accomplished in all of those roles and won admirers from elsewhere, including Ibrox.

The Aberdonian, who grew up in Elgin, was given his debut by Steve Paterson in May 2003 as a 17-year-old and by the time he left to join Rangers on loan seven years later he had clocked up more than 250 first team appearances. He moved on to Bristol in 2011 after a spell as Dons captain.

Jim Forrest

Debut: League Cup, 10 August 1968 v Clyde (a) lost 4-1
Appearances: League 128+3, Scottish Cup 20, League Cup 27+2, Europe 11
Goals: League 44, Scottish Cup 8, League Cup 8, Europe 2
Also played for: Scotland (5 caps), Rangers, Preston North End, Cape Town City, Hong Kong Rangers

When the minnows of Berwick Rangers shocked their Ibrox counterparts with a 1-0 win in the 1967 Scottish Cup the fall out was considerable and for Jim Forrest the game proved to be his last in Light Blue as he was one of the players held accountable for the humiliating defeat. Rangers' loss proved to be Aberdeen's gain.

Forrest, a powerful and pacy forward who was just as adept on the wing, found his escape with Preston North End but by 1968 was back in Scottish football with the Dons following a £25,000 transfer.

The Glaswegian returned with a point to prove and laid the Scottish Cup ghost to rest in grand style when he helped his new club to lift the trophy in 1970 with the 3-1 win over Celtic. It completed a full set of domestic honours for the player who had joined Rangers from school and went on to pick up a championship medal and play in two League Cup wins for the Ibrox men.

Forrest did not score in the Scottish Cup final of 1970 but was regularly on target for Eddie Turnbull and his successor Jimmy Bonthrone. Indeed, in his first season with the Dons he was the club's leading scorer with 23 goals and collected the Aberdeen Supporters' Club player of the year award for his efforts. He also captained the side before handing over that responsibility to Martin Buchan.

He made his debut on August 10, 1968, in a 4-1 League Cup defeat at Clyde and scored the first of those 23 goals just four days later with the winner against Dunfermline at Pittodrie in the same competition.

Aberdeen avoided relegation by just eight points and two league places that season and a series of vital goals from Forrest played a significant part in that mission. In the seasons that followed, the Dons improved steadily, climbing from that 15th place to finish the following campaign eighth before being runners-up to Celtic in both 1970/71 and 1971/72. With the championship just outside their grasp, the Scottish Cup win of 1970 proved to be the crowning glory for Turnbull and his team.

In March, 1971, Forrest confirmed his place as one of the best strikers of his generation when he smashed home his 200th senior goal in Scottish football in a 4-1 win against Ayr United.

In five seasons with the Dons he notched 62 goals in 191 appearances and established himself as a fans' favourite. He also won favour with Scotland managers after making his international debut under Jock Stein in 1965 and going on to win five caps.

Forrest was freed by Bonthrone at the end of the 1972/73 season after being troubled with injuries and rounded off his career in South Africa with Cape Town City and then in Asia with Hong Kong Rangers.

Doug Fraser

Debut: League, 30 April 1960 v Ayr United (h) won 2-0
Appearances: League 65, Scottish Cup 6, League Cup 17
Goals: League 1, Scottish Cup 1
Also played for: Scotland (2 caps), West Brom, Nottingham Forest, Walsall
Managed: Walsall

Defender Doug Fraser was one of the many gems unearthed by legendary west coast scout Bobby Calder. It was Calder who alerted manager Davie Shaw to Fraser's potential, having seen the 17-year-old star for Blantyre Celtic as a centre forward. Fraser even scored a double in a trial match for the Dons against Third Lanark but it was in the back line that he went on to make his name as a speedy and effective left half.

Fraser, who had been on the verge of joining Leeds United before committing to the Dons, pushed his way into the first team in time for the 1960/61 season and made the No.6 shirt his own until the emergence of Dave Smith two years later. With Smith settling quickly into the first team, Fraser was allowed to leave for West Bromwich Albion in September 1963. The English side paid £25,000 to boost Pittodrie coffers already filled by the same fee raked in for George Mulhall by Sunderland a year earlier.

Fraser went on to become a favourite at the Hawthorns and forced his way into Bobby Brown's international side to face the Netherlands in 1968. He made his Scotland debut in a team that also featured former Dons team-mates Dave Smith and Charlie Cooke. It was the first of two caps he won.

After more than 250 appearances for the Baggies he switched to Nottingham Forest in 1971 and then on to Walsall in 1973. He went on to manage Walsall for the 1975/76 and 1976/77 campaigns.

Ryan Fraser

Debut: League, 16 October 2010 v Hearts (h) lost 1-0
Appearances (up to end of 2011/12): League 5

Ryan Fraser was described as small in stature but big in ability when he was introduced to first team life in October 2010. Fraser's drive and determination was a major factor in earning promotion to the top side. After two appearances from the bench inside the space of a week he dropped back down to the under-19 squad.

Tony Fraser

Debut: League, 5 September 1964 v Dundee (a) lost 3-1
Appearances: League 10, Scottish Cup 1, League Cup 2
Goals: League 4
Also played for: Elgin City, Inverness Thistle

Banks o' Dee lost another young star when winger Tony Fraser was picked up by the Dons in 1963. He made his debut under Tommy Pearson early in the 1964/65 campaign and four goals in nine league outings suggested a bright future. Fraser was deemed surplus to requirements under Eddie Turnbull and moved on to Elgin City in 1966 before joining Inverness Thistle and winning the Highland League twice.

Fraser Fyvie

Debut: League, 22 August 2009 v Hamilton (a) won 3-0
Appearances (up to end of 2011/12): League 58, Scottish Cup 6, League Cup 2
Goals (up to end of 2011/12): League 2, Scottish Cup: 1

When Mark McGhee made his entrance as Aberdeen manager as the curtain lifted on the 2009/10 season it looked to be the dawn of a bright new era. A convincing 3-0 victory over Hamilton Accies sounded a clarion call to the Red Army to rally once again and in rookie midfielder Fraser Fyvie there was a symbol of what the fresh regime stood for.

Where Jimmy Calderwood had relied on experience, McGhee arrived with a brief to thrust Aberdeen's youth talent to the fore. When he handed Fyvie his debut he created a new record as the teenage prospect became the youngest ever to feature in a competitive fixture for the Pittodrie side when he ran out at the age of 16 years and four months. He was later usurped by Jack Grimmer, but that does not detract from Fyvie's achievement or the impact he made.

Despite not being old enough to drive, vote or enjoy a post-match beer he looked like a seasoned professional as he set about patrolling the tough midfield beat of the SPL with aplomb. There was not a hint of trepidation as he crunched into tackles and demonstrated composure in possession that belied his age.

Disaster struck in 2010/11 when in only his third match of the campaign he suffered a knee injury in a League Cup tie at Alloa and ended up sidelined for the remainder of the term. In 2012 he announced his intention to move on and clinched a switch to Wigan Athletic.

John Gardiner

Debut: League Cup, 15 November 1978 v Ayr United (h) won 3-1
Appearances: League 2, Scottish Cup 1, League Cup 2
Also played for: Dundee United, Motherwell, Huntly
Managed: Huntly, Inverurie Locos, Formartine United

Goalkeeper John Gardiner had to concede defeat in his efforts to dislodge Bobby Clark from the Dons No.1 shirt. The Glaswegian, recruited from Campsie Black Watch, made five appearances in 1978/79 and won Scotland under-21 honours while at Pittodrie under Alex Ferguson. He joined Dundee United in 1980 for £25,000 to replace Peter Bonetti as reserve to Hamish McAlpine and also turned out for Motherwell before starring in the Highland League as part of the dominant Huntly side of the 1990s. Gardiner went on to manage Huntly, Inverurie Locos and Formartine United in the north game.

Lee Gardner

Debut: League, 16 April 1988 v Morton (a) won 2-0
Appearances: League 1
Also played for: Oxford United (on loan), Ayr United

Ayrshire youth star Lee Gardner first linked up with the Dons while still a schoolboy and joined as a full-time professional straight from school under Alex Ferguson. He made his one and only appearance in Ian Porterfield's team in the 1987/88 campaign before a loan stint with Oxford United in 1991. He joined Ayr United on a free transfer that year.

Willie Garner

Debut: League, 17 January 1976 v Hearts (a) drew 3-3
Appearances: League 113+1, Scottish Cup 11, League Cup 31, Europe 6+1
Goals: League 1, League Cup 2
Also played for: Celtic, Alloa, Keith
Also managed: Alloa, Keith, Deveronvale

It was fitting that Willie Garner emerged from his most consistent season for Aberdeen with a winner's medal in his pocket. The powerful defender was the only ever present for Ally MacLeod in the 1976-77 season and rock in the 11 game League Cup campaign which ended with a 2-1 win over Celtic in the final.

In all the 6ft 2in centre-half played in 50 games that term, all 36 in the league alongside the emerging talent of Willie Miller in central defence. The next season, with Billy McNeill at the helm following MacLeod's switch to the national team, Garner missed just a single game. Significantly the man who deputised for him on that occasion was a youngster called Alex McLeish.

Soon McLeish would take that place permanently, his chance coming when Garner broke his leg in a European Cup Winners' Cup tie against Marek Dimitrov in September, 1978. When he returned to fitness in the 1979/80 season there was still room for Garner in Alex Ferguson's side as they swept to the club's first championship success since 1955, although McLeish was first choice by the time the term ended. The defender played in 21 of the 36 league games that season.

A product of juvenile side Campsie Black Watch, he was spotted by scout Bobby Calder while turning out for Airdrie's reserve side as a trialist. He grew to become an important defensive cog for the club and made 163 appearances over the course of six years, netting three times.

With first team opportunities limited at Pittodrie, Garner switched to Celtic in the summer of 1981 in a £46,000 transfer. Two own goals in a disastrous debut for the Hoops against St Mirren did not make it an easy passage. Garner was not fully fit when he played in that game and struggled to recover from a difficult start to his Parkhead career.

In 1982 he became Britain's youngest manager, combining playing duties with team control at Alloa, and enjoyed success when he kept his side in the First Division following their promotion under predecessor Alex Totten.

That early coaching promise was enough to secure a surprise return to Pittodrie in February, 1984, as assistant manager under his old mentor Ferguson, who had lost right hand man Archie Knox to Dundee. Garner continued to turn out for the reserve team, charged with developing the young players around him, while assisting Ferguson with the running of the first team despite the fact he had not yet celebrated his 29th birthday. It was a profitable pairing, securing the Scottish Cup and Premier Division title in their first season and defending the league crown in the 1984/85 season. The following term brought a League Cup and Scottish Cup double for Ferguson and Garner but in June, 1986, the ties were severed when Knox returned to Pittodrie.

Garner went on to continue playing junior and Highland League football and also managed at that level with Keith and, briefly, Deveronvale before concentrating on his career in the finance industry with Lloyds TSB, joining the company in 1988 and later switching to the Scottish Widows branch of the business and then RBS. He maintains his involvement in football through his role as manager in the junior game.

Hans Gillhaus

Debut: League, 18 November 1989 v Dunfermline (a) won 3-0
Appearances: League 78+6, Scottish Cup 6, League Cup 5, Europe 5
Goals: League 27, Scottish Cup 3, Europe 1
Also played for: Netherlands (3 caps), PSV Eindhoven, Vitesse Arnhem (both Netherlands), Jaro Pietersaari (Finland), Gamba Osaka (Japan)

Aberdeen supporters would give anything to return to the heady days of the late 1980s. Then the Dons were a match for any club on the continent in the transfer market and no talent appeared out of reach at home or abroad as money was readily available and the success of 1983 ensured the reputation was strong enough to lure ambitious stars to the north-east.

Arsenal star Charlie Nicholas was snapped up in a record £500,000 deal in 1988 in a deal that demonstrated the Pittodrie side's clout. With the ink barely dry on the bumper contract that brought Nicholas north, the deal was trumped in November 1989 when the club stumped up £650,000 for the services of a Dutchman who found himself waiting patiently behind Brazilian star Romario in the pecking order at his club.

Hans Gillhaus had hit 19 goals for PSV Eindhoven in the 1988/89 season on their way to the title and had already won three caps for the Netherlands, the type of credentials which would put a striker well out of Aberdeen's reach in the current climate. In 1989, however, the impressive cv was not a barrier.

The prospect of travelling to the continent to pinch one of Holland's rising stars did not deter manager Alex Smith, who already had Theo Snelders and Willem van der Ark on his books, and he got his man.

It proved to be a shrewd investment. Gillhaus did not stay for long in Scotland but his time at Pittodrie left a lasting impression and he rates as one of the most successful imports ever to grace the turf.

He announced his Premier Division arrival with a stunning double on his debut in a 3-0 win against Dunfermline at East End Park on November 18, 1989, which included a memorable overhead kick and a poacher's header from close range. It ranks as arguably the most dynamic debut the club has ever seen and turned Gillhaus into an instant hero.

For good measure he chipped in with the winner against Rangers, an exquisite curling left foot effort, at Pittodrie the following week to confirm his place as the new darling of the stands. He and Charlie Nicholas proved to be a deadly combination and complemented each other with their mix of trickery, vision and goalscoring ability.

Gillhaus had it all. With the ball at his feet he was, in typical Dutch style, eminently comfortable. He could pass the ball with accuracy and vision while physically he was able to look after himself in the rough and tumble of Scottish football. Like all good strikers he came alive in the box and his quick thinking coupled with quick feet let him steal a march over despairing defenders time after time. Crucially he also displayed the killer instinct that separated good strikers from great strikers, scoring an array of goals from all distances.

By his own admission Gillhaus could not maintain the devastating form of his first two games but he was still a prolific player for the Dons, finishing that season with eleven goals in just 24 appearances and starring in the penalty shoot-out victory over Celtic after the 0-0 Scottish Cup final draw to claim his first medal in Aberdeen colours.

In the dramatic 1990/91 season, when the Dons lost the title by two points to Rangers, he finished joint top scorer with Eoin Jess after bagging 15 goals and claimed his first hat-trick for the club in a 4-2 win at Hibs.

It came on the back of his inclusion in the Dutch squad for the World Cup in Italy in the summer, when he served as Marco van Basten's understudy. All in all he picked up nine caps for the Oranje, with his path blocked first by van Basten and then by Ajax star John Bosman. The emergence of a youngster by the name of Dennis Bergkamp proved to be the final nail in the coffin of his international ambitions, although at club level the striker remained in demand.

Romario reportedly asked that PSV brought his former strike partner back to Eindhoven in the summer of 1990 and Gillhaus did nothing to nip talk of a return in the bud, freely admitting his stop in Aberdeen was only temporary.

The message to fans was enjoy it while it lasted, and thanks to his habit of scoring spectacular goals they did. Many were frustrated by the import's laid back approach and lack of long term commitment to the club but nobody could deny his talent.

In the end nothing came of the rumoured £1.2million bid by PSV and in the summer of 1992 the Dutchman took matters into his own hands, taking advantage of his expired Dons contract and returning to Holland to look for alternative employment. By that time Willie Miller had replaced Alex Smith in the top job. He provided a return of 31 goals in 100 games.

It proved to be a long wait. He trained with PSV but there was no prospect of a contract at his old club and he was picky about others on the table despite interest from England and suggestions of a Rangers bid. He spent months in the wilderness before returning to action with Vitesse Arnhem and finishing his career in Japanese football. The disruption stalled his progress and the 1994 World Cup finals in America proved a bridge too far, leaving Italia 90 as his sole experience at the very highest level.

Today Gillhaus continues his career at the very top level as chief scout for Chelsea. He had initially filled a similar role for PSV Eindhoven prior to his Stamford Bridge appointment, having been recruited by the Dutch side by wily coach Frank Arnesen.

Stephen Glass

Debut: League, 29 October 1994 v Dundee United (h) won 3-0
Appearances: League 96+13, Scottish Cup 7+2, League Cup 10, Europe 3
Goals: League 9, League Cup 2, Europe 2
Also played for: Scotland (1 cap), Newcastle United, Watford, Hibs, Dunfermline

A succession of home grown Aberdeen players have been linked with moves to the promised land of the English Premiership but, to date, only three have followed that path directly.

Russell Anderson became the latest when he switched to Fulham while Eoin Jess was the first. Sandwiched neatly in between was Stephen Glass, who became the second to tread the path south in 1998 when Kenny Dalglish, then manager of Newcastle United, homed in on one of the Scottish game's most promising talents.

Others have gone between Pittodrie and the Premiership, including Craig Hignett and Dean Windass, but the elevation of Glass to that level was a vindication of Aberdeen's insistence that the famed Dons youth programme was still capable of delivering top notch players.

There should have been pride when Glass made the move to what was emerging as the world's most entertaining league but in fact there was a sense of injustice. Glass was out of contract and eligible for a Bosman transfer but was the first player to test what was then an unwritten rule that a British club would be liable to pay a compensation fee if taking a player under the age of 24 from another UK side.

Newcastle made a derisory £100,000 offer while the Dons wanted in excess

of £1million for a player they had taken through their youth ranks, blooding him in the man's world of north-east junior football when they farmed him out as a teenager to the now defunct Crombie Sports. In the end a tribunal set a fee of £650,000 and Aberdeen had to settle for it.

The sense of disappointment at losing Glass at 21, coupled with the double blow of losing him at less than market value, did not detract from his achievements during four seasons in the first team.

The quiet and unassuming Dundonian got his big break as an 18-year-old when Willie Miller introduced him as a substitute in a 3-0 win over Dundee United at Pittodrie on October 29, 1994. He entered the team at a turbulent time, as Miller's reign came to an end and the Dons battled against relegation.

Roy Aitken took over from Miller in February, 1995, but shared his predecessor's judgement on Glass and kept faith with him as the fight to beat the drop intensified.

The teenager came into his own when the team was on the ropes, scoring on the final day of the regular league campaign in a 2-0 win over Falkirk to complete a run of three consecutive victories and ensure it was Dundee United in 10th place who fell through the trap door.

The work was not finished as the Dons still had to endure a play-off against Dunfermline, the First Division runners-up, to safeguard their top flight status. Glass played in both and scored in both as his side recorded two 3-1 wins to end the season on a relative high.

The 1995/96 season saw the versatile left sided youngster cement his place in the starting 11, missing only four league games and an ever present in the run to the League Cup final against Dundee. He turned out at left back in the final and produced a man of the match performance as goals from Duncan Shearer and Billy Dodds landed the silverware.

It was the highlight of his Dons career but Glass continued to perform consistently, equally at home on the left side of defence or as an out and out winger. He had all of the makings of a modern player, with a decent helping of pace aided by astute reading of the game and a great range of passes. Add to that the ability to beat a man when required and Glass had all of the qualities to play at the highest level.

Alex Miller was the manager by the time the Premiership scouts began to circle Pittodrie's rising star, with Arsenal reported to have joined Newcastle on the list of admirers, and the deal to take him to the north-east of England was struck before the 1997/98 term was completed. He took his tally to 133 games and 13 goals before departing.

His new Newcastle leader Dalglish was replaced by Ruud Gullit just months after his arrival but Glass held his own in distinguished company, making 29 appearances in his debut season with the Toon and contributing match winning goals against Leicester and Derby. He also experienced FA Cup final day at a packed Wembley, although there was no happy ending as Manchester United lifted the trophy after a 2-0 win. The youngster from the east coast of Scotland had comfortably slotted into what was proudly proclaiming itself to be the best league in the world.

Glass spent three seasons on Tyneside, winning his solitary Scotland cap in a 2-1 win over the Faroe Islands in 1998, before dropping down to the Championship with Watford from 2001 to 2003. He came back to Scotland with Hibs in 2003 to play a key role in the Easter Road club's revival before being farmed out on loan to Dunfermline early in 2007 and switching permanently to Fife and establishing himself as captain. In the summer of 2010, after a bad run of injuries, he was released by the Pars and found himself on the outside looking in for the first time since his debut for the Dons as a teenager. He moved into coaching in Irish football in 2012.

Andy Geoghegan

Debut: League, 18 September 1971 v Airdrie (h) won 5-0
Appearances: League 23, Scottish Cup 2, League Cup 2, Europe 2
Also played for: Ayr United, St Johnstone

Acting as understudy to Pittodrie legend Bobby Clark was a thankless task but Andy Geoghegan fulfilled the role with dedication for five seasons in the 1970s. He was signed from junior side Petershill in 1969 and was introduced to the team by Jimmy Bonthrone in 1971/72, when he kept four consecutive clean sheets before making way for Clark once again. He had his longest run in the first team in 1975/76 when Ally MacLeod put his faith in the shot stopper, although he was released to join Ayr United at the end of the campaign. Geoghan returned to live in the north-east and went on to play for St Johnstone before packing away his gloves to join Grampian Police.

Andy Gibson

Debut: League, 12 October 1991 v Airdrie (h) won 3-1
Appearances: League 8, Europe 1
Goals: League 1
Also played for: Stirling Albion, Stockport County (on loan), Partick Thistle, Clyde, Forfar Athletic

Alex Smith paid £30,000 for Stirling Albion's 19-year-old striker Andy Gibson in the closing weeks of 1988. Dundee United, Hamilton and Norwich City were all keen but he opted to link up with his former Binos mentor Smith. He spent three years as a prolific goal scorer in the reserve team before making the step up to the first team for a handful of appearances. Gibson had a brief loan spell with Stockport County in 1993, joining Partick Thistle later that year for £75,000. Clyde and Forfar were added to his playing cv in the late 1990s.

Bert Gibson

Debut: League, 18 February 1959 v Hibs (a) lost 1-0
Appearances: League 4
Also played for: Lossiemouth

Powerful junior centre half Bert Gibson was signed from Larkhall Thistle as a 19-year-old in 1958. The 6ft tall stopper deputised for Jim Clunie four times before being released in 1960 and signing for Lossiemouth in the Highland League. Gibson went on to serve as a policeman in England.

Bobby Gibson

Debut: League, 29 January 1949 v St Mirren (h) lost 2-0
Appearances: League 1
Also played for: Ashington, Hull City, Lincoln City, Peterborough United, Gateshead

Englishman Bobby Gibson pulled on the famous red No.9 shirt in a 2-0 defeat at home to St Mirren under Dave Halliday in the 1948/49 season. Signed from his hometown club Ashington, he returned south with Hull City in October 1949 and went on to play for Lincoln City, Peterborough United and Gateshead in the 1950s.

Dominico Gibson

Debut: League, 8 May 2010 v St Mirren (a) won 1-0
Appearances: League 1

Mark McGhee handed Nico Gibson his debut as a 17-year-old as the 2009/10 campaign drew to a close and the youth product made a lively start to his Dons career, proving a handful for the Saints defence in the early stages with his energy and enthusiasm.

Gibson dropped back out of the first team picture after his brief taste of top team action to continue to learn his trade with the under-19 side.

Ian Gibson

Debut: League Cup, 13 August 1975 v Dumbarton (h) won 2-0
Appearances: League 15, Scottish Cup 1, League Cup 3
Goals: League 4
Also played for: Nairn County, Kilmarnock

Minister's son Ian Gibson was a schoolboy prodigy when he burst onto the scene in the Highlands. The teenage midfielder trained with Manchester United before being lured to Pittodrie by Jimmy Bonthrone from Nairn County.

He combined his new life as a Dons player with teacher training and made his debut while still a part-time player in the 1975/76 season.

Despite a regular run of games under Billy McNeill, he requested a transfer to a part-time team in the summer of 1978 and joined Kilmarnock in a £15,000 transfer. Gibson emigrated to Australia three years later, where he continued to fit playing commitments around his career in teaching.

Ricky Gillies

Debut: League, 30 August 1997 v Dundee United (h) drew 1-1
Appearances: League 40, League Cup 6
Goals: League 1, League Cup 1
Also played for: St Mirren, Partick Thistle, Stranraer

In demand attacker Ricky Gillies cost £350,000 when Roy Aitken recruited him at the start of the 1997/98 season. Liverpool had taken the St Mirren starlet on trial while the Old Firm and Arsenal were also linked with him before the Dons leapt to the head of the queue with a solid offer. A lot was expected of the new man but he struggled to find his feet and took more than two seasons to score his first goal. Gillies was eventually loaned back to St Mirren in 2000 and helped the Buddies to the First Division championship. Gillies also turned out for Partick Thistle and Stranraer after leaving Love Street in 2005.

Bobby Glennie

Debut: League, 10 December 1977 v St Mirren (h) won 3-1
Appearances: League 3
Also played for: Dundee, Arbroath, Elgin City

Defender Bobby Glennie was converted from centre-half to left-back after joining Aberdeen from Dundee amateur side St Columba's in 1975. He deputised for Chic McLelland in the 1977/78 season under Billy McNeill before being sold to his childhood heroes Dundee later that term for £12,000. Glennie spent 11 years at Dens as defensive lynchpin and skipper before linking up with Arbroath and then Elgin City in the Highland League.

David Gonzalez

Debut: League, 23 July 2011 v St Johnstone (h) drew 0-0
Appearances: League 14, League Cup 1
Also played for: Colombia, Independiente Medellin (Colombia), Deportivo Cali (Colombia), Caykur Rizespor (Turkey), Manchester City, Brighton

When regular No.1 Jamie Langfield suffered a seizure that kept him sidelined for a large chunk of the 2011/12 season as he underwent treatment, the Dons faced a frantic search for a replacement. The man chosen to fill the void was Manchester City reserve David Gonzalez and the Colombian turned in some impressive displays during his loan stint at Pittodrie. He returned to City at the start of2012 and landed a permanent move to Brighton as they pushed for a place in the Championship play-offs.

Ian Good

Debut: League, 5 December v Kilmarnock (a) lost 4-0
Appearances: League 1
Also played for: Forfar Athletic, Peterhead

Glaswegian defender Ian Good joined the ranks of Aberdeen first team players when he appeared from the bench against Kilmarnock in 1998/99. It was his only taste at the top level, joining Arbroath following his release in 2000 before quickly hopping to Forfar Athletic. Good moved to Peterhead in 2003 and made more than a century of appearances for the Blue Toon over five years.

Billy Graham

Debut: League, 28 September 1963 v Airdrie (a) won 7-1
Appearances: League 14, Scottish Cup 1
Goals: League 6, Scottish Cup 1
Also played for: Newcastle United, Gateshead, Queen of the South

A double on his debut in a 7-1 win at Airdrie in 1963 and another strike against Third Lanark, this time in a 1-1 draw, in his next outing were not enough to guarantee English striker Billy Graham a place in Tommy Pearson's side. The strong and direct former Newcastle United reserve player was signed as a 24-year-old from non-league outfit Gateshead for £1,500 after an earlier trial spell. He had a healthy scoring record during his brief time with Aberdeen, scoring seven times in 15 appearances, but was released to join Queen of the South in the summer of 1964.

Alex Grant

Debut: League, 26 November 1977 v Partick Thistle (a) lost 1-0
Appearances: League 4
Also played for: East Stirling, Cowdenbeath

Billy McNeill blooded young midfielder Alex Grant during the 1977/78 season, with two cameo appearances from the bench.

Grant, a product of Lanark United, moved on to East Stirling at the end of that campaign and made well over 100 appearances for the Shire. He also had a short spell with Cowdenbeath.

1989/1990 Scottish Cup Final; Alex McLeish; Brian Grant; Brian Irvine; Charlie Nicholas; David Robertson; Eoin Jess; Gregg Watson; Hans Gillhaus; Jim Bett; Paul Mason; Robert Connor; Stuart McKimmie; Theo Snelders.

Archie Glen

Debut: League, 19 February 1949 v Falkirk (a) won 2-1
Appearances: League 203, Scottish Cup 24, League Cup 42
Goals: League 24, League Cup 3
Also played for: Scotland (2 caps), Annbank United

Aberdeen's captains will always hold a special place in the history of the club. Whether it is Willie Miller holding aloft the European Cup Winners' Cup or even Stewart McKimmie with the League Cup in his hands, for every generation there are certain images that will forever be burnt in the memory to record the triumphs down through the years.

Long before Miller or McKimmie had even kicked a ball, another famous name in Dons history had led the way. Archie Glen put his name in lights in emphatic style. It was the defender who scored the goal that clinched the first championship in 1955 after a 52 year wait. It was fitting that a man of great substance rose to the occasion, confirming what the Pittodrie fans already knew – their skipper was a player they could depend on to deliver when it mattered most.

On April 9 in 1955 the Dons travelled to face Clyde needing a win to secure the coveted prize for the first time. Failure to do that would hand the initiative back to second placed Celtic, who would play host to the Pittodrie side the following week.

The Bully Wee were no pushovers, having won more than they had lost in the top flight and sitting comfortably in the top half of the table, but there was no question that finishing the job at Shawfield was far preferable than heading for Parkhead in need of a result. Aberdeen had to take control and keep their destiny in their own hands and a win at Clyde was the way to do it.

It was a high pressure occasion but that did not trouble Glen, a cool and composed defender who had formed a formidable partnership with Jack Allister and Alec Young. Expectations were high among the supporters who travelled south for the big match, hoping to see their team scale the heights that for periods in Pittodrie history had seemed impossible.

Clyde were the obstacle in their path and the Dons match had to knock them out of the way. In the 13th minute a handball inside the box handed Aberdeen a golden opportunity. Glen had missed from the spot already that season but he shouldered the responsibility for the most crucial penalty in the history of the club to that point and smashed the ball high into the postage stamp corner. No messing around for the reliable defender, just the perfect penalty at the perfect time.

It proved to be the winner and the Dons made the journey back from Glasgow as the champions of the country. For more than half a century the city and the club had been building up to that moment and the celebrations matched the achievement.

Glen, who died in 1998, led by example as skipper of the Dons and was one of only two ever presents in the league winning term. Jackie Hather was the other. The left sided half-back, renowned for his timing and tackling accuracy, was never cautioned by a referee in 269 appearances for the club. His title winning goal was one of 27 he scored in 13 years on the playing staff.

The defender signed for the Dons from junior side Annbank United in Ayrshire when he became one of the first recruits discovered by legendary scout Bobby Calder.

His association began in 1947 but it was in the following decade that he made his mark on the club.

The championship win was followed in the 1955-56 season by the club's first success in the League Cup, although it had been lifted in its previous guise of the Southern League Cup.

The same season brought Glen his two Scotland caps, making his debut at Windsor Park in Belfast in a 2-1 defeat against Northern Ireland in 1955, a game in which a late equaliser was disallowed by the referee in controversial circumstances.

Glen returned to the national fold the following year when he lined up at Hampden in the dark blue jersey and helped his team to a 1-1 draw against the Auld Enemy. Glen and his defensive colleagues excelled against the highly fancied Englishmen, keeping the household names at bay for the bulk of the game. Graham Leggat had put Scotland in front with a well worked goal, giving the home fans among a crowd in excess of 132,000 hope that a famous victory was within touching distance. Cruelly there was a twist in the tale, with Johnny Haynes rifling home from close range in stoppage time to cancel out the Aberdonian's goal and lock the match at 1-1 as the final whistle sounded.

The Lanarkshire born player also represented the Scotland B team and the Scottish Football League. He turned out in 269 games for Aberdeen and scored 27 goals.

A Scottish Cup winner's medal was all that was missing from his collection but he did come close, losing in both the 1954 and 1959 finals. That proved to be his final shot at completing the trophy hat-trick as a serious knee injury in 1959 forced him to retire from the game at the age of 30.

Glen's intelligence extended beyond the boundaries of the football pitch. As a graduate in pure science from Aberdeen University, he went on to become a managing director of an Aberdeen paint firm after hanging up his boots. He remained in the north-east until his death, serving as a church elder and active Rotary Club member in Aberdeen.

Brian Grant

Debut: League Cup, 22 August 1984 v Airdrie (a) lost 3-1
Appearances: League 243+20, Scottish Cup 24+3, League Cup 18+7, Europe 9+4
Goals: League 27, Scottish Cup 2, League Cup 2, Europe 1
Also played for: Stirling Albion, Hibs, Dundee

He was not showy or pretentious but Brian Grant was certainly effective and consistent throughout his 12 year spell at Pittodrie in the 1980s and 1990s. Grant was the type of midfielder every successful side requires, confident in the tackle and a neat passer who always put in a full shift and was never afraid to take hold of the ball. He could even score goals, featuring as a striker in the reserves in his early days, and was the complete midfield player.

He played in three winning Dons side, the dramatic Scottish Cup final penalty shoot out victory over Celtic in 1990 and the League Cup triumphs against Rangers in 1989 and Dundee in 1995. The win against Rangers, when two goals from Paul Mason earned a 2-1 win, is the one Grant classes as the highlight of his career because it brought his first winner's medal. It also gave the Dons the upper hand against their fiercest rivals, with the two clubs dominating the Scottish scene when Grant was in his prime.

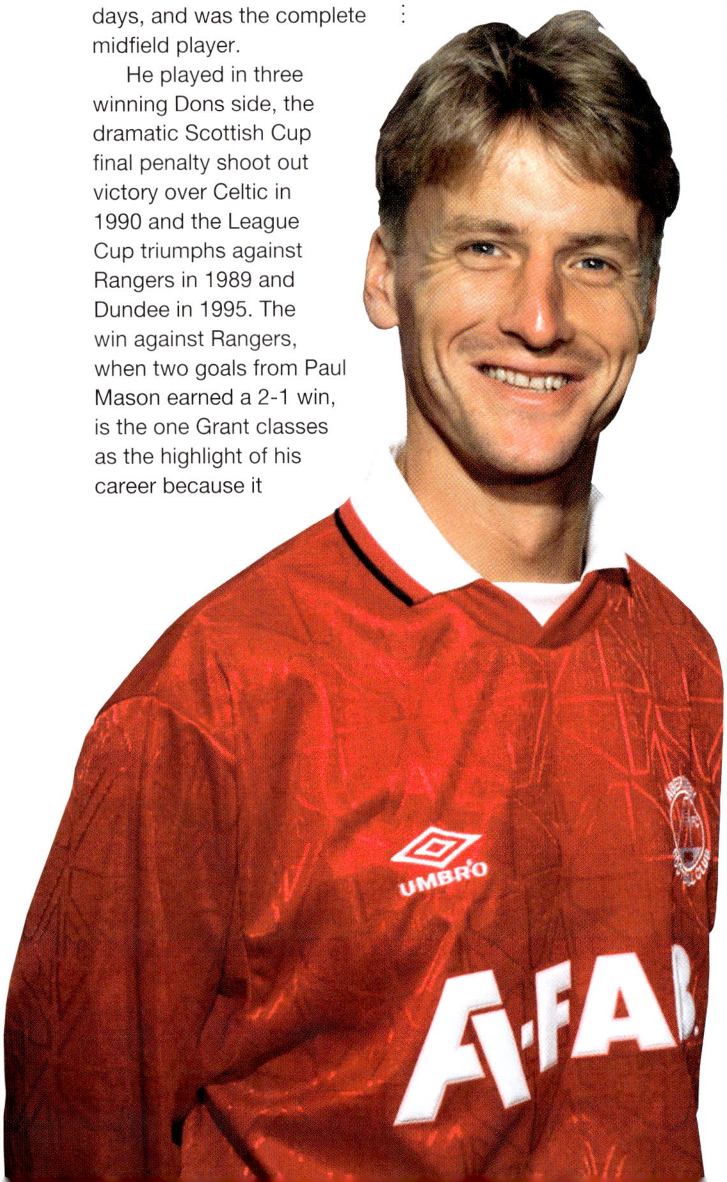

He cut his teeth with Stirling Albion in the early 1980s and played under Alex Smith for the Binos in the Second Division. After less than a full season the teenager was attracting interest from Celtic, Manchester City and Arsenal but there would be only one winner in the race for his signature.

Alex Ferguson took him north to Pittodrie in 1984 in a £40,000 deal but it was not until Grant was reunited with Smith, following his appointment as Aberdeen manager in 1988, that his career with the club really took off.

He made his debut on August 22, 1984, at the age of 20 in a 3-1 League Cup defeat at Airdrie but had to bide his time in the reserves for four years before establishing himself as a regular, taking over from Neil Simpson and forming a partnership with Jim Bett in the middle of the park.

Grant made 329 appearances for the club, scoring 31 goals in the process and collecting three cup winner's medals as well as a league runners-up badge four times in the space of just five seasons between 1989 and 1994. That more than anything is an indicator of how strong the club was in that period, only bettered by Graeme Souness and his multi-million pound Rangers squad.

In August, 1996, a crowd of 9,000 turned out to honour Grant when he was awarded a testimonial match against Joe Royle's Everton, who hadn't read the script and beat their hosts 3-1.

Grant moved to Hibs that year in a £75,000 deal and spent 15 months at Easter Road before moving to Dundee as the Edinburgh side were relegated in 1998 and then winding down his playing days back where it all started with a loan spell at Stirling in 1999.

Grant, living with his family in the central belt, now holds the flourishing McDonald's franchises in Forfar and Arbroath, combining his business commitments with a youth coaching role at Dundee United.

Davide Grassi

Debut: League, 29 August 2009 v Motherwell (h) drew 0-0
Appearances: League 23, League Cup 1
Also played for: Parma (Italy), Cattolica (Italy), Bonifika (Slovenia), Merida (Spain), Sant Andreu (Spain), Sorrento (Italy)

The sunshine and glamour of the Amalfi coast or the more rugged and earthy charms of Scotland's north-east shoreline – that was the choice facing Davide Grassi as he weighed up his options in the summer of 2010. Dons manager Mark McGhee had been keen to retain the services of the versatile Italian, who had performed in midfield and defence for him during the 2009/10 campaign after courageously overcoming a fractured cheekbone early in his Dons days, but the player opted to join Sorrento Calcio in his homeland. Before joining McGhee in Scotland he had played for Parma, Cattolica, Bonifika, Merida and Sant Andreu.

Steve Gray

Debut: League Cup, 28 August 1985 v St Johnstone (a) won 2-0
Appearances: League 37, Scottish Cup 1, League Cup 8, Europe 4
Goals: League 1, Europe 1
Also played for: Airdrie, Huntly

Celtic were three goals up and cruising towards the Scottish Youth Cup in the 1984 final against Aberdeen when Steve Gray took a grip of proceedings. The skilful midfielder drove his team-mates on and helped them to a stunning 5-3 victory, even chipping in with the final goal to cap a memorable match.

By the start of the 1985/86 season the Scotland youth cap, recruited by Aberdeen from Kilmarnock Boys' Club, had forced his way into Alex Ferguson's first team plans and collected a winner's medal as a substitute in the League Cup final victory over Hibs. He went on to represent Scotland at under-21 level.

Big things were expected of the starlet, who had strength and stamina to match his skill on the ball, but he never established himself as a regular in the Dons team under either Ferguson or his successors Ian Porterfield and Alex Smith despite showing promise in the middle of the park and on the wing.

He was sold to Airdrie in August 1989 for £50,000 and helped the Diamonds win the First Division championship under Jimmy Bone. He dropped out of the Broomfield team under Alex MacDonald before being thrown a football lifeline by Huntly manager Steve Paterson in 1993, although his time in the Highland League was hampered by his failure to dedicate himself to the challenge facing him at the north champions. Gray died at his home in Irvine in 2009 at the age of 42.

Jack Grimmer

Debut: League, 7 April 2010 v Rangers (a) lost 3-0
Appearances (up to end of 2010/11): League 2

Jack Grimmer became the SPL's youngest ever player when he entered the fray against Rangers at Ibrox in April 2010. He passed the test well, not fazed in the slightest by the environment. It was the type of form that tempted Fulham to lure the young Don to London in 2012.

Bryan Gunn

Debut: League, 30 October 1982 v Hibs (a) drew 1-1
Appearances: League 15, Scottish Cup 1, League Cup 4, Europe 1
Also played for: Scotland (6 caps), Norwich City

Highlander Bryan Gunn had to wait patiently in the shadow of close friend Jim Leighton for both club and country. The 6ft 2in Thurso-born goalkeeper found himself battling with Leighton for the Dons No.1 shirt after joining Alex Ferguson's squad in the early 1980s. Ferguson claimed to have the best two keepers in the country at that time.

Although he proved an able deputy, making 20 first team appearances over the course of five seasons, the prospect of regular action with Norwich City tempted Gunn to look for a fresh challenge early in the 1986/87 campaign. It proved to be the right choice for Gunn, who spent the rest of his career with the Canaries and established himself as a Carrow Road legend. After returning from playing he continued to work for the club on the commercial staff and also served as manager in 2009.

Gunn's performances for Norwich made him a popular figure with the City supporters but also catapulted him into the Scotland fold. Having won under-21 caps while with Aberdeen, he was promoted to the full international side during the 1990s as a Norwich man. Gunn made his debut in 1990 under Andy Roxburgh and won a further five caps, including his final appearance for Craig Brown's side in 1994.

He had been lined up for a Pittodrie return during Ian Porterfield's tenure but Aberdeen's attempts to persuade the East Anglian outfit to part with their star man proved fruitless.

Danny Griffin

Debut: Scottish Cup, 7 January 2006 v Dundee United (a) won 3-2
Appearances: League 10, Scottish Cup 2
Also played for: St Johnstone, Dundee United, Stockport County, Dundee, Ross County, Livingston, Arbroath

Belfast-born stopper Danny Griffin was one of Scottish football's brightest young talents when he burst onto the scene with St Johnstone in the mid-1990s. He won a £600,000 move to Dundee United in 2000 but, after settling well at Tannadice, began to be plagued by injuries which wrecked his chances of fulfilling his potential. He was signed by Jimmy Calderwood for Aberdeen in January 2006 after being released by Stockport County, having switched to England from United two years previously. Calderwood was confident about his ability but not his fitness and, after a five month extended trial, opted against offering a permanent contract. Griffin went on to play for Dundee, Ross County, Livingston and Arbroath.

Arthur Graham

Debut: League, 21 March 1970 v Dunfermline (h) won 2-0
Appearances: League 220+8, Scottish Cup 22+1, League Cup 44+1, Europe 11
Goals: League 34, Scottish Cup 1, League Cup 9, Europe 2
Also played for: Scotland (11 caps), Leeds United, Manchester United, Bradford

When most boys his age were still dreaming of winning the Scottish Cup at Hampden, Arthur Graham went out and did just that. The Glaswegian was only 17 when he lined up in the No.11 shirt in front of 108,434 supporters at Hampden as Eddie Turnbull's side tackled Celtic on their home turf in the 1970 showdown.

Not for the first time, and not for the last, it was the Dons who had the upper hand in Glasgow and the 2-1 win gave Graham a short and sharp introduction to the joys of the professional game.

Up to that April 11 final he had started just four games for his club, making his debut as a substitute on March 21 in a 2-0 win against Dunfermline at Pittodrie. Four days later he was in the 11 for the first time - scoring in the 2-1 win against the Hoops at Parkhead to announce his arrival in the First Division. He had been a Celtic supporter as a boy, making the moment even sweeter.

Graham scored again in a 2-2 league draw against Kilmarnock five days before the Scottish Cup final and there was no way Turnbull could leave his teenage protégé out for the Hampden showpiece.

Graham missed just three First Division games in the 1970/71 season as the Dons attempted to build on the cup success. They emerged as the only team in Britain to keep an unbeaten home record intact but it was not enough – Celtic won the title by two points. Second place was the club's highest finish since 1956.

Graham made the berth on the left wing at Aberdeen his own between 1970 and his departure in 1977, hardly missing a game. He had pace, trickery and an infectious character – all the ingredients to make him an idol for the Aberdeen fans.

After growing up in Castlemilk, he found work in a Glasgow steelworks while turning out for junior side Cambuslang Rangers. He played just a smattering of games on the left wing when he was snapped up by the Dons, from under the nose of Celtic, and promoted to the first team within a matter of weeks, sampling the high of the Scottish Cup win in his first campaign. He had seen his steelworks wage of £4 increase to £50 when he became a professional football player – but after working night shifts in the unforgiving industrial environment, he knew not to take his new found riches for granted. Graham continued to work hard under both Turnbull and his successor Ally MacLeod.

By 1974/75 he was an ever present and it proved to be his most prolific season in a Dons shirt, his eleven goals putting him just two behind top scorer Drew Jarvie in the final Pittodrie chart.

Having played for his country at youth and under-23 level, his form pushed him into the full Scotland squad but his international career looked to be over before he had even made his debut when - along with Joe Harper, Billy Bremner and Willie Young - an incident in a Copenhagen nightclub after a victory over Denmark led to lifetime bans from the national squad for the trio.

Life did not mean life and the decision was reversed by the SFA. What the interruption did mean was that by the time he made his first Scotland appearance, in a 1-0 defeat at the hands of East Germany in Berlin in 1977, Graham was a Leeds United player.

Over the next four years the Dons youth product represented his country in ten further games. The highlight was Graham's 76th minute winning goal, the only strike of the game, in the 1979 home international showdown with Northern Ireland at Hampden.

Having made his debut under Ally MacLeod, Graham had continued to figure during Jock Stein's reign and it was Stein who was in charge when he netted that maiden goal for the national side. His second goal came less than two weeks later and again it was on the Hampden turf. On that occasion Argentina provided the opposition, with the South Americans emerging with a 3-1 win after a game which had marked Diego Maradona's debut on British soil. Graham left with a goal and Maradona's shirt to show for his efforts.

At club level, the flying winger made the switch to Elland Road in the summer of 1977 after 307 games and 46 goals for Aberdeen. In addition to the Scottish Cup in 1970 he also picked up a Dryburgh Cup winner's medal and a matching badge from the League Cup showpiece in 1976.

Billy McNeill tried to persuade 'Bumper', as he was affectionately known, to stay when he took charge – but the flanker had already made his mind up to move on. After switching to Yorkshire the Glaswegian became a fixture in the Leeds team for six seasons. He became a hero for the Elland Road fans, even though he was part of the side relegated from the English top division in 1982.

Graham spent only a season in the Second Division before Ron Atkinson and Manchester United moved in to take him to Old Trafford in a £45,000 deal, beating Coventry City to the punch. At the age of 30 he helped the club to fourth place in the First Division but was edged out the following term by Jesper Olsen and moved to Bradford in 1985, staying south of the border and moving into coaching at senior and youth level following his playing retirement.

In latter years Graham has run a children's coaching school and also contributed to the Leeds United football academy.

Joe Harper

Debut: League, 4 October 1969 v Ayr United (a) won 2-1
Appearances: League 207+7, Scottish Cup 24+1, League Cup 53, Europe 16
Goals: League 125, Scottish Cup 15, League Cup 51, Europe 8
Also played for: Scotland (4 caps), Morton, Huddersfield, Everton, Hibs
Also managed: Huntly, Peterhead, Deveronvale

The King of the Beach end is unlikely ever to be knocked from his throne, having been crowned as Aberdeen's leading scorer of all time during his heyday in the 1970s. When he retired from the game Harper had been credited with 199 goals but in January 2003 his total was pushed up to 205 when the SFA decreed that his four goals in the short-lived Dryburgh Cup competition could be added to his tally along with two he scored in the Anglo Scottish Cup.

That puts him 50 goals ahead of the next best striker, Matt Armstrong, and 52 clear of the legendary George Hamilton. In more modern times Mark McGhee managed to make it 100 during the 1980s but surely nobody will match Harper's achievement and make it to a double century.

Born in Greenock in 1948, the striker arrived at Pittodrie from Morton less than a month before his 21st birthday celebrations. Even at that tender age he had experienced the merry-go-round of football, having originally joined the Cappielow club as a 15 year-old. He signalled his intent with a debut goal for Ton in a cup game against Partick Thistle and quickly became known as one of the country's best goal getting prospects. In 1967, after finishing as the country's leading scorer with 28 strikes to his credit, he was plucked from Greenock by Huddersfield Town. The move to England was short and by 1968 he was back in the blue of Morton as he regrouped after his flirtation with the game south of the border. It was never more than a minor setback for the irrepressible Harper and, to his club's delight, he attracted another big money bid the following year when Aberdeen finally got their man for £40,000 in 1969.

He made the first of his 308 appearances for Aberdeen on October 4 in a 2-1 win at Ayr United. He netted for the first time in the next match when Partick Thistle fell to a 2-1 defeat at Pittodrie, winning over the supporters with an impressive all round display in his first home outing. The new recruit bagged his first hat-trick in January 1970 in a 5-1 demolition of Raith Rovers on home turf.

He came up trumps in the 1970 Scottish Cup final against Celtic at Hampden, putting the Dons ahead from the spot after just 27 minutes. Thanks to Derek McKay's heroics a 3-1 victory was secured and Harper had his first medal inside his first season at Pittodrie.

In 1970/71 he led the scoring charts with 27 goals, the best total since Ernie Winchester seven years earlier. The best was yet to come though and in the next season Harper became the first Dons player since fellow cult hero Benny Yorton in 1930 to smash

through the 40 goal barrier in a single season. His 42 goal haul made him the third highest scorer anywhere in Europe. It had begun with an incredible run of 19 goals in the first 23 games, including three in just four Uefa Cup ties against Celta Vigo and Juventus.

His efforts did not go unnoticed and before long Everton weighed in with a £180,000 bid which proved too tempting to those who held the Pittodrie purse strings. Harper was an instant hit on Merseyside, forging a partnership with Joe Royle which made the Scottish import the leading scorer at Goodison. Yet again his stop in England was brief, cut short this time by a change in management from Harry Catterick to Billy Bingham, and less than two years later he had rejoined Eddie Turnbull, who had taken charge at Hibs by that point. With the Easter Road club he scored a hat-trick in the 1974/75 League Cup final – but still ended up on the losing side, as Celtic ran out 6-3 winners.

In 1976/77 Harper's career turned full circle as he bowled back into Pittodrie to take his place in Ally MacLeod's red and white army. True to form, the returning hero looked as though he had never been away and scored in his first game back as Kilmarnock were beaten 2-0 in the League Cup. Harper went on to grab nine goals in that competition, including eight in seven consecutive games, as Aberdeen marched to the final to face Celtic again. This time the result was 2-1 and Harper had helped the Dons to another cup success and earned himself another opportunity to celebrate with his adoring public.

The great mystery of Harper's career is why he did not add to his four caps. Even when the obvious factor of his ban from the international team after a Copenhagen nightclub incident in 1975 is taken into account, there was still ample opportunity for the national team to make use of the Aberdeen talisman. He had made a promising start in Dark Blue, scoring on his debut just 19 minutes after being introduced as a 64th minute replacement for Jimmy Bone in a 4-1 victory against Denmark in 1972 in Copenhagen. That earned a start in the return game against the Danes but it was not the start of a beautiful relationship with the international game. He scored against Denmark again in his third appearance for his country in 1975, before the nightclub ruckus which led to his life ban along with Arthur Graham, Billy Bremner, Pat McCluskey and Willie Young. The harsh penalty was later lifted and Ally MacLeod brought his one time Dons signing back into the fold for the 1978 World Cup finals in Argentina, pushing Harper into action in the disastrous 1-1 draw with Iran as a substitute for Kenny Dalglish. And that was that, the international career of one of Scottish club football's most effective forwards of all time.

After 308 games and 205 goals the adventure was over when Alex Ferguson ushered the once unstoppable marksman out of Pittodrie as the 1980s loomed. He went on to manage Huntly, Peterhead and Deveronvale in the Highland League and had a spell as commercial manager with Morton in the late 1990s before a career in after dinner speaking and the media as a football columnist and broadcaster.

Cato Guntveit

Debut: League, 6 November 1999 v Dundee United (a) lost 3-1
Appearances: League 68, Scottish Cup 10, League Cup 4, Europe 1
Goals: League 5, Scottish Cup 1
Also played for: Brann Bergen

Norwegian midfielder Cato Guntveit sampled the best of times and the worst of times as an Aberdeen player. Lured across the North Sea from Brann Bergen in the winter of 1999 by Ebbe Skovdahl, he arrived in time to play in the League Cup and Scottish Cup finals that season. Both ended in the heartache of defeat against Old Firm opposition and in the league the Dons finished rooted to the foot of the table.

Guntveit's energetic performances in the engine room were one of the bright spots of the season. He was a versatile performer, as you would expect of a player who had started life as a full-back with Brann before being moved forward to play in the centre of the park and as a winger. His tenacious tackling and driving runs forward ensured there was always a place for him in Skovdahl's side when he was fit and available.

Had it not been for a series of niggling injuries the Scandinavian would have made far more appearances during his two and a half years in Scotland. The manager was desperate to retain a player he viewed as central to his efforts to stabilise the club – but uncertainty over revenue for SPL television rights forced him to withdraw a contract offer.

Instead of remaining with the Dons, the financial constraints led to Guntveit being released in the summer of 2002. He returned to Brann, where he later became captain and went on to win both the league and cup in Norway.

Gary Hackett

Debut: League, 8 August 1987 v Dundee (a) drew 1-1
Appearances: League 15, Scottish Cup 2, League Cup 3, Europe 2
Also played for: Shrewsbury Town, Stoke City, West Brom, Peterborough United, Chester City

When Ian Porterfield succeeded Alex Ferguson in the manager's office, one of his earliest recruits was Shrewsbury Town winger Gary Hackett, a £75,000 buy who had become a favourite with fans of the Second Division outfit. The speedy flanker, capable of playing on either wing, went straight into the team but soon was relegated to the bench after struggling to settle in Scottish football and, off the park, in the Granite City. He was sold to Stoke City for £110,000.

Ian Hair

Debut: League, 1 September 1973 v Motherwell (a) drew 0-0
Appearances: League 81, Scottish Cup 6, League Cup 14, Europe 4
Goals: League 5, League Cup 1
Also played for: Montrose

Flying full-back Ian Hair burst onto the Aberdeen scene as a youngster and brushed aside any concerns about his inexperience with sure footed displays on the right flank, earning himself the nickname Dan Dare in the process.

Hair was recruited from East Kilbride as a teenager in 1971. He made his first team debut in a 0-0 draw against Motherwell at Fir Park in September 1973 at right back, after impressing in the centre of the defence for the Dons second string.

He had initially been approached by Aberdeen during Eddie Turnbull's tenure but was eventually signed by Jimmy Bonthrone after Turnbull had moved on to Hibs. The rookie burst through the 100 appearance barrier within his first three seasons as he quickly found his stride in the top flight.

The arrival of Stuart Kennedy provided stiff competition for his favoured right back berth and began to limit opportunities, leading Hair to look for regular football away from Pittodrie.

He was only 22 when Montrose paid a club record £10,000 to lure him to Links Park in 1976. After retiring from football he continued to play a key role in a successful wholesale newsagent's firm before branching out into the licensed trade as owner of the Four Mile Inn at Bucksburn.

Derek Hamilton

Debut: League, 1 April 1979 v Morton (a) won 1-0
Appearances: League 44, Scottish Cup 9, League Cup 7
Goals: League 4, Scottish Cup 1
Also played for: Hamilton

Billy McNeill signed Beith juniors full-back Derek Hamilton but it was Alex Ferguson who got the benefit of the reliable squad man over a five season spell in and around the first team squad. He made his debut in 1978/79 and went on to play 13 times in the championship winning team the following term as well as appearing in the Scottish Cup final and subsequent replay defeat against Dundee United in 1980. The versatile Ayrshire player was used in defence and attack, filling both full-back roles as well as playing at sweeper and centre-half. He joined Hamilton in the winter of 1983.

George Hamilton

Debut: League, 13 August 1938 v Partick Thistle (a) lost 2-1
Appearances: League 201, Scottish Cup 32, League Cup 48
Goals: League 102, Scottish Cup 18, League Cup 33
Also played for: Scotland (5 caps), Queen of the South, Hearts, Hamilton

Gentleman George Hamilton, as he will forever be remembered, has gone down in history as one of the finest players ever to pull on an Aberdeen jersey. His scoring record of 153 goals in 281 appearances makes him one of the most potent strikers ever to grace the Scottish game, let alone Pittodrie.

Hamilton, who died in 2001 at the age of 83, spent a decade at Pittodrie either side of World War II. He was 38 by the time he helped the club to the league title in 1955, playing a supporting role as the drama unfolded. He only played four times in that campaign but chipped in with two goals.

The Dons had no hesitation in signing a cheque for £3,000 to complete a record deal to bring the Irvine born striker to the north-east in 1938 from Queen of the South.

The dividends were rich and instant, with the new recruit netting 17 times in 37 league games, 18 in total, to finish leading scorer in his debut season. He made his first appearance in a 2-1 defeat at Partick on August 13, 1938, and grabbed the first goal of many 11 days later in a 3-0 win at home to the same side.

Post war he helped the side to a cup double, part of the Southern League Cup winning side in 1946 when Rangers were beaten 3-2 and a goalscorer in the Scottish Cup final the following year when Hibs were dumped 2-1.

His debut for Scotland followed that Hampden celebration, earning his first cap in November, 1946, in a 0-0 draw against Northern Ireland. Hamilton returned to the national team with a bang in 1951 when he scored a hat-trick against Belgium in a 5-0 win. Three further caps followed up to 1954, when he scored the only goal of the game in a home win against Norway.

At club level, in the final weeks of 1947 he was surprisingly transferred to Hearts at his own request having scored nine goals in 14 games for Aberdeen up to that point. Hearts finished 9th in the 1947/48 campaign, one place and one point above the Dons.

The switch to Tynecastle proved temporary and within six months Hamilton was back in the fold at Pittodrie under his old mentor Dave Halliday. This time the club paid £10,000 for his services.

He topped the club's scoring charts in both the 1948/49 and 1950/51 seasons. The latter was his best for the Dons, with an incredible return of 29 goals in 40 league and cup games.

He left again as the dust settled on the championship success in 1955, playing for six months with Hamilton Accies before retiring due to injury.

At the end of his playing career he returned for a third stint at Pittodrie, serving as reserve team coach before moving into the whisky industry as a sales rep. Hamilton, who was a church elder in the city, proved multi-talented and was crowned champion of Deeside Golf Club in 1967.

TEN: Pittodrie curiosities

1 Home truths: Pittodrie is built on the site of a former dung hill, with the area previously set aside to cater for the waste created by the city's police horses. The site was also known as the Gallows Marsh. The Pittodrie tag is the one that stuck, a Celtic word translating to 'place of manure'.

2 Innovation: Aberdeen can lay claim to being home of the football dugout. Trainer Donald Colman hit upon the idea early in the 20th century as he attempted to get a better view of the feet of his players during games. Colman, a keen dancer, was a great believer that footwork was crucial to every team's success.

3 Broad church: It is not only football that has been a big draw for North-east crowds over the years, with Aberdeen's home ground being turned over to a variety of uses. In 1991 thousands turned out at Pittodrie to listen to touring American evangelist Billy Graham preach, part of a Scottish tour that also saw him address crowds at Murrayfield and Parkhead.

4 Granite rocks: Pittodrie has proved itself as an apt concert venue over the years, with open air performances by Elton John and Rod Stewart pulling in music fans in their droves. The Elton John show in 2004, capping off the club's centenary celebrations, attracted 26,000 and Rod Stewart played to 18,000 in 2011.

5 Set in stone: John Hewitt had the honour of opening the Centenary Walk at Pittodrie to mark 100 years of football. The walk, comprising a display of stone setts inscribed with messages by fans, features a slab dedicated to Gothenburg hero Hewitt. The message on his sett? Quite simply: "I scored it".

6 Famous faces: Aberdeen's sporting heroes are not confined to football but the great and good have a habit of migrating towards the old ground. Open golf champion Paul Lawrie is the highest profile celebrity Dons fan, with boxing's Commonwealth belt winner Lee McAllister also enjoying a lap of honour after his successes in the ring.

7 The big match: The Dons have made the most of changes to rules regarding wedding venues, with Pittodrie offered as a venue for both ceremonies and receptions for Aberdeen fans aiming for a Red twist to their big day. Nothing is off limits for wedding parties – with the Pittodrie boardroom a popular spot for photographs.

8 Beginning of the end: 23 February 2011 was a red letter day for Aberdeen Football Club. City councillors voted 23-17 in favour of approving plans for a new Dons stadium at Loirston Loch in the south of the city. Pittodrie was placed on the market later that year, with permission in place to demolish the ground and build a residential development.

9 Preserving the past: Part of Pittodrie will always remain with Aberdeen, wherever the Dons play. With plans progressing for a new modern stadium, the club has confirmed that the distinctive granite wall at the Merkland turnstiles will be preserved and rebuilt at the new site to provide a lasting reminder of the famous old ground.

10 Grounds for complaint: Finding a suitable site for a new stadium has not been the only quandary for the Dons over the years – with the lack of a dedicated training facility repeatedly cited as a drawback by successive managers. Alex Ferguson thought nothing of putting his players through their paces on Aberdeen beach while the city's Gordon Barracks, Seaton Park and Aberdeen University's playing fields at Balgownie have all been utilised.

Tony Harris

Debut: League, 10 August 1946 v Third Lanark (a) won 3-0
Appearances: League 188, Scottish Cup 31, League Cup 54
Goals: League 18, Scottish Cup 5, League Cup 7
Also played for: Queen's Park, Airdrie.

Tony Harris, or John Robert Harris to give him his full Sunday name, liked the club so much he tried to buy it. You don't get commitment like that too often in football. A Scottish Cup winner in 1947 with Aberdeen, he and former Pittodrie team-mate Don Emery returned in 1969 to try and overthrow the Dons board but the takeover bid failed to get off the ground and Dick Donald went on to take over as chairman.

Nobody will ever know if the Harris and Emery partnership would have been a success but Donald most certainly was and the outcome of the 1960s power struggle proved to be the right one for the club's long term prospects.

Harris first moved to Aberdeen in 1946 after emerging as a centre forward with Queen's Park. He was an amateur international and won a senior cap in 1945 in a war time tie against England.

Dave Halliday added him to the Pittodrie playing staff for the 1946/47 season and marked his debut with a goal in a 3-0 win at Third Lanark on August 10, 1946.

The Dons finished third, behind champions Rangers and Hibs, that term but it was in the Scottish Cup that Halliday's men came to the fore.

Harris, still playing in attack, netted a hat-trick in the 8-0 second round victory over Ayr United and played in every one of the seven ties in the national cup competition up to and including the 2-1 final victory against Hibs. By that time he had switched from No.9 to No.7, the start of a new career as a wing-half.

He was moved initially to the right side of the Dons team before settling down to become a regular on the left.

Harris was renowned as a grafter, a 90-minute man who gave his all for the Aberdeen cause every time he pulled on the jersey.

That type of spirit made him popular with his fellow professionals, who accepted his whole-hearted approach to the game. He was a great friend of Dundee's Billy Steel but that did not transfer on to the pitch and in one encounter at Pittodrie he put Steel out of the game with a crunching challenge inside the first minute. There were no hard feelings - the first name signed on Steel's plaster cast was John R. Harris.

For seven full seasons he was unmovable from the side, missing just a handful of games each term, but in 1954 he made a £1,500 move to Airdrie.

An ankle injury he suffered while playing for the Diamonds forced him out of the game. He played 273 times for Aberdeen and scored 30 goals.

Harris concentrated on his career as a dentist after his playing days and returned to practice in his King Street surgery in Aberdeen in 1956, moving on to Glasgow shortly after his attempt to seize power at Pittodrie in 1969.

He returned to the city in 1973 to continue his work, retiring to the Lake District before his death in 2000.

Jim Hamilton Junior

Debut: League, 3 April 1999 v Dunfermline (h) won 3-1
Appearances: League 14, League Cup 1
Goals: League 1
Also played for: Keith, Hearts, Dundee United, Dunfermline Athletic, Ross County, Livingston, Motherwell, St Mirren, Partick Thistle, Arbroath, East Fife

Pittodrie was one of many stops for football nomad Jim Hamilton during a long and varied life in the Scottish game. The Aberdonian, whose father Jim Hamilton senior had played for the Dons in the late 1960s and early 70s, launched his senior career with Dundee as a teenager. His impressive scoring form earned a move to Hearts in 1996 and the powerful striker continues to rattle in the goals. In 1999 he was snapped up by Paul Hegarty for £300,000 to try and steer the Reds clear of relegation. Hamilton never found his scoring touch with the Dons, netting just a single goal before being sold on to Dundee United for £150,000 in 2000. East Fife became the 12th senior side on his cv when he joined in January 2011.

Jim Hamilton Senior

Debut: League, 5 October 1968 v Hearts (h) lost 2-1
Appearances: League 40, Scottish Cup 9, League Cup 11, Europe 2
Goals: League 5, Scottish Cup 2, League Cup 1
Also played for: Dunfermline, Peterhead, Elgin City
Managed: Peterhead, Keith

When star striker Jim Forrest pulled a hamstring in training on the eve of a league game against Hearts, a window of opportunity flew open for 17-year-old reserve Jim Hamilton. The former Dunipace juvenile starlet, who had been on the Rangers ground staff before joining the Dons, became a regular under Eddie Turnbull and featured for Scotland's youth side. He suffered the cruel blow of being left out of the Scottish Cup final winning squad in 1970 despite playing in all four of the previous ties and was transferred to East Fife the following year. Hamilton moved to Dunfermline in 1974 before moving on to Peterhead and then Elgin City. He enjoyed success as a manager in the Highland League with Peterhead in the 1980s and also took charge of Keith in the 90s.

Hallur Hansson

Debut: League, 27 November 2010 v Kilmarnock (a) lost 2-0
Appearances (to end of 2010/11): League 1

Faroe Islands under-21 international Hallur Hansson was given a brief taste of first team football in the SPL when he came on at half-time in Aberdeen's 2-0 defeat at Kilmarnock in November 2010. He was one of a clutch of teenagers from the Faroes who showed up well during a trial spell in 2008 and chose to accept the offer of a full-time contract.

Chris Harker

Debut: League, 7 November 1959 v Motherwell (a) lost 3-1
Appearances: League 23, Scottish Cup 2, League Cup 3
Also played for: Newcastle United, Bury

Newcastle United answered Aberdeen's SOS when national service robbed the club of the services of goalkeeper John Ogston and injuries struck the other shot stoppers on the books. Magpies reserve Harker was drafted in on loan and made 16 appearances in the 1959/60 season under Davie Shaw.

He was signed permanently the following term and started the campaign as first choice keeper before losing his place. After growing frustrated at playing second fiddle to Ogston, the Englishman hopped back over the border in 1961 to join Bury in search of regular first team football.

Andy Harrow

Debut: Scottish Cup, 14 February 1981 v Morton (a) lost 1-0
Appearances: League 22, Scottish Cup 1, League Cup 7
Goals: League 3, League Cup 1
Also played for: Raith Rovers, Luton Town, Motherwell, Cowdenbeath
Managed: Cowdenbeath

Fifer Andy Harrow was an Alex Ferguson transfer gamble that failed to pay off. Signed from Luton Town for £65,000 in 1981, the bustling striker never scaled the heights with Ferguson's dominant Dons. The former Raith Rovers man spent two seasons knocking on the door of the Aberdeen starting 11 but mustered only a handful of starts. The left-footed 24-year-old asked to leave early in the 1982/83 season and his transfer request was reluctantly granted by a manager who remained an admirer of the forward. He went on to star for Motherwell in a four year stint at Fir Park and also had a spell as manager of Cowdenbeath in the 1990s.

Michael Hart

Debut: League, 29 August 1998 v Dunfermline (a) drew 1-1
Appearances: League 123, Scottish Cup 9, League Cup 7, Europe 6
Also played for: Livingston, Preston North End, Hibs

The decision to bring Michael Hart back to Pittodrie in January 2003 was one of the few legacies from Steve Paterson's time in charge at Aberdeen. Although it was Paterson who signed the defender from Livingston, it was his successor Jimmy Calderwood who reaped the rewards.

Hart's pace was crucial to Calderwood's game plan and, whether playing as a full-back or in the centre of the defence, he provided the perfect insurance policy when the team was stretched. Galloping runs forward added an extra dimension to the side's play and brought Hart to the fore.

For the Glaswegian it was a second chance at success with the Dons and he grasped it with both hands. Hart had initially come through the youth system in the late 1990s but, with first team appearances limited, he was allowed to join Livingston on loan in 2000 before joining the Almondvale side permanently the following year.

He returned north as a stronger and more mature player and for five years he blossomed under Calderwood's tutelage, only curtailed by injury problems that tested his resolve.

He was on the treatment table when Preston North End moved for him in January 2008, agreeing a pre-contract deal to take him south that summer. Protracted negotiations ended with a £100,000 fee being agreed to enable Hart to make the move immediately, although he struggled to regain fitness for any length of time and made only sporadic appearances in England. In 2010 his contract was cancelled by Preston to allow him to return to Scotland with Hibs.

Paul Hartley

Debut: League, 14 August 2010 v Hamilton (h) won 4-0
Appearances (up to end 2010/11): League 24, Scottish Cup 4, League Cup 4
Goals (up to end 2010/11): League 4, League Cup 4
Also played for: Scotland (25 caps), Hamilton, Millwall, Raith Rovers, St Johnstone, Hibs, Hearts, Celtic, Bristol City,
Managed: Alloa Athletic

If Paul Hartley had written the script for his Aberdeen debut he could not have matched reality. The summer recruit from Bristol City ran out at Pittodrie as captain of the Dons on 14 August 2010 and produced a virtuoso display to emerge with the match ball after a hat-trick in a 4-0 opening day demolition of Hamilton. It was no ordinary treble, with the skipper netting each of his goals from the penalty spot in an amazing display of composure and steely nerve.

Hartley had arrived back in Scotland with a point to prove after a year out of sight in English football, having joined City following his surprise release by Celtic in 2009. He had been a regular in Bristol but his return to the SPL put him back in full frame and his form quickly led him to the brink of a Scotland recall as he attempted to add to the 25 caps already in his collection. Injuries went on to hamper his Dons contribution and on the eve of the end of the 2010/11 campaign he announced his retirement from top flight football. Within days he had been appointed played manager of lower league Alloa Athletic as a new chapter opened, winning the Second Division in his first season.

In an incredible playing career, Hartley went from a journeyman winger who had bounced between Hamilton, Millwall, Raith Rovers, Hibs and St Johnstone to a stand out central midfielder with Hearts. His Tynecastle heroics brought international recognition in 2005 and a £1.1million transfer to Celtic two years later. At Celtic the Glaswegian's reputation continued to grow as a star man in Gordon Strachan's side. Tony Mowbray's appointment as manager at Parkhead brought Hartley's career in the Hoops to an end and saw him look south to Bristol City for a new challenge despite interest from clubs at home and abroad.

Jack Hather

Debut: League, 1 January 1949 v Dundee (h) lost 3-1
Appearances: League 264, Scottish Cup 34, League Cup 53
Goals: League 78, Scottish Cup 10, League Cup 16
Also played for: Annfield Plain, Horden Colliery

He had pace, precision, a left foot as good as any in the game and an uncanny knack of scoring at the end of his surging runs down the wing. In the modern game Hather would be worth millions. The Flying Englishman, as he was known, was recruited by Dave Halliday from non league club Annfield Plain for a nominal fee at the tail end of 1948. He was tasked with replacing the veteran Tommy Pearson at outside left and he won the seal of approval from his successor.

In 1955 Pearson, in his new career as a sports writer, voted Hather as Dons player of the year at the end of their historic championship winning campaign. Hather and captain Archie Glen were the only two ever presents in the title winning term but what the Aberdeen fans did not know at the time was that the winger was battling against illness. He required an internal operation at the end of the season to restore him to full fitness, having soldiered on for a year without being able to train properly and needing extra recovery time due to the fatigue the illness caused in the aftermath of match action.

That season he and Harry Yorston, both on 15 goals, were second only to Paddy Buckley in the scoring stakes. In the 1955/56 season he scored a double in the 4-2 quarter-final win against Hearts in the League Cup to ease Aberdeen's passage towards a final which they won 2-1 against St Mirren to earn the Englishman his second winner's medal. Three Scottish Cup final appearances proved fruitless.

Hather appeared frequently on the scoresheet throughout more than 11 years at Pittodrie and his record of 104 goals in 351 games puts him among the all-time leading Aberdeen goalscorers. Many were spectacular long range efforts courtesy of the powerful punch he packed in his left boot.

He made his debut on New Year's day, 1949, in a 3-1 defeat at home to Dundee and was on target for the first time on February 26 to help his side to a 4-2 win against Partick Thistle.

Goalscoring was only a small part of his game – the major asset was his searing pace down the wing. He was regarded the fastest sprinter of his football generation and proved a nightmare for defenders up and down the country. Before signing for Aberdeen, Hather had been offered the chance to become a professional sprinter but opted against a life in athletics.

He was eventually released by the club in August, 1960, to allow him to accept a job offer in his native north-east England. He played on with Horden Colliery in non league football before hanging up his boots.

Hather returned to the Aberdeen area in the 1960s but by the time of his death, in 1996, was back home south of the border. His love of the Dons never left him and passed down through the generations, his son John becoming an Aberdeen fan and even ending up on the Pittodrie books.

TEN: Goal scoring heroes

1 1903/04: Captain Willie MacAulay led by example in Aberdeen's first ever season, finishing leading scorer with 13 goals in his 21 appearances. Highlights included doubles against Montrose and Forfar Athletic as the new team settled into life in the Northern League. Charlie Mackie was second in the scoring stakes after netting 10 times.

2 1921/22: Johnny Miller became the first Dons player to break the 20 goal mark in a single season and he did it in some style. The No.9 bagged 27 goals in the 1921/22 season in a Dons team struggling in the bottom half of the First Division table. Hat-tricks against Clyde and Third Lanark in the space of a fortnight helped Miller on his way to the golden boot.

3 1929/30: Benny Yorston's perfect season saw the frontman notch a staggering total of 46 goals over the course of just 42 games in the league and Scottish Cup. He returned 38 goals in 38 First Division matches and scored the remaining eight in just four cup ties, banging home four hat-tricks during the most memorable of campaigns.

4 1934/35: Matt Armstrong ensured the loss of Yorston was not too painful for the Dons. In 1934/35 the hot shot recorded his best ever season when he hit 39 goals in 43 appearances. It marked the start of a period in which Armstrong finished at the top of the Pittodrie scoring chart for four consecutive seasons.

5 1946/47: War was over and normal service resumed in football, with George Hamilton blowing away the cobwebs for Aberdeen with his exploits in 1946/47. Hamilton scored no less than three hat-tricks and two four goal hauls, not surprisingly finishing the term as leading scorer at Pittodrie on 33 goals. His trebles came against Hamilton, Hearts and Ayr United while Celtic and Falkirk were on the receiving end of his quadruple blasts.

6 1954/55: Paddy Buckley was the man of the moment as the Dons clinched their first ever First Division championship. Buckley's tally of 28 goals, 17 of which came in that glorious league effort, made him by far and away the most potent attacking weapon at manager Dave Halliday's disposal and a hat-trick against title rivals Rangers underlined his ability.

7 1971/72: Joe Harper ruled the roost at Pittodrie in the 1970s and King Joey came close to beating Benny Yorston's record for a single season when he hit the net 42 times in the 1971/72 campaign. He notched 33 goals in 34 First Division matches in the best return of his reign in the North-east, finishing top of the club's scoring list on five occasions.

8 1981/82: Alex Ferguson was not short of attacking talent during his tenure, but it was left to midfield maestro Gordon Strachan to show the strikers how it was done in the 1981/82 season. Strachan was on the scoresheet 20 times, including a goal in the 4-1 win over Rangers in the Scottish Cup final, and made countless others with his creative talents.

9 1984/85: Injury prevented Frank McDougall from fulfilling his potential – but his brief time in the Dons side demonstrated his natural knack for scoring goals. In his maiden season with the club he swept to the top of the scoring chart with 24 goals in 30 outings and he remained top dog the following term, his last full season before being forced to retire.

10 1993/94: After something of a goal famine for Dons followers, Duncan Shearer laid on a feast when he announced his arrival in the Premier Division with 28 goals in league and cup following his arrival from Blackburn Rovers. The Scotland international became the first Aberdeen player to make it past 20 goals since Frank McDougall in 1985/86.

Scott Harvie

Debut: League, 4 May 1988 v Hibs (h) lost 2-0
Appearances: League 3
Also played for: Partick Thistle

Utility man Scott Harvie was a member of the League Cup winning squad in 1989 after being drafted in for experience of the big occasion. The former Eastercraigs Boys Club defender did not play in the victory over Rangers, having been blooded by Ian Porterfield the previous year. He made three appearances before joining Partick in 1990.

John Hather

Debut: League, 27 September 1975 v Ayr United (h) won 3-1
Appearances: League 1
Also played for: Keith (on loan), Blackpool

A cameo from the bench in a 3-1 win at home to Ayr United in 1975 was winger John Hather's taster of life as an Aberdeen first teamer. The son of former Dons hero Jack Hather, he joined as a 16-year-old in 1972 and spent four years on the books. Hather, who had a spell on loan at Keith, was released in 1976 and joined Blackpool.

Hughie Hay

Debut: League Cup, 11 August 1951 v Queen of the South (h) won 5-4
Appearances: League 47, Scottish Cup 4, League Cup 7
Goals: League 23, League Cup 3
Also played for: Dundee United, Arbroath, Fraserburgh, Deveronvale

Dazzling forward Hughie Hay was dreaming of Scottish Cup glory with his home town team when he was cut down in his prime. He was settling comfortably into life as a first team regular in the 1952/53 season, his first as an established star, when he broke his leg and suffered the pain of having to watch his colleagues lose 1-0 to Rangers in the cup final replay at Hampden.

He had averaged close to a goal in every two games after taking over from Archie Baird at inside left but the injury interrupted his career and opportunities became more sporadic despite his impressive return of goals when called upon for first team action.

Hay had served his apprenticeship with Banks o' Dee in the junior game before being snapped up by Aberdeen in 1950 and had a lengthy stay at Pittodrie.

In 1958, at the age of 26, Hay was recruited by Dundee United and spent a season at Tannadice before making the short hop to Arbroath. Spells with Deveronvale and Fraserburgh in the Highland League followed before he retired from football to concentrate on a career in the insurance industry.

He retained an interest in the senior game through the involvement of his footballing cousins Dave Smith, Doug Smith and Hugh Smith. Dave starred for Aberdeen, Rangers and Scotland while Doug went on to captain Dundee United and Hugh turned out for Forfar and Morton.

Markus Heikkinen

Debut: League, 9 August 2003 v Hearts (a) lost 2-0
Appearances: League 68, Scottish Cup 8, League Cup 4
Goals: League 2, Scottish Cup 2
Also played for: Finland, TPS, MyPa, HJK Helsinki, Portsmouth (on loan), Luton Town, Rapid Vienna

If Steve Paterson's eye for a player was demonstrated in his decision to swoop for Michael Hart then the recruitment of Finnish midfielder Markus Heikkinen was the rubber stamp. The uncomplicated but accomplished player was an inspired addition to the Pittodrie roster in time for the 2003/04 season after he had impressed during a trial spell.

Paterson and his assistant Duncan Shearer had plucked Heikkinen's name from a long list of overseas players being touted to SPL clubs and were impressed from the moment he stepped onto the training field.

His solid work ethic, good use of the ball and defensive qualities made the import the perfect player in the centre of the park and he was unmovable from the side when available during his two seasons in the Scottish game.

It was a complete contrast to his first experience of the British game, when he had struggled to get game time while on loan at Portsmouth from HJK Helsinki in the 2002/03 campaign.

Paterson's successor Jimmy Calderwood was desperate to retain the services of the quiet but effective Finland international when his contract expired in 2005 but Heikkinen had set his heart on a change of scene. He opted to join Luton Town and spent two seasons with the Hatters before moving on again to satisfy his wanderlust by landing up in Austrian football with Rapid Vienna in 2007. He settled with Rapid and gained European experience with the club to add to his growing cv.

Jim Hermiston

Debut: League, 15 October 1966 v Ayr United (h) won 2-0
Appearances: League 195+2, Scottish Cup 15, League Cup 45, Europe 15
Goals: League 10, League Cup 5, Europe 1
Also played for: Bonnyrigg, Grange Thistle, Brisbane City, Brisbane Lions

It is impossible to imagine any of the current Aberdeen squad tearing up their Pittodrie contract to switch from parading their skills on the pitch to policing its perimeter but that is exactly what Jim Hermiston did in 1975. The captain made the decision to ditch professional football in exchange for the security of life as a PC with Grampian Police. It was a bold, headline grabbing move which did not lead to any regrets later in life for the Edinburgh born defender.

He had been sickened by Willie Ormond's decision not to include him in Scotland's squad for the 1974 World Cup. That made him desperate to get away from it all and, when a proposed move to Chelsea broke down when Aberedeen held out for £5,000 more than the £75,000 the Londoners had offered, he turned his back on the game altogether. At least for a while.

Shortly after his stunning decision the Hermiston family upped sticks and emigrated to Australia, where he returned to playing before once again entering the police system. In recent years he was honoured by his adopted country with a bravery award after tackling an armed robber outside a bank in Brisbane with the same type of vigour he applied to wingers in Scotland's top flight in his playing prime. He was off duty at the time.

The full-back was signed from Bonnyrigg by Eddie Turnbull in 1965 and made his debut as an 18-year-old in a 2-0 win at home to Ayr United on October 15 the following year. Over the course of the next three years he was gently introduced to the first team but by 1969/70 he had replaced Jim Whyte as the first choice No.3.

That rise to prominence came in time for Hermiston to savour his finest moment in the Dons shirt he wore in 270 first team games as he helped his side to the 3-1 Scottish Cup final victory against Celtic in

The 1970 Scottish Cup winning team display their prize, with Jim Hermiston pictured in the front row to the left of manager Jimmy Bonthrone.

1970. He and Henning Boel became a rock steady full-back pairing for Aberdeen as they challenged for the championship the following year and Hermiston went on to skipper the side as his career at Pittodrie drew to a close.

He revived his playing career when he emigrated to Australia in 1977 and became one of the most respected players in the game in his new homeland. He even released a coaching manual to cater for the growing army of young followers he had.

He was voted player of the year by the country's football writers in 1980 and was being quoted as a contender to captain Australia in the 1982 World Cup. There was a flaw in the plan though, with a 45 minute appearance for Scotland's under-23 team during his time as an Aberdeen player preventing Hermiston from turning out for any other international team. The SFA had to break the bad news that the brief, injury curtailed, appearance had scuppered his hopes of playing for his adopted country.

Hermiston retired from playing in the 1980s to concentrate on reviving his ambitions of a career in policing and continued to rise up the ranks in the Queensland force.

John Hewitt

Debut: League, 15 December 1979 v St Mirren (h) won 2-0
Appearances: League 201+65, Scottish Cup 30+10, League Cup 41+11, Europe 41+14
Goals: League 52, Scottish Cup 8, League Cup 13, Europe 12
Also played for: Celtic, Middlesbrough, St Mirren, Ross County, Cove Rangers.
Managed: Dundalk.

Peter Weir to Mark McGhee, a cross and then bang – John Hewitt was a legend. The Aberdonian's headed winner in the 112th minute of the European Cup Winners' Cup final against Real Madrid on May 11, 1983 was the defining moment in Hewitt's career. It was also the defining moment in sport for his home city, the most famous and important goal ever recorded by the Dons of Pittodrie.

Wherever he went from that moment on, whatever he did, there would be no escape from the glory of Gothenburg. As the only Aberdeen-born player to feature on that momentous occasion, it was fitting that it was Hewitt who had the last word.

Without that man there would not only have been no ECWC win but there would not even have been a final to savour. Hewitt had popped up in the 77th minute of the quarter-final second leg against Bayern Munich to score the winner in the 3-2 win to edge his side into the last four and spark the biggest night of celebration ever seen at Pittodrie.

For a man who had dreamed of gracing the stadium as a youngster growing up playing football on the city's public parks it surely could not get any better. Hewitt was a product of Middlefield Boys' Club and became a schoolboy international after starring for Hilton Academy. His talents as a goal scorer made him stand out from the crowd and he is one of the few players to have rejected Sir Alex Ferguson yet still won a second chance. It took Ferguson two attempts to land the schoolboy sensation, failing to land the hot young property when he was in charge at St Mirren as he competed with Celtic, Manchester United, Sheffield United and Middlesbrough.

Sensibly, Hewitt bided his time and eventually pledged his future to Aberdeen in 1978 when he signed an S-form at the age of 15. Hewitt had been a ball boy at Pittodrie as a youngster and the emerging star's first choice was always to join his home town team.

He was still only 17 when Ferguson handed him his big break, thrown the No.11 shirt for a 2-0 win against St Mirren at Pittodrie on December 15, 1979. He started two games and made two cameos from the bench in that title winning season.

He was eased into the first team over the course of the next year, scoring his

first goal in a 4-1 League Cup win over Berwick Rangers at Shielfield – upstaged by goalkeeper Marc de Clerck, who marked his Dons debut with a goal.

By 1981/82 Hewitt was a permanent fixture in Ferguson's team, with 19 goals in 34 starts including a hat-trick against Rangers in front of an appreciative home crowd in the final league match of the season. A winner's medal from the 4-1 Scottish Cup final victory against the Ibrox side 10 days later capped it all, having set a record earlier in the competition for the fastest ever goal when he netted the winner after just 9.6 seconds in the first round tie against Motherwell.

On top of the European medal in 1983/84 there was a Premier Division championship badge to add to the collection.There was another title success the following year as the Dons dominated, with Hewitt a key player in both legs of the European Super Cup triumph against SV Hamburg for good measure.

A third consecutive championship medal was collected in the 1984/85 season before a cup double the following year. Hewitt played in both finals, bagging a double in the Scottish Cup showdown as Ferguson's troops defeated Hearts 3-0. The man of the match award joined the other accolades on the Hewitt mantelpiece.

He topped the Pittodrie scoring chart for the first time in 1986 as the club entered a transitional period following Ferguson's departure and Ian Porterfield's arrival, scoring 14 to draw level with Billy Stark in the club standings.

After 10 years, 364 appearances and 90 goals Hewitt moved to Celtic in 1989 to link up with Billy McNeill as the Hoops tried to break the dominance Rangers and the Dons were enjoying. Despite all of his experience and success up to that point, he moved to Glasgow as a player who should still have had his peak years ahead of him.

Pittodrie manager Alex Smith could not guarantee the player his preferred role through the centre of the attack, preferring to utilise him on the wing, and that was one of the factors in the decision to part company. An embarrassment of riches when it came to forwards, with Charlie Nicholas in full flow and youngsters such as Scott Booth and Eoin Jess emerging, was another reason cited by Smith for the decision to allow the Gothenburg hero to leave. Queens Park Rangers, Leicester City and Middlesbrough were all keen on the 26-year-old before Celtic won the race with a £225,000 bid.

He struggled to break into the Hoops team and had two periods on loan at Middlesbrough before signing for St Mirren in 1992. A short spell with Ross County followed before a stint as a manager with Irish side Dundalk.

He also featured as a player and assistant manager to former team-mate Doug Rougvie with Highland League club Cove Rangers in the late 1990s. Hewitt has gone on to carve out a career in the north-east business community after hanging up his boots, getting his sporting fix from regular appearances on the competitive amateur golf circuit in his home city.

Jim Henry

Debut: League, 12 January 1974 v Rangers (a) drew 1-1
Appearances: League 18, Scottish Cup 5, League Cup 3
Also played for: Dundee United, San Antonio Thunder (USA), Forfar Athletic

The American dream proved a major lure for midfielder Jim Henry when the Dons called time on his career at Pittodrie in 1975. Henry had established himself as a first team regular under Jimmy Bonthrone in the 1974/75 campaign but fell out of favour the following season when Ally MacLeod took charge and grabbed the opportunity to join San Antonio Thunder. He had arrived in the north-east as a £20,000 player from Dundee United in 1974, where he had been a rising star in his home city as he attracted big money interest from Fulham. After his spell in the US, including a stint in Hawaii, he returned to Scotland to turn out for Forfar Athletic.

Des Herron

Debut: League Cup, 13 August 1960 v Ayr United (h) won 4-3
Appearances: League 3, League Cup 6
Goals: League 1, League Cup 1
Also played for: Ayr United, Arbroath, Montrose, Dumbarton, East Stirling

Winger Des Herron scored on his debut against Ayr United at the start of the 1960/61 season, just weeks after joining from junior side Duntocher Hibs. Herron struggled to continue his progress and joined Ayr on a free transfer in 1962. He also sampled Canadian football before embarking on a tour of the lower leagues with Arbroath, Montrose, Dumbarton and East Stirling.

Peter Hetherston

Debut: League, 13 August 1994 v Hearts (h) won 3-1
Appearances: League 35, Scottish Cup 1, League Cup 6, Europe 1
Also played for: Falkirk, Watford, Sheffield United, Raith Rovers, Airdrie, Partick Thistle, Queen of the South

League Cup winner Peter Hetherston's career with Aberdeen was short but eventful. Signed by Willie Miller for £175,000 from Raith Rovers, the midfielder's nickname

of 'Silky' hinted at his talents as a playmaker. The former Falkirk schemer had established himself as a cultured operator with the Bairns and then Rovers. With the Dons he was restricted to sporadic appearances, with injury restricting his contribution. Hetherston appeared as a substitute in the League Cup final win against Dundee in 1995 but moved on to Airdrie at the end of that season, having been given the all clear to continue playing despite a hip injury being traced to the early signs of arthritis in the joint. He played on with Partick, Raith and then Queen of the South and had a brief spell in charge of Albion Rovers.

Craig Higgins

Debut: League, 18 April 2004 v Motherwell (h) lost 2-0
Appearances: League 4
Also played for: Elgin City (on loan), Stranraer, Montrose, Dundee, Ayr United

Central defender Craig Higgins was playing only his second top team game for Aberdeen when he went head to head with Henrik Larsson and Celtic's star studded attack – and won. Higgins was part of the Dons side that defeated the Hoops 2-1 in 2004 in one of the few bright spots of Steve Paterson's reign. It broke an unbeaten home run for the Parkhead side of 77 games.

Higgins struggled to retain his place in the squad following Jimmy Calderwood's appointment as manager and was loaned to Elgin City in 2005 before moves to Stranraer, Montrose, Dundee and Ayr. He then switched to the junior ranks with Arthurlie.

Craig Hignett

Debut: League, 1 August 1998 v Dundee (a) won 2-0
Appearances: League 13, League Cup 2
Goals: League 2
Also played for: Middlesbrough, Barnsley, Blackburn Rovers, Leicester City, Leeds United, Darlington, Hartlepool, Coventry City (on loan), Crewe (on loan)

The transfer dealings surrounding Craig Hignett were a roaring success for Aberdeen, on paper at least. The Englishman arrived on a free transfer from Middlesbrough in time for the 1998/99 season and within five months had been sold on to Barnsley at an £800,000 profit.

The Englishman made a scoring debut in the opening game of the league campaign at Dundee and was a hero in his next Premier Division outing when his strike helped put Celtic to the sword in a 3-2 victory at Pittodrie.

And then he was gone. Hignett, who became the highest earner in the club's history when he joined, admits he had second thoughts about the move almost as soon as he agreed to the switch. His form quickly dipped after the short honeymoon period as he struggled to cope with the distance between his new base in the north-east of Scotland and his young children in England.

Within two years of escaping to Barnsley he sealed a £2.25million move to Blackburn Rovers and spent three seasons at Ewood Park before moves to Leicester, Leeds United, Darlington and Hartlepool. Hignett also featured on loan at Coventry and Crewe during the latter stages of his career.

Frank Hill

Debut: League, 1 September 1928 v St Mirren (a) lost 5-2
Appearances: League 98, Scottish Cup 8
Goals: League 9, Scottish Cup 1
Also played for: Scotland (3 caps), Forfar Athletic, Arsenal, Blackpool, Southampton.
Managed: Crewe, Burnley, Preston, Notts County and Charlton.

In 2006 the football bandwagon was briefly rocked as it thundered through another season when allegations of a multi-million pound betting culture amongst managers in the English Premiership were made. Suggestions that coaches were gambling on the outcomes of games involving their own teams caused consternation among the paying public but it was far from the first time the game had been embroiled in that type of controversy. One of the earliest cases came in Aberdeen in the 1930s and caused the premature end of a player who looked set for a long and prosperous career with the Dons.

Frank Hill made a sharp exit along with Benny Yorston, Jimmy Black, Hugh McLaren, and David Galloway in 1932. The decision to allow the group to leave was shrouded in mystery but Yorston, decades later, confirmed that they were accused of betting on Aberdeen to draw the first half of a series of games before winning after the break. Suspicions arose when Yorston missed an easy chance in a game and the striker never denied the allegations.

Nobody can tell what might have been had it not been for the forced exit but it is clear Hill was already well on his way to proving himself as one of the finest performers the club had had in its brief history.

He had joined from hometown club Forfar Athletic in 1928, making his debut in a 5-2 defeat at St Mirren on September 1 that year. Hill featured 14 times in his first season but missed just three in 1929/30 as Aberdeen's stock began to rise, climbing from seventh in the First Division the previous year to third in the table.

It is easy to become complacent about international recognition but in Hill's era appearances by Aberdeen players in Scotland colours were few and far between.

When he made his debut for the national side in 1930, in a 2-0 win against France in Paris, he became only the fifth Dons star to make it to the top level. He was capped again that year in a 1-1 draw against Wales at Hampden and made his third and final international appearance in a 0-0 draw against Northern Ireland in Belfast.

Hill had made 106 appearances for Aberdeen by the time he played his last game, a 1-1 draw against Kilmarnock on November 14, 1931.

Leaving Pittodrie under a cloud did not spell the end of Hill's top flight career and with Arsenal, who paid the Dons £3,000 for his services, he took English football by storm, winning three consecutive championships in the 1930s.

Hill, who died in 1970, rounded off his playing days at Blackpool and Southampton before moving into management with Crewe, Burnley, Preston, Notts County and Charlton. Manchester City continued to utilise Hill as a scout until his death.

TEN: Coaches who played a part

1 John Clark: The arrival of Celtic legend Billy McNeill as manager in 1977 brought the advent of the high profile assistant manager at Pittodrie, with McNeill opting to raid Parkhead for coaching talent and take John Clark, a fellow Lisbon Lion, with him to Pittodrie. Clark had cut his teeth under Jock Stein, looking after the Hoops reserves, before joining the Dons.

2 Pat Stanton: When Alex Ferguson checked in, he turned to Pat Stanton for support. Stanton, a playing star with Hibs and then Celtic, was appointed assistant manager but returned south to his roots after a short stint in the North-east and went on to have spells in charge of Cowdenbeath, Dunfermline and then Hibs between 1982 and 84.

3 Archie Knox: Pat Stanton and Willie Garner both had spells as Alex Ferguson's right hand man, but it was Archie Knox who proved to be the ideal foil. Knox, the gruff and tough coach who had been a player with Dundee United and manager with Forfar, followed Ferguson to Manchester United. After spells with Rangers and various other clubs, he found his way back to Pittodrie as assistant to Craig Brown.

4 Jimmy Mullen: The appointment of Ian Porterfield as Aberdeen manager in 1986 was a gamble by the Dons board and the new man did not look locally for an assistant. Instead he opted for former Sheffield Wednesday and Rotherham player Jimmy Mullen, who later went on to serve as a boss in his own right with Blackpool, Burnley, Sligo Rovers and Walsall.

5 Paul Hegarty: Dundee United stalwart Paul Hegarty had served on the coaching staff at Tannadice and with Hearts before new Dons manager Roy Aitken swooped to take him to Pittodrie as assistant manager. Hegarty went on to have a spell as caretaker manager following Aitken's departure and was a serious contender to take over permanently. He has since served with Livington and back at Dundee United as a coach.

6 Tommy Moller-Neilson: Aberdeen appeared to have pulled off a backroom coup when they lured Tommy Moller-Neilson onto the coaching staff to join fellow Dane Ebbe Skovdahl in 1999. Having been on the staff at Rangers he had a solid reputation, but medical problems and an apparent clash of personalities with Skovdahl led to his departure after less than a year. Skovdahl chose to put his faith in Gardner Speirs, his trusted assistant.

7 Oshor Williams: Man of mystery Oshor Williams was a surprise appointment to Steve Paterson's coaching team in 2002, joining the familiar face of Duncan Shearer. Williams had been a colleague of Paterson's at Manchester United as a young player and, having worked behind the scenes with the PFA in England, was drafted in to give a new dimension to the Dons staff. Williams, an intelligent football man, won the respect of players and fellow coaches during his brief stint in Scotland.

8 Jimmy Nicholl: The arrival of Jimmy Calderwood from Dunfermline in 2004 also brought Jimmy Nicholl to Pittodrie as assistant manager, with the pair first having worked together with the Pars. The former Rangers and Manchester United star, who famously led Raith Rovers to the League Cup as manager, added steel and huge experience.

9 Sandy Clark: Calderwood, Nicholl and Sandy Clark. The trio were very much one package during their tenure at Pittodrie, with former Rangers player Clark adding more experience to the mix having bossed Hearts and St Johnstone previously. Tasked particularly with improving the club's strikers, Clark's son Nicky joined him on the staff.

10 Scott Leitch: Mark McGhee had first worked with Scott Leitch when he inherited him as part of the coaching staff at Motherwell. The Gothenburg Great liked what he saw, and invited Leitch, the former Well midfielder and Ross County manager, to follow him to Pittodrie. Leitch, with a reputation for a no-nonsense approach, departed with McGhee in 2010.

Leigh Hinds

Debut: League, 1 February 2003 v Rangers (a) lost 2-1
Appearances: League 42, Scottish Cup 5, League Cup 2
Goals: League 8, League Cup 2
Also played for: Wimbledon, Clyde, Partick Thistle, Stranraer

English striker Leigh Hinds was typical of the signing Steve Paterson was expected to make during his tenure at Aberdeen. The forward was snapped up for £20,000 from Clyde in January 2003, having already agreed a pre-contract deal with the Dons with a view to a summer move. Hinds, who had started his career with Wimbledon, had been a regular scorer for the Bully Wee and fitted the profile of a young player capable of fulfilling his full potential at Pittodrie. He scored a handful of goals for the Dons but fell out of favour when Jimmy Calderwood took over in 2004, criticised by the new boss for a lack of effort in training. Hinds went on to see service with Partick, who he joined in 2004, and Stranraer.

Jared Hodgkiss

Debut: League Cup, 24 September 2008 v Kilmarnock (a) lost 4-2
Appearances: League 7, League Cup 1
Also played for: West Brom, Northampton, Forest Green

The search for new talent took Jimmy Calderwood and his coaching team on the highways and byways of Britain as they racked up the miles on scouting trips. Full-back Jared Hodgkiss was one of the results, picked up from West Brom on loan in August 2008 to provide cover at right-back. The young Englishman played eight games during four months in the SPL without settling fully before returning to the Hawthorns to try and push for a place in the Baggies team, having made a handful of first team appearances prior to his Aberdeen move. Hodgkiss was later loaned to Northampton before moving permanently to Forest Green in 2009.

Billy Hogg

Debut: League, 23 November 1957 v Kilmarnock (h) lost 2-1
Appearances: League 13, Scottish Cup 1
Goals: League 4
Also played for: Rangers, Morton

When Billy Hogg moved north from Glasgow junior side Petershill to join Dave Shaw's Aberdeen team he made a decent fist of his opportunity. The inside forward, who had won the Scottish Junior Cup in 1956, scored four times in 14 appearances for the Dons before being released at the end of the 1957/58 season. The lively forward, still only 25, was a man in demand and was snapped up by Rangers after a trial with the Ibrox men. Despite scoring on his debut for the Light Blues, he played only two games for the first team and was freed in the summer of 1959 and moved on to Morton.

Jimmy Hogg

Debut: League Cup, 18 August 1956 v Rangers (h) lost 6-2
Appearances: League 213, Scottish Cup 22, League Cup 43
Goals: League 1
Also played for: Preston North End, Inverness Caledonian, Fraserburgh, Huntly, Rothes

A 6-2 defeat at the hands of Rangers on their debut would be enough to have many players running for cover. Not Jimmy Hogg. The resilient defender bounced back from the pain of that result on his first appearance for the Dons in 1956 by establishing himself as an Aberdeen stalwart and eventually going on to captain the team.

Hogg had launched his career with Preston North End and was recruited by David Halliday for the Pittodrie squad in 1953. National service delayed his introduction to the Reds team but once he made the breakthrough there was no stopping the left-back.

An ever present in 1959/60 and then again in 1962/63, it was a period in which the club struggled to recapture the form that had seen them bring a succession of trophies north in the 1940s and 50s.

In 1965 Hogg was granted a free transfer and moved into Highland League football with Inverness Caledonian, Fraserburgh, Huntly and Rothes. The veteran defender finally brought the curtain down on his playing days in 1972 but continued his involvement in football as a junior coach with Stonehaven and then Lewis United. He also served as a committee member with Lewis prior to his death in 1984 at the age of 51, by which time his son, Graeme Hogg, had broken into the first team at Manchester United.

Jock Hutton

Debut: League, 16 August 1919 v Albion Rovers (h) won 2-0
Appearances: League 241, Scottish Cup 39
Goals: League 13, Scottish Cup 4
Also played for: Scotland (10 caps), Hall Russells, Bellshill Athletic, Blackburn Rovers

The exploits of Aberdeen's tank like defender became the stuff of legend on both sides of the border in the 1920s. Standing just 5ft 8in tall, Jock Hutton was built like an ox. His weight was officially logged at under 14 stone but that was considered a gross underestimate by the reporters of the time.

He is said to have wowed team-mates with amazing feats of strength, once picking up a Blackburn Rovers team-mate at training. Nothing too staggering in that, until you consider Hutton used his teeth for that particular party trick.

Despite his bulk, the Glaswegian also had tremendous pace and was a feared opponent both in Scottish and English football.

He first caught the eye of the Dons while turning out for junior side Hall Russells in the city during his service with the Gordon Highlanders. Aberdeen began rebuilding their team when the First World War ended and in 1919 turned to Hutton, signing him from Bellshill Athletic.

He spent his first season as an inside forward, making his debut in a 2-0 win at home to Albion Rovers on August 16, 1919. The following term manager Jimmy Philip switched him to defence and the No.2 shirt became Hutton's property for seven seasons.

In that time he emerged as one of Scotland's finest defenders, captaining the Scottish League select side four times and capped for the first time in a 1-0 win in Northern Ireland in 1923.

Hutton played 10 times over the course of five years, skippering the national team to a 2-0 win at home to Northern Ireland a year after his debut and scoring his solitary Scotland goal in a 2-2 draw against Wales in 1927. Hutton's cap haul, seven appearances as a Dons player, was an Aberdeen record for more than four decades.

To catch the eye of international selectors was not easy for Aberdeen players of Hutton's era. In his time at the club they never finished above fifth place in the First Division, battling just to get out of the bottom half of the table.

He was more than just a star in Scottish football and his unique physique and consistent performances drew attention from England, with Blackburn Rovers stumping up £5,000 in 1926 to take him to Lancashire after 282 games and 17 goals for the Dons. It was a record breaking deal for the Dons and a considerable sum of money – in the 1920s you could have the house of your dreams built for £850.

It proved to be a fruitful relationship and within two years he had helped Rovers to lift the FA Cup with a 3-1 win over Huddersfield under the twin towers of Wembley.

A larger than life character who played the game with a smile on his face, Hutton retired from the senior game in 1933 before moving to Northern Ireland.

Jim Hosie

Debut: League, 2 January 1960 v Dunfermline (h) drew 1-1
Appearances: League 10, Scottish Cup 1
Goals: Scottish Cup 1
Also played for: Barnsley, Ross County, Nairn County

Grace and ball artistry were among the qualities Jim Hosie was credited with during his career in Scotland and England. The former King Street and East End player was called up by Aberdeen in 1958 and made his debut early in 1960. Capable of playing on the wing or across the forward line, Hosie was confined to a support role in three seasons with the Dons and moved to Barnsley in the summer of 1962. He was a regular at Oakwell for his single season south of the border and returned north of the border to sign for Ross County. The Aberdonian was a huge hit in the Highland League with the Dingwall side and also served with Nairn County before retiring in the early 1970s.

Mark Howard

Debut: League, 14 August 2010 v Hamilton (h) won 4-0
Appearances: League 9, League Cup 2
Also played for: Falkirk (on loan), Cardiff City, Swansea City (on loan), St Mirren

Londoner Mark Howard began his career with Arsenal before joining Cardiff City in 2006. He had a loan spell with Falkirk while still a Gunners player and a temporary stint at Swansea after his move to Cardiff.

A move to St Mirren in 2007 gave Howard regular first team football and he was snapped up by Mark McGhee in 2010 to provide cover for Jamie Langfield.

Stephen Hughes

Debut: League, 28 January 2012 v Dunfermline (h) won 1-0
Appearances (up to the end of 2011/12) : League 5, Scottish Cup 3
Also played for: Rangers, Motherwell, Norwich City

Experienced former Rangers midfielder Stephen Hughes was free and was snapped up by Craig Brown in January 2012, handed a two and half year deal at Pittodrie. Hughes, who had completed a short stint at Motherwell, his second period with the club, was viewed as vital midfield cover at a time when the squad was stretched by a succession of injuries.

Bobby Hume

Debut: League Cup, 10 August 1963 v Dundee United (a) drew 1-1
Appearances: League 33, Scottish Cup 4, League Cup 9
Goals: League 4, Scottish Cup 2, League Cup 6
Also played for: Rangers, Middlesbrough, Highland Park (South Africa)

Six goals in his first six games suggested a star had been born when Bobby Hume settled into Pittodrie life in the 1963/64 season. The former Rangers winger had joined Tommy Pearson's team from Middlesbrough and was an instant hit, although he struggled to maintain that form and fell out of the team under Eddie Turnbull the following term. Hume moved to South Africa, where he continued his playing career with Highland Park, and remained in the country after hanging up his boots.

The former Dons man was killed when he was shot by thieves in a carjacking incident in Johannesburg in 1997 at the age of 56.

Mark Humphries

Debut: League, 4 April 1992 v Dunfermline (a) drew 0-0
Appearances: League 2
Also played for: Leeds United, Bristol City, Raith Rovers

Aberdeen beat a host of clubs to the signature of left-back Mark Humphries when he graduated from the city's juvenile ranks with Cove Rangers A. He made his debut under Willie Miller, deputising for David Winnie in two games late in the 1991/92 season, but was released in 1993. Humphries joined Leeds United and also played for Bristol City before returning to Scotland with Raith Rovers in 1995.

Willie Hume

Debut: League, 13 August 1938 v Partick Thistle (a) lost 2-1
Appearances: League 9, League Cup 1
Goals: League 1
Also played for: Dundee United

The Second World War was sandwiched between forward Willie Hume's two spells in the Aberdeen team.

He first appeared in 1938/39 season and returned to the fold in 1945/46 for three seasons which brought only fleeting first team appearances. Hume moved to Dundee United in 1948 before turning junior with Penicuik Athletic.

Jerel Ifil

Debut: League, 15 August 2009 v Celtic (h) lost 3-1
Appearances: League 44, Scottish Cup 3, League Cup 4
Also played for: Watford, Huddersfield Town (on loan), Swindon Town, Bristol Rovers

Imposing defender Jerel Ifil became known as 'The Beast' after landing in Scottish football in 2010 when he moved from Swindon Town to join Mark McGhee's rebuilding programme. The Englishman looked destined to become a crowd favourite but faltered early in his Dons team, particularly when pressed into

action as an emergency full-back. Performances became more erratic as the team's fortunes took a turn for the worse and the stopper was released soon after Craig Brown's appointment as manager. He found a new football home with Bristol Rovers as he attempted to revive his career after the disappointment of his Scottish excursion.

John Inglis

Debut: League, 5 November 1994 v Falkirk (a) lost 2-1
Appearances: League 101+1, Scottish Cup 4+1, League Cup 14, Europe 4
Goals: League 4, League Cup 1
Also played for: East Fife, Meadowbank Thistle, Brechin City, St Johnstone, Levski Sofia, Carlisle United, Raith Rovers

When Alex McLeish departed Pittodrie in 1994 to take over as manager at Motherwell he left a huge defensive void for manager Willie Miller to try and fill. He experimented with Gary Smith alongside Brian Irvine before switching to an Irvine partnership with Stephen Wright at the start of the 1994/95 season but was not happy.

As a player he knew a thing or two about defending and as a manager Miller was convinced John Inglis was the man to cure his headache. He was vigorous in his pursuit of the St Johnstone stopper, having two bids rejected before finally getting his man for £400,000 in October, 1994, to head off competition from Bolton Wanderers.

The powerfully built centre-half, known as Zeus to team-mates at Pittodrie because of his physique, made it to the top the hard way. He progressed from East Fife, Meadowbank Thistle and Brechin City before establishing himself in more than 140 games for Saints.

The Edinburgh born player was 28 when Miller handed him the biggest opportunity of his career, hoping to build Aberdeen's future around a central defensive team of Inglis and Smith.

Before that duo could find their feet the manager had been replaced by Roy Aitken, who kept faith with his predecessor's masterplan as the 1995/96 season opened. Inglis marked the opening day with a goal in a 3-2 win at Falkirk but saved his most important contribution for that department of the League Cup quarter-final, on target as Motherwell were beaten 2-1 en route to the final against Dundee. Inglis was an ever present in the successful campaign, in his usual No.5 shirt for the 2-0 win which clinched the trophy.

The arrival of Toni Kombouare, a £400,000 recruit from Sion in 1996, put pressure on Inglis and a move to Fulham only fell through at the last minute in 1997.

As it happened he outlasted the Frenchman, reclaiming his place and going on to become an important player for both Aitken and his successor Alex Miller until he was deemed surplus to requirements early in 1999.

In February that year he made a shock switch to Levski Sofia, becoming the first Scot ever to play in Bulgaria, having been freed by the Dons.

Never totally accepted by the Aberdeen fans, it was an entirely different story for the 6ft defender in his new country. He spent 18 months with Levski and became a hero, helping the club to the championship and turning out in Europe. Inglis married a Bulgarian model and they became the nation's star couple.

If his meteoric rise on foreign soil was a shock to the Dons supporters he had left behind, his return to Pittodrie in August, 2000, was a total bolt from the blue. It was Ebbe Skovdahl, with his squad riddled with injuries, who turned to the former League Cup winner in his hour of need.

In the end his short term stay ended without an appearance to add to the 121 he had made in his first stint, with Inglis briefly playing for Carlisle and Raith Rovers before returning to Bulgaria and settling. He has established himself in Sofia as a football agent.

Brian Irvine

Debut: League, 3 May 1986 v Clydebank (a) won 6-0
Appearances: League 294+14, Scottish Cup 29+1, League Cup 23+3, Europe 19
Goals: League 30, Scottish Cup 4, League Cup 4, Europe 2
Also played for: Scotland (9 caps), Falkirk, Dundee, Ross County
Managed: Elgin City

Brian Irvine's boots have long been cast to one side but he is a man who retains a burning ambition in football. A huge favourite with the Aberdeen fans as a player, Irvine yearns for a return to the Pittodrie staff one day.

He cut his managerial teeth with Elgin City in 2006, having taken his first steps on the coaching ladder with Ross County, but left the club in the same year and returned to his media role as a summariser with BBC Radio Scotland.

Already a frequent visitor to his old stomping ground in that capacity, Irvine makes no secret of his passion for the Dons. In fact, he still pays through the gate to take his Dons mad family to Aberdeen games.

A return to coaching appears a certainty for a man with a wealth of experience and the same measure of integrity. That dream ticket back to the Dons is the incentive.

Irvine was the epitomy of the no-nonsense centre half. Dominant in the air, he posed a threat in attack and his haul of 40 goals in his 338 Aberdeen appearances is an illustration of that.

His most important contribution did not come with his head but from his boot in the most dramatic of circumstances. The 1990 Scottish Cup final against Celtic had ended locked at 0-0 after extra-time. The penalty shoot-out also struggled to find a winner, with the teams tied at an amazing 8-8 when Irvine stepped up to bury the decisive spot kick and take the trophy back to Pittodrie. The towering defender's wild celebrations told their own story.

After 22 years the emotion of the moment is still as strong and Irvine said: "It was a unique moment for me and having been an Aberdeen supporter since I was a boy it was extra special. Although I was brought up in Glasgow, among Rangers and Celtic fans, I always followed the Dons because my family's roots were in the north-east. To have the chance to score the penalty which would win the Scottish Cup was special.

"I was far from first choice for taking penalties - only the goalkeepers were left after me. The shoot out went on and on until Anton Rogan stepped up to take his - at that point Theo Snelders roused the Aberdeen supporters behind the goal and made it difficult for Anton, who still struck a good penalty but saw Theo pull off a magnificent save.

"The walk from the half way line to the penalty spot went quickly for me – I was in a no lose situation really. If I scored then we won the cup, if I missed then it was still level at 8-8. There was less pressure on me than those who had gone before me. The feeling I experienced when the ball hit the back of the net, and the noise from the fans behind the goal, will live with me forever. I became the first player ever to score the winning penalty in a Scottish Cup shoot-out because a final had never gone to spot kicks. Even in the one since then, when Hearts beat Gretna, there wasn't a winning penalty because it was decided on a miss. I never had a good record with penalties when I was at school and in senior football I only ever took one - to decide the cup final. I never took one before or after that game."

The Bellshill born player, a Dons supporter in his youth, was recruited from Falkirk in 1985 by Alex Ferguson after establishing himself in the Bairns first team as a teenager. He had just turned 20 when he arrived at Pittodrie and found himself rubbing shoulders with the stars of the Scottish game, joining a team who had just been crowned champions of Scotland for the third year in succession.

The Dons surrendered their crown that term but Irvine at least achieved a personal goal, making his first start for the club in the final league game of the season when Clydebank were humbled 6-0 on May 3, 1986.

Irvine had to wait patiently behind Miller and McLeish but that did not limit his opportunities in the first team. He stepped in to fill the No.5 or No.6 shirt close to 100 times over the course of just four full seasons before Miller's retirement at the start of the 1990/91 season paved the way for a permanent role in Alex Smith's team.

Prior to that he had been a substitute in the 2-1 League Cup final win over Rangers in 1989/90 before standing in for Miller in the Scottish Cup final to collect his second winner's medal after the penalty shoot-out.

As first choice central defender, Irvine was promoted to the Scotland scene and made his debut under Andy Roxburgh in a 2-1 win over Romania in September, 1990.

He retained his place when Craig Brown took charge of the national team and went on to earn eight further caps over four years. His international career coincided with an almost unbroken run of appearances in the Aberdeen first team, missing just eight league games over the course of three seasons between 1991/92 and 1993/94.

The on-field efforts took a back seat when Irvine was diagnosed with Multiple Sclerosis. Strong Christian beliefs helped Irvine through his darkest days and he amazed doctors by reviving his football career, playing on with the Dons until his transfer to Dundee in 1997.

He made 79 appearances for the Dens Park side over two seasons before Ross County took him north in 1999. Irvine played 143 games for County before joining the coaching staff following his final appearance in May, 2003, when he was just three weeks from his 38th birthday.

His appointment as manager at Elgin at the start of 2006 sparked an upturn in fortunes and he steered the club to the Third Division play-offs, although promotion proved a bridge too far and he parted company.

Irvine has since had stints coaching in the US and also branched out into the world of publishing when he released *Winning Through* in 2006, an innovative book designed at developing readers and which received a seal of approval from adult literacy experts. It came a decade after his more traditional autobiography *What a Difference a Day Makes* was released.

Harald Ingolfsson

Debut: League, 26 October 1996 v Raith Rovers (h) won 1-0
Appearances: League 6
Also played for: Iceland, Akranes

An exceptional display against Rangers reserves in a trial match won Icelandic international winger Harald Ingolfsson an Aberdeen contract in 1996 following his release by Akranes in his homeland. Two goals in that trial game proved to be the highlight of his six months in Scotland and he was released after just one start and five appearances from the bench.

Jimmy Ingram

Debut: League, 29 October 1955 v East Fife (a) drew 1-1
Appearances: League 2
Goals: League 1
Also played for: East Fife, Inverness Caledonian

Forward Jimmy Ingram was another of the talented youngsters to roll off the Sunnybank conveyor belt. He scored on his first team debut for the Dons in a 1-1 draw at East Fife in 1955 but made just one further appearance, in a 4-1 defeat at home to Clyde in the next game, before a two season spell with East Fife in the late 1950s. Ingram also featured for Inverness Caledonian in the Highland League.

Ryan Jack

Debut: League Cup, 22 September 2010 v Raith Rovers (h) won 3-2
Appearances (up to end of 2011/12): League 61, Scottish Cup 8, League Cup 5
Goals (up to end of 2011/12): League 4

Modest, hard working and with a great future in the game. That was Craig Brown's assessment of teenage midfielder Ryan Jack after watching the youngster at close quarters in training and in match action. Jack became the latest player to make the leap at Pittodrie when he made his entrance early in the 2010/11 season.

He quickly progressed from squad man and substitute to win a regular place in the first eleven, making up for the loss of Fraser Fyvie through injury by adding youthful enthusiasm to the Aberdeen side with his bursting runs from midfield.

Ian Jamieson

Debut: League, 2 November 1946 v Queen of the South (h) lost 3-1
Appearances: League 1
Also played for: Peterhead (on loan), Coventry City

Right winger Ian Jamieson was released after one season and one game on the staff in the post-war years. The former Jamestown Athletic player had a spell on loan with Peterhead after swapping Dunbartonshire for the north-east and, after leaving Pittodrie, went on to star for Coventry City throughout the 1950s. Jamieson rose to succeed Jimmy Hill as chairman of Coventry in 1983.

Dean Jarvis

Debut: League, 2 October 2010 v Caley Thistle (a) lost 2-0
Appearances (up to end of 2010/11): League 1
Also played for: Derry City

Dean Jarvis will always look back on 2010 with fond memories. In the space of a year he was promoted to the Northern Ireland under-21 squad and made his debut for Aberdeen. The left-back was capped by his country at under-16 and under-17 level before moving from Derry City to the Dons to further his career.

David Johnston

Debut: League, 17 December 1966 v Stirling Albion (a) won 6-2
Appearances: League 77, Scottish Cup 15, League Cup 6, Europe 2
Goals: League 32, Scottish Cup 5
Also played for: Nairn County, Hearts, Inverness Caledonian

The Highland League has been a rich source of talent for Scotland's senior clubs over the years and winger David Johnston was one of the youngsters from the north to make the transition to the full-time game.

It was Hearts, not Aberdeen, who swooped to sign the 17-year-old Nairn County left winger in 1960 in the face of competition from Celtic and Arbroath as well as Portsmouth, Cardiff City and Preston North End.

Despite quickly earning a place in the Tynecastle first team, he returned to Nairn a year later after failing to settle in Edinburgh - but got a second bite at the First Division cherry when Aberdeen, under Eddie Turnbull, made their move in the winter of 1966.

By then Johnston had matured into a potent centre forward who had shattered the Highland League's scoring record with a 72 goal haul in the 1963/64 season. He rejected overtures from St Johnstone, both Dundee clubs and Falkirk before finally agreeing to join the Dons.

Johnston finished leading scorer at Pittodrie in 1967/68, his first full season in the red shirt, with 14 strikes. He played just one further term with the Dons before returning to the Highland League with Inverness Caledonian in the summer of 1969. He remained with Caley until 1975 and had a final season back with his home town team Nairn County before retiring. He guided junior side Nairn St Ninian to successive championships in the late 1970s and had a second spell in charge in the early 80s.

Tom Jones

Debut: League, 10 October 1987 v Dundee (h) drew 0-0
Appearances: League 28, Scottish Cup 3
Goals: League 3
Also played for: Swindon Town, Reading

English non-league international midfielder Tom Jones was signed by Ian Porterfield from Weymouth for £30,000 as he prepared for his first full season in charge. The 22-year-old had impressed while on trial in Scotland and featured regularly during the 1987/88 campaign. When Alex Smith replaced Porterfield there was no place for Jones, and he was allowed to move to Swindon in an £80,000 deal just two months into his second term with the club. Jones established himself with the Robins and also featured for Reading and Woking in the 1990s.

George Johnstone

Debut: League, 6 February 1937 v Motherwell (a) lost 1-0
Appearances: League 151, Scottish Cup 25, League Cup 24
Also played for: Benburb, Dunfermline, Morton, Cowdenbeath

In the first 100 years of the club's existence only six goalkeepers collected league or cup winner's medals. George Johnstone was the first in a group which included Fred Martin, Bobby Clark, Jim Leighton, Theo Snelders and Michael Watt.

Johnstone left Pittodrie with two coveted badges tucked in his pocket, the first coming from the 1946 Southern League Cup final against Rangers when his side won 3-2. The competition was the forerunner to the League Cup and represented Aberdeen's first triumph on the national stage.

The following year Johnstone was again the No.1 as the Scottish Cup was claimed with a 2-1 victory over Hibs – when the Dons keeper feared he had made the most costly error of his career within 30 seconds of kick-off at Hampden. Johnstone allowed a harmless looking backpass from George Taylor to slip past him and into the net but he recovered from that nervous start to keep the Leith side at bay as his outfield colleagues hit back with two first half goals.

Johnstone was not a Scottish Cup final rookie in 1947, a survivor from the club's appearance at the same stage in 1937. On that occasion it had ended in a 2-1 defeat against Celtic.

A year before that game Johnstone had played in goal for the Benburb side that won the Scottish Junior Cup, recruited from that victorious side by Aberdeen alongside Frank Dunlop.

He took over from Steve Smith on February 6, 1937, and, despite a 1-0 defeat at Motherwell, never looked back as he played the final nine First Division games in a Dons team which finished runners-up to Rangers.

He went on to become an ever present in his first full season at Pittodrie, keeping 11 clean sheets.

In 1947, the same year as the Scottish Cup was won, Johnstone was part of the team which shipped four goals without reply against Rangers in the League Cup final but it did not dent his reputation. A fierce wind and driving rain ensured it was not a day to judge goalkeepers.

A succession of men tried and failed to dislodge Johnstone from the first team during his 12 years at the club, including Pat Kelly and Tom Rennie, but he always bounced back to win favour with Dave Halliday until his departure in 1949.

A 2-0 defeat at home to St Mirren on January 29 proved to be the death knell for Johnstone's position as Aberdeen's No.1. He was replaced by John Curran and never played another first team game.

Johnstone played in 200 games for Aberdeen before his switch to Dunfermline and then Raith Rovers. In the twilight of his career, after turning to coaching, he also pulled the gloves back on to come to the aid of Morton and Cowdenbeath.

Johnstone went on to coach Newburgh juniors in Fife before becoming trainer of Darlington in 1963. He died in Kirkcaldy in 1974.

TEN: facts about the glory of Gothenburg

1 Early days: Gothenburg greats Jim Leighton and Alex McLeish were club colleagues as youngsters with Glasgow United, plucked from the west coast juvenile side by the Dons and the club's ever alert scouting network to join the youth ranks at Pittodrie and learn their trade under Alex Ferguson and his coaching team.

2 Money, money, money: The run to the final of the European Cup Winners' Cup in 1982/83 took Aberdeen's turnover through the £1million barrier for the first time and brought the club a healthy £200,000 profit that was carefully looked after by wily chairman Dick Donald and his vice-chairman Chris Anderson as they looked to the future.

3 Sing when you're winning: The European Song, penned to commemorate the Gothenburg final by musician Harry Barry, sold 55,000 copies to Dons fans desperate to join the fun. Despite selling out, no additional copies of the record were made because the company behind it went into liquidation at the height of the interest.

4 Legendary praise: Shattered Real Madrid coach Alfredo Di Stefano singled out Peter Weir and Gordon Strachan for special praise after watching his Spanish superstars being humbled by the slick Dons in Gothenburg in the 1983 final. His assessment was shared by Alex Ferguson in post-match interviews.

5 Exotic influences: The Gothenburg greats were not all Scots born and bred. Neale Cooper's passport shows India as his birthplace, courtesy of his parents' posting to the sub continent through work in the tea plantations, even though he returned to Aberdeen as a youngster and grew up in the city. Neil Simpson is a Londoner by birth despite his upbringing in Aberdeenshire.

6 Come fly with me: Aberdeen's official travel agents chartered 20 planes from across Europe to meet demand for air travel to the final in Gothenburg. More than 2,500 passengers booked places on those flights, including the team and club staff who travelled in an aircraft emblazoned with 'The Flying Dons' on its nose.

7 High spirits on the high seas: For those not lucky enough to land a plane seat, the alternative was to travel by boat to Sweden. More than 500 fans were accommodated on the P&O ferry St Clair as it sailed from Aberdeen on a special voyage to take the Red Army to Scandinavia for the big date with Real Madrid.

8 Back to the future: One of Willie Miller's first acts upon taking a seat on the Dons board in 2004 was to invite fellow Gothenburg hero Peter Weir to return to the fold. Weir was recruited to beef up the youth development programme, working on the scouting and coaching network on the west coast.

9 Milne's pride: Current Aberdeen chairman Stewart Milne was an enthusiastic supporter when the Dons enjoyed their finest hour. Milne, still early in his business career, took 20 of the managers and staff from his construction company to Gothenburg to take in the 1983 final and join the celebrations in the aftermath of the triumph.

10 Economic sense: It cost less than £500,000 to build the team that shocked Real Madrid. The same group of players raised more than £3million when they were sold on at various stages in the years that followed, with Jim Leighton's £750,000 transfer to Manchester United raking in the biggest single fee for the club.

Drew Jarvie

Debut: League Cup, 12 August 1972 v Queen of the South (a) won 4-0
Appearances: League 275+35, Scottish Cup 28+3, League Cup 66+14, Europe 17+1
Goals: League 85, Scottish Cup 6, League Cup 29, Europe 10
Also played for: Scotland (3 caps), Kilsyth Rangers, Airdrie, St Mirren

Under the stewardship of Dick Donald, Aberdeen was a club which prided itself on prudence and a solid fiscal approach. There was no place for extravagance and a dislike of risky gambles, so when manager Jimmy Bonthrone went knocking on the boardroom door in 1972 looking for a transfer fee larger than anything the club had ever spent previously he must have presented a good case.

The target was Drew Jarvie and the £70,000 the Dons paid to wrest him from Airdrie's grasp proved to be a bargain. It was a record buy for Aberdeen, using the proceeds from Martin Buchan's £125,000 switch to Manchester United two years previously. With a surplus still resting in the club coffers, a cultured and imperious central defender had in effect been traded for a livewire forward with the ability to torment his opponents with his energy and movement.

For Jarvie it continued an upward spiral in the game which started when he helped Kilsyth Rangers to the Scottish Junior Cup in 1967, earning caps for the junior international side along the way and getting an early taste for success.

Airdrie snapped him up after that cup triumph and he continued his football apprenticeship with the Diamonds. His performances won Scotland under-23 recognition before he stepped up to the full national team in 1971 when he played in three internationals under Bobby Brown, surprisingly the only caps he collected in a long career at the top level. He was ignored by a succession of Scotland coaches during his Pittodrie days but the fact he was able to earn international recognition while playing with tiny Airdrie was testament to his talent.

Jarvie was recruited to form what Bonthrone expected to be a lethal partnership with Joe Harper and those hopes were

boosted when the new boy made a scoring debut in a 4-0 League Cup win against Queen of the South on August 12, 1972.

The budding pairing got off to a solid start in the 1972/73 season but Harper's move to Everton within four months ripped it apart. Harper had thrived on Jarvie's creativity and unselfishness but it was after he had left to move to Goodison that his former strike partner came into his own.

Jarvie bagged 28 goals to finish leading scorer in his first season at Pittodrie, haunting his former club Airdrie when he hammered home his first Aberdeen hat-trick along the way, and again topped the chart in 1973/74 with a haul of 24 which included four in a single game against Falkirk. He made it a hat-trick the following term when his tally of 13 put him one ahead of Arthur Graham on the Dons scoring list.

While those personal triumphs flowed thick and fast, Jarvie had to wait until the 1976/77 campaign for the team glory he craved. When it came, he proved to be a key player.

He scored two goals in the League Cup run which ended when the Dons lifted the trophy with a 2-1 win against Celtic and both came against the Old Firm. He opened his account in the competition with a screaming volley from outside of the box in the semi-final against Rangers to help his side to a memorable 5-1 victory but the real trump card came in the final against Celtic.

The Hoops were old hands, having appeared in every one of the previous 12 League Cup finals, but for Aberdeen it was the first time since 1955. Celtic looked to be putting their experience to good use when Kenny Dalglish put them ahead from the spot in the 11th minute but Jarvie hit back within 13 minutes when he headed home the equaliser. Davie Robb snatched the winner in extra time for Ally MacLeod's side and Jarvie had his first senior medal tucked in his pocket.

The next came in 1980 when a Premier Division championship badge joined the Jarvie collection and his contribution to that first title success for a quarter of a century should not be underestimated.

Steve Archibald was leading scorer overall for Alex Ferguson's team that season but in the league he and Jarvie shared the workload with 12 goals each. That included a run of six in eight games for Jarvie as the season entered a crucial stage in February and March.

Alex Ferguson's young guns began to edge the seasoned campaigner out of the first team in the following seasons but Jarvie remained a hero to the Dons fans, who turned out to honour him in a testimonial match against Ipswich in 1982 to put a cap on his career with the club.

In October, 1982, at the age of 34 he switched back to Airdrie with a glowing tribute from Ferguson ringing in his ears and spent a year at Broomfield before his appointment as assistant manager to Alex Miller at St Mirren.

It marked the first step on a long road in coaching which continued at Dundee before he arrived back at Pittodrie as assistant to co-managers Alex Smith and Jocky Scott in 1988.

Jarvie helped to mastermind the Scottish Cup and League Cup double of the 1989/90 season and continued, alongside Roy Aitken, as one of two right hand men to Willie Miller when he took over from Smith in the manager's office.

In 1995, following Aitken's promotion to the top job, Jarvie switched roles to take charge of Aberdeen's youth system and remained on the coaching staff until parting company with the club in 2002 following Steve Paterson's appointment.

He is now back in Aberdeen after a spell as assistant manager to another Pittodrie old-boy, Ian Porterfield, at Korean side Busan Icons.

Eoin Jess

Debut: League, 6 May 1989 v Motherwell (h) drew 0-0
Appearances: League 275+36, Scottish Cup 21+2, League Cup 29+5, Europe 9
Goals: League 74, Scottish Cup 3, League Cup 5, Europe 6
Also played for: Scotland (18 caps), Coventry City, Bradford City, Nottingham Forest, Northampton Town.

For Aberdeen supporters there are few greater pleasures than getting one over on Rangers and in the case of Eoin Jess the Dons certainly had the last laugh. Targeted by Rangers as a schoolboy, Jess was close to signing at Ibrox until a delay in completing the paperwork allowed for a change of heart. He eventually ended up committing his future to Aberdeen and the rest, as they say, is history.

Jess went on to torment the Light Blues time and time again as the two clubs became locked in a fierce battle for supremacy in the late 1980s and early 1990s. Despite his childhood connection to Ibrox, Jess falls very much into the category of homegrown talent for Aberdeen. Born and raised in the north-east town of Portsoy, he has commanded in excess of £3million in the transfer market.

He was toughened up in the welfare leagues of Moray, a relative late starter in competitive football but a youngster whose brain allowed him to compete in surroundings more recognised for brawn. It was his form as a teenager that brought him to the attention of senior clubs and, after his dalliance with Rangers, it was the Dons who snared him.

Alex Smith gave the Reds fans a taste of what was to follow when he introduced Jess as an 18-year-old on May 6, 1989, in a 0-0 draw against Motherwell at Pittodrie. One week later he played as a substitute in a

3-0 league win against champions Rangers at Ibrox and the seeds for a love of the big stage were sown.

That was confirmed in October, 1989, when Jess played from the start in the 2-1 League Cup final win against the club who had released him just two years earlier. It was a sweet victory for the rising Dons star, who would prove adept in almost every attacking role in the side. Whether cutting in from wide, leading the line in attack or offering intelligent promptings from midfield he comfortably slotted in.

Jess had scored his first goal in a red shirt earlier that season, hitting the only goal in a game against Dundee but it was in the 1990/91 season that he truly established himself as one of Scottish football's biggest threats.

He tied with Dutch international Hans Gillhaus on 15 goals at the top of the scoring chart and proved a valuable match-

winner, scoring all of the goals in a 4-1 win against Dunfermline at East End Park and shattering Dundee United with a hat-trick in a 3-2 win at Pittodrie.

Late in 1992 the first of 18 caps for Scotland was won in a 0-0 draw with Italy at Ibrox when he came off the bench to replace Gordon Durie. Jess, who featured fleetingly in the Euro 96 thriller against England at Wembley, scored against the Czech Republic and San Marino in a seven year stint with the national team.

Just months after his Scotland debut the versatile attacker, who was equally at home in midfield as he was leading the forward line, broke his leg in a Scottish Cup tie against Clydebank but he bounced back quickly and rediscovered his best form.

He gained his second winner's medal in the 1995 League Cup when the Dons defeated Dundee 2-0 but less than three months later was off the Pittodrie pay-roll.

Coventry City tempted Aberdeen with a £1.7million offer and that record breaking fee was too good to turn down, although it didn't turn out to be pure profit.

After just one full season with the Sky Blues, Jess returned to Aberdeen in a £700,000 deal in the summer of 1997 to team up once again with manager Roy Aitken.

Bred on a diet of cup success and title challenges, he found himself at a club now classed as perennial strugglers. His brief time in England would have to be classed as a disappointment, with his subtle talents perhaps not best suited to playing for a Coventry side that had to scrap for survival, but it was an itch that had to be scratched.

Having sampled life on the other side of the border, he returned to lend a hand to Aberdeen's own battles against relegation. In 2000 it was only Falkirk's inability to meet SPL stadium standards which prevented a relegation play-off against the Bairns after Ebbe Skovdahl's Dons had finished 10th in the 10 team division.

Jess, disenchanted with the fortunes of a club that had once been challenging for the championship during his first spell on the books, spent the second half of that term on loan at Bradford City. The Yorkshire side were attempting to retain their place in the English Premier League and presented the Scot with another opportunity to test himself against the likes of Manchester United, Liverpool and Arsenal.

The Bantams eventually fell through the relegation trap door but snapped up Jess on a free transfer in the summer of 2001 as they regrouped, with Jess becoming a fixture in their side for the following term in the Championship. With his Aberdeen days behind him, he threw himself into English football as he entered the veteran stage of his career.

The attacker left for Nottingham Forest in 2002 and spent three seasons with the Midlands outfit before joining Northampton Town in 2005 for a two year stint. He helped the Cobblers to promotion from League Two in 2005/06 as they finished runners-up to Carlisle under manager Colin Calderwood.

Jess, who suffered a stroke in 2009 and also had an operation to cure a heart condition which had gone undetected throughout his career, rejoined Nottingham Forest as part of the club's youth academy coaching team before moving to Peterborough as a coach in 2012.

Paul Kane

Debut: League, 23 November 1991 v Hibs (a) lost 1-0
Appearances: League 119, Scottish Cup 10, League Cup 7, Europe 5
Goals: League 11, League Cup 1, Europe 1
Also played for: Hibs, Oldham Athletic, Viking Stavanger, St Johnstone, Clyde

Had it not been from the cruellest of twists in the 1992/93 season then midfielder Paul Kane could have joined the ranks of trophy winning Aberdeen stars. Kane was a vital member of the squad that term and looked certain for a central part in the Scottish Cup final against Rangers until manager Willie Miller took a huge gamble with his team selection.

Kane, who had played in both the quarter-final and semi-final ties, was bombed out and Eoin Jess, on the road back to fitness after a lengthy injury lay-off, was in. The gamble failed, with Jess struggling to keep up with the frenetic pace and the Dons lost 2-1 as midfield schemer Kane kicked his heels in the stand.

The Edinburgh-born player had been signed by Miller's predecessor Alex Smith in the winter of 1991 for £350,000. Kane joined from Oldham Athletic, having moved to England from his boyhood heroes Hibs just ten months earlier in a £325,000 transfer. He was 26 when he moved to Pittodrie and, with Scotland under-21 caps under his belt from his time at Easter Road, ready to hit his peak.

His tenacious displays in the engine room made Kane a popular Dons player, although first team opportunities began to dwindle. He joined Norwegian outfit Viking Stavanger under freedom of contract in the summer of 1996 but returned to Scotland with St Johnstone a year later. Five years with Saints, bringing more than 150 appearances for the Perth side, were followed by a year with Clyde from March 2002.

Archie Kelly

Debut: League, 25 December 1947 v Third Lanark (a) lost 3-2
Appearances: League 36, Scottish Cup 1, League Cup 8
Goals: League 21, Scottish Cup 2, League Cup 3
Also played for: Hearts, Motherwell, Stirling Albion, Ayr United

Filling the shoes of the legendary George Hamilton was the task facing forward Archie Kelly when he joined midway through the 1947/48 season. He moved from Hearts as part of the deal brokered to take Hamilton in the opposite direction and slotted comfortably into Dave Halliday's side, scoring 12 goals in just 17 games and banging in a hat-trick against Clyde in the process. He scored another treble, this time against East Fife, the following term but fell out of the first team picture and was sold to Motherwell during the 1949/50 season. He won the Scottish Cup with Well in 1952 and also had spells with Stirling Albion and Ayr United.

Bernard Kelly

Debut: League, 26 September 1959 v Airdrie (a) lost 1-0
Appearances: League 4
Goals: League 1
Also played for: Raith Rovers, Leicester City, Cowdenbeath

Forward Bernard Kelly was signed from Nottingham Forest early in the 1959/60 season for £4,000. He had also had a spell with Leicester City after initially rising to prominence with Raith Rovers. Despite a reputation as a goal scorer, Kelly netted just once for the Dons after struggling to break into the team. He returned to Raith for £2,000 in the summer of 1960 and moved on to Cowdenbeath the following year.

George Kelly

Debut: League, 7 November 1953 v Rangers (h) drew 1-1
Appearances: League 2
Also played for: Stoke City, Cardiff City, Stockport County, Keith, Fraserburgh, Forfar

Versatile sportsman George Kelly became a tennis champion in the north-east and played for Scotland in the sport after his Dons days. He had signed from Banks o' Dee in 1952 as an 18-year-old and played two games at inside forward during three seasons. Kelly went on to play for Stoke, Cardiff and Stockport County before returning to play in the Highland League with Keith and Fraserburgh. He also featured for Forfar. He died in 1998 at the age of 65.

Robert Kelly

Debut: League Cup, 27 August 1958 v Hibs (a) lost 4-2
Appearances: League 1, League Cup 2
Goals: League Cup 1
Also played for: Alloa Athletic

Young striker Robert Kelly enjoyed a meteoric rise. In the space of a week he went from junior player with Musselburgh Athletic to top flight forward with the Dons in the 1958/59 season after impressing on trial. He scored on his debut but played just two further games before dropping out of the team. He was released in 1959 and signed for Alloa Athletic.

Andy Kerr

Debut: League, 24 April 1964 v Dunfermline (a) lost 3-1
Appearances: League 14, League Cup 2
Goals: League 7, League Cup 1
Also played for: Scotland (2 caps), Kilmarnock, Sunderland

Former Scotland international Andy Kerr was recruited by Tommy Pearson and made his debut in 1964. The Ayrshire man, who made his name with Partick Thistle and won two caps in 1955, had starred with Kilmarnock and Sunderland before switching to Pittodrie. Kerr's record of eight goals in 16 appearances in the 1964/65 season did not prevent his release by Eddie Turnbull in 1965. He went on to play for Glentoran and Inverness Caledonian.

Mark Kerr

Debut: League, 9 August 2008 v Caley Thistle (h) lost 2-1
Appearances: League 69, Scottish Cup 7, League Cup 3, Europe 2
Goals: League 1
Also played for: Falkirk, Dundee United, Asteras Tripolis (Greece)

Mark Kerr joined illustrious company when he was

made captain of Aberdeen football club in 2009. He was appointed by manager Mark McGhee, a man who knew better than most the responsibilities that went with the role having himself served under the greatest skipper in the team's history in Willie Miller during his playing days in the 1980s.

Kerr was picked ahead of contenders Zander Diamond and Gary McDonald for the honour. His season wearing the armband proved disappointing, with the team toiling and the player himself struggling to live up to expectations.

He was unveiled as a Dons player in the summer of 2008 after being recruited on a free transfer from Dundee United by Jimmy Calderwood. He had spent five years on Tayside and carved out a reputation as a solid holding midfielder. Calderwood praised Kerr's athleticism and tactical awareness when he secured his services and saw him as the ideal man to stiffen a midfield that had been weakened by Barry Nicholson's departure.

Kerr, only 26 when he moved to Pittodrie, was already experienced after playing more than 100 games for Falkirk as a youngster. He moved to United in 2003, plumping for Tannadice despite interest from Aberdeen, and quickly settled into SPL life.

He was a consistent performer under Calderwood in his first season in a red shirt but Kerr's form dipped during McGhee's tenure and he took the opportunity to move abroad when his contract expired in 2010. The Glaswegian won a surprise move to Greek side Asteras Tripolis, a team seeking to strengthen after scraping clear of relegation the previous term.

Don Kerrigan

Debut: League, 26 October 1963 v Falkirk (h) won 3-0
Appearances: League 52, Scottish Cup 6, League Cup 5
Goals: League 26, Scottish Cup 2, League Cup 1
Also played for: St Mirren, Hearts, Dunfermline, Fulham, Portadown

Tommy Pearson swapped Willie Allan for St Mirren star Don Kerrigan during the 1963/64 season and got a good return on the deal. The versatile attacker, who played in all five forward positions for the Dons, was tied with Ernie Winchester at the head of the club's scoring chart the following season with 15 goals. He was exchanged for Hearts forward Tommy White by Eddie Turnbull in the summer of 1965 and also had stints with Dunfermline, Fulham and Irish outfit Portadown. Kerrigan died in a work accident in 1990 at the age of 49.

Alec Kiddie

Debut: League, 18 August 1945 v Kilmarnock (a) won 4-1
Appearances: League 38, League Cup 10
Goals: League 11, League Cup 2
Also played for: Celtic, Falkirk

Winger Alec Kiddie cut his teeth with Dundee junior side Stobswell before stepping up to the senior game with Celtic. He moved from Parkhead to Pittodrie in 1945 as football returned to normality after the war and was Dave Halliday's first choice on the right flank for two seasons until Peter Rice took possession of the No.7 shirt. Kiddie was a key man in the Southern League Cup final victory against Rangers at the end of the 1945/46 season, setting up two goals in the 3-2 thriller. He moved on to Falkirk in 1950.

George Kinnell

Debut: Scottish Cup, 30 January 1960 v Brechin City (h) drew 0-0
Appearances: League 129, Scottish Cup 12, League Cup 23
Goals: League 20, Scottish Cup 4, League Cup 1
Also played for: Stoke City, Oldham Athletic, Sunderland, Middlesbrough

His younger brother was a professional player with St Johnstone but it was a cousin by the name of Jim Baxter who led the family's charge to make a major impact at the highest level. While Baxter was a silky skilled midfield maestro, Kinnell was an uncompromising defender and one who stepped out of his famous relative's shadow to carve out a fruitful career of his own. Like his illustrious cousin, he was a character who enjoyed life to the full.

Kinnell signed for the Dons from junior side Crossgates Primrose in his native Fife in 1958 and went on to captain Aberdeen. He spent five years as a lynchpin of the Pittodrie back line before his form attracted the attention of Stoke City, who tempted the board to part with their key man by offering a £35,000 bounty that shattered the previous record transfer receipt in 1964.

Kinnell also played for Oldham Athletic and was later reunited with Baxter when he joined his cousin at Sunderland, recruited as a stopper first and foremost but also, in theory, as a calming influence to keep his relative in check. He skippered the Roker Park side before moving to Middlesbrough in 1968 and then on to Australia for a nine-year stint that included a move into coaching. Kinnell returned to Aberdeen in the late 1970s to concentrate on building a life outside of football.

Stuart Kennedy

Debut: League Cup, 14 August 1976 v Kilmarnock (h) won 2-0
Appearances: League 223, Scottish Cup 29, League Cup 55+1, Europe 26+1
Goals: League 3, League Cup 5, Europe 1
Also played for: Scotland (8 caps), Falkirk

The European Cup Winners' Cup final in 1983 brought amazing highs and terrible lows for defender Stuart Kennedy as the Scotland international's career came to a shuddering end on that glorious night in the most tragic of circumstances. Amid the scenes of joy and triumph, not even the man himself could have predicted the life changing impact the events in Gothenburg would have on his life and his career.

Not fit enough to take his usual place at right back against Real Madrid due to a knee injury, Kennedy was named among the substitutes and leapt from the bench to celebrate John Hewitt's winner – catching his studs between the track and pitch, aggravating the knee injury which kept him out of the game in the first place and ending his playing days in the process. It is one of the cruellest chapters in the long story of Aberdeen Football Club and a moment too often forgotten when the triumph of 1983 is remembered.

Up to that point Kennedy had been a shining light for the Dons and established himself as one of Scotland's leading defenders thanks to blistering pace and impeccable timing. With those crucial attributes he was able to tame the trickiest of wingers, proving a formidable opponent during an era in which the Scottish Premier Division was blessed with a clutch of talented wide men. Few could claim to have got the better of Kennedy during his exemplary service at Pittodrie, a stint where he displayed passion and loyalty to go with his skills on the pitch.

In the build-up to the European Cup Winners' Cup final he had played in nine of the previous ten ties, scoring in the opening game against Sion, but his dream of playing in the big one was dealt a cruel blow when a challenge from Roy Aitken in the Scottish Cup semi-final against Celtic left him crumpled on the turf. He answered Alex Ferguson's plea to haul himself back into the team for the European semi-final ties against Waterschei but twisted his already damaged knee against the Belgian side and the chance was gone. It proved to be the ultimate sacrifice, putting his body on the line to help the Dons into the final before being forced to bring down the curtain on a career that had yet to reach its peak.

Kennedy, now back living in his home town of Grangemouth, did not play again and chose to sever his ties with the club and football after brief stints coaching and scouting for Ferguson. The pain of remaining in and around the game which had been snatched away from him proved to be hard to take.

The pair's relationship went back beyond their time together at Pittodrie, with Kennedy a part-time player with Falkirk and apprentice electrician in the shipyards of the Clyde when Ferguson was part of the same Bairns squad as his own playing career was winding down in the early 1970s. Ferguson, of course, came from shipyard stock himself.

Kennedy was 18 when he first played for Falkirk in 1971. Five years later Ally MacLeod took him to Aberdeen on the back of the club's desperate, but successful, fight against relegation in the 1975/76 season.

There was an instant and dramatic upturn in fortunes as MacLeod led his team to third in the Premier Division and to the League Cup with a 2-1 victory over Celtic in the final. Kennedy, who had made his Dons debut in a 2-0 win against Kilmarnock at Pittodrie in the first game of that cup run on August 14, 1976, was an automatic pick and wore his traditional No.2 shirt in the Hampden showdown. He had missed just a handful of games, notching 43 appearances in his first term at Pittodrie. Between then and his retirement in 1983 he made in excess of 40 starts in all but two seasons.

Just as he had given Kennedy his big break with Aberdeen, it was MacLeod who thrust the defender into the international limelight. He made his first Scotland appearance in a 1-1 draw with England at Hampden in May, 1978, in time to book his place on the plane to the World Cup finals in Argentina. His No.13 shirt proved unlucky in the 3-1 defeat against Peru on the game's biggest stage but Kennedy experienced the other end of the spectrum when he made his second, and last, appearance in football's showpiece in the 3-2 win against Holland. As Scotland surfed the Ally MacLeod wave of euphoria and crushing disappointment, Kennedy could say 'I was there'.

He collected eight caps between 1978 and 1981 but could well have added to the collection if his career had

not been cut short by injury before he had passed his 30th birthday. In addition to those matches against the Auld Enemy, Peru and the Dutch masters he played in a home nations draw against Wales as well as two

defeats against Portugal in World Cup and European Championship qualifiers, a 2-1 friendly win against Bulgaria and a Euro qualifier defeat in Austria.

Domestically Kennedy completed a coveted clean sweep, missing just a single game in the championship win of 1980 and adding the Scottish Cup to his honours list when he starred in the 4-1 extra time win over Rangers in 1982. That day in the sunshine at Hampden proved to be his final honour as a player, although his contribution to the European run of 1983 ensures he will always be remembered as a Gothenburg great.

The defender took a conscious decision to walk away from the prospect of a career in coaching as he reeled from the abrupt end to his playing days after 335 Dons appearances and nine goals, moving into the hospitality trade in the central belt.

Ilian Kiriakov

Debut: Uefa Cup, 6 August 1996 v Zalgiris Vilnius (a) won 4-1
Appearances: League 73, Scottish Cup 4, League Cup 6, Europe 6
Goals: League 1
Also played for: Bulgaria, Deportivo La Coruna, Anorthosis Famagusta, Raith Rovers

Bulgarian midfielder Ilian Kiriakov was as near to a World Cup winner as Aberdeen have yet to get. The flame haired star was part of the squad which finished fourth in the 1994 World Cup.and was still in the thick of the international action when he signed for the Dons in the summer of 1996.

He already had 52 caps in his locker and weeks later he was playing to a global audience at Euro 96. Kiriakov's arrival represented a major coup for manager Roy Aitken, who had spent £400,000 on a player who was cut from the same cloth as he was. Kiriakov was a fiery character who could mix it as well as play the game.

He had been turning out for Cypriot side Anorthosis Famagusta and had caught the eye in 1995 when he overshadowed Rangers counterpart Paul Gascoigne during a European tie. He had experience of the continental game at the highest level after previously featuring for Deportivo La Coruna in Spain's La Liga.

He signed a four year contract at Pittodrie, designed to tie him to the club until he was 32, but did not get off to the ideal start when, during his first pre-season trip with his new team-mates, he was fined for breaking curfew with five fellow players while at their Austrian training camp.

Kiriakov, an undoubtedly talented player, then missed the last two months of the 1996/97 season due to hepatitis. At the start of the following season he was transfer listed by Aitken as questions about the player's commitment to the cause began to surface. He went on to turn out for Raith Rovers.

Jim Kirkland

Debut: European Cup Winners' Cup, 13 September 1967 v KR Reykjavik (a) won 4-1
Appearances: League 13, Scottish Cup 2, Europe 1
Also played for: Grimsby Town

Five years of patience paid off for defender Jim Kirkland when he made his Dons debut in the 1967 European Cup Winners' Cup tie against KR Reykjavik in Iceland. Having joined from Lanarkshire youth football in 1962, it marked his transition from boy to man having risen to skipper the Dons second string. Kirkland, a natural left-back, had his path to the top team blocked by Ally Shewan and then Jim Hermiston. He had a spell as a regular under Eddie Turnbull in the 1969/70 season but was released in the summer of 1970 and joined Grimsby Town.

Peter Kjaer

Debut: League, 27 October 2010 v Hearts (h) won 3-2
Appearances: League 46, Scottish Cup 2, League Cup 2, Europe 4
Also played for: Denmark, Silkeborg (Denmark), Besiktas (Turkey)

During a time when international stars gracing Pittodrie were few and far between, the arrival of Denmark goalkeeper Peter Kjaer caused a flutter of excitement among Dons fans. The great Dane lived up to his pedigree and provided a calming influence to counter the eccentricities of the Ebbe Skovdahl era.

The former Silkeborg star was a 35-year-old veteran when he flew in to answer Skovdahl's call in October 2001 after a short stop with Turkish side Besiktas. Ryan Esson and David Preece had been vying for the keeper's jersey up to that point but were bowled out of the way by the imposing import. With physical presence that allowed him to command his box and defence in equal measure, Kjaer also displayed reflexes that made a mockery of his advancing years. He had an important role to play in the impressive run of nine home league wins in succession and provided the foundation for the results which led the club to a fourth place finish in 2001/02.

His form with the Dons extended his international career and ensured Aberdeen fans had a genuine interest in

the 2002 World Cup despite Scotland's absence, with the club's shot stopper part of the Danish squad for the finals in Korea and Japan.

When Skovdahl departed during the 2002/03 season it set the clock ticking on his compatriot Kjaer's time in Scotland. New manager Steve Paterson put his faith in Preece and allowed the more experienced man to return to Scandinavia and concentrate on building a career in the media industry as a football pundit on Danish television.

Antoine Kombouare

Debut: League Cup, 3 September 1996 v Morton (a) won 7-3 (after extra time)
Appearances: League 43, Scottish Cup 2, League Cup 5
Goals: League 3
Also played for: Nantes, Paris Saint Germain, Sion, RC Paris
Managed: Strasbourg, Valenciennes, Paris Saint Germain

Aberdeen do not throw open the doors of the Pittodrie boardroom for any signing and when the Dons convened a press call within those four walls to welcome French defender Antoine Kombouare a sense of expectation was whipped up.

The quietly spoken continental star, better known as Toni, was already the talk of the club, having made a major impact during his first training sessions with his new team-mates, and after clinching his £300,000 transfer from Swiss side Sion in August 1996 he went straight into Roy Aitken's side.

The former Paris Saint Germain captain, who had been a league and cup winner with the capital side, was already 32 when he landed on Scottish soil, tempted to the north-east by the opportunity to indulge his passion for golf and by tales of the country's quality of life from former Nantes team-mate Mo Johnston.

Kombouare, a ball playing centre-half with a steely core, had a promising start to his Dons career and acted as stand-in skipper during his first season. A dip in form and niggling injuries saw him drop out of the team and return to France to concentrate on establishing himself as a coach after a final season as a player with RC Paris. He worked with PSG's reserve side before managing Strasbourg and Valenciennes. In 2009 the former French international star was appointed manager of PSG and led his side to domestic cup success, having previously guided Valenciennes to promotion to the top flight to establish his credentials as a talented coach.

Malcolm Kpedekpo

Debut: League, 13 May 1995 v Falkirk (a) won 2-0
Appearances: League 11, Europe 1

Today Malcolm Kpedekpo is a founding partner in venture capitalists Panoramic Growth Equity, dealing in funds totalling tens of millions of pounds after carving out a glowing career in investment banking. Where did it all go wrong? Kpedekpo's decision to turn his back on football in the 1990s to concentrate on his business career may have raised eyebrows at the time but the decision has reaped rich rewards for the Aberdonian. The Aberdeen University graduate was seen as a rising striking star by Roy Aitken and was in and around the Dons first team squad for three seasons before hanging up his boots at the age of 20.

Thorarinn Kristjansson

Debut: League, 16 January 2005 v Celtic (h) lost 1-0
Appearances: League 3
Also played for: Keflavik (Iceland), Prottur (Iceland)

Trial spells with Hibernian and Dundee United proved fruitless for Icelandic striker Thorarinn Kristjansson. It was third time lucky for the attacker when he crossed the North Sea once again to finally win himself a shot at SPL football by doing enough to convince Jimmy Calderwood to award him a six-month contract in January 2005. The former Iceland under-21 starlet struggled to make an impact at Pittodrie and made just one start before heading for the Pittodrie exit. Having joined from Keflavik in his homeland he returned to his domestic league with Prottur.

Jamie Langfield

Debut: League Cup, 23 August 2005 v Berwick Rangers (h) won 3-0
Appearances (up to end 2011/12: League 191, Scottish Cup 19, League Cup 8, Europe 9
Also played for: Dundee, Raith Rovers (on loan), Partick Thistle (on loan), Dunfermline

With more than 200 appearances under his belt, goalkeeper Jamie Langfield is part of a select band of players to have hit that considerable landmark while wearing Aberdeen colours. The fact he galloped past the target in less than six years is testament to his consistency and staying power, having seen off a number of challengers for the No.1 jersey during his time with the Dons.

Langfield has come through turbulent times at Pittodrie, not least his infamous Majorcan bust-up with manager Jimmy Calderwood during the summer break in 2007. He was dumped from the side for a period on the back of that incident but knuckled down and forced his way back to re-establish himself as the main man under Calderwood, Mark McGhee and then Craig Brown.

He was a Calderwood recruit during the close

season in 2005, having also been signed by his new boss for Dunfermline a year previously. He had arrived at the Pars via a successful spell at Dundee, where he launched his career and became a Scotland under-21 international, and short stops at Raith Rovers and Partick Thistle.

The move to the north-east proved to be the catalyst to finally establishing himself as one of the best goalkeepers in the SPL and the Paisley-born shot stopper has been involved in the Scotland squad on several occasions during his time at Pittodrie. He blossomed under the tutelage of Jim Leighton during Calderwood's time in charge to learn from the best and push for Scotland honours.

David Lilley

Debut: League, 2 October 1999 v Hibs (h) drew 2-2
Appearances: League 22, Scottish Cup 3
Also played for: Queen of the South, Partick Thistle, Kilmarnock, Queen of the South

Glaswegian defender David Lilley was making a name for himself with Queen of the South when the window of Premier Division opportunity swung open for him at Aberdeen in 1999. He was signed by Ebbe Skovdahl but in three seasons at Pittodrie had to be content with a role as understudy, filling in as a centre-half and full-back. Lilley joined Partick Thistle, who had just been promoted to the top flight, in 2002 and was moved on to Kilmarnock in a £30,000 deal early in 2004. He spent more than five years at Rugby Park and made over 100 appearances before going back to Queen of the South in 2009.

Billy Little

Debut: League Cup, 14 September 1957 v Clyde (a) lost 4-2
Appearances: League 238, Scottish Cup 24, League Cup 45, Europe 1
Goals: League 78, Scottish Cup 8, League Cup 12
Also played for: Juventus (Australia), Inverness Caledonian, Falkirk, Stirling Albion, East Stirling
Managed: Falkirk, Queen of the South, East Stirling

Billy Little was a Scottish youth international forward and was being tracked by a whole pack of clubs from both sides of the border when Aberdeen took him north from Dumfries in 1957 to link up with the Pittodrie squad.

He made his debut within months and netted a hat-trick against Hibs in 1958, still only 18, to signal his potential. A burst of four goals in the last four games of 1959/60 set him up for the following term, when he took permanent possession of the No.9 shirt and hit double figures for the first time with his 13 goal haul.

By the end of 1961/62 he had finished as leading scorer for the Dons, bagging 25 goals in all competitions. A hat-trick on the opening day of the First Division marathon set him off and running.

That proved to be the pinnacle of his time in a red shirt, although Little remained with the Dons until 1969. During that time he completed a degree at Aberdeen University.

When Little severed his 12 year association with Aberdeen it was for a complete contrast. He left to join Melbourne club Juventus in Australian football, aiming to combine playing commitments with a career in teaching, but returned after a short spell to settle again in Aberdeen and turn out in the Highland League for Inverness Caledonian. He returned to the senior game with Falkirk in 1970 and went on to play for Stirling Albion and East Stirling. Little served as a coach with St Johnstone before managing Falkirk, Queen of the South and, during two stints at Firs Park, East Stirling.

Ian Lister

Debut: League, 19 October 1963 v Kilmarnock (a) lost 2-0
Appearances: League 22, League Cup 1
Goals: League 2
Also played for: Dunfermline, St Mirren, Raith Rovers, Inverness Caledonian

Manchester United trialist Ian Lister opted to accept Aberdeen's signing invitation when he made his big decision in 1963, choosing the Dons ahead of a number of clubs who were keen on recruiting the right winger after he had completed his school studies in Fife. Lister went on to be capped by Scotland's youth team while on the Dons books and was blooded in the first team by Tommy Pearson in the 1963/64 season. He was released by Eddie Turnbull after Billy Little's emergence as first choice No.7 and went on to play for Dunfermline, St Mirren, Raith Rovers and Inverness Caledonian.

Willie Logie

Debut: League, 1 August 1958 v Airdrie (h) lost 1-0
Appearances: League 5, Scottish Cup 2
Also played for: Rangers, Arbroath, Brechin City, Alloa

It was second time lucky for Aberdeen when they recruited defender Willie Logie in 1958. Logie, who was born in Montreal but moved to Scotland as a child, was a star with Cambuslang Rangers when the Dons had first expressed an interest. Leeds United, West Ham, Everton, Fulham and Falkirk were also keen but it was Rangers who landed the 6ft 1in prospect.

He sampled European Cup football with the Ibrox side before joining Aberdeen after a stint in the Rangers second string. He started the 1958/59 season in Dave Shaw's first 11 but was used mainly as an understudy to defender Ian Burns that term. He left to play out his career with spells at Arbroath, Brechin and Alloa.

Michele Lombardi

Debut: League, 8 May 2004 v Hibs (h) lost 1-0
Appearances: League 1
Also played for: Ross County, Forfar Athletic, Huntly, Deveronvale

Ayrshire lad Michele Lombardi was introduced to Dons fans as a substitute by Steve Paterson in the final weeks of his time as Dons manager in 2004.

The forward moved to Ross County and also saw service with Forfar before switching to the Highland League with Huntly and then Deveronvale.

Willie Lennie

Debut: League, 19 August 1905 v Partick Thistle (h) lost 1-0
Appearances: League 227, Scottish Cup 24
Goals: League 62, Scottish Cup 5
Also played for: Scotland (2 caps)

Aberdeen has carved out a proud reputation as a source of patriotic players for the Scotland team as well as a hotbed for recruiting passionate members of the Tartan Army. Willie Lennie was the man who launched the Pittodrie side's relationship with the national team in fine style in 1908.

Lennie was Aberdeen's first tartan foot soldier and he announced the club's arrival on the big stage with a bang. He made his debut against Wales in the British International Championship against Wales on March 7 that year at Dens Park in Dundee. He and his team-mates trailed 1-0 at the interval but a goal from Alec Bennett on the hour gave the home fans in the 18,000 crowd hope of victory – and it was Lennie who delivered with an 87th minute winner.

It was only four years and seven months since Aberdeen had played their first competitive match and Lennie's inclusion was an indication of his club's rising status in the game after humble beginnings.

The Dons had played the 1903/04 season in the Northern League but could only finish third behind Montrose and Arbroath, crashing out of the Scottish Cup in a first round tie against Alloa. It was not the dream start the founding fathers had hoped for.

Aberdeen went national the following season, finishing seventh in the Second Division, and by the time Lennie arrived in 1905 were a First Division side.

Lennie was installed as manager Jimmy Philip's first choice No.11 at the start of the 1905/06 season, making his debut in a 1-0 defeat at home to Partick Thistle on August 19. He was sidelined only once that term as the Dons found their feet in their new league, 12th in the 16 team competition.

The following season Lennie was joint top scorer with Henry Low, both hitting nine as the club moved up one place on Scottish football's ladder.

He was goal king in his own right in 1908/09 with 14 strikes but surprisingly had fallen out of the Scotland reckoning by the time he hit his peak with his club side. Lennie gained his second and last cap seven days after making his international debut, playing in a 5-0 win against Northern Ireland at Dalymount Park.

Lennie's career with Aberdeen ended in 1913, by which time he had made another unique claim for a place in the club's history books.

In the 1909/10 season he became the first Dons player to earn a benefit game and 3,000 supporters turned out for his moment in the spotlight, when Dundee provided the opposition.

The highlight of Lennie's time with the club was undoubtedly the 1910/11 campaign when he and his team-mates were just four points behind champions Rangers as they collected runners-up medals.

The Glaswegian was only 31 when he played his last game for the club. Lennie emigrated to America but returned to the north-east and ran a newsagent's shop in Aberdeen.

MAGIC MOMENTS

9 April 1955
CLYDE 0, ABERDEEN 1

It took more than half a century of trying, but at last the moment had arrived – Aberdeen were champions of Scotland. It had a nice ring to it for the Dons fans who had lived long enough to see their team grow from newcomers to overtake the establishment and reach the front of the pack. A new order was forming.

That glorious 1954/55 season was a case in point, with Hearts vying with Aberdeen for the title right up to the closing weeks of the campaign.

On the April afternoon that the Dons travelled to Shawfield to tackle Clyde, the equation was simple. Dave Halliday's team needed to win and for the Jambos not to collect maximum points when they travelled to face Rangers at Ibrox at the same time. If those blocks fell into place, the Reds would win the First Division championship for the first time in the club's history.

On paper it was simple but in practice it would be far trickier against the stuffy Bully Wee on their home patch. Just days earlier Clyde had dumped Aberdeen out of the Scottish Cup at the semi-final stage when they won the replay 1-0, suggesting another tight match was on the cards.

And that is exactly the way it played out, with the Dons not helped by the fact stars Paddy Buckley and Jack Allister were ruled out through injury. A scrappy match ensued, with chances at a premium.

One of those rare opportunities arose just 13 minutes in, when a corner from Graham Leggat caused panic in the Clyde box. George Hamilton's header was half cleared and when Bobby Wishart returned it with interest the ball was punched clear by a Clyde defender to give Aberdeen a penalty.

Allister would have been on duty had he made the team but it was left to Archie Glen to step up to the spot in his absence. Glen, who had shared penalty responsibility with Allister that season, was the coolest man on the park as he sent the ball soaring into the postage stamp corner to give his team the lead – a lead that they would preserve through to the final whistle.

Clyde piled on the pressure in the closing stages but met a resolute and determined defence who played like a unit who knew exactly what was required of them.

It was only after the match had finished that confirmation was received about Rangers' victory over Hearts in Glasgow. The 'what ifs' that had preoccupied everyone connected with Aberdeen at the start of the day had vanished and in their place was a league table that showed the Dons clear at the top – the title flag would flutter over Pittodrie after all.

The champagne flowed deep inside Shawfield as the championship winning stars marked their achievement, having secured their place as legends who would forever be part of the success story of Aberdeen Football Club.

ABERDEEN: Martin, Mitchell, Caldwell, O'Neil, Young, Glen, Leggat, Yorston, Hamilton, Wishart, Hather.

Graham Leggat

Debut: League, 12 September 1953 v Stirling Albion (a) lost 1-0
Appearances: League 109, Scottish Cup 16, League Cup 26
Goals: League 64, Scottish Cup 7, League Cup 21
Also played for: Scotland (18 caps), Banks o' Dee, Fulham, Birmingham, Rotherham, Toronto Metros
Managed: Toronto Metros

In only his 67th game as a professional football player for his home town team, Graham Leggat won the prize hundreds of Aberdeen players before him had fought so hard for over the course of more than half a century.

The former Woodside Primary School and Central Secondary School pupil was still only 20 when the Dons clinched the 1955 First Division championship and in only his second season in the first team, having signed as a 17 year-old from junior outfit Banks o' Dee.

In that time he had made the right wing berth in Dave Halliday's team his own and missed just four games in the victorious league run, weighing in with 11 goals in his 26 First Division appearances. He was exciting and inventive, a wide man with a mind of his own and an attacking verve that made him an overwhelming hit with the Pittodrie faithful.

His contribution to the League Cup triumph the following season was just as telling, bagging a hat-trick in the 5-3 win over Hearts in the first leg of the quarter-final and scoring again in the 4-2 second leg win to complete the job. Rangers were the semi-final opposition and Leggat was again on target, opening the scoring in a 2-1 win before being rushed to hospital with a shoulder injury. He overcame that pain to take his usual place in the side for the final against St Mirren and it was a good thing for the Dons that he did – popping up in the 80th minute to score with a bizarre shot from the right flank which looked harmless until it was missed by the Saints goalkeeper and nestled in the net to secure another trophy for the Pittodrie boardroom display. He finished leading scorer for his club that term with 29 goals.

International honours soon followed for a player who had already been capped at youth and under-23 level. Leggat, who had taken his bow for the Dons in 1953 in a 1-0 defeat at Stirling Albion on September 12, made his debut for Scotland on April 14, 1956, against the Auld Enemy at Hampden. It was a happy afternoon for Leggat, who marked his milestone with a goal in the 1-1 draw against England in front of 132,817 supporters.

The Aberdonian went on to win 18 caps and scored eight vital goals – on target in another 1-1 draw against England and earning the same result for Scotland in games against Wales and Northern Ireland as well as scoring in a 2-1 win against Holland and a 3-2 win against West Germany amongst others. He also earned the distinction of playing in the 1958 World Cup finals in Sweden as Scotland drew 1-1 with Yugoslavia and fell to a 3-2 defeat against Paraguay. Had it not been for a policy of concentrating on players who were turning out in the Scottish domestic league, there would undoubtedly have been further caps for one of the most naturally gifted players of his generation.

At club level, Leggat enhanced his growing reputation when he once again topped the Pittodrie scoring chart in the 1956/57 season.

In July, 1958, Fulham got themselves a bargain when they took one of Scotland's greatest talents to London for a fee of just £15,000. Leggat, with his filmstar looks and glamorous persona, had become a major figure in Aberdeen. He was one of the city's most recognised faces and had become a big fish in the small pond of the Granite City, with the attention at times proving a frustration.

His talents had not gone unnoticed by the wider audience and when the opportunity to swim in the big sea of London arose it presented an ideal opportunity for the Aberdonian star. He grasped that chance with both hands and left his home city behind, presented with an escape from the intense pressure of playing in a one team city and also benefiting from significantly improved terms and conditions with the English club. He had been unsettled for two seasons prior to his move and believed the switch south of the border was a chance to kick-start his career and prevent him from stagnating.

Leggat was an instant hit with Fulham, scoring on his debut and in the next six games he played for the Craven Cottage side. He spent eight seasons with the Cottagers before switching to Birmingham City in 1966. He stayed for two seasons with the club before a stint as a youth coach with city rivals Aston Villa.

In 1971 Leggat opened a new chapter in his life when the Toronto Metros tempted him to Canada with a player-coach role in the North American Soccer League.

While so many British players made fleeting excursions into the burgeoning US and Canadian soccer scene, for the Aberdonian it proved to be a life changing decision. The emigration was permanent and led to a shift in direction that he could not have predicted.

Within a year on foreign soil his expertise was

being put to good use in an entirely different way, with the Scotsman appointed to CBC's commentary team covering the NASL. His broadcasting career has taken in World Cup finals, Olympic games and a host of other top level events as Leggat established himself as one of the best known faces in Canadian sports television.

In 2001 he won a place in Canadian football's hall of fame but his legend lives on the other side of the world. In 2006 he joined Martin Buchan as the only two former Dons players in the city of Aberdeen's sporting hall of fame.

Jim Leighton

Debut: League, 12 August 1978 v Hearts (a) won 4-1
Appearances: League 382, Scottish Cup 49, League Cup 54, Europe 43
Also played for: Scotland (91 caps), Manchester United, Dundee, Hibs

Never before had an Aberdeen player represented Scotland as often as Jim Leighton and there is no sign on the horizon that the club's most decorated player's record will ever be broken.

Leighton made 91 appearances for his country and could have passed the magical 100 mark had he not decided to call time on his international career in controversial circumstances in 1998, when he rejected the international manager Craig Brown's plea to continue and stood by his decision to retire due to a troubled relationship with Scotland's goalkeeping coach Alan Hodgkinson. His amazing run in the national team ended on his own terms and with Leighton holding the record as the most capped goalkeeper the country has ever seen.

The Scotland journey began in October, 1982, when he made his debut in a 2-0 win against East Germany. It spanned a staggering 16 years, to his final appearance in a 3-2 win over Estonia.

In between the Johnstone born keeper had played in three World Cup finals, savouring that experience for the first time in Mexico in 1986 when he was an ever present. It was the same story in Italy four years later and again in France in 1998.

It was an amazing adventure, mirrored by a club career which had more than its share of twists, turns and fairytale moments.

Leighton was an Alex Ferguson protégé, thrown into the melting pot at the tender age of 20 when he made his debut in a 4-1 win against Hearts at Tynecastle on August 12, 1978, in place of the veteran Bobby Clark.

Clark returned to see out the season and remained No.1 until Leighton emerged from his considerable shadow in the 1980/81 campaign when he missed just two games in a marathon 48 match season.

That was nothing compared to the following season, when he and Willie Miller were the only two men to play in every single one of the 58 games the Dons played in all competitions. The reward at the end of that gruelling effort was a Scottish Cup winner's medal after the 4-1 final win against Rangers.

Leighton made another 58 appearances the next season, sitting out just one fixture, a 1-1 league draw against Hibs, and shut out Rangers in the Scottish Cup final to earn another domestic prize.

He was an ever present in the run to victory in the

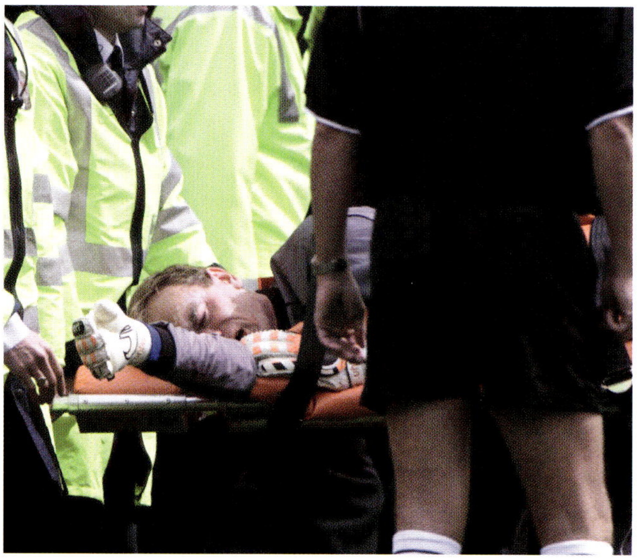

European Cup Winners' Cup, conceding just six goals in the 11 matches in the most famous sequence of encounters in the history of the club.

Aberdeen's steely defence, with Leighton as its anchor, was renowned. Despite finishing third behind Dundee United and Celtic in 1983, they conceded a miserly 12 goals in 36 games to finish the season as Scotland's meanest rearguard.

In the 1983/84 season that amazing resolve was strengthened even further as Aberdeen, with Leighton as their only ever present, lost just nine goals in 36 games on their way to the Premier Division championship. A 2-1 win against Celtic in the Scottish Cup rounded off a memorable term for the club and its goalkeeper, who had turned out 63 times between August 20, 1983, and that final against the Hoops on May 19 the following year.

Success came thick and fast for Leighton in that glorious period, with another league winner's medal secured in 1985 to join the League Cup and Scottish Cup double of the 1985/86 season.

Alex Ferguson's departure upset the rhythm at Pittodrie but Leighton remained a rock solid fixture under his successor Ian Porterfield, an ever present in 1987/88 and set a new Dons record with a remarkable 35 clean sheets in 55 games.

In the summer of 1988 he was reunited with Ferguson in a £750,000 transfer to Manchester United.

The Scotland international took over as United's first pick keeper but within two years the dream had turned to a nightmare and Leighton's relationship with his manager hit an all time low. The root cause was Ferguson's decision to drop Leighton from the 1990 FA Cup final replay against Crystal Palace, after being held up as a scapegoat for the shock 3-3 result in the first final and left in the wilderness at United after that.

He got the chance to rebuild his career when Dundee took him back to Scotland in 1992 in a £200,000 deal. A First Division championship medal was added to the Leighton collection with the Dark Blues, courtesy of 13 league games after his arrival from Old Trafford, before his 1993 switch to Hibs where the comeback was completed when the keeper returned to the Scotland team in 1994 after a four year absence.

He made 178 appearances for the Easter Road club before his homecoming to Pittodrie in 1997 when Roy Aitken took him back to Aberdeen. Leighton made 100 appearances in his second spell at Pittodrie, his playing career ending in the agony of a severe facial injury which forced him out of the 2000 Scottish Cup final against Rangers in the opening minutes. He was 41 when he played that game, his 531st and last match.

The end of one chapter marked the beginning of another as the experienced and battle scarred campaigner was called upon to pass on his expertise as a goalkeeping coach at Pittodrie, serving first under Ebbe Skovdahl and then as part of Steve Paterson's team before linking up with Jimmy Calderwood. It was during his time on Calderwood's staff that Leighton helped propel Jamie Langfield to the fringes of the national team.

Leighton's coaching credentials saw him brought into the Scotland fold, working with the country's young keepers, but were not enough to keep him in a job when former team-mate Mark McGhee took over as manager in 2009. Leighton was dismissed, replaced by McGhee's former Motherwell goalkeeping and fitness coach Colin Meldrum, but earned a reprieve when he was reappointed to the staff following Craig Brown's installation as team boss at the end of 2010.

MAGIC MOMENTS

19 April 1947
ABERDEEN 2, HIBERNIAN 1

The post war years brought a series of firsts for Aberdeen Football Club. The first championship in 1955, the first trophy with the Southern League Cup in 1946. The one that meant as much as any of the others to the Dons faithful was the first Scottish Cup in 1947.

It had marked Aberdeen out as serious contenders on the national stage and was a platform for all of the good work that followed in the years and decades afterwards.

The Red Army turned out in their thousands to welcome their triumphant heroes back to the Granite City after their Hampden exploits in the type of scenes never before witnessed in Aberdeen. It was a truly momentous occasion, with the prize claimed in dramatic fashion.

The road to the showdown with Hibs was far from easy, with close run ties in all but one of the rounds. Partick Thistle were beaten 2-1 in the opening match and then Ayr United thrashed 8-0 at the second hurdle. It took a replay to overcome Morton in the third round, with a 2-1 win at Cappielow after the first match at Pittodrie finished pegged at 1-1, before Dave Halliday's side edged past Dundee with a 2-1 win in the quarter-final. A hard fought 2-0 victory over Arbroath in the semis teed up a glittering final against Hibs, the team who would finish runners-up to Rangers in the title race and just two points off the league crown, at Hampden on an April afternoon.

The stadium was packed to the rafters as the two east coast sides ran out and there was barely time for the supporters to catch breath before the scoring was opened.

A mix-up between George Taylor and Aberdeen goalkeeper George Johnstone allowed Hibs star Johnny Cuthbertson to give the Easter Road side an early lead.

It was time for Dons legend George Hamilton to take control. His glorious header after 36 minutes brought the final all square and Stan Williams edged the Dons ahead six minutes later.

The advantage could have been even greater if Hamilton had converted from the penalty spot in the closing stages of the final. Instead Aberdeen had to cling onto their slender lead as the talented Hibs side pushed for an equaliser.

Try as they might, there was no way through for the Leith outfit as the committed Dons team defended admirably and continued to push forward looking for a killer third goal.

That never came, but it was not needed. A 2-1 win in front of 82,000 thrilled spectators in Glasgow was enough to take the Scottish Cup to Pittodrie for the first time in the club's history.

There were further appearances in the final in the years that followed, but it would be more than 20 years before that piece of silverware came to rest in the North-east again, making the significance of the 1947 success even greater.

ABERDEEN: Johnstone, McKenna, Taylor, McLaughlin, Dunlop, Waddell, Harris, Hamilton, Williams, Baird, McCall.

Andy Love

Debut: League, 21 November 1925 v St Johnstone (h) lost 1-0
Appearances: League 215, Scottish Cup 22
Goals: League 79, Scottish Cup 4
Also played for: Scotland (3 caps), Kirkintilloch Rob Roy, Aldershot, Montrose

Andy Love was another of the Dons who wore the dark blue of Scotland with pride in the early days of the club. His international career was a whirlwind affair lasting just eight days but including three games and one goal.

His first cap came in Vienna in a 5-0 defeat against Austria on May 16, 1931. Four days later he was in the touring side which lost 3-0 to Italy in Rome. By May 24 he and his team-mates were in Geneva to face Switzerland and the Dons man had the last word, scoring an 89th minute winner as Scotland returned home with a 3-2 win to atone for at least some of the disappointment caused by the first two results.

Love, a powerfully built winger adept on either flank, arrived at Pittodrie from Kirkintilloch Rob Roy in 1925 and his committed approach and powerful two-footed shooting drew favourable comparisons with star turn Alex Jackson.

The Pat Travers signing made his debut on November 21, 1925, in a 1-0 defeat at home to St Johnstone. He was used sparingly the following campaign but did score in one of the most dramatic games Pittodrie has ever seen, his goal making it 1-1 against Hearts on the first anniversary of his debut in a First Division game which ended 6-5 in Aberdeen's favour. In the 1927/28 season Love finally established himself as a regular in the first team and his scoring ratio of one goal in every three games from the wings made him a valuable weapon.

The next term he improved on that, notching 15 goals in 30 league games, and he remained a potent scoring threat until the end of his career with the club. In all, between 1925 and 1934, he scored 83 goals in 237 games and finished leading scorer in the 1931/32 campaign. He had picked up where he had left off the previous term, when he had scored his one and only Aberdeen hat-trick in an 8-1 demolition of Clyde on the last day of the season.

The Pittodrie fans appreciated Love's fearless approach to the game as much as they did his goals but it was that attitude which eventually proved his downfall. He left the Dons in 1935 and spent two years in England with Aldershot before returning for a short spell with Montrose in 1937, where a knee injury forced him out of the game. It was the last in a long line of scars inflicted in his duels with opposition defenders on both sides of the border.

His last game for the club at which he made his name as an international came in a 0-0 draw at home to St Mirren on March 14, 1934, without getting his hands on any domestic prizes. The closest call was in 1929/30 when he and his Pittodrie team-mates streaked ahead early in the First Division before slipping to third, despite boasting the only unbeaten home record in British football.

After his playing retirement Love accepted a job as a groundsman at Kings College, where he coached the Aberdeen University football team. The Renfrew born player died in 1962 at the age of 57.

Steve Lovell

Debut: League, 6 August 2005 v Kilmarnock (h) lost 2-1
Appearances: League 76, Scottish Cup 6, League Cup 1, Europe 5
Goals: League 20, Scottish Cup 1, League Cup 1, Europe 1
Also played for: Portsmouth, Dundee, Partick Thistle, Bournemouth

A price tag of £250,000 made Steve Lovell one of the grandstand signings at Aberdeen in the modern era. He was levered away from Dundee following their relegation to the First Division in 2005 and commanded that hefty fee on the back of a strong run of scoring for the Dark Blues.

He had developed a reputation as a natural goal scorer and had been pursued doggedly by Jimmy Calderwood for months before he finally sealed his move to Pittodrie in the build-up to the 2005/06 season. Leicester City had been favourites to secure the Englishman's services but had not bargained on his inclination to ignore a far better financial package at the Walkers Stadium in favour of the challenge of SPL football with the Dons.

Lovell had launched his career with home town club Bournemouth before stepping up to join Portsmouth in 1999 in a £250,000 deal. He moved north to join Dundee in 2002 and made a big impact.

With Aberdeen he provided a serious goal threat, although concerns about his workrate during games and training did surface as he toiled with injuries during three years in the north-east. Those worries were negated by his frequent appearance on the score sheet, but there was no new contract on the table in 2008 when his deal expired.

Falkirk stepped in to sign the 27-year-old and a season with the Bairns was followed by a further year with Partick Thistle before he packed his bags to head for home and sign for first club Bournemouth in 2010.

Nicky Low

Debut: League, 27 January 2010 v Hearts (a) won 3-0
Appearances (up to end of 2011/12): League 4

Promising midfielder Nicky Low had just celebrated his 18th birthday when he was handed his Dons debut by Mark McGhee. Low came back into the side under Craig Brown at the tail end of the 2010/11 season and has been tipped to cement a regular berth in the first team squad.

Tommy Lowrie

Debut: League, 17 March 1951 v Motherwell (a) drew 1-1
Appearances: League 29, League Cup 6
Goals: League 1
Also played for: Manchester United, Oldham Athletic

Defender Tommy Lowrie was one of Matt Busby's protégés at Manchester United. He spent four years at Old Trafford and saw first team action with the English side before returning to home soil with Aberdeen in the spring of 1951 in a bid to kick-start his career. Lowrie went straight into the side at the expense of Chris Anderson and kept his place for the following season. He was sold to Oldham in 1953 after a stint in the Dons reserves and spent three years with the Latics. He later returned to his native Glasgow and was one of the founding members of East Kilbride juniors.

Jamie McAllister

Debut: League, 1 August 1999 v Celtic (h) lost 5-0
Appearances: League 117, Scottish Cup 15, League Cup 8, Europe 4
Goals: Scottish Cup 1
Also played for: Scotland (1 caps up to end 2010/11), Queen of the South, Livingston, Hearts, Bristol City

Determined defender Jamie McAllister raced past a century of appearances for Aberdeen in the space of less than four top team seasons. While he was a prolific performer, McAllister never truly won over the Dons support during a period in which the club was in almost constant flux.

He was recruited as a promising young player from Queen of the South, having been part of the Doonhamers squad that won the SFL Challenge Cup in 1997, and was quickly promoted to the first team, operating predominantly at left-back under Ebbe Skovdahl and, briefly, in the early months of Steve Paterson's reign.

Despite standing just 5ft 8in tall he proved to be a dogged defender with the ability to burst forward and join in attacks, helped by pace and stamina in equal measure.

A veteran of both cup final disappointments in 1999/2000 with Aberdeen, it was after leaving Pittodrie in 2003 to join Livingston that the Glaswegian's career took off. He scored for Livi in the League Cup final victory over Hibs in the 2003/04 campaign and rounded off the season in style when he picked up a Scotland cap in a 4-1 win over Trinidad and Tobago at Easter Road.

His form won the defender a move to Hearts in 2004 and he spent two seasons at Tynecastle before heading south to Bristol City. He broke through the 200 appearance mark with the English side during the 2010/11 season having firmly established himself in the No.3 shirt.

Rory McArdle

Debut: League, 14 August 2010 v Hamilton (h) won 4-0
Appearances: League 54, Scottish Cup 9, League Cup 6
Goals: League 2, Scottish Cup 1, League Cup 2
Also played for: Northern Ireland, Sheffield Wednesday, Rochdale,

The summer of 2010 will always figure prominently for Rory McArdle when he looks back on his football memories. Not only did the Ulsterman earn a move to Aberdeen but he also became a fully fledged international player during a whirlwind week in May of that year.

He arrived at Pittodrie under freedom of contract after helping Rochdale win promotion from League Two. He was a veteran of the Dale side, despite being just 23 when he left, and had firmly established himself as a hard working defender during three and a half years as a permanent member of staff and two earlier loan stints with the same club during his days as a youngster learning his trade at Sheffield Wednesday.

Just days after pledging his future to Aberdeen he was whisked away on Northern Ireland's tour of North America and made his debut in a match against Turkey before also featuring against Chile. McArdle continued to gain international experience when he lined up against Scotland, including Dons team-mate Chris Maguire, in the Carling Cup of Nations early in 2011. Before his promotion to the full squad he had been a regular for his country's under-21 side with 17 caps to his name.

At club level his versatility was welcomed by both McGhee and Brown as he made appearances in the centre of the defence and at full-back before he was released in 2012.

Mike McArthur

Debut: League, 16 April 1988 v Morton (a) won 2-0
Appearances: League 3
Also played for: Kilmarnock

Impressive performances for Cove Rangers' under-18 side won Mike McArthur his break with Aberdeen in 1987. Ian Porterfield gave the winger a chance to shine at the tail end of the 1987/88 campaign, with two substitute appearances and one start, but he was sold to Kilmarnock for £15,000 in 1990 after drifting out of the first team scene under Alex Smith.

Kyle Macaulay

Debut: League, 4 February 2006 v Hearts (a) lost 3-0
Appearances: League 5, Scottish Cup 1, League Cup 1
Also played for: Peterhead, Alloa Athletic, Elgin City, Huntly, Formartine United

Assured and confident displays in his early days as a first team squad member under Jimmy Calderwood in the 2005/06 season ensured midfielder Kyle Macaulay was earmarked as one for the future by the Dons coaching team. Macaulay, who had served his apprenticeship with Derby County after being tempted south by the English side from his Moray stomping ground, was quickly offered improved terms after making his breakthrough but failed to live up to expectations and was loaned out to Peterhead in November 2006, where he played under his uncle Steve Paterson for the Blue Toon. He joined the Balmoor men permanently in 2007 and went on to turn out for Alloa after moving south to study in Glasgow. He returned to the north-east with Elgin City in 2009/10 before being reunited with his uncle at Huntly and then Formartine United.

John McBride

Debut: League, 12 September 1959 v Dunfermline (a) won 3-1
Appearances: League 2
Also played for: Third Lanark, Reading, Shrewsbury

Globetrotting goalkeeper John McBride was on holiday in Aberdeen when he offered his services to manager Dave Shaw, who was facing an injury crisis early in the 1959/60 season. The veteran stood in for two matches and then took off for a coaching role in Egypt, having already filled a similar role in Pakistan. The former Third Lanark, Reading and Shrewsbury shot stopper went on to coach in Australia after his Cairo posting.

Benny McCabe

Debut: League, 4 February 1967 v Ayr United (a) won 5-2
Appearances: League 1
Also played for: Berwick Rangers

When Bathgate juniors defender Benny McCabe joined Aberdeen he suffered a painful debut. Playing against Ayr United at Somerset Park early in 1967, the 18-year-old had to be replaced at half-time due to a head injury. Those 45 minutes proved to be his only first team action as McCabe, a former Celtic trialist, was released in 1969 and joined Berwick Rangers.

John McCall

Debut: League, 19 August 1959 v Hibs (a) lost 2-1
Appearances: League 1
Also played for: Airdrie, Dumbarton

Glasgow University student John McCall was interesting Rangers and Dundee when Davie Shaw stepped in and signed him for the Dons in 1959. The 18-year-old Dalry Thistle player made his debut in the first league game of the 1959/60 campaign, when Dickie Ewen was unavailable due to illness, but did not feature again.

He moved on to Ayr United in the summer of 1960 and had spells with Airdrie and Dumbarton before returning to the juniors with Glenafton in 1966.

Billy McCall

Debut: League, 10 August 1946 v Third Lanark (a) won 3-0
Appearances: League 42, Scottish Cup 7, League Cup 16
Goals: League 8, Scottish Cup 2, League Cup 5
Also played for: Newcastle, Motherwell, Third Lanark, Worcester City

Aberdeen's name would not have been engraved on the Scottish Cup for the very first time in 1947 if it had not been for the goals of inside forward Billy McCall. He was a key player in the club's passage to the 2-1 win against Hibs in the final, playing in all seven of the ties on that successful run. In fact, he sat out just a single league game that term to head the appearance chart with 46 matches to his credit.

Cup finals are one thing, but the leg work is done in the early stages and in McCall the club had a player who could be relied on to get the difficult jobs done. The Scottish Cup effort was launched against Partick Thistle in the first round when 34,000 made their way to Pittodrie. McCall settled the nerves with the opener after 30 minutes but, after a Partick equaliser in the second half, it was a rare Willie Cooper strike which put the Dons through.

An 8-0 second round triumph at home to Ayr United set-up a Pittodrie clash with Morton which ended locked at 1-1. In the replay McCall was again on target, his 16th minute strike sending Aberdeen on their way to a 2-1 win and into the quarter-final draw. Dundee, Arbroath and Hibs were swept away as McCall and his team-mates marched to the club's maiden Scottish Cup success.

It capped a memorable season for McCall, who not only made more appearances than any other player on the books but also provided a constant attacking threat. His twelve goals in all competitions put him third in the scoring chart behind George Hamilton and Tony Harris. He was playing in esteemed company in a Dons side that was a match, on their day, for any team in the land.

The club, in addition to lifting the cup, finished third and only seven points behind champions Rangers. It was the Ibrox side who had prevented the Dons from claiming a cup double, with McCall part of the team which was beaten 4-0 in the League Cup final.

It was his second season with the club and brought his second winner's medal. The first had come in the Southern League Cup of 1946 when Rangers were defeated 3-2 in the final.

Two seasons, two trophies. It couldn't get any better for McCall and he spent just one further season on the playing staff, making his farewell appearance at Pittodrie in a 2-1 win over Motherwell on January 3, 1948.

He went on to add Newcastle, Motherwell and Third Lanark to his playing credits before joining non-league English outfit Worcester City in 1953 as a career that had peaked in the north-east with Aberdeen wound down south of the border.

MAGIC MOMENTS

11 April 1970
ABERDEEN 3, CELTIC 1

Bookmakers never get it wrong. Or do they? Sometimes even those who should know better can be blinded by the allure of the Old Firm and in 1970 that was certainly the case as Celtic were installed as 6-1 favourites to dump the Dons in the Scottish Cup final to complete a domestic double.

The First Division champions, who had romped clear of Rangers at the head of the table that term, were expected to blow away an Aberdeen side that, under Eddie Turnbull, had just scraped into the top half of the league.

Jock Stein's well oiled machine, on their way to nine-in-a-row, had not bargained on the nature of the emerging Dons side that Turnbull was sculpting. With influential young captain Martin Buchan epitomising the ethos developing at Pittodrie, there was confidence from front to back in the starting 11 that day.

They had carefully negotiated a path through to the final by defeating Clyde 4-0 in the first round and then Clydebank 2-1 at the next stage. That was when Derek McKay came into his own, scoring the only goal of the quarter-final against Falkirk and then netting the winner in the semi-final against Kilmarnock when again his was the only name on the score sheet.

With a place in the final secure, there was a long build-up for the eager Dons fans to endure and time for Turnbull to carefully formulate his plan to get the better of the country's dominant football force.

A crowd of 108,434 gathered in Glasgow, the bulk cheering for the local team. That sizeable green and white contingent were in for a rocky ride and after just 27 minutes they had that confirmed as Joe Harper put his side 1-0 up from the penalty spot.

Scottish Cup talisman Derek McKay had a role to play, firing in the cross which was handled by Bobby Murdoch to concede the spot kick. Tensions were running high, with Tommy Gemmell booked for hurling the ball at the referee after the penalty award.

Aberdeen weathered the storm and doubled their lead in the 83rd minute when that man Cup Tie McKay gathered a loose ball following a save by Evan Williams from Jim Forrest's run and shot before firing home a perfect shot from a tight angle.

Celtic had a lifeline six minutes later when Bobby Lennox scored to set up a grandstand finish.

What nobody predicted was that Aberdeen would be stung into an immediate response, scoring in the 90th minute to put clear water between them and Celtic.

This time Harper broke on the right as Celtic pushed for an equaliser, faked to go one way but instead picked out McKay with a pass in the opposite direction and the hero of the hour lashed home the decisive goal.

Skipper Buchan held aloft the Scottish Cup and the celebrations began, carrying on at the team hotel and than back in Aberdeen as more than 100,000 supporters turned out to welcome home the winning players.

ABERDEEN: Clark, Boel, G. Murray, Hermiston, McMillan, M. Buchan, McKay, Robb, Forrest, Harper, Graham.

Frank McDougall

Debut: League, 18 August 1984 v St Mirren (a) won 2-0
Appearances: League 54+5, Scottish Cup 6, League Cup 6, Europe 3+1
Goals: League 36, Scottish Cup 3, League Cup 4, Europe 1
Also played for: Clydebank, St Mirren

Achieving legendary status can take some players an entire career but for Frank McDougall it happened in the space of 90 minutes inside his first season at the club. A hat-trick in a 5-1 rout against Rangers at a packed Pittodrie early in 1985 did the trick, the Pittodrie fans revelling in their team's demolition of the Light Blues and their new recruit's goalscoring knack.

It was a sweet moment for McDougall, who was a Celtic fan as a boy, but he did not reserve his most devastating displays for games against the Ibrox men. Later that year he destroyed the Hoops with a four goal blitz in a 4-1 win at Pittodrie to become the first player since 1975 to score hat-tricks against both halves of the Old Firm and there has yet to be a repeat. They were heady days for the player and fans alike and the bond remains strong in the north-east.

He played for just two full seasons but picked up more honours and scored more goals than many players do in a lifetime, including a sought after Premier Division winner's medal from the 1984/85 season.

He completed the clean sweep in his second season with matching 3-0 wins against both Edinburgh sides in the League Cup and Scottish Cup finals, Hibs steamrollered in the first competition and Hearts in the second.

In both of his seasons as Aberdeen's No.9 the striker finished leading scorer, bagging 24 in his first term and 20 in his second. He scored three hat-tricks in the space of those two seasons, with Hearts sunk by a McDougall treble at the end of 1984/85 to join Celtic and Rangers on the list of victims.

In terms of sheer impact there have been few to match McDougall. Would he have gone on to surpass Joe Harper had his career in red been prolonged? We will never know, but he had the potential to do just that. Only Hans Gillhaus and Duncan Shearer have had the same type of instant appeal in the decades since McDougall made his mark.

He made his debut on August 18, 1984, back on his old haunt at Love Street as the Dons beat his former St Mirren team-mates 2-0. The first of many goals came a fortnight later in a 4-1 win against Hibs at Pittodrie.

He was prolific and consistent, going on a run of seven consecutive games on target between October 6 and November 24 that year to help the team to 12 points from a possible 14.

After one year and 360 days, 75 games and 44 goals it was all over. A serious back injury cut McDougall down in his prime, with a solitary appearance from the bench

at the start of the 1986/87 season in a 4-0 win at home to Hibs marking the end of his career at the age of 28. He had limped out of that game, struck down again by back pain that had forced him to take injections simply to get through matches. His training was also hindered, leading to concerns about fitness and match sharpness even before the injury took him out of the picture completely.

Doctors had found a small bone floating around his spine, a condition that may have been present from birth. The player expected surgery or a lengthy period of rest, but six months later he received the devastating news that he would never kick another ball in anger. The news was delivered on his 29th birthday. He returned from the trip to the specialist, was handed a modest pay off by the Dons and bid a tearful farewell to his colleagues at the end of a short but dramatic stay at Pittodrie.

By his own admission he was not what would be classed as a model professional in modern terms - his favourite meal on the eve of a big game was vindaloo washed down with lager - but he was a model goalscorer.

The Glaswegian, who grew up in the tough Cadder area of the city, was a schoolboy international and was picked up by Hearts at the age of 16. Homesickness led to a return to the west coast with Partick Thistle and spells with Glasgow Perthshire and Clydebank followed. He had been a champion amateur boxer in his youth but chose to concentrate his sporting efforts on football.

It was with the Bankies that McDougall's reputation was built, netting 40 goals in his only season at Kilbowie.

That led to a record breaking £180,000 switch to St Mirren in 1979, with the Paisley side out-bidding Celtic to complete the deal. He starred in black and white alongside Frank McAvennie, with the duo proving as dangerous off the pitch as they were on it as they embraced their star status.

In 1984 Aberdeen paid £100,000 to add McDougall to Alex Ferguson's illustrious squad and his goals proved vital to the success the club enjoyed in the short time he was on the books. In the league winning season of 1984/85 he was the golden boot winner in the Premier Division with 22 league goals and third in the European pecking order - yet that form was still not good enough to earn international recognition, with not a single cap to the striker's name by the time he was forced out of the game.

Following his injury McDougall relocated to England and for a spell ran a pub in Bury. He returned to Aberdeen in 2008 to take over the running of The Criterion bar on Guild Street and in 2010 released his autobiography *McDougoal* to a Dons audience still appreciative of his impressive contribution to the cause.

Walker McCall

Debut: League, 5 January 1974 v St Johnstone (h) lost 1-0
Appearances: League 68, Scottish Cup 2, League Cup 10, Europe 2
Goals: League 22, League Cup 1
Also played for: Ayr United, San Diego Sockers, Atlanta Chiefs, Dundee

The influence of Aberdeen scout Bobby Calder persuaded Walker McCall to snub interest from Ayr United and Kilmarnock in his native Ayrshire and commit to the Dons as a young man. It proved a life changing decision, with the Irvine-born star still living and working in the north-east long after hanging up his boots.

McCall signed from Hurlford United juniors in 1970 with an impressive track record as a goal scorer in juvenile football, although it was two years later that he was called up full-time by the Dons. He eventually made his first top team appearance early in 1974 and was a regular goal scorer during his appearances in the starting line-up until his departure for Ayr in 1976.

A spell in the USA with the San Diego Sockers and Atlanta Chiefs was sandwiched between another stint with Aberdeen, which came about after his brother in law Dougie Bell asked Alex Ferguson if McCall could train with the Dons in 1980 to keep himself ticking over. He impressed in those sessions and was offered a short term deal - a short term deal that ended up with a three year stay as a valuable squad man during the glory days.

It was during the course of the 1982/83 campaign that the popular attacker finally called time on his Pittodrie career. Periods in Hong Kong and then back on home soil with Dundee capped his career in the professional game and McCall settled into a life in the oil industry.

John McConnachie

Debut: League Cup, 29 August 1959 v Kilmarnock (h) lost 4-2
Appearances: League 2, League Cup 1

Defender John McConnachie filled in for Jim Clunie in three matches during he 1959/60 season. All three ended in defeat, with 11 goals conceded, and the Kilsyth Rangers youth product's dreams of a long career in an Aberdeen shirt were shattered. He was one of 33 players used during a turbulent season that saw manager Dave Shaw replaced by Tommy Pearson.

John McCormick

Debut: League, 17 October 1964 v Motherwell (h) lost 1-0
Appearances: League 28, Scottish Cup 2, League Cup 2
Also played for: Third Lanark, Crystal Palace, Queens Park Rangers (on loan)

Experienced and strong centre-half John McCormick cost close to £10,000 when he was lured from Third Lanark in the autumn of 1964. The Glaswegian had spent five years in the Cathkin Park side's first team and was the man Tommy Pearson hoped would shore up a leaky defence as he took possession of the No.5 shirt. The emergence of Tom McMillan the following season led to limited opportunities and McCormick moved on to Crystal Palace in time for the 1966/67 season. He spent seven years with the London club, which included a loan spell with Queens Park Rangers in which he helped his new side to promotion to the First Division, before dropping into non-league football with Wealdstone.

Murray McCulloch

Debut: League, 8 May 2004 v Hibs (h) lost 1-0
Appearances: League 3
Also played for: Inverurie Locos, Cove Rangers

Defender Murray McCulloch had already been told he was being released when he was blooded by Steve Paterson in 2004. McCulloch started one match and appeared from the bench in two others before heading to England to qualify as a PE teacher. He combined his new profession with playing commitments in the Highland League and, after a spell with Inverurie Locos, won the title with Cove Rangers in 2009.

Frank McDonald

Debut: League, 3 May 1947 v St Mirren (h) won 4-2
Appearances: League 1

Frank McDonald was one of four players used to fill the left-back berth in the six matches regular No.3 Pat McKenna missed in the 1946/47 season. McDonald's contribution was to help Aberdeen to a 4-2 win against St Mirren at Pittodrie before being released by Dave Halliday.

Gary McDonald

Debut: League, 9 August 2008 v Caley Thistle (h) lost 2-0
Appearances: League 52, Scottish Cup 3, League Cup 3, Europe 2
Goals: League 8, Scottish Cup 1, League Cup 1
Also Played for: Kilmarnock, Oldham Athletic, Hamilton

Gary McDonald was the model of midfield consistency with an average of 30 games and five goals per season during his two year stay in Aberdeen. He was not a household name when he was landed on a free transfer from Oldham Athletic in August 2008 but the Ayrshire man quickly settled into Jimmy Calderwood's team at Pittodrie and became an indispensable component in the engine room with his drive and stamina.

The Irvine-born player, who appeared in the Scotland Future team in 2005, spent five years with Kilmarnock after bursting onto the first team scene in 2001. After more than a century of appearances for Killie he was lured south by Oldham in 2006, notably scoring the winning goal for the Latics against Everton in the FA Cup in 2008.

He was invited to extend his stay at Boundary Park but chose instead to accept Calderwood's contract offer. His impressive first season with Aberdeen was followed by an indifferent second campaign under Mark McGhee, during which his reluctance to commit to the club along with captain Mark Kerr led to a cooling in the support from the Red Army for the midfield duo.

When McDonald departed in the summer of 2010 it was not for a bigger club, instead returning closer to his west coast roots by linking up with Billy Reid at Hamilton Accies as the Lanarkshire side prepared for another fight to retain their SPL status.

Ian MacFarlane

Debut: League, 15 October 1955 v St Mirren (a) won 3-0
Appearances: League 16, Scottish Cup 1
Also played for: Chelsea, Leicester City, Bath City
Managed: Carlisle United

Glaswegian Ian McFarlane played as a goalkeeper in youth and junior football before his conversion to become a top flight defender. MacFarlane, recruited from junior side Douglas Walter Thistle in 1954, played in both full-back positions during the 1955/56 season before being headhunted by Chelsea at the end of his first term. The Stamford Bridge side paid £12,000 for the emerging Dons talent and he went on to play for Leicester City and non-league Bath City before embarking on a coaching career which took him to Sheffield Wednesday and Sunderland.

He stepped up to become manager of Carlisle United before coaching with Middlesbrough, Manchester City, Sunderland, Leicester City and Burnley.

Neil MacFarlane

Debut: League, 28 January 2006 v Kilmarnock (h) drew 2-2
Appearances: League 6
Also played for: Queen's Park, Kilmarnock, Clyde, Hearts, Gretna, Queen of the South, Morton, Airdrie United, Annan Athletic

Experienced, reliable, professional, committed and available for free. Hearts midfielder Neil MacFarlane ticked all of the boxes for Jimmy Calderwood in the

January transfer window of 2006. MacFarlane, who had spent four years as a squad man at Tynecastle after cutting his teeth with Queen's Park, Kilmarnock and Clyde, was viewed as the ideal deputy for Scott Severin at the heart of the engine room but struggled to make an impact and was released after just half a season. He went on to wear the colours of Gretna, Queen of the South, Morton and Airdrie United before landing at Annan Athletic early in 2011.

Phil McGuire

Debut: League, 11 December 1999 v Celtic (h) lost 6-0
Appearances: League 152, Scottish Cup 14, League Cup 8, Europe 6
Goals: League 10
Also played for: Doncaster Rovers, Caley Thistle, Formartine United, Arbroath

Liverpool were among the clubs linked with a move for Phil McGuire when he was at the peak of his powers as one of Scotland's most promising young defenders. Having broken into the Aberdeen team as a teenager, McGuire emerged as a cool and composed player with confidence that belied his tender years.

Those qualities helped him make close to 200 appearances for the side during barren years, establishing himself as a Scotland under-21 and B international player along the way and drawing admiring glances from rival teams.

Questions over McGuire's pace and a lack of height for a central defender appeared the chink in the armour and the big move never did materialise. Instead it was Doncaster who provided the exit route after Jimmy Calderwood decided against renewing the defender's contract at the end of the 2004/05 season.

He spent just a year south of the border, appearing in less than half of his new side's games, before popping up in Fife with Dunfermline Athletic. A season with the Pars got McGuire back into the swing of first team football and he was signed by Inverness Caledonian Thistle boss Craig Brewster for the 2007/08 campaign. After two years in the Highlands he was released by the Caley Jags and made a surprise move to Highland League newcomers Formartine United. A spell with Arbroath followed in 2010 before hopes of a switch to Cypriot football were scuppered by financial problems in his country of choice. McGuire signed for ambitious Dundee junior outfit Lochee United in January 2011.

Mark McGhee

Debut: League, 1 April 1979 v Morton (a) won 1-0
Aberdeen record:
Appearances: 164+12, Scottish Cup 20, League Cup 34+1, Europe 31+1
Goals: League 61, Scottish Cup 7, League Cup 18, Europe 14
Also played for: Scotland (4 caps), Morton, Newcastle, SV Hamburg, Celtic
Managed: Reading, Leicester City, Wolverhampton Wanderers, Millwall, Brighton

You should never go back. It was left to Mark McGhee to prove that particular football rule in spectacular fashion late in 2010 as his dream return to Pittodrie lurched into a recurring nightmare.

The Gothenburg Great will forever be a legend at Aberdeen after inspiring the Dons to European success in 1983. When the call to return to his spiritual home came from director of football and old friend Willie Miller in the summer of 2009 it proved just too strong a pull to resist.

He was tempted away from Motherwell to succeed Jimmy Calderwood and arrived with lofty ambitions and grand plans. Those were quickly shot to pieces when Sigma Olomouc defeated the Dons 8-1 on aggregate in his first European tie and domestic results were also shaky, not least cup reverses at the hands of First Division outfits Raith Rovers and Dundee during his first season. The 2010/11 campaign started in positive fashion but an embarrassing 9-0 defeat at Celtic was the beginning of the end for McGhee, who was eventually dismissed following a 2-0 loss at Kilmarnock.

The sorry saga proved that playing credentials provide no guarantee of managerial success. While supporters began to grow weary of his efforts to breathe life into the modern day Dons team, nobody could question his achievements during his playing heyday in the 1980s.

John Hewitt scored the winner in Gothenburg but it was McGhee who finished the European Cup Winners' Cup campaign as Aberdeen's top scorer in the competition. His cross for Hewitt's match-winner in the final against Real Madrid was his decisive contribution to that stunning run but his six goals in the 10 games prior to Gothenburg were as important.

He got off and running with a strike in the first leg of the preliminary round against Sion at Pittodrie as the Dons brushed their Swiss opponents aside with a 7-1 win and notched a double in the 4-1 victory in the return leg.

His second round goal at Pittodrie in the first leg against Polish outfit Lech Poznan was crucial, breaking the deadlock against stuffy opponents with the opener in a 2-0 win. His double in the first leg of the semi-final against Belgian side Waterschei at home gave Aberdeen a 5-1 cushion to take across the channel and virtually guaranteed the final berth.

McGhee proved he could score in European competition but he was equally emphatic on the domestic scene, with 16 goals in the league on top of four in the League Cup and one in the Scottish Cup to make him leading scorer with 27 in total as the club won both the European prize and the Scottish Cup.

He led the way in the Pittodrie stakes three times in just five

full seasons to justify the £80,000 fee Alex Ferguson paid to sign him from Newcastle United in 1979. He was just 21 at the time and claimed his main aim was simply to establish himself in the first team.

McGhee need not have worried about that. He made his debut in a 1-0 win away to Morton, the club where he launched his career, on April 1, just days after signing and was a permanent fixture for the remaining 10 games of the season.

He opened his Aberdeen scoring account in his third game with the only goal of the game away to Partick and made the healthy return of four goals in 11 appearances.

In 1979/80 he made 21 league appearances to earn a Premier Division winner's medal and was leading scorer for the first time the following season with 17 goals, although the Dons ended up empty handed.

His first Scottish Cup medal came in dramatic circumstances in the 1982 final. Rangers and Aberdeen were locked at 1-1 going into extra time but McGhee's 93rd minute header put them on their way to success. Ten minutes later he turned provider, flicking the ball back for Gordon Strachan to make it 3-1 before Neale Cooper added a fourth in the 110th minute. McGhee had also opened the scoring in the 3-2 semi-final replay win against St Mirren.

After the double celebration of the 1983/84 campaign he remained bang in form the following term with 24 goals, including 13 in the Premier Division as Aberdeen stormed to the title. The west coast striker added another Scottish Cup goal to his collection, along with another medal, when he scored the only goal of extra time from a Strachan assist to secure a 2-1 victory against a Celtic side reduced to 10-men when Roy Aitken was dismissed for an assault on McGhee after just 40 minutes.

It proved to be the striker's final game in the red of the Dons as he secured a lucrative and life changing move to German club SV Hamburg in the summer of 1984. He used the freedom of contract rules as they stood at the time to secure a £280,000 move.

Injuries wrecked the Scotsman's hopes of making it big on the continent and in 1985 he returned to home soil with Celtic. He rounded off his playing career with Newcastle before moving into coaching as manager of Reading in 1991.

As a player McGhee won four caps, all while on the Dons staff, in the space of a year. He marked his June, 1983, debut with a goal in a 2-0 win in Canada and scored his only other international goal on his final appearance in Dark Blue when he hit the net in a 1-1 draw against England at Hampden in May, 1984.

McGhee quickly established himself as a promising boss and his ruthless ambition led to quickfire moves to first Leicester, in 1994, and then Wolves from 1995 to 1998. He managed Millwall between 2000 and 2003 before a three year stint in charge of Brighton which ended in 2006. He was given his first Scottish assignment by Motherwell and was a revelation at Fir Park as he pieced together an attacking and attractive side that qualified for Europe, leading to his switch to Aberdeen in 2009. He joined Bristol Rovers in 2012.

Ernie McGarr

Debut: League, 21 October 1967 v Hearts (h) lost 2-1
Appearances: League 43, Scottish Cup 7, League Cup 8
Also played for: Scotland (2 caps), Kilbirnie Ladeside, Dunfermline, East Fife, Cowdenbeath, Airdrie, Berwick Rangers

Ernie McGarr is a legend of football trivia. He did not win medals, he did not play many games but the goalkeeper did win two international caps to make Aberdeen the answer to a favourite with pub quiz comperes everywhere: which club provided Scotland with two international goalkeepers in one season?

McGarr and Bobby Clark both forced their way into Bobby Brown's first team within months of each other in a bizarre series of events sparked by a dip in form Clark suffered in the 1968/69 season. After shipping 11 goals in just two games, six against Hibs and five against Dunfermline, Clark found himself banished to the touchlines by Eddie Turnbull.

That opened the door for McGarr, who had made his one and only appearance for the club up to that point in a 2-1 home defeat at the hands of Hearts on October 21, 1967. His re-introduction to the Dons team came in December the following year but he was again on the losing side, with Airdrie winning 2-0.

Despite the result the new No.1 did enough to persuade Turnbull to keep the faith and he kept the gloves for the remaining 25 games of the season, 19 in the league as the Dons steered clear of the relegation places and six in a Scottish Cup run that ended with a shattering 6-1 semi-final defeat against a Rangers side inspired by a Willie Johnston hat-trick.

McGarr was not held responsible for the dramatic collapse and won the affection of the Aberdeen fans over the course of the season with a flamboyant style and habit of producing spectacular saves.

When Aberdeen started the 1969/70 season he retained the goalkeeper's jersey and caught the attention of the Scotland manager. Brown handed McGarr his first cap on September 21, 1969, against the Republic of Ireland in Dublin.

The national team was gearing up for a vital World Cup qualifier against West Germany but injury wrecked McGarr's hopes of securing a place in that game. He went into the game against Ireland carrying a thigh strain and lasted just 35 minutes before he had to be replaced by James Herriot, who retained his place for the clash with the Germans a month later with McGarr as his understudy.

He did make it into the starting 11 for the World Cup qualifier against Austria in Vienna in November, 1969. A 2-0 defeat in that game was the latest blow to the qualification hopes of the struggling national side.

Any hopes McGarr had of making it back into the Scotland team were shattered when he lost his club place to Clark in February, 1970. Clark took McGarr's jersey at Aberdeen and completed his rapid return to favour when Brown fielded him as the country's No.1 against Northern Ireland in the British International Championship just two months later.

He asked for a transfer in 1970 and won a move to Dunfermline early the following year after five years with Aberdeen, where he had arrived in October 1965 as a 20 year-old recruited from Kilbirnie Ladeside. In 1972 he made the short hop to East Fife, playing out his senior career with Cowdenbeath, Airdrie and Berwick before packing away his gloves in 1980.

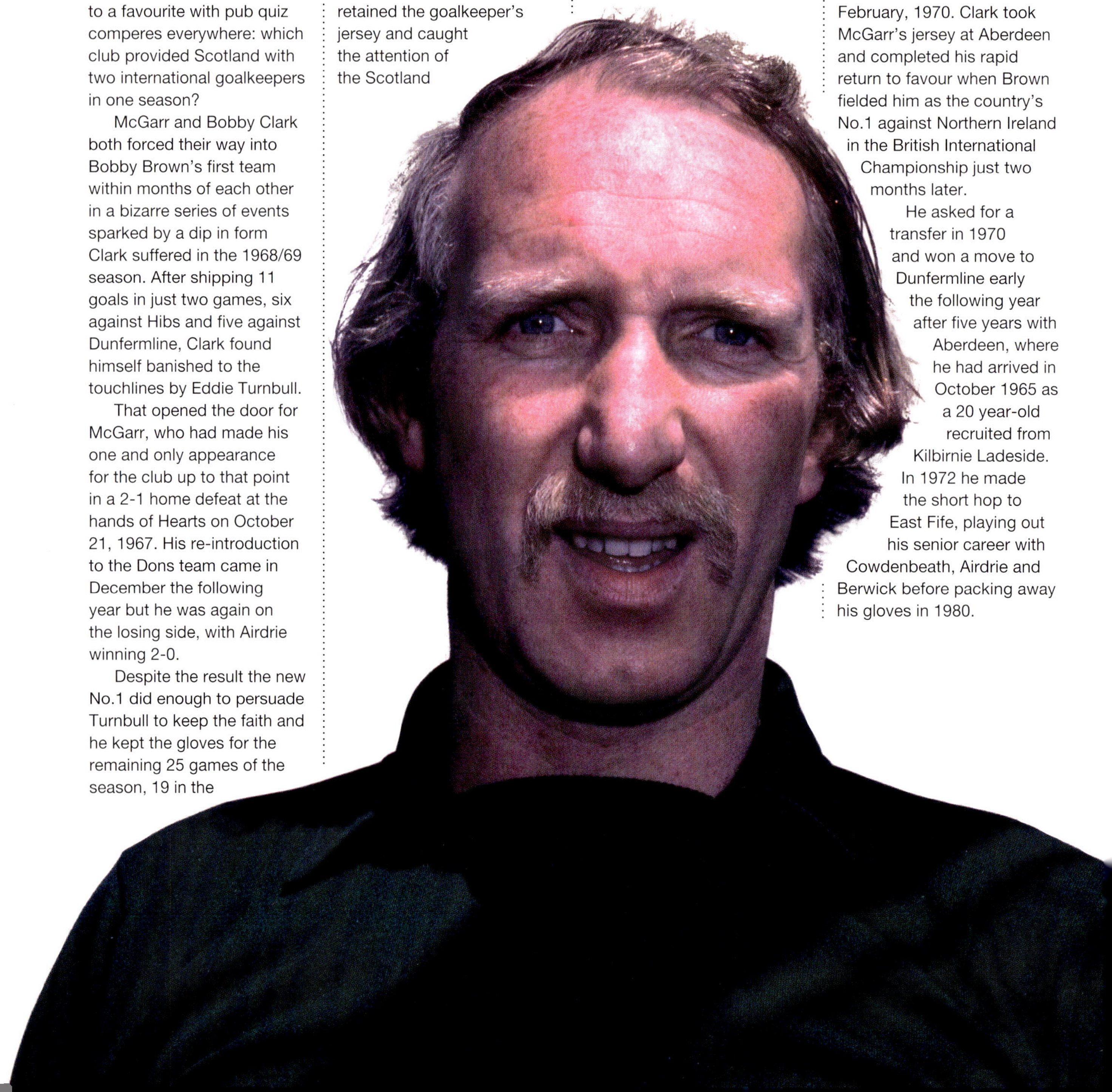

Brian McIlroy

Debut: League, 29 October 1969 v Celtic (h) lost 3-2
Appearances: League 6
Also played for: Rangers, Kilmarnock

Championship winning Kilmarnock winger Brian McIlroy was in the twilight of his career when he moved north to Pittodrie in 1969. The 29-year-old, who had been on Rangers' books as a teenager, was released after a decade of service at Rugby Park and filled in for half a dozen games after joining the Dons. He was released in 1970 and retired from the senior game.

Graham McInnes

Debut: League, 22 November 1958 v Clyde (a) lost 4-0
Appearances: League 1
Also played for: Morton, Elgin City, Inverness Caledonian, Clachnacuddin

Davie Shaw's first signing as Aberdeen manager was young forward Graham McInnes from now defunct junior side 25th Old Boys in August 1955. McInnes, a member of the city's junior select, played a single game on the right wing just three months after joining. He joined Bury in 1959 and had a short spell in Canadian football before returning to Scotland with Morton and then starring in the Highland League with Elgin City and Inverness clubs Caledonian and Clach.

Willie McIntosh

Debut: League Cup, 8 August 1964 v Rangers (a) lost 4-0
Appearances: League 7, League Cup 6
Goals: League 1, League Cup 1
Also played for: East Stirling, Highland Park (South Africa), Atlanta Chiefs (USA)

When East Stirling stormed to promotion to the First Division in 1964 they had dashing winger Willie McIntosh among their heroes. The Firs Park minnows turned full-time in a bid to make the most of their top flight opportunity but were relegated, leading to McIntosh's decision to look for an alternative club to preserve his full-time status. Tommy Pearson and Aberdeen obliged when he wrote a £4,000 cheque and McIntosh started 1964/65 in possession of the No.11 jersey before being replaced by Bobby Hume, Andy Kerr and then import Leif Mortensen. Following his Pittodrie release in 1965 the former Hearts youngster moved to South Africa to play for Highland Park and also had a stint in America with the Atlanta Chiefs.

Jimmy McIntyre

Debut: League, 3 January 1950 v Hibs (h) lost 3-0
Appearances: League 2
Also played for: Arbroath

Forward Jimmy McIntyre played two matches under Dave Halliday in 1949/50. Both ended in defeat and the former Kilbirnie Ladeside player was allowed to join Arbroath at the end of that campaign. McIntyre, who had been called upon to deputise for Archie Baird by the Dons, spent a season with the Red Lichties in the Second Division.

Tommy McIntyre

Debut: League, 8 October 1983 v St Mirren (h) won 5-0
Appearances: League 29, League Cup 3
Also played for: Hibs, Airdrie

Alex Ferguson rated young defender Tommy McIntyre highly and handed the Fir Park Boys' Club youth product his debut less than six months after the glory of Gothenburg in 1983. He proved an able deputy for Doug Rougvie at right-back but was restricted to a bit part role and was snapped up by Hibs manager Alex Miller at the start of 1987 to mark the start of a seven year association with the Easter Road side which brought more than a century of appearances. McIntyre also served with Airdrie before retiring in the late 1990s.

Pat McKenna

Debut: League, 1 September 1945 v Celtic (a) drew 1-1
Appearances: League 134, Scottish Cup 17, League Cup 30
Also played for: Blantyre Celtic, Plymouth Argyle, Arbroath, Fraserburgh

Only four players were ever present in both of Aberdeen's victorious runs in consecutive seasons in the Southern League Cup and Scottish Cup in the 1940s. Frank Dunlop, Billy McCall and Stan Williams were three and Pat McKenna completed the quartet.

The Glaswegian was an unspectacular player but totally dependable and his record of two trophy wins in seven seasons at Pittodrie stands up to scrutiny.

The full-back played 181 games for the Dons without scoring a single goal but his forte was defending. He proved to be a formidable member of the rearguard.

Speed was central to McKenna's role within the team and one of the qualities which persuaded Dave Halliday to gamble on the Blantyre Celtic player in 1944, taking him north as a 24 year-old. He made his post-war debut in a 1-1 draw at Parkhead on September 1, 1945, in a team which was proving to be capable of mixing with the big guns of the Scottish game. That season the Dons lost just one game at home, when Clyde escaped with full points, and went on to finish third as Celtic won the league and Hibs took the runners-up spot.

The next visit ended in disappointment, with a 4-0 defeat in the 1946/47 League Cup final against Rangers.

Fourteen days after that shattering blow McKenna was back in his No.3 shirt for the Scottish Cup final against Hibs to play his part in the famous 2-1 victory.

The Dons had once again finished third in the league, the best they could do during McKenna's seven year stay. When he was hospitalized for an appendix operation in the summer of 1950 he missed the start of the season and struggled to force his way back into Halliday's plans as Dave Shaw established himself in the left back berth.

In August, 1952, McKenna moved from the north-east coast of Scotland to the southern shore of England when he linked up with Plymouth Argyle at the age of 32. He spent a season with Argyle as they finished fourth in the Second Division before returning to Scotland with Arbroath in Division 2. McKenna wound down his playing days in the Highland League with Fraserburgh.

Derek McKay

Debut: Scottish Cup, 21 February 1970 v Falkirk (a) won 1-0
Appearances: League 15, Scottish Cup 3, Europe 1
Goals: Scottish Cup 4
Also played for: Deveronvale, Dundee, Forres Mechanics, Barrow, Siu Fong, Durban United, Keith, Kiev, Ross County

Derek McKay played football on three continents and for an array of clubs but one place will always have a special place in his heart. That place is Hampden Park, the scene of the far travelled player's legendary heroics.

The date was April 11, 1970, and more than 108,000 were shoe-horned into the national stadium to watch champions Celtic tackle Eddie Turnbull's unfancied Aberdeen side.

Joe Harper's 27th minute penalty gave the Dons the initiative but one goal was never likely to be enough to keep the Hoops at bay. When McKay tucked home the rebound after a Jim Forrest shot had been parried in the 83rd minute the impossible dream looked almost probable. Bobby Lennox looked to have set-up a tense final minute when he reduced the deficit to 2-1 in the 89th minute but within seconds McKay had completed his double and won the trophy for the Dons with a neat left footed goal.

Without McKay's goals the club would not have even reached the final, let alone won it. A close range 66th minute goal in the quarter-final, part of a man of the match performance, secured a 1-0 win against Falkirk. In the semi-final he scored the only goal of the match against Kilmarnock in the 22nd minute to take the Dons through to the Celtic showdown.

The legend of Cup Tie McKay was born, with the Scottish Cup return of four goals in his only three games in that season's competition a stunning contribution from a player who only mustered 12 league starts and not a single First Division goal in his Pittodrie career.

He arrived at Aberdeen just in time for the cup quarter-final against the Bairns, making his debut in that tie on February 21, 1970. He had moved to Dens Park as a 16-year-old, having caught their eye playing as a winger for Deveronvale in his native Banffshire, but was freed by the Dark Blues less than four years later.

After stealing the show in the cup final he completed the league season with two top team starts and looked set for a key role in the 1970/71 campaign, in the first 11 for two of the three league openers and in the 3-1 European Cup Winners' Cup first round first leg victory against Honved at Pittodrie.

That proved to be the final appearance of a short but very sweet stay with the Dons, with McKay freed by Turnbull in April, 1971.

He returned to the Highland League with Forres that summer but within weeks, and after three appearances, had switched to English Fourth Division side Barrow.

In 1972 McKay accepted his first foreign assignment, joining Hong Kong side Siu Fong, and sampled Australian football briefly before joining Durban United in South Africa late in 1973.

Within a year he was back in the north-east with Keith but before long was back on his travels, adding Australian club Kiev to his growing list of attachments. Ross County, in 1978, became the 15th club on his playing cv. McKay soon returned to Australia, where he remained until his death in 2008.

Billy McKenzie

Debut: League Cup, 22 August 1959 v Stirling Albion (a) won 5-2
Appearances: League 2, League Cup 1
Goals: League Cup 1
Also played for: Arbroath, Elgin City, Peterhead

More than a century of goals for junior side Banks o' Dee, not to mention a Scottish Junior Cup winner's medal, persuaded Aberdeen to give the inside forward his big break. The 20-year-old scored against Stirling Albion on his debut but made just three more appearances before joining Arbroath on a free transfer in 1960. After a year at Gayfield he moved to the Highland League with Elgin City and then Peterhead.

Ralph MacKenzie

Debut: League, 5 May 1947 v Morton (h) drew 2-2
Appearances: League 12, Scottish Cup 5, League Cup 4
Also played for: Dundee United (on loan), Arbroath (on loan), Falkirk, Dundee

Defender Ralph MacKenzie was a man a series of managers turned to throughout the 1940s and 50s in times of need. He joined Aberdeen in the post-war years and featured sporadically for the Dons for four years, during which time he was loaned first to Dundee United in the 1947/48 campaign and then to Arbroath the following term.

It was Falkirk, the club he joined when he was released by Aberdeen in 1950, that MacKenzie enjoyed his most consistent run of first team football, as he made more than a century of appearances before moving on to Dundee in 1956. He later served as coach to Elgin's contingent of Aberdeen-based players.

Tony McKeown

Debut: League, 7 January 1950 v Third Lanark (a) lost 3-1
Appearances: League 2
Also played for: Pike Rovers

Tony McKeown had a reputation as one of Irish football's rising stars when he was snapped up by Aberdeen in 1949. The former Pike Rovers player, who had taken part in league representative matches in his home country while playing for Rovers in Limerick, made two appearances at right-back, in place of Don Emery, but struggled to make an impact and was released.

Darren Mackie

Debut: League, 14 August 1999 v Dundee (h) lost 2-0
Appearances: League 313, Scottish Cup 19, League Cup 28, Europe 9
Goals: League 58, Scottish Cup 6, League Cup 3, Europe 2
Also played for: Caley Thistle (on loan)

He is the ultimate Marmite player. For every Aberdeen supporter who loved Darren Mackie for his dedication and never say die spirit there appeared to be another who remained unconvinced. Regardless of public opinion, Mackie outlasted player after player on his way to becoming one of his side's longest serving players.

Managers have come and gone since he made his first appearance way back in 1999 but each one of them has seen the merit of relying upon the pace and dogged qualities of the striker. From joining the

Dons as a youth signing from Inverurie juvenile outfit Colony Park there was only one interruption to Mackie's career with Aberdeen. In the second half of the 2003/04 campaign he was loaned to Inverness Caley Thistle by Steve Paterson but he has rejected any notion of a permanent move away from Pittodrie.

He went on to become Aberdeen record goal scorer in the SPL and also contributed vital goals at vital times. The most important was his goal in the Uefa Cup qualifier against Dnipro in the Ukraine in 2007/08 to earn a passage to the lucrative group stages of the competiton. Mackie's early goal was cancelled out by a late Dnipro equaliser but it was enough to clinch a win on the away goal rule. It was his 50th goal for the club and a vital one.

Mackie, entitled to a testimonial after more than a decade of service for the Dons, turned 29 at the end of the 2010/11 season and already had well over 300 appearances in the bag by then. He was released in 2012.

Ray McKinnon

Debut: League, 2 April 1994 v Rangers (a) drew 1-1
Appearances: League 26, Scottish Cup 3, League Cup 5, Europe 2
Also played for: Dundee United, Nottingham Forest, Luton Town, Livingston, Raith Rovers, Ayr United, East Fife, Montrose

Many managers tried to get the best out of Ray McKinnon but only one truly succeeded. It was as a youngster under Jim McLean at Dundee United that McKinnon showed the best form of his career, earning a £750,000 move to Brian Clough's Nottingham Forest in 1992. He failed to hit the heights in England and was offered an escape route by Willie Miller and Aberdeen in 1994 with a £300,000 move. McKinnon, a skilful and creative midfielder, never fully settled at Pittodrie and drifted in and out of the side under Miller and then Roy Aitken. He returned to Tannadice in 1995, sold for £200,000, and also had spells with Luton and Livingston as well as a string of lower league sides in Scotland before moving into management with junior side Lochee United.

Joe McLaughlin

Debut: League Cup, 12 October 1946 v Falkirk (a) won 1-0
Appearances: League 47, Scottish Cup 8, League Cup 15
Also played for: Hamilton Academical, Raith Rovers

Scottish Cup winning wing-half Joe McLaughlin cut his teeth with Celtic before returning to competitive action after the war with Hamilton Accies. The left sided player was quickly lured north by Aberdeen and spent three years as a dependable servant at Pittodrie before moving on for a matching tour of duty with Raith Rovers. McLaughlin switched to Irish football in 1952 when Sligo Rovers tempted the experienced campaigner across the sea. McLaughlin was one of the stars of the Scottish Cup winning team in 1946/47, an ever-present in the run to the 2-1 victory against Hibs in the Hampden final and a lynchpin of that famous side.

Steven MacLean

Debut: League, 2 February 2010 v Falkirk (h) lost 1-0
Appearances: League 16, Scottish Cup 2
Goals: League 5
Also played for: Rangers, Scunthorpe (on loan), Sheffield Wednesday, Cardiff, Plymouth, Oxford United (on loan)

Steven MacLean returned to Scotland in January 2010 with a point to prove after more than five years in exile. The former Rangers trainee had built an impressive track record in the English leagues with Scunthorpe, Sheffield Wednesday and Cardiff City before a £500,000 move to Plymouth Argyle in 2008 stalled his progress. He fell out of favour at the south coast club and was loaned to Mark McGhee and the Dons to kick-start his career, a process helped by five goals in 18 Aberdeen appearances – including a double in a pulsating 4-4 draw against Celtic at Pittodrie. MacLean returned to Plymouth at the end of his temporary stint in a red shirt but was loaned to Oxford United in 2010/11.

Ally MacLean

Debut: League Cup, 14 August 1976 v Kilmarnock (h) won 2-0
Appearances: League 9, League Cup 3
Also played for: Ayr United, Partick Thistle

Agile goalkeeper Ally MacLean started and finished the 1976/77 season as first choice goalkeeper after following manager Ally MacLeod's path from Ayr United to Aberdeen. The former Scotland amateur international made eleven appearances in Dons colours but could not keep Bobby Clark out of the reckoning and, when Clark returned from illness, had to concede defeat in his efforts to cement his place in the side. In 1978 the penalty save specialist moved back to Ayr and later turned out for Partick Thistle and then Irvine Meadow in the junior ranks.

Chic McLelland

Debut: League, 9 February 1964 v Dumbarton (h) won 3-0
Appearances: League 181, Scottish Cup 18, League Cup 35, Europe 6
Goals: League 3, League Cup 1, Europe 1
Also played for: Motherwell, Dundee, Montrose
Managed: Montrose

Chic McLelland was a fixture in the Aberdeen team for the bulk of the 1970s. The reliable left-back made his debut under Jimmy Bonthrone, was a regular for Ally MacLeod, featured prominently for Billy McNeill and also played in the vast majority of fixtures in Alex Ferguson's maiden season at Pittodrie.

Between 1973 and 1979 he clocked up 240 appearances across all competitions – the only thing he lacked was a winner's medal, having missed out on the semi-final and final during the successful Scottish Cup run in 1976/77 and suffering the pain of Hampden defeat in the League Cup final two seasons later.

By the time the Dons won the championship in 1980, the No.3 shirt was shared between Doug Considine and Doug Rougvie. McLelland by then was plying his trade with Motherwell, having joined the Fir Park outfit in the summer of 1979 when his former Dons boss MacLeod came calling and invited him to move to Lanarkshire.

The Glasgow boy, who had joined Aberdeen as a teenager from Eastercraigs in his native Glasgow in 1969 and went on to win youth international caps, also played for Dundee before accepting a player-coach role with Montrose in 1983. He also served as a youth coach with the Angus side before stepping up to become co-manager with Rougvie in 1990 for a season in charge. He moved into a community coaching role with the SFA in the north-east in 1992 and then with Aberdeen, as part of the community and youth coaching staff, until his departure from Pittodrie in 2007.

Andy MacLeod

Debut: League, 3 September 1988 v Hibs (h) drew 0-0
Appearances: League 1
Also played for: Fortuna Sittard (Netherlands), Ross County, Brora Rangers

Highlander Andy MacLeod made just a single appearance in a 0-0 draw against Hibs at Pittodrie before being released by Alex Smith in the summer of 1989. The Invergordon youngster, who had come through the Dons youth ranks, won a move to Dutch outfit Fortuna Sittard and spent 15 months in the Netherlands before returning to win the Highland League title twice with Ross County. He later moved to Brora Rangers.

George McMillan

Debut: League, 6 January 1951 v St Mirren (h) drew 1-1
Appearances: League 1
Also played for: Forres Mechanics, Huntly, Fraserburgh, Newport, Wrexham, Peterhead

A broken neck early in his days with the Dons did not prevent winger George McMillan from carving out a long career in football at home and abroad. After recovering from that sickening injury, suffered in an accident at work outside of the game, he made a single appearance in a red shirt in 1951 before a tour of the Highland League which took him to Forres, Huntly and Fraserburgh. The former Bridgeton Waverley man also featured for Peterhead after spells with Newport and Wrexham in Wales and then emigrated to Australia to continue playing and coaching in the 1960s.

Declan McManus

Debut: League, 28 April 2012 v Dunfermline (a) lost 3-0
Appearances (up to the end of 2011/12) : League 2

Teenage hot-shot Declan McManus emerged at the tail end of the 2011/12 season as the senior team drew a blank in the SPL. Having averaged close to a goal a game for the under-19 side, Craig Brown gave McManus a brief taste of top team life with cameos from the bench against Dunfermline and Kilmarnock and tipped the 17-year-old to have a bright future with the club.

Jackie McNamara

Debut: League, 4 August 2007 v Dundee United (a) lost 1-0
Appearances: League 17, Scottish Cup 3, League Cup 2, Europe 3
Also played for: Dunfermline, Celtic, Wolves, Falkirk, Partick Thistle
Managed: Partick Thistle

With 31 Scotland caps and a trophy cabinet of honours from a decade of service at Celtic, there was no question Aberdeen had found a man with experience and pedigree to bolster the Pittodrie squad when he agreed to join Jimmy Calderwood's squad in May 2007. He had returned to Scotland after an injury hit two year spell with Wolves and hoped for a fresh start. McNamara suffered from a dip in form and fitness before moving on to Falkirk in the summer of 2008. Two years with the Bairns included a loan period at Partick Thistle and the defender joined the Jags permanently in time for the 2010/11 season. McNamara, who was appointed manager of Partick in 2011, had launched his career with Dunfermline in the early 1990s.

Stewart McKimmie

Debut: League, 17 December 1983 v Hibs (h) won 2-1
Appearances: League 430+1, Scottish Cup 47, League Cup 48, Europe 39+1
Goals: League 9
Also played for: Scotland (40 caps), Dundee, Dundee United

When it comes to Aberdeen legends, Stewart McKimmie ticks every box. An Aberdonian born and bred, the defender was a loyal servant and captain as well as winner of every domestic honour and a star on the international stage.

McKimmie also has continental success on his list of honours courtesy of the European Super Cup medal he won in only his second game as an Aberdeen player.

A product of Aberdeen juvenile club Deeside, he clocked up more than 100 appearances for Dundee before being taken home to Aberdeen by Alex Ferguson in December,1983, in a £90,000 deal. It was a significant fee at the time but one that the manager was prepared to pay for a player who was yet to hit his peak.

At the age of 21 he made his Dons debut in a 2-1 home win against Hibs on December 17 and three days later retained his place for the second leg of the Super Cup showdown with Hamburg. After a 0-0 draw in Germany, a 2-0 home victory secured the title.

It was an early taste of what was to follow in a trophy laden fourteen year stay with the club, with a Premier Division medal collected in his debut season thanks to 17 appearances and another joining it when the championship was retained in 1984/85 when he missed just two league games. It was an appearance record only beaten by Willie Miller and matched by Jim Leighton.

Despite his tender years he smashed through the century mark of games for the Dons in the 1985/86 campaign on his way to adding League Cup and Scottish Cup winner's medals to his burgeoning collection.

Ferguson, who had considered buying Tosh McKinlay before opting for the McKimmie signing, had once again proved a shrewd judge in the transfer market and a succession of managers benefited from his neat piece of business. McKinlay, who was a team-mate of McKimmie's at Dundee, later got his big break with Celtic and Scotland but few Dons fans would attempt to argue that the Hoops got the better deal.

Under Ian Porterfield and then the team of Alex Smith and Jocky Scott the defender proved to be an automatic selection as a right back who was a tenacious tackler and an enthusiastic attacker on the wing. With a young and spritely David Roberston on one flank and McKimmie on the other, the Dons had the best pair of full-backs in the business during the late 1980s and their promptings from wide proved valuable in the triumphs of the time.

McKimmie was an ever present in the two runs which brought both the League Cup and Scottish Cup in the 1989/90 season for Smith and Scott's team.

By that time he was a fully fledged member of the Scotland squad, having made his debut in May, 1989, in a 2-0 defeat against England in the Rous Cup. Days later Andy Roxburgh gave the Pittodrie player his second cap in a 2-0 win against Chile in the same event but it was against the world champions Argentina early in 1990 that he sealed his place in the international party for the World Cup in Italy that summer.

McKimmie scored the most famous goal of his career at Hampden Park when he ventured forward in the 32nd minute to rifle home a spectacular winner. It proved to be one of the defining moments of his career, a goal that was a fitting highlight to his dedicated service at international level.

He played against Brazil and Costa Rica in Italia 90, adding to his big stage experience in Euro 92 and Euro 96 when he played all three group games in Sweden and in the huge ties against Holland and hosts England in 1996.

The Euro 96 adventure, which brought his 40th and final cap, came just months after one of McKimmie's proudest moments as an Aberdeen player when he joined a select band of trophy winning Dons captains as he led his side forward to collect the League Cup in the 1995/96 season after the 2-0 victory over his former club Dundee. The only other Aberdonian ever to lift a prize while wearing the red shirt was Martin Buchan more than

quarter of a century earlier, putting the 1990s captain in esteemed company.

He had taken over the skipper's armband from Alex McLeish following his departure for Motherwell in 1994, the same year in which McKimmie was honoured with a testimonial against Blackburn. He was passionate about his club, a quality that brought him into conflict with supporters on occasion as tensions ran high, and a heart on sleeve skipper who was prepared to lead from the front. Those are the leadership qualities that have proved so elusive in the post-Millennium years, a period in which success has proved just as hard to find.

Like Ferguson, Porterfield, Smith and Willie Miller before him, Roy Aitken relied on McKimmie as a defensive mainstay. Having launched his career as a full-back, he became adept as a central defender in the second half of his Pittodrie career and his versatility proved valuable. Despite not having the height of McLeish or Brian Irvine, pace and sharpness allowed him to function through the centre of the back four and allowed him a berth which brought his organizational skills to the fore.

The League Cup proved to be the last of many cup final appearances for the club. He was released in March 1997 and made the short move to Dundee United, where he remained for a further season before retiring at the age of 35. McKimmie, who made 564 appearances for Aberdeen and scored nine goals, retains his involvement in football through his role as a newspaper columnist with the *Evening Express* and contributions to radio coverage of the Dons.

Alex McLeish

Debut: League, 2 January 1978 v Dundee United (h) won 1-0
Appearances: League 493+2, Scottish Cup 68+3, League Cup 74+1, Europe 56+1
Goals: League 25, Scottish Cup 2, League Cup 2, Europe 1
Also played for: Scotland (77 caps).
Managed: Scotland, Motherwell, Hibs, Rangers, Birmingham.

Never let it be said there is no room for humour in football. During a 0-0 draw at Ibrox, with Aberdeen inflicting more pain on Alex McLeish and his toiling Rangers team in 2005, the Dons fans unfurled a banner with a cutting message.

Signed off with Willie Miller's name, it simply read: Agent McLeish, mission accomplished, return to base.

While the Pittodrie faithful revelled in the fall from grace their arch rivals suffered under their one time playing hero, in truth most would welcome him back with open arms if he were to decide to test his managerial skills in Scottish club football at some point in the future.

Most, but not all. Moving to Rangers is an unforgivable act in the eyes of some Aberdeen fans, as many who have made the switch have found in the past, but for the majority McLeish will always be considered a Don first and foremost.

Before the prospect of a return to the club game even loomed on the horizon he has far bigger fish to fry as manager of the national side, a job inherited from Walter Smith. For one of Scotland's most revered and respected players it truly was the dream job.

The football journey started almost 30 years ago, with the first glimpse of the McLeish-Miller partnership coming two days into 1978. Willie Garner had broken the team's curfew and manager Billy McNeill thrust a flame-haired 17 year-old into action in his place.

It was a one-off move that season but the birth of one of Scottish football's greatest defensive partnerships. For the record, it also marked the first clean sheet for the duo as the Dons defeated Dundee United 1-0.

It was under Alex Ferguson that the Barrhead born central defender truly blossomed, bedded in over the course of the 1978/79 season before cementing his place the following term as Ferguson claimed the Premier Division championship for the first time. He relied heavily on McLeish, who turned 21 mid way through the season, and nobody played more games than he did in that nail-biting league race which went right to the final match.

His list of honours with Aberdeen is phenomenal. The Scottish Cup in 1982 and again in 1983 and 1984, the European Cup Winners' Cup and the European Super Cup, two further league championships, another Scottish Cup in 1986 and then a cup double in the 1989/90 season. That double winning season also saw him recognized as Scotland's player of the year.

McLeish outlasted every one of his Pittodrie contemporaries during his career. By the time he left in 1994, Miller had graduated to become team boss.

In 17 years as a first team player he played in 696 games and scored some vital goals among his career total of 30.

Among the most memorable goals was the sublime curling equaliser against Rangers in the 1982 Scottish Cup final, one

facet of a man of the match performance in a game his side went on to win 4-1 after extra time.

Against Bayern Munich in the second leg of the European Cup Winners' Cup semi-final in 1984, he once again moved forward from the heart of the defence to level the scores at 2-2 with a typically imperious header from a Gordon Strachan free-kick. A minute later John Hewitt made it 3-2 and the Dons were on their way to the most famous victory Pittodrie has ever seen.

Of course it was as a defender of international standing that McLeish made his biggest mark on the game. He and Miller took their vaunted partnership into the world arena with Scotland throughout the 1980s.

McLeish made his debut for the national team in March, 1980, in a 4-1 win against Portugal under Jock Stein. A further 76 caps followed to catapult him into the SFA's hall of fame.

His international career coincided with a purple patch for Scotland and allowed him to play in the World Cup finals in 1982, 1986 and 1990. He was booked only once in those 77 internationals, a measure of his talents as a defender who did not have to rely on muscle to compete at the top level.

In 1994 it took an offer McLeish could not refuse to break his bond with the Dons. The chance to follow Miller onto the managerial ladder with Motherwell tempted him south and he got his coaching career off to a promising start when he led the Steelmen to second place in his rookie season as a manager.

He switched to Hibs in 1998 to join a club in turmoil and could not prevent their relegation. The First Division championship in 1999 followed and in 2001, with Hibs chasing the Old Firm at the head of the SPL table, Rangers made their move.

McLeish enjoyed tremendous success initially, winning the championship in 2003 and 2005 as well as the Scottish Cup twice and the League Cup three times. Even as his exit loomed after a run of poor domestic form, McLeish became the first manager to lead a Scottish team into the last 16 of the Champions League. He left Ibrox at the end of the 2005/06 season to be replaced by Paul Le Guen and rejected several approaches from English clubs before accepting the role of Scotland manager at the start of 2007.

He proved an accomplished coach at international level, most notably masterminding the stunning James McFadden inspired 1-0 victory over France in Paris inside his first year in the Hampden job. In November 2007 the former Dons defender left the Scotland post to become manager at Birmingham, failing to save the Blues from relegation but steering them back to the top flight at the first attempt and establishing himself as one of English football's most respected managers by building a solid and well drilled side at St Andrews without breaking the bank. Success in the League Cup in 2010/11, when the highly fancied Arsenal were defeated in the Wembley final, cemented his reputation, before his cross-city switch to Aston Villa for a solitary season.

1969-70: Arthur Graham; Derek McKay; Bobby Clark; Davie Robb; George Buchan; George Murray; Henning Boel; Jim Forrest; Jim Hermiston; Joe Harper; Martin Buchan; Tommy McMillan.

Tommy McMillan

Debut: League Cup, 21 August 1965 v Rangers (h) won 2-1
Appearances: League 172, Scottish Cup 23, League Cup 45, Europe 8
Goals: League 1, Europe 1
Also played for: Neilston, Falkirk, Inverness Thistle
Managed: Inverness Thistle, Fraserburgh

Martin Buchan played the captain's role in the 1970 Scottish Cup final victory against Celtic but playing a key supporting role was his defensive partner Tommy McMillan. Both men were given their big break by Eddie Turnbull in the second half of the 1960s and both were at the heart of the defining moment of that era, when the Dons collected the club's first piece of silverware for 15 years with a 3-1 win against the Hoops.

The McMillan and Buchan partnership which served Turnbull so well in every one of the five Scottish Cup ties in 1970 never had the chance to flourish, with the skipper's departure after the Hampden final taking him on to bigger and better things in England.

While Buchan's career was still in its infancy when the trophy was claimed, McMillan was an experienced campaigner. He was a robust centre-half but, having played as an inside forward as a schoolboy, was also prone to attacking excursions up field.

Aberdeen came within a whisker of missing out on their target when Turnbull moved in for McMillan, who had been starring for Neilston Juniors, in the mid 1960s. He was preparing to board a plane, bound for a new life in Australia, when he got the call from Pittodrie. Without hesitation he ditched his plans to emigrate and travelled north, leaving behind his job as an electrician to become part of the recently recruited vision for a new-look Aberdeen team.

He made his debut in a League Cup tie against Rangers on August 21, 1965, and got off to a winning start as goals from Jorg Ravn and Billy Little earned a 2-1 victory.

He went on to miss only two league games in his debut season, quickly established as a key player for his new club.

His arrival coincided with an improvement in form for the club, finishing eighth in the First Division compared to 11th the previous term. The 1966/67 season proved even more fruitful. McMillan played 48 times, missing just a single game, and helped the Dons up to fourth in the table. His form at the heart of the defence ensured his first taste of international football, called up by the Scotland under-23 team in November, 1966, for a game against Wales and again in March the following year. They were his only caps at any level and brought two victories.

The 1970/71 season marked the beginning of the end of his Pittodrie career, with Willie Young emerging to take over as the defensive pivot Turnbull's side revolved around.

The Paisley born former under-23 cap moved to Falkirk in a £10,000 deal in 1972 and spent 15 months at Brockville before switching to the Highland League with Inverness Thistle in 1973. He went on to become a successful manager of the north side, winning a succession of cups before resigning to take a job in the North Sea oil industry. A stint in charge of Fraserburgh followed in 1978.

David McNamee

Debut: League, 1 January 2011 v Dundee United (h) drew 1-1
Appearances: League 9, Scottish Cup 2, League Cup 1
Also played for: Scotland (4 caps), St Mirren, Blackburn Rovers, Coventry City, Plymouth Argyle

Scotland international defender David McNamee holds the distinction of being Craig Brown's first signing as Aberdeen manager. The Glaswegian arrived on a free transfer from Plymouth Argyle at the end of 2010 to give Brown a natural choice for the left-back berth. McNamee, capped four times between 2004 and 2006, emerged with St Mirren before being snapped up by Blackburn Rovers in 1999. He returned north to play for Livingston in 2002 before joining Coventry four years later and then moving on to Plymouth. After being deemed surplus to requirements by the cash strapped south coast club he trained under Craig Brown at Motherwell and was on the verge of signing for the Steelmen when the manager moved to Pittodrie, taking his Fir Park trialist with him.

Ian McNeill

Debut: League, 6 January 1951 v St Mirren (h) drew 1-1
Appearances: League 7, League Cup 3
Goals: League 1
Also played for: Leicester City, Brighton
Managed: Shrewsbury Town, Wigan Athletic

Chelsea and Leeds United both benefited from the expertise and experience of renowned talent spotter Ian McNeill. He served as chief scout for the English giants before retiring to Aberdeen as his 80th birthday loomed, returning to the city where he had started his football adventure. McNeill joined from Glasgow side Bridgeton Waverley at the start of the 1950s and made his debut in 1952. He remained in and around the first team squad, playing on the wing and as a forward, until the end of the 1955/56 campaign when he moved to Leicester City under former Dons manager Dave Halliday. He also played for Brighton and coached Ross County, managed Shrewsbury and also Wigan, on two occasions, as well as serving as assistant manager at Chelsea in the 1980s before embarking on his scouting career.

Jamie McQuilken

Debut: League, 9 August 2003 v Hearts (a) lost 2-0
Appearances: League 7, League Cup 1
Also played for: Celtic, Dundee United, Hibs, Falkirk, St Johnstone, Gretna, Queen of the South

There were high hopes for energetic full-back Jamie McQuilken when he travelled north to complete his £60,000 move from Falkirk in the summer of 2003. He had displayed excellent pace, endeavour and determination during five years with the Bairns after initially making his breakthrough with Celtic, Dundee United and then Hibs. McQuilken went straight into Steve Paterson's team but struggled to impose himself in the top flight and was made available for transfer just six months later. He spent a season with St Johnstone before two and a half years with Gretna preceded three seasons with Queen of the South in the First Division.

John McMaster

Debut: League Cup, 24 August 1974 v Dunfermline (h) won 3-0
Appearances: League 205+32, Scottish Cup 29+5, League Cup 54+7, Europe 28+3
Goals: League 20, Scottish Cup 4, League Cup 9
Also played for: Peterhead, Morton

Aberdeen supporters do not suffer fools gladly and when 16,500 of them turned out to pay tribute to the sophisticated skills of John McMaster in his 1985 testimonial against a Billy McNeill Select it served as a significant gauge of the regard in which he was held by the paying public in the Granite City.

He was a hero to the masses and nobody grudged him a lucrative benefit year to recognise his dedication to the Dons cause. It was fitting that Liverpool manager Kenny Dalglish made a contribution – since it was one of the Merseyside club's players who came close to ending McMaster's career prematurely.

Five years prior to his testimonial, in a European Cup tie against the Anfield club at Pittodrie, he was scythed down by Ray Kennedy. He had a knee operation within hours and surgeons informed the Pittodrie heirachy that their player, cut down in his prime, would never play again.

McMaster defied the odds to return to the game he loved and, after almost a year on the sidelines it was business as usual for the versatile left sided player. The easy route would have been to take the initial medical advice and retire, but there was enough hope remaining for the dedicated star to believe there was light at the end of the tunnel. He had tasted success and was desperate for more.

By the time he suffered that injury setback McMaster was already the proud owner of a Premier Division championship medal having played in all but three of Aberdeen's league games on the way to the 1980 title. He was also knocking on the door of the Scotland squad but his hopes were dashed by Kennedy's rash challenge and in the end he never won the cap he craved.

At club level, his return to action in 1981/82 allowed him to take his place in the side for the 4-1 Scottish Cup final win against Rangers and he again played in the 1983 final against the Ibrox men when the Dons recorded a 1-0 win.

By then McMaster and his team-mates were champions in the European Cup Winners' Cup. He started seven of the 11 games in that campaign, making two additional contributions from the bench – with his substitute's appearance against Bayern Munich in the 3-2 success in the second leg of the quarter-final particularly telling.

McMaster turned from player to play actor as he and Gordon Strachan feigned a mix-up over who was to take an attacking free-kick as Aberdeen trailed 2-1. After pretending to collide, Strachan turned swiftly to swing in the free-kick which provided Alex McLeish with the chance to head home the equaliser and set-up John Hewitt's winner. The audacious McMaster and Strachan move bamboozled the German defenders.

He forced his way back into the starting 11 for the second leg of the semi-final against Waterschei and was handed the No.3 shirt for the tumultuous 2-1 final win against Real Madrid in Gothenburg.

He was 28 at the time of the final and, not surprisingly, it proved to be the peak of his career. McMaster played a third of the 1983/84 league campaign to earn another championship medal, adding a European Super Cup badge to the collection, but a serious ankle injury kept him out of the successful defence of that title.

After struggling to regain his place in the side, Ian Porterfield granted McMaster a free transfer as a thank you for his service to the club which had spanned fifteen years and brought an incredible array of trophy highs and injury lows.

McMaster first caught the attention of Aberdeen scout Bobby Calder while turning out for Port Glasgow Rovers, champions of the Paisley and District Under Age League, in 1971. The Reds kept a close eye on his progress and McMaster shone in a Dons trial match against East Fife the following year, alongside Rovers team-mate Bobby Street. Both youngsters were signed.

McMaster, a 16-year-old left winger, made his reserve team debut just 10 days after moving to the club and the following season was loaned to Peterhead in the Highland League. He scored two goals for the Blue Toon in a 2-2 draw against the Dons in a friendly towards the end of that campaign, having also scored a double for the Buchan side in a 2-1 win against the Pittodrie reserves weeks earlier, and that form persuaded Aberdeen to recall him immediately.

He made his first team debut on August 24, 1974, in a 3-0 League Cup win against Dunfermline at Pittodrie, and went on to appear 363 times and score 33 goals. He never ventured away from the club he joined as a teenager despite interest from various sides during his time in the north-east, most notably from Ayr United after McMaster had fallen out of the side in 1977. The move looked certain to be pushed through, but the player opted

out and vowed to fight for his place with typical spirit. It proved to be a blessing for both McMaster and Aberdeen as his best years were ahead of him and success soon followed at home and abroad.

When he eventually was told his Dons days were numbered, he switched to his hometown club Morton to serve as player coach under Alan McGraw and Jackie McNamara senior and then assistant manager. In more recent years McMaster's vast knowledge has been put to use by Middlesbrough and Aberdeen as he has embarked on a new career as a scout. He worked as part of Jimmy Calderwood's team at Pittodrie, compiling reports on opposition teams, and also formed part of the club's talent spotting network for the youth academy in the Glasgow area.

Kevin McNaughton

Debut: League, 5 August 2000 v St Mirren (h) won 2-1
Appearances: League 165+10, Scottish Cup 13, League Cup 9, Europe 5
Goals: League 3
Also played for: Scotland (4 caps to end of 2010/11), Cardiff City

When a home grown player rejects a new contract in favour of searching for greener grass on the other side of the border the traditional feelings of outrage and betrayal from the supporters in the stand are understandable.

The fact Kevin McNaughton left with the blessing of both his management team and the fans despite exiting Pittodrie in those circumstances hints at the regard in which he was held at the club which nurtured him on his path from schoolboy to fully fledged international.

Jimmy Calderwood desperately wanted to retain McNaughton's services when his Aberdeen deal expired in the summer of 2006 but there was no bitterness when the final decision was made and the versatile Dundonian moved on to Cardiff City to help the Welsh club in its quest for a Premiership place.

Despite uncertainty over his future for the last five months of his final season, there was never any question among the management team or the fans that he would continue to give his all to the cause.

McNaughton was part of a crop of youngsters blooded within the space of two seasons by Ebbe Skovdahl. Jamie McAllister, Darren Mackie, Kevin Rutkiewicz, Phil McGuire, David Lilley, Calum Bett, Fergus Tiernan, Ross O'Donoghue and Scott Michie were all catapulted into the first team as the Danish coach raided the youth ranks in an attempt to boost the club's flagging fortunes.

McNaughton is the only one of that group to have gone on to play for Scotland's national team and truly thrive in the club game.

He came into the team at the start of the 2000/2001 season. The previous season the club had finished rock bottom of the SPL and only avoided a relegation play-off because First Division promotion hopefuls Falkirk could not meet top flight stadium criteria.

It was a gloomy time for the club but McNaughton's introduction as a substitute in a 2-1 home win against St Mirren on August 5, 2000, provided a spark to give hope of brighter times ahead.

From that point on he was assured of a starting place, fitness permitting, and as an 18 year-old made 38 appearances in his rookie season. McNaughton, who had come through the coveted Pittodrie youth system, began his career as a left-back but went on to become a victim of his own versatility – playing on both sides of the defence, as a sweeper and in every position across the midfield during his six years of first team duty.

In only his second season McNaughton was crowned Scotland's young player of the year, the accolade coming on the back of his selection for the international side. He took his Scotland bow in front of an appreciative Pittodrie crowd on April 17, 2002, in a friendly against Nigeria. McNaughton, who was the first Dons player to turn out for the national team since 1999, played 90 minutes in a 2-1 defeat against the powerful and talented Africans.

Berti Vogts was the coach who gave McNaughton his big break and heaped praise on his new boy following his first appearance – but the German did as much to damage his career at that level as he did to aid it.

Vogts withdrew McNaughton from his starting 11 the day before he was due to make his debut against World champions France in Paris a month before the Nigeria game. Vogts claimed the Dons player was too nervous to play, a bizarre explanation and one of the first of the blunders which would become familiar as Vogts' tenure progressed.

The national coach criticised McNaughton for a second time following his second appearance for the team, in a 1-0 defeat against Denmark in 2002, after withdrawing him at half-time. Not surprisingly it damaged the relationship between the pair further and McNaughton did not appear again under Vogts.

He returned for his third cap, a 4-1 defeat against Sweden, when Tommy Burns took control on a temporary basis and returned to the international fold under Walter Smith in 2006.

At club level McNaughton, who played 202 games and scored three goals, was unfortunate to arrive at Aberdeen during troubled times and domestic honours proved only a dream as the Dons toiled under Skovdahl, Paul Hegarty and Steve Paterson before Calderwood's arrival sparked a revival.

His decision to leave at a time when the club was on the up was bold but paid off when Cardiff mounted an immediate challenge for promotion to the Premiership and the Scottish recruit emerged as a valued defensive cog for an ambitious team with dreams of making it to the big time.

At the time of writing, in 2012, the Dundonian is approaching his seventh season as a Blues player to surpass his achievement of making more than 200 appearances for Aberdeen. While Cardiff continue to knock on the door of promotion from the Championship, the highlight for the former Dons starlet was the FA Cup run of 2007/08. It ended at Wembley in the final, when Portsmouth lined up against their Welsh opponents in the showpiece match.

McNaughton won a place in the starting eleven and was integral to the side as the underdogs set about the Premier League favourites with vigour, playing to an audience of almost 90,000. A goal from Nigerian star Kanu was all that separated the sides, handing Pompey the prize and sending Cardiff back across the border to think again.

It was a heartbreaking experience for McNaughton and his team-mates, and one repeated in 2011/12 when they lost on penalties to Liverpool in the Carling Cup Final, after a 2-2 draw.

Atlantic
31

Tommy McQueen

Debut: League, 11 August 1984 v Dundee (h) won 3-2
Appearances: League 53+4, Scottish Cup 6+1, League Cup 3, Europe 3
Goals: League 4, League Cup 1
Also played for: Clyde, West Ham, Falkirk, Dundee

Ever since David Robertson's departure to Rangers in 1991 Aberdeen have searched in vain for a long term solution to the traditionally difficult to fill left back berth. In sharp contrast, the 1980s brought an embarrassment of riches in that department.

Robertson was the most famous Dons No.3 of that era but his predecessor also played his part in the club's success.

Tommy McQueen was an Alex Ferguson signing in the summer of 1984, going from an electrical salesman who combined his day job with his football commitments with Clyde under Craig Brown to a member of Scottish football's most feared squad of players.

The Glaswegian was just 21 when Ferguson clinched the deal with a £40,000 cheque, nipping in to scupper the hopes of Hibs after the Easter Road club had agreed a fee with the Bully Wee.

With Doug Rougvie off the books and John McMaster sidelined after surgery, there was an immediate passage to the first team for the new boy and he made his debut on the opening day of the season in a 3-2 win at home to Dundee on August 11.

He started 33 of the 36 Premier Division games that season on the way to Aberdeen's seven point championship win over Celtic. He made the transition from part-time football to life with the elite with ease, even assuming penalty duty for the Dons and eventually leaving with a record of seven goals from seven spot kicks.

In a lightning introduction to life at football's top table, McQueen made his European Cup debut just a month after his first game as a Dons player. Aberdeen and Dinamo Berlin ended locked 3-3 on aggregate after two legs and, despite McQueen converting his effort the Germans won in a penalty shoot-out.

There was consolation in knock-out competition in the 1985/86 season when he won a place in Ferguson's side for the Scottish Cup final against Hearts. The Jambos, who had suffered the crushing disappointment of being pipped to the league title on goal difference by Celtc just days earlier, had their misery compounded when John Hewitt's double and a Billy Stark goal took the trophy back to Pittodrie thanks to a 3-0 win.

It was another winner's medal for McQueen and looked certain to be just the start of a long and profitable relationship between him and the Dons. Instead he found himself battling with Brian Mitchell for the No.3 jersey in the 1986/87 campaign before suffering a leg fracture in training just three months into the season. By the time he returned there had been two crucial changes at the club: Ferguson had left and been replaced by Ian Porterfield while David Robertson had established himself as one of the country's emerging talents and first choice in McQueen's position for Aberdeen.

In March, 1987, a £125,000 offer from West Ham was accepted by Porterfield and McQueen, still only 23, linked up with the London club in the English top flight.

After 36 appearances for the Hammers he returned to Scotland with Falkirk in 1990 in a £60,000 transfer. In August, 1995, he moved to Dundee but had his hopes of ending his career on a high dashed when Aberdeen defeated his new club 2-0 in that season's League Cup final.

1985-86: Aberdeen skipper Willie Miller holds the Scottish Cup. Also pictured are, back row left; Alex McLeish; Frank McDougall; Jim Bett; Joe Miller; John McMaster; John Hewitt. Front row: Neale Cooper; Peter Weir; Stewart McKimmie; Tommy McQueen.

Hugh McVean

Debut: League, 18 October 1947 v Falkirk (h) lost 2-1
Appearances: League 9
Also played for: Clydebank, Sunshine George Cross (Australia)

Tall and powerful wing half Hugh McVean cut his teeth with Vale of Leven, Shawfield juniors and Clydebank before joining Aberdeen in the post war years. He made nine first team appearances at Pittodrie over two seasons in the late 1940s before joining Australian outfit Sunshine George Cross in Melbourne.

Josh Magennis

Debut: League, 14 August 2010 v Hamilton (h) won 4-0
Appearances (up to end of 2011/12): League 52, Scottish Cup 7, League Cup 4
Goals (up to end of 2011/12): League 4, Scottish Cup 1
Also played for: Northern Ireland, Cardiff City, Grimsby Town (on loan)

Sometimes football throws up a story more suited to a Roy of the Rovers comic strip than real life and Josh Magennis is the star of one of those scripts. He began his senior career with Cardiff City as a goalkeeper before his pace, physical presence and ability in the air led Dave Jones to transform him into a striker. Magennis has not looked back and since then has won a move to the Scottish top flight with Aberdeen and made his debut for Northern Ireland.

The powerfully built Ulsterman arrived on a free transfer in the summer of 2010 and became a valuable squad man.

Chris Maguire

Debut: League, 7 May 2006 v Celtic (h) drew 2-2
Appearances (up to end of 2010/11): League 131, Scottish Cup 14, League Cup 7, Europe 6
Goals (up to end of 2010/11): League 16, Scottish Cup 6, League Cup 2
Also played for: Scotland (1 cap up to end of 2010/11), Kilmarnock (on loan)

When Chris Maguire ran on to replace James Morrison in Scotland's match against Northern Ireland in the Carling Cup of Nations in Dublin in 2011 he joined the elite band of dark blue Dons. The young striker, just 22 when he helped Craig Levein's side to a 3-0 victory, took a huge step towards fulfilling his full potential when he won that first cap. Levein had made no secret of his admiration for the Reds star and is hopeful he will become a regular at the top level.

Maguire had been part of Aberdeen's first team squad for more than four years by the time he made his international debut, having arrived in style by scoring on his debut against Kilmarnock on Boxing Day in 2006. The Glaswegian, who had been capped as a schoolboy and went on to progress through the Scotland age groups through to the full team, had a reputation as one of the most naturally gifted players in the youth system, confident on the ball and with excellent close control, but had to be patient in his pursuit of a permanent place in the side.

Manager Jimmy Calderwood raved about Maguire's talents but was careful not to push him too far too soon, dipping him in and out of the side at regular intervals. He pushed through the 100 appearance barrier

while still only 21 – but almost half of those were from the bench, as the youngster found a niche as an impact player.

It was not until 2010/11 that Maguire took major strides forward. Calderwood had departed by then, although he did have a role to play having helped put the spark back in the Pittodrie prospect's game by taking him to Kilmarnock on loan for a successful spell in 2009/10. He successfully helped the Rugby Park side clear of relegation and his impressive performances raised questions about Aberdeen's decision to allow him to farm him out.

He returned to the Dons the following term and hit the ground running. As the team toiled and Mark McGhee gave way for Craig Brown to take the helm, Maguire's increasingly mature performances were one of the bright spots. His ability to play wide or as a central attacker ensured the assured forward became a permanent fixture and he provided a genuine goal threat, hitting double figures for the first time. Having been a prolific striker for Scotland's under-21 team, that promise translated to consistent displays at club level. A hat-trick against East Fife in the Scottish Cup was one of the highlights and another achievement to add to the Dons starlet's list.

His best run of form for the Dons coincided with the final year of his contract with the club and his imminent availability sparked interest from an army of scouts. A new deal was tabled by Brown as he attempted to retain the club's most saleable asset and prevent him from walking away under freedom of contract, with the player deciding to join Derby County. He moved to Sheffield Wednesday in 2012.

Fred Martin

Debut: League, 14 April 1950 v East Fife (a) lost 3-1
Appearances: League 206, Scottish Cup 33, League Cup 52
Also played for: Scotland (6 caps), Carnoustie Panmure

Fred Martin was the man behind the rock solid defence that helped Aberdeen to the club's first championship success. But it could all have been so different if his career had not taken a dramatic twist during national service.

Martin was signed by the Dons from Carnoustie Panmure in 1946 as an inside forward but national service followed. For some players the outbreak of war ended their career before it had begun in earnest, but for others there were opportunities emerging from the grim circumstances.

Martin found himself based south of the border and, like so many of his peers, soon found football provided a welcome relief. While turning out as a striker for Woolwich Royal Artillery, an injury to the English side's keeper forced Martin between the sticks and it became a permanent transformation.

It took until the final games of the 1949/50 season for Martin to establish himself as Aberdeen's No.1. He made his debut in a 3-1 defeat against East Fife at Bayview on April 14, 1950, but the result did not count against him.

By the start of the next campaign he was the first name on Dave Halliday's team sheet and came close to his first club honour when the Dons took Rangers to a replay in the 1953 Scottish Cup final before falling to a 1-0 defeat in the second game. Aberdeen returned to Hampden for a second bite at the Scottish Cup in 1954 but this time it was Celtic who inflicted pain in the final, winning 2-1.

The Pittodrie men refused to lick their wounds and inflicted revenge on both halves of the Old Firm with league success the following year. Rangers, Celtic and Hibs had dominated for more than two decades but Martin helped upset Scottish football's traditional pecking order.

In the 1954/55 season he and his defensive colleagues conceded just 17 goals in 30 league games as they pipped Celtic to the prize by just two points. The Hoops proved to be more of an attacking threat that year but could not match the Pittodrie side's resilience and that proved telling. Martin recorded eleven shut-outs in his 28 appearances in the league and that proved as valuable as the exploits of the famous goalscorers Paddy Buckley and Harry Yorston.

By then he was also a star on the international stage. The Angus man made his debut for Scotland in May 1954 when he was picked by national coach Andy Beattie for a challenge match against Norway at Hampden, helping his new team-mates to a 1-0 victory. The match carried more significance than a regular friendly, given it was played just weeks before the country made its debut in the World Cup finals in Switzerland.

It was an opportunity to put Scotland on football's map and competition for places was strong. After his introduction against the Norwegians in Glasgow, the Dons keeper kept his place in the team for the return match in Oslo a fortnight later. This time the sides were locked at 1-1 and Beattie's men went into the World Cup confident of giving a good account.

Martin, flying the flag for Aberdeen as well as Scotland, took his place in the No.1 shirt for the opener against Austria. A single goal defeat was disappointing but respectable – what followed was a shock to the system, not least for the goalkeeper. The second game brought a 7-0 mauling at the hands of Uruguay, the defending champions and a prime example of why European football faced a massive challenge to keep pace with developments in South America. The Uruguayans eventually fell at the semi-final hurdle, with Germany going on to lift the World Cup by getting the better of pre-tournament favourites Hungary.

The Hungarians provided Martin with his next test in a friendly six months after the Uruguay rout. Again it was not a happy day's work for the Dons keeper, who was powerless to prevent the visitors running out 4-2 winners.

Heavy defeats were part and parcel of life in dark blue during that period and Martin's international career ended on another low note, when he took his place between the posts in an Auld Enemy showdown at Wembley. The keeper fumbled in the opening minute to gift England the opener and the day got worse from then on in. At the end of a torrid afternoon, the scoresheet read England 7, Scotland 2. It was not a side devoid of talent, with legends Tommy Docherty and Lawrie Reilly on target, but everything that could have gone wrong did.

While the Wembley debacle in 1955 proved to be Martin's last contribution in international football, he was not hindered at club level. In the same season he had a Scottish championship medal safely in his hip pocket and his career with Aberdeen lasted until 1961. A series of injuries took their toll and it was time for the Dons to inject some fresh blood.

Filling his gloves would not be easy, with six different replacements tried by the club in his final season at Pittodrie. It was John Ogston who eventually won the battle to become the next No.1.

Martin's final appearance came in a 2-2 draw against Airdrie at Pittodrie on January 16, 1961. After 291 games he retired from football, becoming a sales manager in the whisky industry in Perthshire as he embraced his second career with the same professionalism and efficiency that had marked him out as an international football player.

Paul Mason

Debut: League Cup, 17 August 1988 v Arbroath (h) won 4-0
Appearances: League 138+20, Scottish Cup 11+1, League Cup 13+2, Europe 7+1
Goals: League 23, Scottish Cup 1, League Cup 8, Europe 1
Also played for: Groningen, Ipswich Town

Behind every great manager lies tactical awareness, masterful motivational skills and an aptitude for man management. On top of that the best bosses need an almighty slice of luck and Alex Smith had that good fortune handed on a plate in 1988 when he unearthed a player who went on to become an Aberdeen legend. Smith was on a scouting mission in Europe to watch future Pittodrie goalkeeper Theo Snelders in action. While Snelders lived up to his expectations, an opposition winger by the name of Paul Mason also caught the wylie manager's eye.

Mason, a Liverpudlian, was turning out for Groningen in the Dutch league and it took an offer of £200,000 to snatch him from their grasp. His path to the Netherlands was a winding one, rejected by Everton and Tranmere as a youngster he played non league football in England before a leg break and job loss forced him to rethink his future. Mason moved to Holland to join his brother, relaunched his football career in the amateur leagues and finally made his mark on the professional game.

He became one of Smith's first signings at the start of a successful era for the club and despite being far from the most high profile he was certainly one of the most effective. Mason, a versatile player most at home on the right wing, was the main man when Smith clinched his first trophy as boss at Pittodrie.

The magic date was October 22, the year was 1989. A crowd of 61,190 had gathered at Hampden to watch Aberdeen attempt to beat Rangers in the final of the League Cup and end a run of 19 straight wins over three years in the competition. Aberdeen had been the runners-up to Graeme Souness and his men in each of the two previous finals but thanks to Mason the unwanted hat-trick was avoided.

Mason got Aberdeen off to the perfect start when he headed a Robert Connor cross past Gers keeper Chris Woods but Mark Walters levelled with a penalty. A tense final was settled by the Englishman in the second half when he swept home the winner from a Charlie Nicholas flick-on to clinch the first trophy of the Scottish season. The Dons also won the last trophy of the campaign when Mason and his team-mates collected the Scottish Cup win a penalty shoot-out victory against Celtic.

Mason was an ever-present in both cup runs and instrumental in both.

Mason made his debut from the bench in a 4-0 League Cup canter against Arbroath on August 17 in 1988 and went on to make 193 appearances and score 37 goals. The Scottish Cup final of 1993, when the Light Blues won 2-1, proved to be Mason's final appearance in a red shirt.

The Dons, by that time managed by Willie Miller, doubled their money when they sold their talented midfielder to Ipswich Town for £400,000 soon after. He spent five seasons at Portman Road, the first two in the Premiership, before retiring from the game to concentrate on a new career in the hospitality trade in Suffolk.

Lee Mair

Debut: League Cup, 27 August 2008 v Ayr United (a) won 1-0
Appearances: League 42, Scottish Cup 5, League Cup 3, Europe 3
Goals: League 1
Also played for: Dundee, East Fife (on loan), Falkirk (on loan), Stockport, Dundee United, St Mirren

Two years, 53 appearances and one goal. Lee Mair's career with his home town club was short but did enable the defender to tick the box of playing in the red shirt of Aberdeen.

His arrival ahead of the pre-season trip to Egypt in 2007 proved the Aberdonian had impeccable timing as he slotted into a squad preparing to embark on a Uefa Cup adventure that would pit them against Bayern Munich and Atletico Madrid amongst others. Mair made appearances from the bench against Dnipro and Panathinaikos before being promoted to the starting 11 for the pulsating 2-2 draw against Bayern at Pittodrie in what was a dream start to his life as a Dons player.

Mair had to overcome injury problems while at Pittodrie, as well as contending with being played out of position as a full-back rather than his preferred place in the centre of defence at regular intervals, but carved out a healthy appearance record during his two years on the staff.

Mair had started life as a professional with Dundee, farmed out to both Falkirk and East Fife along the way, before joining Stockport County in 2004. He moved to Dundee United early in 2005 for a two and a half year stay at Tannadice before earning his shot at glory with Aberdeen.

Gordon Marshall

Debut: League, 29 January 1972 v Kilmarnock (h) won 4-2
Appearances: League 7, Scottish Cup 2
Also played for: Hearts, Newcastle United, Nottingham Forest, Hibs, Celtic, Arbroath

Gordon Marshall played eight games as deputy to the injured Bobby Clark early in 1972 after being brought in as cover by Jimmy Bonthrone. Marshall made his name with Hearts and Newcastle United in the 1960s and also had stints with Nottingham Forest, Hibs and Celtic reserves before arriving in the north-east. He was released in the summer of 1972 and joined Arbroath, playing on past his 40s for the Gayfield side.

Paul Marshall

Debut: League, 2 January 2010 v Dundee United (a) won 1-0
Appearances: League 9, Scottish Cup 1
Also played for: Manchester City, Blackpool (on loan), Port Vale (on loan), Walsall

England under-20 international Paul Marshall set off on the road he hoped would lead to football stardom with Manchester City as a starry eyed 11-year-old. The left sided midfielder could not have predicted the direction his club would take in the years ahead and when the billionaires moved in, he was forced out. Marshall's lifeline was a loan spell with Aberdeen in the second half of the 2009/10 campaign after similar spells with Blackpool and Port Vale. Marshall was steady but returned to join Walsall on a free transfer in the summer of 2010.

Jamie Masson

Debut: League, 28 April 2012 v Dunfermline (a) lost 3-0
Appearances (up to the end of 2011/12) : League 4
Goals (up to the end of 2011/12): League 1

The emergence of teenager Jamie Masson was cited by Craig Brown as one of the few high spots of the 2011/12 season and one that gave him hope for the future. Masson, who made his first start playing on the left side of midfield, made a handful of appearances as the campaign drew to a disappointing close and made a name for himself when he opened his goal scoring account with the opener against Kilmarnock in a 1-1 draw at Rugby Park.

Alan Massie

Debut: League Cup, 11 September 1948 v St Mirren (h) won 3-1
Appearances: League 8, League Cup 3
Also played for: Dundee, Dundee United, Fraserburgh

Alan Massie played eleven games at right-back for his hometown team after joining from Banks o' Dee in 1948. He moved on to Dundee the following year and spent five years at Dens, captaining the reserves and making occasional first team appearances, before crossing the street to join Dundee United in 1954. A spell in the Highland League with Fraserburgh preceded a switch to Canadian football in the late 1950s.

Youl Mawene

Debut: League, 23 July 2011 v St Johnstone (h) drew 0-0
Appearances (up to the end of 2011/12): League 22, Scottish Cup 2, League Cup 1
Goals (up to the end of 2011/12): League 2
Also played for: Lens (France), Derby County, Preston North End, Panserraikos (Greece)

Experienced French defender Youl Mawene had worked with Craig Brown at Preston North End and the pair were reunited at Pittodrie in time for the 2011/12 season. He had also sampled British football with Derby County after they paid £500,000 to French club, Lens, before leaving on a free transfer.

Like many of his fellow summer recruits, he lasted just a single term with Aberdeen after injury and indifferent performances hampered his chances of earning another Dons deal.

Alan Maybury

Debut: Scottish Cup, 2 February 2008 v Hamilton (h) won 1-0
Appearances: League 13, Scottish Cup 4, Europe 2
Also played for: Republic of Ireland, Leeds United, Reading (on loan), Crewe (on loan), Hearts, Leicester City, Colchester, St Johnstone

Recruited by Jimmy Calderwood from Leicester City, the powerful Republic of Ireland international proved to be a calming influence and was offered a permanent deal on the back of some impressive displays which had won over the Pittodrie crowd. The former Hearts and Leeds United man, who had a highly successful three year stint at Tynecastle after joining in 2001, opted to reject the Dons deal and ended up joining Colchester before resurfacing in the SPL with St Johnstone in 2010.

Andreas Mayer

Debut: League, 30 January 1999 v Rangers (h) lost 4-2
Appearances: League 41, Scottish Cup 3, League Cup 3
Goals: League 3
Also played for: Bayern Munich (Germany), Rosenborg (Norway), KSV Hessen Kassel (Germany)

With Bayern Munich on his playing credits there was a ringing endorsement for midfielder Andreas Mayer's playing credentials before he had even kicked a ball for Aberdeen. Signed from Norwegian side Rosenborg for £200,000 by Paul Hegarty early in 1999, the import was installed at the heart of the team that staved off the threat of relegation. He remained part of Ebbe Skovdahl's plans in the 1999/2000 season, appearing as a substitute in the League Cup final defeat against Celtic, but was deemed surplus to requirements after Cato Guntveit, Rachid Belabed and Hicham Zerouali were brought in. Mayer returned to German football in January 2001.

Mitchel Megginson

Debut: Europa League, 6 August 2009 v Sigma Olomouc (a) lost 3-0
Appearances (up to end of 2011/12): League 34, League Cup 3, Scottish Cup 4, Europe 1
Also played for: Arbroath (on loan), Brechin City (on loan)

A mini-tour of Angus was part of Mitchel Megginson's apprenticeship. The Aberdonian, who had just turned 17 when he made his debut in 2009, was loaned to Arbroath in the 2009/10 season and then Brechin City the following term as Aberdeen aimed to give the forward vital first team experience.

Harry Melrose

Debut: League, 9 October 1965 v Hamilton (a) won 4-0
Appearances: League 64, Scottish Cup 11, League Cup 11, Europe 2
Goals: League 13, Scottish Cup 3, League Cup 2, Europe 1
Also played for: Rangers, Dunfermline Athletic, Berwick Rangers
Managed: Berwick Rangers, Dunfermline Athletic

If anyone could testify to what a provincial club is capable of it is surely Harry Melrose. Released by Rangers early in his career, the popular attacker shot to glory as part of the Dunfermline side that famously won the Scottish Cup under the tutelage of Jock Stein in 1961. He starred for the Pars on the wing and as an inside forward and won many admirers along the way. One of those was Aberdeen manager Eddie Turnbull, who made Melrose one of his first signings to the Dons squad.

He joined the Pittodrie revolution in 1965, spending two seasons in the top team and replacing Ally Shewan as captain as well as playing in every game in the Scottish Cup run of 1966/67. Unlike his cup final experience with Dunfermline, the Hampden day out ended in despondency as Celtic won 2-0.

Melrose stepped back from frontline duties in 1967 to become reserve team coach under Turnbull before pulling on his boots again two years later when he accepted the offer of the player-manager's role with Berwick Rangers.

Melrose spent six years learning his trade with the Borderers before switching to the top job at Dunfermline. During five years in charge he suffered relegation from the First Division and promotion from the Second Division. He returned to Dunfermline in 1990 as general manager and secretary and spent four years at East End Park before severing his ties.

Scott Michie

Debut: League, 20 May 2001 v Dundee United (h) lost 2-1
Appearances: League 22, League Cup 2, Europe 1
Goals: League Cup 1
Also played for: Peterhead, Montrose, Inverurie Locos

The stage was set at Hampden Park, the Scottish Youth Cup sat awaiting the winners as Aberdeen's young guns went toe to toe with their Celtic rivals. The year was 2001, the Dons were the winners in the final showdown and Scott Michie and Fergus Tiernan were the goal scoring heroes. Michie's reward was a first team debut within a fortnight of the trophy triumph. He went on to spend three seasons on the fringes of the first team before conceding defeat in his battle to establish himself and moving on to Peterhead in 2004. A spell with Montrose and in the Highland League with Inverurie Locos preceded a return to Peterhead for 2009/10.

Leon Mike

Debut: League, 16 February 2002 v Dundee United (h) won 4-0
Appearances: League 33, Scottish Cup 1, League Cup 2, Europe 3
Goals: League 5, League Cup 1
Also played for: Manchester City, Oxford (on loan), Halifax (on loan)

Leon Mike is the first, and possibly last, Aberdeen player who can lay claim to an appearance in *Coronation Street*. A budding thespian as a teenager, the striker had a cameo in the soap before football leapfrogged drama on his career ladder when he began to edge his way into Manchester City's first team.

Not that there was any reason to doubt that it would be on a football field rather than television set that Mike would get his big break. He had been picked for England at every level from under-13 to under-18 and appeared destined for big things thanks to his strength on the ball and fierce shot.

He had been with City throughout his teenage years but, after just a handful of opportunities, looked to Aberdeen to give him the big stage he craved. Ebbe Skovdahl made a £50,000 bid in February 2002 to secure the services of the 20-year-old forward and impressive early displays suggested the Dane had unearthed a gem. Skovdahl himself described the new boy as 'raw' but was confident he could smooth the edges.

Mike failed to live up to the early promise he demonstrated and drifted out of the first team picture, eventually leaving in the summer of 2003 after agreeing an early exit from his Pittodrie contract. It proved to be Mike's final involvement in the senior game as he returned to his home patch in the north west of England.

Joe Miller

Debut: League, 22 December 1984 v Dundee United (h) lost 1-0
Appearances: League 184+31, Scottish Cup 14+8, League Cup 19+5, Europe 12+2
Goals: League 32, Scottish Cup 3, League Cup 10, Europe 2
Also played for: Celtic, Dundee United, Raith Rovers, Parramatta Power, Clydebank, Clyde
Managed: Clyde

At the tender age of sixteen Joe Miller was billed as Scotland's answer to Roy of the Rovers by Andy Roxburgh. The comparison came after the youngster had waltzed past six England defenders to earn a 2-1 win for his country in a youth international. Roxburgh was bowled over by the promise of a young player who also drew comparisons with George Best from the Scotland youth coach at the time thanks to his fluent style and ability to ghost past defenders.

Alex Ferguson did not share Roxburgh's passion for dramatic comparisons but the two coaches did share a common appreciation of his ability. At club level Ferguson showed his faith when he thrust Miller into first team action just 14 days after his seventeenth birthday in 1984.

His debut was his only taste of first team action in his first season in the top squad but by the 1985/86 season he was a key squad man. He started eighteen games but it was one of his four cameos from the bench which brought him his first winner's medal. Miller came on for John Hewitt in the Scottish Cup final against Hearts as his side coasted to a 3-0 win and the occasion whetted his appetite and further success followed both with the Dons and Celtic.

The Hoops pulled off a stunning transfer coup when they beat Liverpool, who had a substantial bid rejected, as well as Manchester United and Tottenham in a hotly contested signing race late in 1987. Billy McNeill broke the record for a transfer between two Scottish clubs with his £650,000 swoop for the Scotland under-21 international.

The new recruit, who had been released as a schoolboy by Celtic, won a Premier Division winner's medal with the Parkhead club that season and added another Scottish Cup badge to his collection when Celtic defeated Dundee United in the final. His love affair with the national cup competition continued in 1989 when he was part of the Hoops side which defeated Rangers 1-0 to lift the trophy again – with Miller scoring the winner.

In 1993, at the age of 25, Miller returned to Aberdeen when manager Willie Miller invested £300,000 to land his first choice for the right wing berth vacated by Paul Mason. In 1995/96 the flying winger won his second Dons winner's medal when he starred in the 2-0 League Cup final win against Dundee and he remained with the club until May 1998.

His fourteen year association with the club was brought to an end when he signed for Dundee United on a free transfer. After two seasons with United he played a handful of games for Raith and Clydebank, as well as enjoying two stints in Australia, before his surprise appointment as assistant manager to former Old Firm rival Graeme Roberts at Clyde in 2005. After a year he was promoted to manager following the club's acrimonious split with Roberts and Miller led the Bully Wee to the Challenge Cup final in 2006.

Dave Millar

Debut: League Cup, 4 September 1965 v Rangers (a) lost 4-0
Appearances: League 17, League Cup 10
Also played for: Queen's Park, Raith Rovers, St Mirren

Eddie Turnbull's first move as Aberdeen manager was to mount a double signing swoop on his former club Queen's Park to land amateur internationals Bobby Clark and Dave Millar. Clark became a legend for the Dons but his former Hampden team-mate struggled to make an impact after turning professional. Millar, who continued to study accountancy after making the switch, joined as a forward but dropped back to the midfield and defence as cover during his three seasons in the north-east. He left to join Raith Rovers early in 1968.

Willie Millar

Debut: League, 14 September 1946 v Partick Thistle (h) drew 2-2
Appearances: League 27, Scottish Cup 2, League Cup 13
Goals: League 4, Scottish Cup 1, League Cup 8
Also played for: Partick Thistle, Stirling Albion, Gillingham

One is the European Cup Winners' Cup winning hero and Scotland international defender of some repute. The other is a post-war winger who played a support role for four seasons in the late 1940s. The differences between Willie Miller and Willie Millar are many and varied but both have a place on the list of Aberdeen FPs. Millar, a former Partick Thistle man, displayed a nose for goal during his appearances in Dons colours but moved on to Stirling Albion after finding first team opportunities limited and went on to star with Gillingham in the 1950s.

Bertie Miller

Debut: League, 25 September 1971 v Rangers (a) won 2-0
Appearances: League 56, Scottish Cup 4, League Cup 23, Europe 8
Goals: League 6, Scottish Cup 1, League Cup 1, Europe 2
Also played for: Celtic, Rangers, East Fife, Montrose, Cowdenbeath

Can you name the Aberdeen player who has been signed by both halves of the Old Firm? It is one of the lost pieces of Pittodrie trivia, but 1970s winger Bertie Miller is that man. The Fifer was on the books of Rangers and Celtic as a teenager but eventually got his senior break closer to home with East Fife.

It was from the Bayview side that manager Jimmy Bonthrone, who had himself been in charge of East Fife and had the player under his wing during that time, recruited the flanker to add to the Dons squad early in the 1971/72 campaign. Forward Jim Hamilton was the Pittodrie man exchanged in a deal believed to value Miller in the £20,000 bracket. Hibs, managed by Eddie Turnbull, were the rival suitors but the lure of working with mentor Bonthrone was too strong to resist. Miller had been a regular goal scorer for the Methil side during five seasons in the first team, although it was for his contribution from wide areas that he was signed. His early displays made him a favourite with the Pittodrie crowd as the new man slotted straight into Bonthrone's starting line-up.

He was sold back to East Fife for £10,000 at the end of 1973. Miller also had a stint with Montrose and Cowdenbeath, going on to coach with the Blue Brazil in the early 1980s.

Jimmy Miller

Debut: League, 10 November 1973 v Falkirk (a) won 3-1
Appearances: League 6, League Cup 1
Also played for: Leicester City, Queen of the South

Teenage attacker Jimmy Miller had been released by Leicester City when Jimmy Bonthrone threw a lifeline that pulled him to Pittodrie. The 18-year-old from Greenock had initially turned down Aberdeen to move to Filbert Street but got a second chance. He tasted first team football within two years of signing for the Dons but was released in 1974 and moved on to Queen of the South.

Robert Milsom

Debut: League, 15 January 2011 v St Mirren (h) won 2-0
Appearances (up to end of 2011/12): League 39, Scottish Cup 4, League Cup 1
Goals (up to end of 2011/12) : League 2
Also played for: Fulham, TPS Turku (Finland, on loan), Brentford (on loan), Southend United (on loan)

Fulham midfielder Robert Milsom breezed into life in the SPL when he joined on a free transfer from the London club in January 2011. The athletic playmaker slotted straight into Craig Brown's side and became one of the first names on the team-sheet after some composed and imposing performances at the heart of the team. The Englishman, who made his debut for Fulham during the 2008/09 season, had loan stints with Brentford and Southend as well as in Finland with TPS during his twelve years at Craven Cottage as a youth and senior player. He was released by Mark Hughes at the turn of 2011 and moved to Pittodrie on a short term deal before penning a permanent contract in time for the 2011/12 campaign.

Bobby Mimms

Debut: League, 17 February 1990 v Celtic (h) 1-1
Appearances: League 6, Scottish Cup 2
Also played for: Rotherham, Everton, Notts County (on loan), Sunderland (on loan), Manchester City (on loan), Tottenham, Blackburn, Crystal Palace, Preston, York, Mansfield

Championship chasing manager Alex Smith turned to experienced goalkeeper Bobby Mimms when Theo Snelders joined the Aberdeen casualty list in the closing stages of the 1989/90 season. Youngster Michael Watt had deputised for the Dutchman, but the opportunity to install the Spurs man in the No.1 jersey was too good to ignore. Mimms played eight times for the Dons, including two Scottish Cup wins on the run to the victory in the competition, before returning to London. He had made his name with Everton before landing at Tottenham. After his Dons stint he linked up with Kenny Dalglish at Blackburn Rovers and starred in more than 100 games for the Lancashire club, returning to Ewood Park in 2008 as goalkeeping coach.

Lee Miller

Debut: League, 9 September 2006 v Celtic (h) lost 1-0
Appearances: League 119, Scottish Cup 11, League Cup 5, Europe 9
Goals: League 29, Scottish Cup 2, League Cup 2
Also played for: Scotland (3 caps up to end of 2010/11), Falkirk, Bristol City, Hearts (on loan), Dundee United, Middlesbrough, Notts County (on loan), Scunthorpe (on loan)

When the dust settles on Lee Miller's career, there is every chance the Scotland striker will reflect that he hit his peak while wearing the red shirt of Aberdeen. The Lanark-born forward made his international debut just months before joining the Dons from Dundee United in the summer of 2006 and went on to make two further appearances in dark blue while on the Pittodrie books.

The first of those was as a half-time substitute against Argentina in 2008 and the next was a year later in Yokohama when he made his first start for the national side in a 1-0 defeat against Japan, both during George Burley's tenure at Hampden. He had made his entrance on the international stage under Walter Smith in another match against the Japanese.

The ability that had tempted Smith to promote the attacker to Scotland colours was what tempted Jimmy Calderwood to lure him north after the player's relations with his Tannadice club had reached breaking point. The Arabs' loss was Aberdeen's gain as Miller added a new dimension to Calderwood's side, with his intelligent play and ability to hold the ball up proving just as important as his goal scoring contribution.

While at Pittodrie he rolled back the years, hitting the type of form that had made him one of the outstanding prospects of his generation when he burst into the Falkirk side in the 2000/01 campaign.

In three seasons as a Bairns player, Miller was courted by a string of clubs – with Aberdeen, under Steve Paterson, among the suitors. In the end he plumped for the bright lights and bulging pay packets of the English game and joined Bristol City in a £300,000 deal in 2003.

It was not an enjoyable experience for the young attacker and he spent the second half of the 2004/05 campaign on loan at Hearts, where his performances convinced Dundee United to invest £225,000 in the summer of 2005 to take him back to Scotland permanently.

It was after his subsequent transfer to Aberdeen that he hit top gear, finishing leading scorer at Aberdeen in each of his first two seasons. While his third and final campaign was less convincing, it did not prevent attention from elsewhere.

The Bristol disappointment left Miller with unfinished business south of the border and when Middlesbrough, led by Gordon Strachan, lodged a £500,000 bid for the Aberdeen star in the January transfer window in 2010 it was an enticing prospect for both club and player. During times of financial strain, the fee was a welcome boost during an era in which saleable assets have been in short supply at Pittodrie.

Miller made the move to Teesside but endured more turbulent times in England, struggling to make an impact as Strachan's rebuilding exercise faltered. The manager fell on his sword and when Tony Mowbray took charge at Boro there was no place for Miller, who was sent out on loan to Notts County and then Scunthorpe in the 2010/11 campaign, before joining Carlisle.

Willie Miller

Debut: League, 28 April 1973 v Morton (a) won 2-1
Appearances: League 560+1, Scottish Cup 66, League Cup 109, Europe 61
Goals: League 19, Scottish Cup 6, League Cup 3, Europe 2
Aberdeen manager: February 1992-February 1995
Also played for: Scotland (65 caps)

For generations of Aberdeen followers, Willie Miller is *the* all time great. He is the man more than any other who epitomises their club and symbolises the success story of football in the Granite City. The contradiction is that the legendary captain, former manager and current director is a Glaswegian who has negotiated the east-west divide with perfection.

He turned his back on his home town when Aberdeen came calling during his teenage years and has never looked back, making the north-east his home and becoming the most iconic individual in the proud history of the Dons. He was a one club man and a loyal servant to the cause.

Miller first pulled on the famous red jersey as a 15 year-old in a youth tournament, having been spotted starring in the Glasgow schools league. He began his youth career as a goalkeeper, representing his city select as a shot stopper, but carved out a niche as a striker during his teenage years. That provoked Aberdeen's interest and after his youth team cameo for the Dons he was signed as a professional and shipped off from the family home in Glasgow to start a new life in the north-east along with so many other hopefuls from the central belt. His successful loan stint with Peterhead, during which he was a prolific scorer, led to a recall to the Dons squad before his transformation from attacker to defender in the Pittodrie reserves.

He made his debut for the Aberdeen first team on April 28, 1973, in a 2-1 win at Morton. It was the final game of the 1972/73 campaign and when the next season began Miller was at its heart – transformed from attacker to defender in Jimmy Bonthrone's side.

The teenager missed only three league games in his rookie season and for 17 full seasons he was the Aberdeen bedrock. In that time he was ever present five times and made a staggering 561 league appearances to set a record which is unlikely ever to be equalled.

He went on to play under Ally MacLeod, Billy McNeill, Alex Ferguson and Ian Porterfield before retiring while Alex Smith and Jocky Scott were at the helm. Every one of those managers depended upon him more than any other player.

Miller had a relatively long wait for his first taste of success, at least compared to the frequency in which honours would follow.

By the time Celtic were beaten 2-1 in the 1976 League Cup final he was captain of the side, having replaced goalkeeper Bobby Clark. It was Clark who recommended Miller take over as skipper, impressed by the young stopper's leadership qualities despite his tender age.

What followed was an amazing run which earned the defender a total of three Premier Division championships, four Scottish Cup and three League Cup winner's medals and the European Cup Winners' Cup and European Super Cup.

The image of Miller holding aloft the club's first European trophy is the most iconic in the history of the Dons and more than two decades on is still being snapped up by supporters desperate for a lasting reminder of that famous night in Gothenburg when Real Madrid were humbled by Miller and his troops.

He scored 30 goals during the course of his distinguished playing career, by far the most important coming in 1985 when, on April 27, a 1-1 draw against Celtic at Pittodrie clinched the championship. A Roy Aitken penalty had given the Hoops a first half lead but Miller's typically powerful header from a 61st minute Ian Porteous free-kick smashed off the post and flew into the net to leave the visitors shattered.

It took a serious knee injury to force Miller out of the team. At the age of 35 he attempted to battle on despite the pain but, after playing in a 2-1 League Cup win at Hampden against Queen's Park on the opening day of the 1990/91 season, he was forced to concede

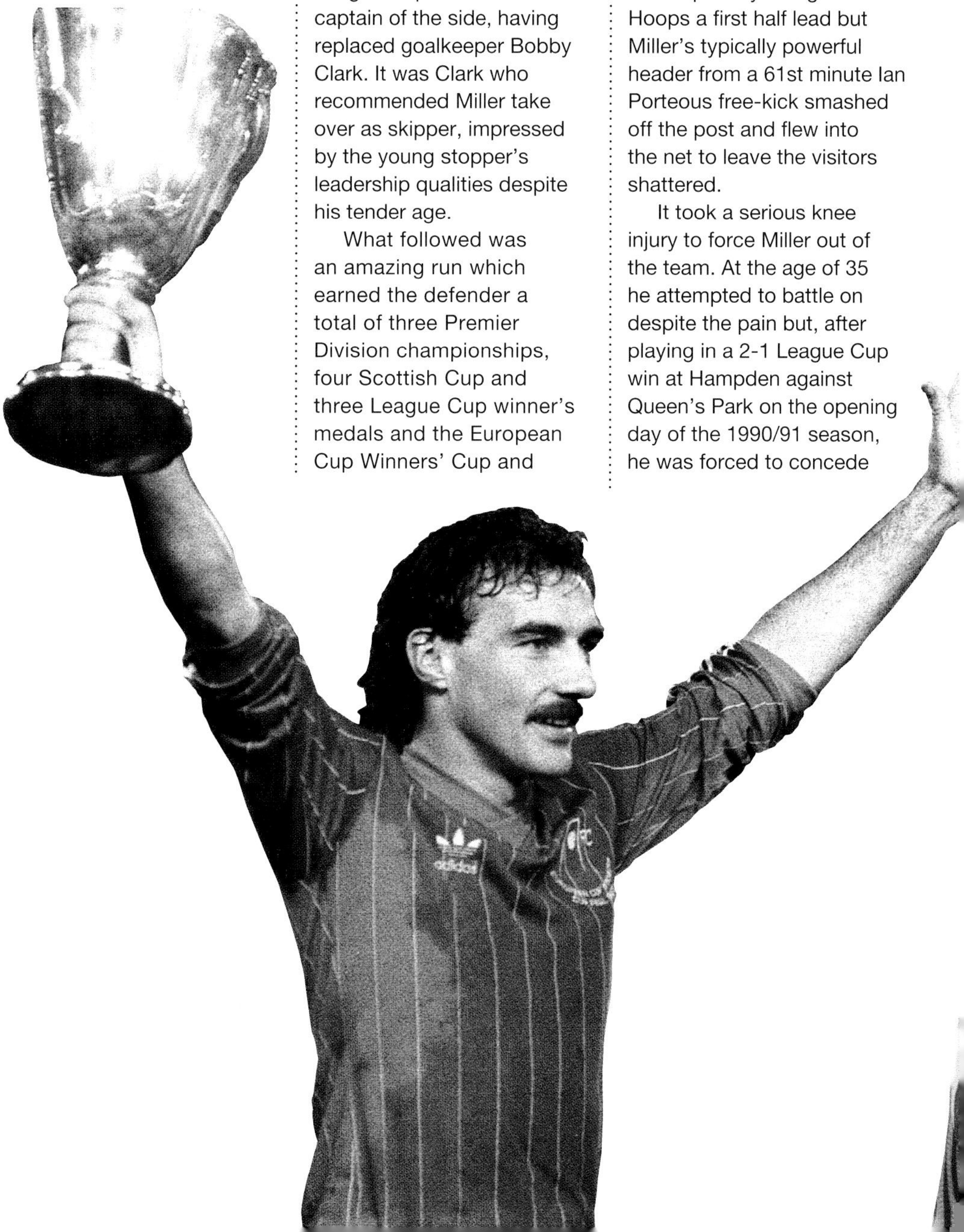

defeat and concentrate on his role as a member of Smith and Scott's coaching team.

He retired having established himself not just as a legend at club level, where he was Scotland's player of the year in 1984, but also on the international stage. Miller made 65 appearances for Scotland between 1975 and 1989, captaining the national team 11 times and taking part in the World Cup finals of 1982 and 1986. His solitary goal in Dark Blue was the winner against Wales in 1980.

William Ferguson Miller MBE, as he became in the 1980s as a reward for his services to football, had charged through his first two decades in the game collecting trophies at every turn. He has since been described by Sir Alex Ferguson as "the best penalty box defender I have ever seen". To back up that claim, he was crowned Scotland's player of the year in 1984.

After retiring from playing, Miller concentrated on his new life as a coach. At first serving under Alex Smith, it was only a matter of time before Miller took the helm.

That happened following Smith's dismissal in 1992 and initially the results were impressive. Miller steered his side to the runners-up spot in all three domestic competitions in his first season. They finished second in the league again in 1994 but second best was never going to be enough for a man who built his reputation as a winner, and Miller the manager set about demolishing the team he had inherited and starting virtually from scratch.

The project was not a success, and in 1995 he left the club and took a sabbatical from frontline duties which lasted until his reintroduction at Pittodrie as director of football in 2004.

Between 2004 and 2012 he set about developing the Pittodrie youth system. If there was ever an example of what can be achieved with hard work and determination then the man who skippered the club to its finest achievement, the European Cup Winners' Cup final victory against the mighty Real Madrid, must be that man.

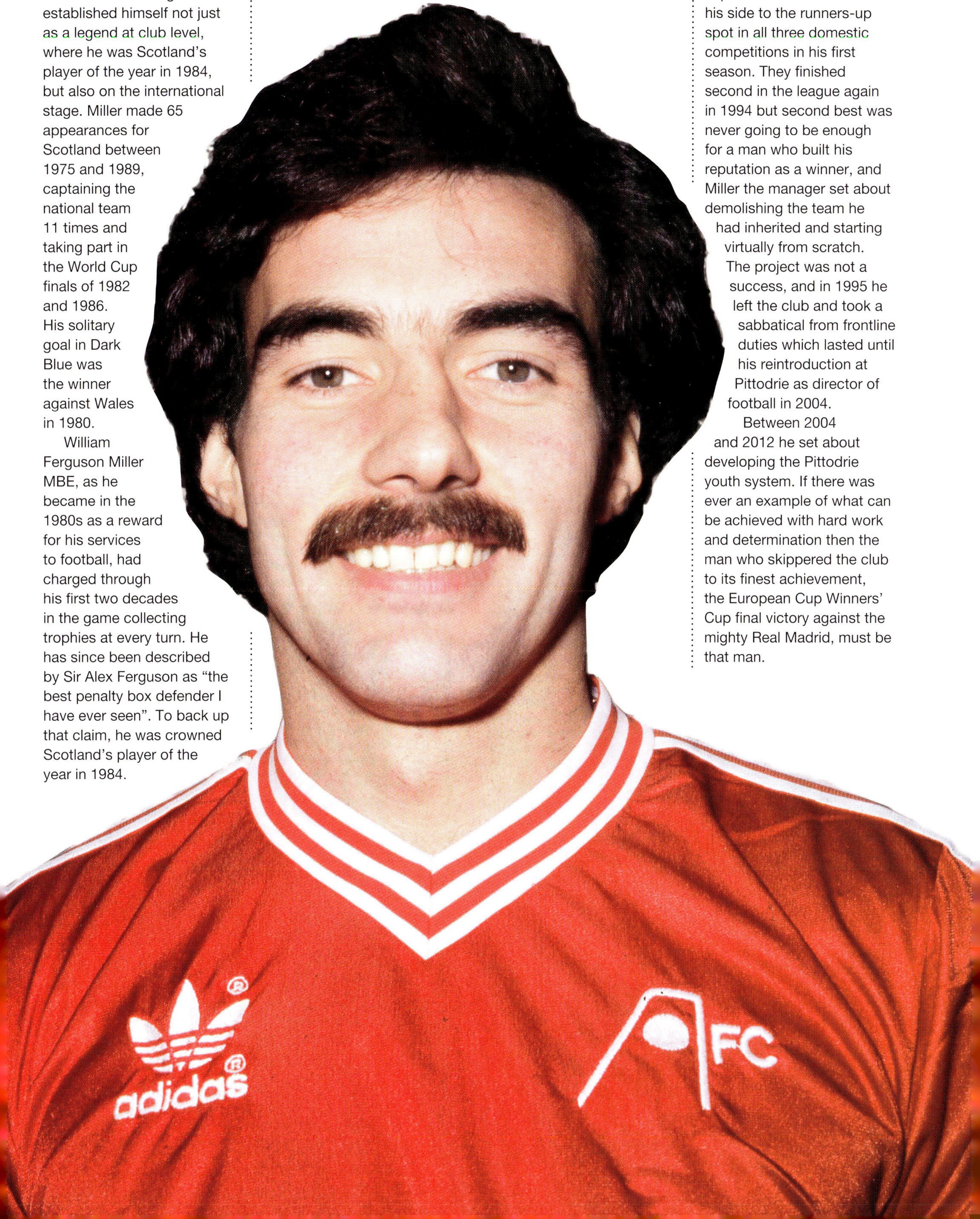

Willie Mills

Debut: League, 20 August 1932 v Motherwell (h) drew 1-1
Appearances: League 182, Scottish Cup 28
Goals: League 102, Scottish Cup 12
Also played for: Scotland (3 caps), Bridgeton Waverley, Huddersfield Town, Huntly, Keith, Lossiemouth

The names Harper and Jarvie struck fear into the heart of defences in the 1970s while in the 1980s it was Hewitt and McGhee. Before any of those players had even been born the mention of Armstrong and Mills sent a shiver down the spine.

Armstrong's scoring exploits are well documented but the all round contribution of Willie Mills was another reason to cheer for the Pittodrie fans. Long after his retirement, Mills was still being lauded as the finest inside forward the Dons ever had on their books.

His legendary status was confirmed by the Scotland selectors who handed him three full caps as well as a place in the team for touring matches in his heyday. Mills took his Scotland bow on October 5, 1935, in a 1-1 draw against Wales in Cardiff and went on to help the national side to a 2-1 win against Northern Ireland later that year. Mills made his final appearance in Dark Blue in a 2-1 home defeat at the hands of the Welsh in 1936 – wearing No.10, lining up alongside club-mate Matt Armstrong at No.9.

The outbreak of war halted competitive football but did not stop Mills in his tracks. He teamed up with Sir Stanley Matthews in a select side to tackle the Scottish Command during the conflict and outshone the English legend, scoring once to help his team to a 2-1 win in 1941.

Nine years earlier he had turned up for a trial at Pittodrie as a raw seventeen-year-old who had been starring for Bridgeton Waverley. His chance to impress came in a reserve game against Celtic and manager Pat Travers was left with little option when the new boy scored the winner against the Hoops.

He was signed on the strength of that performance and played just one further reserve game before being promoted to the starting 11 for his debut in a 1-1 draw against Motherwell at Pittodrie on August 20, 1932. Four days later he scored his first goal in a fine 7-1 win against Kilmarnock. Within three months he completed another landmark when he notched his first hat-trick in an 8-1 victory against Clyde. The teenager could play.

A ratio of 18 goals in just 31 games made him a key ally to leading scorer Paddy Moore but the tables were turned in 1933/34 when it was Mills who topped the goal chart with an incredible 28 strikes in 35 league games, including hat-tricks against Airdrie and Cowdenbeath.

The following season the Mills and Armstrong dream team truly came into its own, Mills grabbing 16 to add to the 38 scored by his strike partner. Between them they scored 54 of the club's 83 goals that season.

A shock cup exit at the hands of Second Division side East Fife in 1938 prompted a changing of the guard at Pittodrie and Mills found himself on the way out, joining Huddersfield Town in a £6,500 deal soon after. He had scored 114 goals in 210 games.

Mills died in Aberdeen in 1990.

Barrie Mitchell

Debut: League, 21 October 1972 v Ayr United (a) won 3-2
Appearances: League 13, Scottish Cup 1, League Cup 1, Europe 2
Goals: League 1, Scottish Cup 2
Also played for: Arbroath, Tranmere Rovers, Preston North End, York City, Vancouver Whitecaps, Morton

A fee of £25,000 put a weight on the shoulders of former Sunnybank forward Barrie Mitchell when he moved from Dunfermline Athletic to join his hometown team in 1972. He was converted to a defensive role during his time at Pittodrie but, after struggling with a back injury, was restricted to a handful of appearances and was allowed to join Tranmere Rovers on a free transfer in 1974. Mitchell, who had got his senior break with Arbroath after starring in junior football, also featured for Preston, York City and in the North American Soccer League with Vancouver before returning to Scotland with Morton.

Jimmy Mitchell

Debut: League Cup, 9 August 1952 v Motherwell (a) lost 5-2
Appearances: League 129, Scottish Cup 21, League Cup 34
Also played for: Queen's Park, Morton, Cowdenbeath
Also managed: Cowdenbeath

Jimmy Mitchell is a player with the unique distinction of conceding three penalties in one game and missing four in another after an unexpected twist in his sporting career. Mitchell's series of fouls came while playing for Aberdeen in 1953, leading to a 3-0 defeat against Celtic as Bobby Collins scored a hat-trick from the spot. His combination of misses came in 1961 – after switching to rugby with Bellahouston FPs in his home city. This time it was an Aberdeen side, Gordonians, who took advantage of his misfortune.

For a man who built his reputation as a sturdy and reliable defender, failing to score a single goal as he stuck to his duties with discipline and tenacity, Mitchell's career was far from dull.

The highlight was the 1955 league championship success with the Dons, when the No.2 missed just a single game in the gallop to the title flag.

He also suffered heartbreak in three Scottish Cup finals at Hampden, once with Morton in 1948 and then twice with Aberdeen in 1953 and 1954.

That pain was offset by the glory of the 1955/56 League Cup final when Mitchell skippered the Dons to a 2-1 triumph over St Mirren to lift the trophy.

Mitchell was no stranger to the national stadium, having launched his life in football in Mount Florida with the amateurs of Queen's Park in 1943. After serving his time in the Royal Navy, the defender turned professional in 1947 with Morton and spent five years at Cappielow before Pittodrie manager Dave Halliday came calling as he ended his search for a right back to take over from Don Emery.

His first appearance came in a 5-2 defeat at Motherwell in the League Cup on August 9 in the 1952/53 campaign and from that moment he became a mainstay for the Dons, making more appearances than any other player in his first season at the club.

Mitchell, who helped the Scottish League select to victory against England in his only representative appearance, was a loyal and dedicated servant throughout his time with the club. He made 184 appearances in just five full seasons at Pittodrie before a broken rib at the start of 1957/58 sidelined him and allowed Dave Caldwell to retain the jersey he had won at the tail end of the previous term.

He left to take charge of Cowdenbeath in the summer of 1958, playing on for a further year, before turning his back on management to launch a new career in the insurance industry in Glasgow. It was back on home turf in 1959 that he revived his sporting ambitions by turning to rugby with Bellahouston, where he had played the oval ball game as a schoolboy. Mitchell died in 2004.

Brian Mitchell

Debut: League, 10 April 1982 v Hibs (a) won 3-0
Appearances: League 82, Scottish Cup 6, League Cup 11
Goals: League 1
Also played for: Bradford City, Bristol City, Hull City

Good in the air, quick on the ground and with a bright future ahead of him. That was the assessment of Alex Ferguson as he cast an eye over impressive teenage defender Brian Mitchell during his early days as a star of the Pittodrie reserve side.

The former Harlaw Academy pupil was a powerfully built player who established himself as an imposing centre half for the second string. However, it was as a full-back that he was introduced to the first team in 1982 when he played at right-back against Hibs in a 3-0 win at Easter Road.

Mitchell also served at left-back during five years in the first team, proving an able deputy for a string of established stars including Stuart Kennedy, Stewart McKimmie and Tommy McQueen.

It was as McQueen's replacement that Mitchell entered the 1985/86 League Cup run at the quarter-final stage, retaining his place right through to the 3-0 victory over Hibs in the final at Hampden to collect a cherished winner's medal.

In February 1987 the Stonehaven-born player was sold to Bradford City for £70,000. The Scot was a big hit with the Bantams in the Second Division, making more than 200 appearances before moving on to Bristol City and then Hull City in the early 1990s. It was while with Hull that Mitchell was forced to retire from the game due to a knee injury at the age of 31 in 1995.

He completed his coaching qualifications to take up an appointment with the SFA's community team in the north-east.

Reg Morrison

Debut: League, 20 April 1953 v Falkirk (a) lost 4-1
Appearances: League 68, Scottish Cup 6, League Cup 13
Also played for: Dundee, Stirling Albion, Deveronvale, Rothes

Behind every strong goalkeeper is an able deputy and Aberdeen had that man in Reg Morrison. World Cup star Fred Martin was the man in possession of the No.1 jersey in the 1950s when Morrison joined from city junior side Lewis United and continued to hold the position for the lion's share of the time the duo spent together as colleagues.

Whenever called upon, Morrison stepped up to first team duties with consummate ease. He was a squad man in the 1954/55 championship winning year, making two league appearances and emerging with an unblemished record after turning out in matching 4-0 wins against St Mirren and Rangers.

It was in the 1957/58 campaign that he finally edged Martin out of the team and took over as the first choice keeper for Davie Shaw, retaining his place the following term before surprisingly being released in the summer of 1959 as the young John Ogston began to stake a claim for the goalkeeping berth.

Morrison had won Scotland under-23 honours while with the Dons and was quickly snapped up by Dundee, although Dens Park was a temporary staging post as he moved on to Stirling Albion soon after. He moved into Highland League football with Deveronvale in 1960 and also represented Rothes before taking a step back from the game to embark on a career as a prison officer.

Scott Morrison

Debut: League, 10 May 2003 v Partick Thistle (h) won 2-1
Appearances: League 40, Scottish Cup 7, League Cup 1
Goals: League 1
Also played for: Dunfermline, Ross County

From the moment Scott Morrison made his debut as a substitute against Hearts in November 2003 it looked like there would be no turning back. Within a fortnight he had been elevated to the starting 11 as he impressed manager Steve Paterson with his sure-footed performances on the left flank.

It was a difficult time to be an Aberdeen player as Paterson's team lurched through the campaign with a sense of inevitability in a season culminating in the manager's departure and the appointment of Jimmy Calderwood.

While Morrison had been a fixture in Paterson's team, he found first team football more difficult to secure under the new boss. For a player who had first linked up with the Dons at the age of 10, the realisation that he would have to leave Pittodrie in search of regular football was a body blow.

Morrison, a former Robert Gordon's College pupil, did not fit the gallus and brash identikit Calderwood laid down as he searched for players to fit his system and was allowed to leave for Dunfermline in 2005.

A serious knee injury suffered while on duty with Scotland's under-21 side dented his chances with the Pars, occurring just weeks into his first season in Fife. He battled back to fitness to put in three years of service at East End Park before joining Ross County in 2008. The Aberdonian, who grew up in Kemnay, was part of the County side that made a fairytale run to the Scottish Cup final in 2010 and was part of the Snaggies team that won promotion to the SPL in 2012.

Tommy Morrison

Debut: League, 12 October 1963 v Celtic (a) lost 3-0
Appearances: League 21
Goals: League 7
Also played for: Port Vale, Sligo Rovers, Partick Thistle, St Johnstone

A strong football pedigree stood youngster Tommy Morrison in good stead when he stepped up from junior side Kilsyth Rangers to the senior game in 1963 as an 18-year-old. His father had played for Celtic and his brother starred for Queen of the South, giving the inside forward a headstart in the game. He made his debut as understudy to Charlie Cooke early in the 1963/64 season and was a regular scorer during his appearances in the top team, although his performances were not enough to spare him from Eddie Turnbull's clearance in 1965. Morrison was snapped up by Port Vale on a free transfer before a spell in Ireland with Sligo Rovers and then back in Scotland with Partick and St Johnstone until his return to the junior ranks in the early 1970s.

Leif Mortensen

Debut: League, 27 January 1965 v Third Lanark (h) won 3-1
Appearances: League 15, Scottish Cup 3
Goals: League 1
Also played for: Udinese, Copenhagen

Danish winger Leif Mortensen arrived as part of the bundle which brought Jens Peterson and Jorg Ravn to Pittodrie. The recruitment of the trio by Tommy Pearson created waves designed to placate a support smarting by the sale of Charlie Cooke to Dundee. Mortensen made the No.11 shirt his own after arriving in January 1965 but was usurped by Jimmy Wilson by the start of the 1965/66 campaign as new boss Eddie Turnbull made his mark. Mortensen, who had a spell in Italian football with Udinese before joining Aberdeen from Copenhagen, was released in April 1966 to return to his homeland.

Scott Muirhead

Debut: League, 30 November 2002 v Dundee United (a) drew 1-1
Appearances: League 64, Scottish Cup 5, League Cup 7
Goals: Scottish Cup 1, League Cup 1
Also played for: Dunfermline, Stirling Lions (Australia)

Paisley-born winger Scott Muirhead was edging towards a century of Aberdeen appearances when he was moved on by Jimmy Calderwood during the January transfer window in 2006. The Pittodrie young gun's ability to play on the left flank helped boost his appearance tally and he chalked up a decent record while on the Dons books without ever establishing himself as a likely contender for a long lasting career in the top team.

Muirhead was initially secured on a two and a half year contract by Dunfermline, who had an earlier approach rejected before finally landing their target. Pars manager Jim Leishman was finally successful after Aberdeen had bolstered their midfield options with the recruitment of Neil MacFarlane.

Ironically it was the injury suffered by former Aberdeen colleague Scott Morrison earlier in the season that opened the door for Muirhead at Dunfermline, with Leishman desperate to find left-footed cover.

Muirhead found a place on the left wing and went on to outlast Morrison in Fife, remaining with the club until his release at the end of the 2009/10 campaign after signing an extension to his original deal and again going close to 100 appearances.

The former Dons youngster took the opportunity to broaden his horizons and joined the growing band of Scottish players sampling life in Australia when he linked up with FW State Premier Division side Stirling Lions in Perth. Former Deveronvale and Montrose striker Jamie Watt was among his team-mates at the club.

Charlie Mulgrew

Debut: League, 9 August 2008 v Caley Thistle (h) lost 2-0
Appearances: League 72, Scottish Cup 6, League Cup 3, Europe 2
Goals: League 9, Europe 1
Also played for: Celtic, Dundee United (on loan), Wolves, Southend United

Charlie Mulgrew became a Dons hero with his match winning repertoire of free-kicks. After a nomadic start to his career, which had taken him from boyhood team Celtic to Dundee United on loan and then south to Wolves and Southend United, it was at Pittodrie that he finally found his stride and turned promise into consistent performances.

The Scotland under-21 cap's cultured left foot and intelligent dead ball deliveries added a sense of anticipation to the Dons' offensive play. Whether whipping in dangerous crosses or giving goalkeepers nightmares with curling efforts at goal, Mulgrew posed a genuine threat every time he ventured forward.

A central defender in his youth, Mulgrew was converted to play at left-back as he matured. Concerns about his defensive capabilities reared their head but his attacking prowess outweighed those negatives and his potential tempted Aberdeen to part with a rare transfer fee in the summer of 2008. A cheque in the region

of £50,000 persuaded Wolves to allow the Glaswegian to link up with Jimmy Calderwood in the north-east.

Mulgrew emerged as a star man for the Dons and his decision to turn his back on the club in 2010 when his contract expired was a bitter blow for the Red Army. Interest from Sheffield United had turned the defender's head and he was set to join the Blades until Neil Lennon and Celtic came calling, offering him a second chance to make a name for himself with the team he had supported as a boy.

MAGIC MOMENTS

11 May 1983
ABERDEEN 2, REAL MADRID 1

It was the match that changed Aberdeen Football Club forever. The Dons, in an instant, were transformed from a successful provincial team to a side that would forever be listed among Europe's elite.

The achievements of Alex Ferguson and his Gothenburg Greats were momentous in 1983 – but the passage of time has served only to heighten the importance of events on that most glorious of nights as the European Cup Winners' Cup was claimed in considerable style at the Ullevi Stadium in Sweden.

It was undoubtedly Aberdeen's finest football moment and it is unlikely to be matched in an era in which the continental superpowers have stretched away from rivals from smaller leagues.

In 1983 the gap was close enough to bridge, not least because of the unique talents of the incredible team that Ferguson had built. Even with their class and ability, the Reds entered the final against the mighty Real Madrid as underdogs. What unfolded was a wondrous story of David slaying Goliath.

Aberdeen made a dream start when Eric Black opened the scoring after just six minutes, knocking home the rebound after an Alex McLeish header from a Gordon Strachan corner had been blocked inside the box. Eight minutes later the match was deadlocked again. A McLeish pass back, held up by surface water on a rain soaked evening, left goalkeeper Jim Leighton in a race against Real skipper Carlos Santillana and when he tumbled the referee pointed to the spot. Juanito stepped up to tuck home the penalty and make it 1-1.

Despite sustained pressure, particularly after the interval, Aberdeen could find no way to restore their lead inside the 90 minutes and the final moved into a tense period of extra-time.

The superiority that the plucky Scots had shown throughout was continued as the match entered its final half hour and what became apparent was that Ferguson's men had the fitness and stamina to press home their advantage.

Aberdeen had claims for a penalty of their own denied, after Neale Cooper went down in the box, and Mark McGhee also took a tumble in an incident that brought no more than a corner.

It was in the 111th minute that the tie was finally settled and it was left to John Hewitt, the substitute who had replaced the injured Eric Black earlier in the game, to do the honours.

Peter Weir broke down the left and fed the ball to McGhee, who cut into the box and crossed for Hewitt to head home the most dramatic of diving headers. The iconic goal and subsequent celebrations have stood the test of time, a passage of play no Dons supporter will ever tire of seeing.

A brief flutter of panic when Real Madrid won a late, late free-kick deep in Reds territory proved unfounded – the chance was wasted, the name of Aberdeen Football Club was ready to be engraved on the famous old trophy.

ABERDEEN – Leighton, Rougvie, McMaster, Cooper, McLeish, Miller, Strachan, Simpson, McGhee, Black (Hewitt), Weir.

George Mulhall

Debut: League Cup, 13 August 1956 v Hibs (a) won 1-0
Appearances: League 110, Scottish Cup 9, League Cup 31
Goals: League 30, Scottish Cup 2, League Cup 10
Also played for: Scotland (3 caps), Kilysth Rangers, Sunderland, Cape Town City, Morton
Managed: Halifax Town, Bradford City, Bolton Wanderers

Aberdeen have rarely missed a trick in the transfer market but in the case of George Mulhall the English press were in no doubt that the Pittodrie club had made a grave error of judgement when they sanctioned his 1962 transfer to Sunderland. The Roker Park club paid £25,000 for the winger and it was classed as a stroke of genius on the part of manager Alan Brown. Three months into his career south of the border Mulhall was described in reports as the finest left winger in British football after a succession of flawless performances and glittering displays.

Mulhall played for the Dons in an era when success was thin on the ground but he confirmed his place among the club's greats when he made his international debut on October 3, 1959, against Northern Ireland in Belfast.

It was a proud day for Aberdonians as homegrown talents Denis Law and Graham Leggat lined up in the same team as Pittodrie starlet Mulhall. The winger was a product of Kilsyth but he was Aberdeen's own, at least for a spell.

He marked his Scotland debut with the fourth goal in a 4-0 win, finishing the job Fulham striker Leggat had started with the opener at Windsor Park. By the time Mulhall made his second and third appearances for the national side in 1962 and 1963, he was a Sunderland man.

He signed for Aberdeen under Dave Shaw and joined a club on the crest of a wave, a regular in the reserves as the first team clinched the 1955 championship. The young recruit went on to play 12 games in the 1955/56 season and made an early contribution to the League Cup success the Dons enjoyed that term. He played five of the six Section 3 games as Shaw's side topped the group. The experienced Jackie Hather reclaimed the No.11 shirt for the knock-out stages, including the final victory against St Mirren, and Mulhall's hopes of a medal were dashed.

After four seasons as a squad man he stepped up to become a regular in the 1959/60 campaign and remained camped in the first 11 until his switch to Sunderland in 1962. For the Dons he played 150 games and scored 42 goals.

He stayed at Roker until 1969, when he switched to South Africa to play for Cape Town City. In 1971 Mulhall had a short spell with Morton before embarking on a long career in management, starting with his appointment as boss at Halifax in 1974. He moved on to become assistant manager at Bolton Wanderers and helped the club to promotion to the First Division before leaving to take the top job at Bradford in 1979. The former Dons winger returned to Bolton as manager soon after but departed in 1982. In 1996, at the age of 60, he spent two further seasons at Halifax Town and helped the club win promotion back to the Football League as Conference champions in 1998.

Frank Munro

Debut: League, 15 October 1966 v Ayr United (h) won 2-0
Appearances: League 44, Scottish Cup 6, League Cup 6, Europe 4
Goals: League 8, League Cup 1, Europe 5
Also played for: Chelsea, Dundee United, Wolves, Celtic

Dundonian Frank Munro was a schoolboy prospect who attracted interest from both sides of the border as a youngster. He chose Chelsea at the tender age of 15, although he returned home to join Dundee United soon after.

The tough tackling player, then turning out in midfield, won caps for the Scotland amateur and youth teams along the path to establishing himself as a senior player. It was while playing for the young Scots under Eddie Turnbull that he caught the eye of the Dons coach and was snapped up in a £10,000 transfer in 1966, still only 18 when he joined the Pittodrie cause.

Munro was a key part of the squad that ran to the final of the Scottish Cup in his debut season, suffering the pain of defeat against Celtic, and had the added strength of versatility as he put his powerful tackling and good distribution to use.

Early in 1968 a shock £40,000 bid from Wolves proved too good to resist for the Aberdeen board and the emerging talent was on his way to England. He spent close to ten years with the Molineux side, winning five caps while with Wanderers and skippering them to promotion in 1977 after emerging as a dominant centre-half, before earning a dream move to Celtic under Jock Stein. His time with his boyhood heroes was short and Munro returned to the Midlands to settle.

George Murray

Debut: League, 9 December 1967 v Kilmarnock (a) lost 3-0
Appearances: League 89+3, Scottish Cup 11, League Cup 20, Europe 7+2
Goals: League 4
Also played for: Drumchapel Amateurs, Motherwell
Managed: Odds-Ball, Canberra Arrows

In 1970 the famous double from Derek McKay and Joe Harper's goal won the Scottish Cup for Aberdeen. While the goalscorers deservedly stole the headlines, in a quiet corner of Hampden one man said a quiet thank you to an unsung hero in the Dons ranks as the Pittodrie playing staff celebrated.

Goalkeeper Bobby Clark cut through the euphoria in the aftermath of that glorious day in Glasgow to single out one moment which helped the club realise its dream.

It came in the first half of the semi-final against Kilmarnock at Muirton Park in Perth, a game settled by another McKay cup goal. A man who had a smaller but equally significant part to play was George Murray, who popped up on the line after Killie defender Jackie McGrory had beaten Clark with a powerful header from

a corner. Murray cleared and the Dons sailed through to the final.

The 3-1 Scottish Cup win against Celtic came at the end of a landmark season for Murray, who had started life as a midfielder with Motherwell and continued in the centre of the park after being brought to the Dons in 1967 in a swap deal involving Jimmy Wilson. He had spent seven years at Fir Park.

The Drumchapel Amateurs youth product was capped by Scotland at under-23 level and for the Scottish League select as a midfielder but found it difficult to break into an Aberdeen side well covered in that department as he made just 23 appearances in his first two seasons. He made his debut as a substitute in a 3-0 defeat at Kilmarnock on December 9, 1967, just days after signing but made only 12 further appearances that term.

In 1969/70 Eddie Turnbull converted him into a left back and Murray's Pittodrie career took off. He was the only player to start every single one of the 34 First Division games that term, missed just three League Cup ties and was an ever present in the Scottish Cup campaign.

He was a key man in 1970/71 for Turnbull and his side as they finished agonisingly just two points behind champions Celtic but in 1972 he hung up his boots to concentrate on a new role as coach under Turnbull's successor Jimmy Bonthrone. He had first taken on coaching duties at Pittodrie as a 29 year-old the previous year and proved a valuable asset on the training ground, eager to innovate but with a firm approach to discipline at work.

In 1975 he took charge of the Dons team as caretaker manager following Bonthrone's departure but the club opted not to promote from within and recruited Ally MacLeod instead.

He continued to serve on MacLeod's coaching staff and under Billy McNeill before resigning less than three weeks into 1978 to seek a fresh challenge after a decade with the Dons. That challenge took the form of a coaching post with Norwegian club Odds-Ball four months after his resignation from Aberdeen. In 1980 he swapped the hostile weather conditions of Norway for the heat of Australia when he was appointed coach to the Canberra Arrows in the country's fledgling National League.

Steve Murray

Debut: League, 18 March 1970 v St Mirren (h) drew 1-1
Appearances: League 101, Scottish Cup 10, League Cup 22, Europe 7
Goals: League 20, Scottish Cup 1, League Cup 1, Europe 3
Also played for: Scotland (1 cap), Dundee, Celtic, Dundee United
Managed: Forfar, Montrose.

Three months into 1970 Eddie Turnbull rocked the North-east when he set a new Aberdeen transfer record. Dundee captain Steve Murray was the man the Dons boss was forced to dig deep for and it took £50,000 to convince the Dens Park club to part with their midfield star.

Murray, who took over the record signing tag from Joe Harper, made his debut on March 18 in a 1-1 draw at home to St Mirren. It was less than a month before the Scottish Cup final win against Celtic but, having played in the competition for Dundee in the earlier rounds, he was forced to sit out the biggest game the club played during his three years in the north-east.

By the time he was installed as captain in place of the departed Martin Buchan in 1972, Murray was a Scotland international. He had played alongside Buchan and Dons team-mate Bobby Clark in a 1-0 European Championship qualifying group win over Belgium in November, 1971. That game was played at Pittodrie and it proved to be Murray's solitary cap, with Tommy Docherty preferring to rely on his clutch of English-based players in place of home based stars. John O'Hare scored the winner after five minutes to give Murray a short but perfect Scotland record.

Following his arrival at Pittodrie he played out the seven league games remaining on the card and missed just two games in the 1970/71 season as he made his mark on his new club with 44 appearances and nine goals in domestic and European competition. Aberdeen finished second and the future looked bright as Turnbull attempted to break Celtic's dominance.

It proved to be an impossible task, with the Dons runners-up to Jock Stein's Hoops again in 1972 as Murray played out what proved to be his final full season at Pittodrie. The Dumbarton-born player was aware of his value and refused to accept the re-signing terms tabled by Dick Donald and his board at the start of the 1972/73 season. The club refused to give up hope of convincing him to stay and even rejected a £100,000 offer from Sheffield United before conceding defeat and accepting a deal worth half as much.

Celtic's £50,000 offer was approved in May, 1973, and came three months after the player had asked to be relieved of the Dons captaincy as his unrest at the club grew. He made 140 appearances and scored 25 goals for Aberdeen.

After two years at Parkhead, winning the league in 1974 and the Scottish Cup, a foot injury forced his retirement from the game. Murray, who went on to become a bank manager, had his involvement in the game revived in 1979 when he was appointed as a scout by Dundee United, leading to a short playing comeback with the club that brought a League Cup winner's medal. He went on to have brief spells in charge of Forfar and Montrose before rejoining Dundee United as assistant manager to Jim McLean in 1989. He parted company with the Arabs less than a season later in favour of a return to the banking sector.

Stuart Nelson

Debut: League, 20 February 2010 v Falkirk (a) lost 3-1
Appearances: League 3
Also played for: Doncaster Rovers, Brentford, Leyton Orient, Norwich City, Notts County

Goalkeeper Stuart Nelson had three chances to prove he was worthy of taking over the gloves from Jamie Langfield after being lured north from Norwich City by Mark McGhee in the summer of 2009. The Englishman failed to keep a clean sheet in any of those appearances as he played his part in defeats against Falkirk and Kilmarnock and a draw at St Johnstone. The former Doncaster, Hucknall, Brentford and Leyton Orient player joined Notts County in 2010 after rejecting the chance to extend his stay with the Dons and established himself as first choice for the Magpies.

Mike Newell

Debut: League, 2 August 1997 v Kilmarnock (h) drew 0-0
Appearances: League 44, Scottish Cup 2, League Cup 4, Europe
Goals: League 6, League Cup 4
Also played for: Liverpool, Crewe, Wigan Athletic, Luton Town, Leicester City, Everton, Blackburn, Birmingham, Doncaster, Blackpool
Managed: Hartlepool, Luton Town, Grimsby Town

Mike Newell, with a championship medal in his collection from four and a half years with Blackburn Rovers appeared to be a snip at £160,000 when he was bought from Birmingham City.

He had been shipped out on loan by the Blues to West Ham and Bradford and was looking to get his career back on the right note by establishing himself in the Scottish game. A League Cup hat-trick against Dumbarton in only his second appearance for Aberdeen set him on the right path, although Newell proved more of a provider than an out and out scorer during two seasons at Pittodrie, in which time he played under Aitken as well as Alex Miller and Paul Hegarty during dark days for the club.

Newell launched his career with Liverpool and embarked on a tour of the lower leagues with Crewe, Wigan, Luton Town and Leicester in his early days in the game before becoming a £1.1million player when he moved to Everton in 1989. The same fee took him to Blackburn two years later. After leaving Aberdeen he played out his days with Crewe, Doncaster and Blackpool and managed Hartlepool, Luton and Grimsby.

Doug Newlands

Debut: League, 13 October 1951 v Queen of the South (a) drew 1-1
Appearances: League 3
Also played for: Burnley, Stoke City, St Johnstone, Airdrie, Forfar Athletic
Managed: Forfar

Impressive displays for RAF teams while stationed in the north gained Doug Newlands a break with Aberdeen. The right winger from Edinburgh played in a trio of first team games in the 1951/52 season before moving on to Burnley and then Stoke City. He returned to Scotland as St Johnstone's record signing in 1960 and also featured for Airdrie and Forfar. Newlands also managed Forfar for a year in the late 1960s.

Peter Nicholas

Debut: League, 8 August 1987 v Dundee (a) drew 1-1
Appearances: League 30, Scottish Cup 6, League Cup 5, Europe 4
Goals: League 3
Also played for: Crystal Palace, Arsenal, Luton Town, Chelsea, Watford

Welshman Peter Nicholas was a £350,000 signing from Luton Town ahead of the 1987/88 season. The talented midfielder sparkled for Ian Porterfield's team early in the campaign and was a key man in the run to the League Cup final, suffering the disappointment of defeat on penalties in the Hampden showdown against Rangers. Nicholas, who played an impressive 54 games in his single season at Pittodrie, had launched his career with Crystal Palace and had two spells with the Selhurst Park club wrapped around a spell with Arsenal. When he left the Dons it was to return to London with Chelsea, who paid £350,000 for his services.

Barry Nicholson

Debut: League, 30 July 2005 v Dundee United (a) drew 1-1
Appearances: League 102, Scottish Cup 9, League Cup 7, Europe 7
Goals: League 13, Scottish Cup 4, League Cup 4
Also played for: Scotland (3 caps up to end 2010/11), Rangers, Dunfermline, Preston North End

Making every penny count is vital when money is tight and the post-Millennium years saw Scottish football finances stretched to breaking point. When the Aberdeen board sanctioned the £250,000 purchase of Barry Nicholson in June 2005 it represented a courageous decision and an impressive notice of the support that the directors gave Jimmy Calderwood.

The manager had worked with the signing target while he was in charge at Dunfermline and those who held the purse strings were willing to back his judgement with hard cash.

Nicholson, who was 26 when he signed, got off to a steady but unspectacular start to his Aberdeen career. By the time he left he had established himself as a firm favourite among Dons followers with his livewire performances in midfield and incisive attacking promptings.

The Dumfries-born player was one of the heroes of the outstanding European run of 2007/08, the campaign which proved to be his swansong with the club. Despite Calderwood's efforts to secure the Scotland cap on a new contract, Nicholson opted for a lucrative move to England with Preston North End when his Dons deal expired in the summer of 2008.

Injury problems, including a broken leg, restricted his appearances for his new club but he bounced back in the 2010/11 season to join Preston's fight against relegation from the Championship. That battle was a far cry from his early days in football as part of the dominant Rangers squad of the 1990s. He made a handful of appearances for the Ibrox side before moving to Dunfermline in 2000 for a successful five year spell at East End Park.

Charlie Nicholas

Debut: League, 9 January 1989 v Hibs (a) drew 0-0
Appearances: League 59+2, Scottish Cup 10, League Cup 8, Europe 3
Goals: League 27, Scottish Cup 3, League Cup 1
Also played for: Scotland (20 caps), Celtic, Arsenal, Clyde

Charlie Nicholas is a Celtic man through and through. He grew up idolising the Hoops players of the 1960s and 1970s, made his name as a teenage starlet at Parkhead in the 1980s and left Aberdeen behind in the 1990s to return for a second spell with his boyhood heroes.

Despite his unbreakable ties to the Glasgow club, his final act as a Dons player was one which underlined his claim for a place in Pittodrie folklore. In the build-up to the 1990 Scottish Cup final between Aberdeen and Celtic the worst kept secret in the game was that Nicholas was ready to leave the north-east to sign up at Parkhead.

Before then he had a game to take care of and when it ended tied at 0-0 after extra-time the spectre of a penalty shoot-out loomed. Nicholas, never one to shirk his responsibility, was nominated as a penalty taker and struck a crippling blow against the men who would soon be his team-mates when he rifled home his contribution to the shoot-out on the way to Aberdeen's 9-8 victory.

It was a bitter-sweet moment for Nicholas but one he has never regretted. Despite his Champagne Charlie nickname and superstar status in his heyday, he always prided himself on his professionalism.

He explained: "The Scottish Cup was the only medal that I hadn't won in Scotland and it had always been an unlucky tournament for me. Every time it came up and the big games came around I had always missed out with injury. I was beginning to think I would never complete the domestic set and then the 1990 final happened. Obviously it was bitter sweet for me, beating old friends and guys who would soon be my team-mates, but I was an Aberdeen player and the cup was there to be won.

"When I scored against Celtic in any game there were never celebrations from me, the Aberdeen supporters knew where I was from and what I was about and I think they respected that. When it came down to it I was an Aberdeen player and I did whatever I could to help the team win every game.

"When you are sitting alongside people like Willie Miller, Alex McLeish, Jim Bett and the rest of the Aberdeen team there was no way you give anything less than 100 per cent and there is no way I would have let that happen anyway. I was going down to Hampden to get the set of medals completed.

"I remember getting back to Aberdeen for the open top bus parade, we were all still a bit boozy after a wild party in Anstruther on the way back up the road. I will never forget the reception I got when I stepped out at the town house – that was the day that showed me the supporters respected me and appreciated that I had never tried to con anyone. Fans aren't mugs and they know if a player isn't giving their

all for the team. The people of Aberdeen, more than the club, will always be in my heart."

In 30 months with the Dons he collected two winner's medals, one from the Scottish Cup showdown with his future employers and the other in the 2-1 1989 League Cup final victory against Rangers.

Nicholas cost £500,000 when Ian Porterfield swooped to take him back to Scotland from Highbury in January, 1988. Arguably he is the biggest signing the club has ever made. Paul Bernard is the record signing, but his arrival was put in the shade by the Nicholas deal.

The Glaswegian had been the darling of Celtic and Scottish football after bursting onto the scene in 1980 as a 19 year-old for the Hoops. The cultured attacker was named Scottish player of the year in 1983 and also collected the Scottish Professional Footballers' Association award in the same year.

He was coveted by the English giants Arsenal and Liverpool but it was the Londoners who won him over and in 1983 Nicholas switched to the Gunners in an £800,000 deal.

He won a League Cup winner's medal when he scored a double against Liverpool in the 1987 final but under George Graham his free flowing attacking style did not fit. The result was his shock move to Aberdeen and a brief but entertaining glimpse of his star quality for the Dons fans.

Nicholas made his debut in a 0-0 draw against Hibs at Easter Road on January 9, 1988. One week later a crowd of over 20,000 turned out to see their new hero on home turf for the first time, a staggering turn out considering lowly Dunfermline were the opposition. To put it in context, just over 11,000 had paid through the gate to watch the same fixture at Pittodrie in the first half of the same season.

Within months Porterfield had been replaced by Alex Smith and Jocky Scott but Nicholas was still in the thick of things. Under Smith the gifted striker struck up a lethal partnership with Hans Gillhaus, another high profile recruit.

Between them they scored 17 goals in the 17 Premier Division matches they played together in the 1989/90 season. Opponents soon realised that if one didn't get you, the other certainly would.

Following his return to Celtic in 1990 he spent five years at Parkhead. In two spells with the Hoops he won the league title two times and the League Cup once.

The last of 20 Scotland caps was won while he was on the Pittodrie payroll, a 2-1 win against Cyprus at Hampden in 1989 under Andy Roxburgh. His international career brought five goals and spanned six years, including the 1986 World Cup in Mexico in which he made two appearances.

At club level, Nicholas was reunited with Alex Smith at Clyde in 1995 when he made the move with a view to launching a coaching career but played on for a year before making a change in direction.

He retired from playing in 1996 and quickly forged a new career in the media industry as a football analyst with Sky television and newspaper columnist. The on field achievements are a fading memory but Nicholas is playing to a larger audience than ever before.

Alex Notman

Debut: League, 20 February 1999 v Dundee United (a) lost 3-0
Appearances: League 2
Also played for: Manchester United, Sheffield United (on loan), Norwich City, King's Lynn, Formartine United.

As Aberdeen struggled to retain Premier Division status in 1998/99, the old boys network swung into action. Scotland under-21 starlet Alex Notman was parachuted into Pittodrie by Manchester United boss Alex Ferguson in the hour of need, although the loan deal did not work out as either party would have hoped. Notman made two low key appearances as a substitute, on the losing side on both occasions, before returning to Old Trafford. The Edinburgh-born forward was transferred to Norwich City in 2000 and spent three years at Carrow Road before retiring due to an ankle injury. He returned in non-league football south of the border and was a surprise signing for Highland League side Formartine United in 2010.

Ross O'Donoghue

Debut: League, 28 April 2001 v St Johnstone (a) won 3-0
Appearances: League 8, Scottish Cup 3
Also played for: Elgin City, Dumbarton

Diminutive midfielder Ross O'Donoghue's lack of height was compensated for by his ability on the ball, with a maturity to his passing that belied his tender years when he was introduced to the first team by Ebbe Skovdahl in 2001. The 5ft 7in playmaker looked set for a long future with the Dons after impressive early displays but was restricted to cameo appearances and was eventually released in the summer of 2003. After dropping out of the senior game he reappeared with Elgin City in 2007, with a single campaign with Dumbarton sandwiched between two stints with the Moray outfit.

John Ogston

Debut: League, 20 December 1958 v Rangers (h) lost 3-1
Appearances: League 179, Scottish Cup 17, League Cup 34
Also played for: Liverpool, Doncaster Rovers, Buckie Thistle, Huntly, Fraserburgh, Deveronvale

The Banks o' Dee team that defeated Kilsyth Rangers 1-0 in the junior Scottish Cup final at Hampden in 1957 has gone down in Aberdeen football folklore. The achievement was momentous at the time as the revered city side followed in the footsteps of local rivals Sunnybank in getting their hands on the coveted prize. The fact it has not been repeated by a north-east team in more than 50 years since the final serves to highlight the scale of the accomplishment.

John Tubby Ogston was the goalkeeper for the victorious Dee side that day and was a man in demand, snubbing Rangers as well as Sheffield Wednesday and Aston Villa to commit to his home town team and sign for Aberdeen in 1957.

He made his debut the following year and over the next eight years made more than 200 appearances for the Dons until the new broom of Eddie Turnbull began to sweep clean. With new boy Bobby Clark in position, the Scotland under-23 international was allowed to move on and it was Liverpool who won the race for his signature in 1965 with a hefty £12,000 bid.

He spent three years on Merseyside, making a single appearance for his new club, before switching to Doncaster Rovers for regular first team football. He won the Fourth Division championship with Doncaster before returning to the north-east to play with Buckie, Huntly, Fraserburgh and Deveronvale before retiring at the age of 35. Outside of football he took up a position as a porter at Aberdeen's fish market and also served as a porter at Aberdeen Royal Infirmary.

Ryan O'Leary

Debut: League, 8 May 2004 v Hibs (h) lost 1-0
Appearances: League 2
Also played for: Kilmarnock, Dundee (on loan)

Aberdeen have lost homegrown players for a variety of reasons over the years – but homesickness was a new one. That was the factor cited in Ryan O'Leary's decision to move on in 2005 at a time when Jimmy Calderwood was hoping to push him into the first team reckoning following his brief taste of action as a 16-year-old under Steve Paterson the previous year. The teenager was snapped up by Kilmarnock after deciding to move back to the west coast to be nearer his family. O'Leary emerged as a solid SPL defender with the Rugby Park club before moving to Dundee on loan in 2010. He was released by Killie that year and went on trial with the Vancouver Whitecaps in Canada.

Brian O'Neil

Debut: League, 2 August 1997 v Kilmarnock (h) drew 0-0
Appearances: League 27, Scottish Cup 1, League Cup 4
Goals: League 1
Also played for: Scotland (7 caps), Celtic, Wolfsburg, Derby County, Preston North End

The defender failed to live up to his £750,000 price tag after being lured from Celtic by Roy Aitken in the summer of 1997. He had all the right credentials. At the age of 24 he still had his best years in front of him and had the benefit of an impressive apprenticeship with Celtic behind him. More than 100 appearances in the Hoops had won him Scotland recognition from Craig Brown in 1996 and the Paisley-born stopper appeared a shrewd acquisition for the Dons.

Although he was a regular under both Aitken and his successor Alex Miller in the 1997/98 campaign, O'Neil was ushered out of Pittodrie in July 1998 when Wolfsburg offered £350,000 for his services.

He carved out a solid reputation in the tough arena of German football during two years on the continent and only landed back on British soil when his club opted to use him as bait in a swap deal that took Derby player Stefan Schoor back to his homeland in 2000. O'Neil moved from Derby to Preston North End in January 2003 and made over 100 appearances in four years before retiring through injury.

Between leaving Aberdeen in 1998 and hanging up his boots in 2006 he won six further caps to add to the appearance he made while on Celtic's books, making his last Scotland contribution in a 2-2 friendly draw in Austria in 2005.

Joe O'Neil

Debut: League, 17 February 1951 v Partick Thistle (h) won 4-1
Appearances: League 23, Scottish Cup 4, League Cup 7
Goals: League 9, Scottish Cup 4, League Cup 2
Also played for: Southend (loan), Leicester City, Northampton

The word 'hero' is often overused in football but forward Joe O'Neil is a worthy man to wear that tag. O'Neil was a valuable squad man in the 1955 league championship success, playing a dozen of the 30 top flight games, but is best remembered for his stunning hat-trick in the 6-0 Scottish Cup semi-final demolition of Rangers the previous year. What made the performance even more incredible was the fact he had played in that tie less than a fortnight after fracturing his skull and having surgery to repair the damage. O'Neil, who was loaned to Southend during his national service, went on to play in England with Leicester City, Northampton, Bath City, Weston-super-Mare and Trowbridge Town. He had joined Aberdeen from junior side Bridgeton Waverley.

Michael O'Neill

Debut: League, 10 January 1998 v Rangers (a) lost 2-0
Appearances: League 7, Scottish Cup 1
Also played for: Northern Ireland, Newcastle United, Dundee United, Hibs, Coventry City, Reading (on loan), Wigan, St Johnstone, Clydebank, Glentoran, Ayr United.
Managed: Brechin City, Shamrock Rovers

Northern Ireland international Michael O'Neill played on loan from Coventry City in the 1997/98 campaign. The Ulsterman starred for Dundee United and Hibs before his £500,000 move to the Midlands in 1996. The cultured midfielder, who had served his apprenticeship at Newcastle before moving to Tannadice in 1989, played eight times for the Dons before returning to Coventry. A loan spell with Reading was followed by permanent stints with Wigan Athletic, St Johnstone, Clydebank, Glentoran and Ayr United before he moved into management with Brechin City. He took charge of Shamrock Rovers in 2008, guiding them to the championship two years later, and was appointed boss of Northern Ireland in 2012.

Isaac Osbourne

Debut: League, 23 July 2011 v St Johnstone (h) drew 0-0
Appearances (up to the end of 2011/12): League 22, Scottish Cup 1, League Cup 2
Also played for: Coventry City

Englishman Isaac Osbourne was among a clutch of new faces introduced as the curtain came up on the 2011/12 season with a visit from St Johnstone. He had been sidelined by injury for the bulk of the previous season at Coventry City but had convinced the Dons he was back to full fitness. Osbourne, a defensive midfielder, was seen as the man to add steel to the core of the Aberdeen team and made a solid start to his career in the SPL before being struck by a hamstring problem that saw him return to the treatment room.

Jimmy Owens

Debut: League, 31 January 1948 v Falkirk (a) lost 3-1
Appearances: League 1

A 3-1 defeat against Falkirk at Brockville in the top flight was the only taste of top team football for Jimmy Owens. That appearance, under Dave Halliday in the 1947/48 season marked the beginning and the end of Owens' career as the forward struggled to negotiate a path past Tony Harris and Archie Baird.

Mixu Paatelainen

Debut: League, 4 April 1992 v Dunfermline (a) drew 0-0
Appearances: League 75, Scottish Cup 9, League Cup 6, Europe 3
Goals: League 23, Scottish Cup 1, League Cup 3, Europe 1
Also played for: Finland, Dundee United, Bolton Wanderers, Hibs, Strasbourg, St Johnstone, St Mirren
Managed: Cowdenbeath, TPS Turku (Finland), Hibs, Kilmarnock, Finland

As a manager Mixu Paatelainen has gained a reputation as a shrewd operator and a coach capable of creating teams with silk and steel. As a player he was no different, mating his incredible power and physique with a natural goal scorer's touch and the ability to link play.

The Finland international was signed by Willie Miller from Dundee United for £400,000 in 1992 as the new manager put his stamp on the Pittodrie squad. The bustling forward's committed style made him an instant hit, both with supporters and his team-mates. He was no stranger to the Scottish game, having first arrived in 1987 when he succeeded in winning a contract after a trial with Jim McLean at Tannadice.

With an embarrassment of attacking riches, the Dons decided to cash in their chips in 1994 when Bolton beat Stoke City and Millwall in a race for the Scandinavian's signature and succeeded with a £300,000 offer. He won the First Division title with Wanderers before moving on to Wolves and then back to Scotland with Hibs, enjoying two spells at Easter Road. He also served with French outfit Strasbourg, St Johnstone and St Mirren before cutting his managerial teeth with Cowdenbeath. The Third Division championship with the Blue Brazil won the chance to manage

the ambitious TPS Turku in his homeland before a disappointing spell with Hibs. He bounced back in style with Kilmarnock in the 2010/11 campaign, earning plaudits for turning the Rugby Park side into an attractive attacking force and promotion to the Finland national manager's job before the season ended.

Fernando Pasquinelli

Debut: League, 28 August 2004 v Livingston (h) won 2-0
Appearances: League 10
Goals: League 3
Also played for: Boca Juniors, Livingston

In the list of eccentric Aberdeen signings, the name of Fernando Pasquinelli looms large. The Argentinian striker had spent a season with Livingston, winning the League Cup with the Almondvale side, before he was picked up by Jimmy Calderwood ahead of the 2004/05 season. He was tall, tricky and had a decent pedigree after learning his trade with Boca Juniors. The forward scored three times in his first ten appearances for the Dons before a muscle tear left him confined to the treatment table. Pasquinelli's contract was terminated after just six months to allow him to return to Argentina to kick-start his career.

Arthur Paterson

Debut: League, 22 November 1958 v Clyde (a) lost 4-0
Appearances: League 2
Also played for: Ayr United, Clydebank

The transition from junior player to Dons first team man took all of five months for left winger Arthur Paterson. He joined from Inverurie Locos in the summer of 1958 and played two games in his first season on the Dons books. He was released after two years and returned to the junior game with Irvine Meadow, winning the Scottish Junior Cup and capped at that level by Scotland, before stepping back up a grade with Ayr United and Clydebank in the 1960s.

Bobby Paterson

Debut: League, 10 October 1953 v Hamilton (h) won 5-1
Appearances: League 8, League Cup 1
Also played for: Queen's Park, Dumbarton

Scotland amateur international right-back Bobby Paterson was recruited from Queen's Park in 1952 after starring for the Hampden side. He provided reliable cover for regular No.2 Jimmy Mitchell until his release in 1958 and returned to his home city to combine his accountancy studies with part-time football at Dumbarton.

Jim Paterson

Debut: League, 2 February 2010 v Falkirk (h) lost 1-0
Appearances: League 7, Scottish Cup 2
Also played for: Dundee United, Motherwell, Plymouth

Injury halted Jim Paterson's run in the Aberdeen team before it had got into full swing. The wily former Dundee United and Motherwell midfielder moved north on loan from Plymouth Argyle early in 2010 but was injured in what was only his ninth appearance for the club and returned to England to nurse the damaged Achilles tendon for the remainder of the campaign.

Manager Mark McGhee admitted Paterson would be outwith Aberdeen's reach financially as a permanent recruit and the interest ended. The Glaswegian forced his way back into the Plymouth first team after his brief dalliance with the Dons.

Alistair Patience

Debut: League, 1 January 1959 v Dundee (h) drew 1-1
Appearances: League 2
Also played for: Clachnacuddin, Inverness Caledonian

Super passing ability marked wing half Alistair Patience out as one of the most gifted Highlanders of his generation. His ability on the ball persuaded the Dons to recruit him from Clachnacuddin in 1957 and Patience made two appearances for the first team before being called away for national service. Patience went on to star for Inverness Caledonian in the Highland League but died in 1973, at the age of 38, after a long illness.

Michael Paton

Debut: League, 20 December 2008 v Caley Thistle (a) won 3-0
Appearances (up to end of 2010/11): League 49, Scottish Cup 4, League Cup 1, Europe 1
Goals (up to end of 2010/11): League 4, League Cup 2
Also played for: Brechin City (on loan)

Youth product Michael Paton came back from the point of what appeared to be no return when Craig Brown took over as manager. Paton, who had been part of the first team under Jimmy Calderwood after a loan spell with Brechin City in 2008, fell dramatically out of favour under Mark McGhee. The Greenock-born striker rejected a loan move to Dundee but appeared destined for the exit door when he went on trial with Wacker Innsbruck in the winter of 2010. Then McGhee was gone, Brown was in and Paton returned to the first team fold to challenge for a berth in the attack. He was released in the summer of 2012.

Billy Paul

Debut: League, 1 February 1969 v Partick Thistle (h) drew 1-1
Appearances: League 2
Also played for: Rangers, Stirling Albion

Winger Billy Paul had briefly filled the shoes of Willie Henderson while starting out in the game with Rangers. The former Irvine Meadow junior star made just a single appearance for the Ibrox side before moving to Aberdeen in 1969, where he again played a solitary game before switching to Stirling Albion and then back into junior football with Kirkintilloch Rob Roy.

Peter Pawlett

Debut: Scottish Cup, 17 February 2009 v East Fife (h) won 5-0
Appearances (up to end of 2010/11): League 32, Scottish Cup 5, League Cup 1
Goals (up to end of 2010/11): League 1

Aberdeen have been short of players capable of thrilling the Pittodrie crowd in modern times. In Peter Pawlett the club has unearthed a talent who promises to do just that. The Hull-born youngster, brought up in the north-east and capped by Scotland at under-19 level to confirm his allegiance to the country, was blooded by Jimmy Calderwood early in 2009 and looked assured at top team level. A knee injury stalled his progress but Pawlett, who has been used as a central attacker as well as in his preferred right wing role, looks set to emerge as a key man for the Dons.

Stephen Payne

Debut: League, 2 January 2003 v Celtic (h) drew 1-1
Appearances: League 8, Scottish Cup 2
Also played for: Queen of the South, Stranraer

The joy of playing in a one team city can occasionally be a curse and Stephen Payne discovered that to his cost. When manager Steve Paterson compared his crossing ability to that of David Beckham, a throw away line became headline news under the intense media spotlight in the Granite City. Payne, freshly tagged as the 'new Beckham' in the media, toiled in the face of close scrutiny and the right sided wing-back was released by Paterson to join Queen of the South in January 2004. Payne spent two years with the Doonhamers and had a brief spell with Stranraer before moving to junior football with Bathgate Thistle.

Jim Pearson

Debut: League, 17 January 1962 v Dundee (a) lost 2-1
Appearances: League 3
Goals: League 1
Also played for: Morton, East Stirling, Melbourne HSC (Australia)

Forward Jimmy Pearson swapped the wind and rain of Aberdeen for the sunshine of Australia when he left Pittodrie in 1962 to join Melbourne HSC. The former Neilston juniors player got his senior break with Morton in the late 1950s before joining East Stirling and then Aberdeen. He scored one goal, against Partick, in three appearances for Tommy Pearson's side in the 1961/62 campaign.

Mark Peat

Debut: League, 13 April 2002 v Hearts (h) lost 3-2
Appearances: League 1
Also played for: Arbroath, Albion Rovers, Forfar Athletic, Montrose, East Stirling, Berwick Rangers

Glaswegian goalkeeper Mark Peat was propelled into the first team as deputy to Peter Kjaer and Ryan Esson in 2002. He was released the following year and established himself with Arbroath before spells with Albion Rovers, Forfar, Arbroath for a second spell and then Montrose. After a loan spell at East Stirling he signed for Berwick Rangers in the summer of 2009.

Mark Perry

Debut: League, 1 August 1998 v Dundee (a) won 2-0
Appearances: League 59, Scottish Cup 4, League Cup 5, Europe 1
Goals: League 5
Also played for: Dundee United, Ross County, Peterhead, Keith

Defender Mark Perry is another of the Aberdonian players who had to take a step away from the Granite City to eventually find a path back to Pittodrie. Perry was snapped up by Dundee United from Cove Rangers as a youngster in the late 1980s and emerged as a Tannadice stalwart throughout the 90s, making more than 150 appearances for the Arabs as a central defender and right-back.

His strength, height, versatility, experience and reliability were some of the qualities that attracted Dons manager Alex Miller to the stopper when he became available in the summer of 1998. He was 27-years-old by then and was brought north to add another old head to a squad that relied heavily on seasoned professionals.

He missed just a handful of matches during his maiden season, slotting into a defence marshalled by Jim Leighton and also featuring Derek Whyte and Gary Smith. It had the makings of a solid unit but came together in a season in which the club flirted with relegation and ended up replacing Miller with Paul Hegarty.Opportunities became more limited following Ebbe Skovdahl's arrival the following year and Perry was allowed to join Ross County on a free transfer midway through the 2000/01 season. He remained with the Dingwall side for two years before returning to the north-east for a four and a half year spell with Peterhead. Perry dropped down to the Highland League with Keith after leaving Balmoor in June 2007.

Nigel Pepper

Debut: League, 28 November 1998 v Dundee United (h) lost 3-0
Appearances: League 14, League Cup 1
Also played for: Rotherham, York City, Bradford City, Southend United (on loan), Scunthorpe United

English battler Nigel Pepper's dubious Aberdeen record is unlikely ever to be beaten. When the midfielder was red carded 17 seconds after his introduction from the bench against Dundee United in 1999 his name went down as the fastest ordering off in Dons history. To rub salt into the wounds, it was his first appearance since a suspension after being sent off against Celtic just six minutes after entering the play as a substitute. Alex Miller paid £300,000 to secure the services of the Bradford City player in 1998. Pepper was loaned to Southend United before landing a permanent move to Scunthorpe. He also played for Barrow before forging a career as a social worker in York.

Jens Petersen

Debut: League, 27 January 1965 v Third Lanark (h) won 3-1
Appearances: League 145, Scottish Cup 22, League Cup 31, Europe 7
Goals: League 7, Scottish Cup 1, League Cup 1, Europe 1
Also played for: Denmark, Esbjerg

With more than 200 Aberdeen appearances to his credit, Jens Petersen can be lauded as one of the club's most successful imports. The Danish star was among the first continental players to grace the Scottish top flight and he was a key man at Pittodrie in the 1960s as he rose to become captain in succession to Harry Melrose.

Petersen took a huge gamble when he made the move from Esbjerg in January 1965. Because of rules adopted by the Danish authorities during that era, turning professional meant the defender had to sacrifice his international career to make the move happen.

By that stage he had 22 caps under his belt and, as the reigning Danish player of the year on the back of his club's triumph in the domestic league, looked destined for a long and illustrious stint in the red of his country.

Instead he chose to pull on the red of Tommy Pearson's Aberdeen, going on to play under Eddie Turnbull during a six season spell on the Pittodrie staff. Pearson had thrown his net wide to attempt to improve the fortunes of his struggling Dons, recruiting Petersen along with Jorg Ravn and Leif Mortensen at a time when foreign markets were largely untapped.

Persuading the cultured stopper to call time on his international career was not the only obstacle the Dons had to negotiate to clinch the deal, having first targeted the player when he was in the midst of national service with the armed forces in his homeland. He eventually secured early release from those duties - but had to serve out the remaining months of his service upon his return to Scandinavia at the end of his playing career.

He lost his place to the emerging talent Martin Buchan towards the end of the 1969/70 campaign, meaning his missed out on that season's Scottish Cup final victory. He had come close to success in the national tournament, playing in the 1967 Scottish Cup showdown with Celtic, but fell at the final hurdle when he and his team-mates were beaten 2-0 by the Hoops. By the time the club reached the final again three years later the chance was gone for the popular foreigner, with Buchan not only taking his place in the back line but also inheriting the captaincy.

After being released by Aberdeen the Dane moved to fresh pastures, turning out in Austrian and Belgian football before returning to Denmark. In recent years he worked as sports development officer at his first club Esbjerg. He also become a prolific marathon runner and has completed the races in Berlin, London, Prague and New York.

Billy Pirie

Debut: League, 16 March 1974 v Falkirk (h) won 6-0
Appearances: League 52, Scottish Cup 2, League Cup 9
Goals: League 11
Also played for: Arbroath, Dundee

Aberdonian striker Billy Pirie proved he had an eye for goal during his three seasons in and around the Dons team. Pirie, a former Sunnybank A and Banks o' Dee player, was first blooded by manager Jimmy Bonthrone in 1974 and after settling into his stride proved a potent deputy for Drew Jarvie as he bagged four goals in six starts in the 1974/75 season. Seven strikes in eight starts the next term did not secure a long term future with his home town club and Pirie moved on to Arbroath and Dundee before sampling football in South Africa, America and Australia.

Ian Porteous

Debut: League, 5 May 1983 v Kilmarnock (h) won 5-0
Appearances: League 70, Scottish Cup 10, League Cup 7, Europe 4
Goals: League 6, Scottish Cup 1, League Cup 2
Also played for: Herfolge (Denmark), Kilmarnock, Elgin City, Arbroath

May 1983 will forever be etched in the memory of Aberdeen supporters who revel in the glory of Gothenburg. For young midfielder Ian Porteous the date is memorable for a different reason as it marks the month in which he made his first team debut, stepping into the top team for a 5-0 demolition of Kilmarnock at Pittodrie in the final game before the European Cup Winners' Cup final against Real Madrid. Porteous remained on the staff until 1989, used mainly as an impact player from the bench, before joining Danish outfit Herfolge.

He returned to Scottish soil with Kilmarnock and also turned out for Elgin City in the Highland League before a spell with Arbroath in the mid-1990s.

David Preece

Debut: League, 1 August 1999 v Celtic (h) lost 5-0
Appearances: League 89, Scottish Cup 10, League Cup 7
Also played for: Sunderland, Darlington, Silkeborg, OB Odense, Barnsley

Affable English goalkeeper David Preece is one of the few players who can blame a piece of furniture for stalling their career. The Wearsider's comeuppance came as the result of a wardrobe falling on his foot during a spot of amateur removals at his city home and left him kicking his heels in the physio's room.

It was one of a clutch of setbacks for a man who had arrived at Pittodrie in a £300,000 deal from Darlington ahead of the 1999/2000 season. He was an Ebbe Skovdahl recruit and was installed as the first choice goalkeeper.

By the end of the maiden season he had been usurped by veteran Jim Leighton and throughout his six years in Scotland he faced a series of challenges for the No.1 jersey. Leighton, Ryan Esson and Peter Kjaer all jumped ahead in the queue at various stages.

Preece, who had started his career with Sunderland before moving on to become a regular in the first team at Darlington, had an extended spell in the first team under Steve Paterson but found it was a false dawn.

The arrival of Jimmy Calderwood in the manager's office led to the recruitment of Jamie Langfield and Preece's days were numbered. In 2005 he departed for Danish side Silkeborg and settled in Scandinavian football. He moved across his adopted country to OB Odense in 2008 and spent a year with the club before opting for a return to England with Barnsley in 2009 to serve as reserve keeper.

Horace Preston

Debut: League, 26 April 1947 v Queen's Park (a) drew 0-0
Appearances: League 3

South African defender Horace Preston spent three seasons with Aberdeen in the post-war years. He made his debut in the spring of 1947, when he was pressed into action at right-back, and remained a valuable squad man through to the summer of 1949.

Bryan Prunty

Debut: Scottish Cup, 21 January 2004 v Dundee (a) won 3-2
Appearances: League 17, Scottish Cup 4
Goals: League 2
Also played for: Celtic, Caley Thistle, Airdrie United, Ayr United, Stirling Albion, Alloa Athletic

A stunning 2-1 win against Celtic at Parkhead in April 2004 was the highlight of Bryan Prunty's short time with the Dons. He had arrived at Pittodrie from the Hoops, where he had served his apprenticeship, in January that year and cancelled out Henrik Larsson's opener in a game settled by David Zdrilic's dramatic late winner. It was a sweet moment for the striker, but not enough to prolong his Aberdeen career. He joined Caley Thistle on a free transfer in August 2004 and has gone on to play for Airdrie United, Ayr United, Stirling Albion and Alloa Athletic.

Ian Purdie

Debut: League, 15 April 1972 v Clyde (a) drew 0-0
Appearances: League 40, Scottish Cup 6, League Cup 12, Europe 2
Goals: League 10, Scottish Cup 1, League Cup 3
Also played for: Dundee, Motherwell, Wigan Athletic

A Scotland under-23 cap won while making a name for himself with Aberdeen in the early 1970s robbed winger Ian Purdie of an international career with Australia. The Socceroos hoped to adopt the former Dons man during a successful spell with the Canberra Arrows but had to concede defeat. The left flanker had joined Aberdeen from junior side Larkhall Thistle in 1970 and became known for his powerful shot. His departure to Dundee was as a makeweight in the deal that brought Jocky Scott to the north-east in 1975. Spells with Motherwell and Wigan Athletic followed before he moved to Australia to star for several clubs.

Gavin Rae

Debut: League, 19 February 2012 v St Johnstone (h) drew 0-0
Appearances (up to the end of 2011/12): League 12
Also played for: Scotland (14 caps), Dundee, Rangers, Cardiff City

Gavin Rae eventually landed at his hometown club in January 2012. Rae had starred in Aberdeen juvenile football and was snapped up by Dundee straight from school. He went on to shine for Scotland, Rangers and Cardiff before landing back at Dens Park and then moving on to Aberdeen in the twilight of his career. Rae, 34 when he joined, rejected overtures from Hibs to commit himself to the Dons.

Tommy Rae

Debut: League Cup, 10 August 1968 v Clyde (a) lost 4-1
Appearances: League 14, League Cup 7, Europe 2
Goals: League 2
Also played for: Partick Thistle, Cowdenbeath, Morton, East Stirling

Free-scoring winger Tommy Rae was viewed as a key signing for Eddie Turnbull in the summer of 1968 as the Dons splashed out £20,000 on the 22-year-old right sided Partick Thistle star. The Glaswegian had started life as a forward before moving wide and maintained his goal touch after the switch of position.

Despite going straight into Turnbull's team he was quickly edged out by Dave Johnston and returned to Partick in 1969. Rae remained at Firhill until 1975 and returned for a third spell in 1977 after stops with Cowdenbeath, Morton and East Stirling.

Jorg Ravn

Debut: League, 27 January 1965 v Third Lanark (h) won 3-1
Appearances: League 25, Scottish Cup 7, League Cup 1
Goals: League 9, Scottish Cup 2, League Cup 1
Also played for: Copenhagen

An average of a goal for every two games was a decent return for Danish forward Jorg Ravn following his arrival midway through the 1964/65 season, with his reputation enhanced by a goal on his debut at home to Third Lanark.

The powerfully built Copenhagen striker, a Danish under-23 cap before his transfer, had been leading scorer in Denmark's league for the three years prior to his move to Scotland with the Dons. He lost his place under Eddie Turnbull and was released in April 1966 to allow him to return to Scandinavia.

John Reilly

Debut: League, 2 April 1977 v Kilmarnock (a) won 2-1
Appearances: League 1
Also played for: Hamilton Academical

Glaswegian midfielder John Reilly made his solitary first team appearance in a 2-1 Premier Division win at Kilmarnock under Ally MacLeod in 1977. The youth product, who joined the club as a 13-year-old, was released by Billy McNeill the following year and was picked up by Hamilton Accies.

Mark Reynolds

Debut: Scottish Cup, 7 January 2012 v Forfar (a) won 4-0
Appearances: League 16, Scottish Cup 5
Also played for: Motherwell, Sheffield Wednesday

Former Scotland under-21 international Mark Reynolds will go down as one of the most successful temporary signings made by Aberdeen. Recruited on loan from Sheffield Wednesday, the ex-Motherwell stopper, who played over 200 games for the Steelmen, was a reliable and consistent performer for Craig Brown's side as defensive frailties of previous regimes were ironed out.

Reynolds opted to return to Sheffield Wednesday at the end of the 2011/12 season, with them having just won promotion to the Championship, and fight for his place, having seen opportunities with the Owls limited up to that point.

Peter Rice

Debut: League, 18 December 1948 v Morton (a) drew 1-1
Appearances: League 23, Scottish Cup 1, League Cup 3
Goals: League 3
Also played for: Hibs, St Mirren

Winger Peter Rice was one of a clutch of players blooded by Aberdeen as football settled back to normality in the post-war years. The Hibs youth product had his chances of regular action blocked by the emergence of Alan Boyd as first choice for the role on the right flank and moved on to St Mirren in 1950 for a four year stint at Love Street. Rice went on to turn out for Raith Rovers and Albion Rovers before being appointed as a youth coach by the SFA and taking the national under-16 and under-18 sides under his wing. Rice, who died in 1990 at the age of 65, also coached with Glasgow University and Westerlands.

Lee Richardson

Debut: League, 19 September 1992 v Partick Thistle (h) won 2-0
Appearances: League 64, Scottish Cup 8, League Cup 4, Europe 3
Goals: League 6, Scottish Cup 2, League Cup 1, Europe 1
Also played for: Halifax, Watford, Blackburn Rovers, Oldham, Stockport (on loan), Huddersfield, Bury (on loan), Livingston, Chesterfield
Managed: Chesterfield

Snarling midfielder Lee Richardson once claimed he would rather play drums for heavy metal heavyweights AC/DC than turn out for Inter Milan. It may have been tongue in cheek, but the star's taste in music was no surprise to anyone who watched him perform on the pitch. He was loud and abrasive and not easily intimidated.

While Richardson became something of an enemy to Scotland's referees, with perceived persecution one of the reasons cited when he cut short his Dons days, there were also subtleties to his play. As well as snapping into tackles he could carve open defences with a deft pass or thunder home breathtaking goals with power and accuracy. He was a midfielder who had it all, including the appreciation of the Red Army.

The Englishman arrived from Blackburn Rovers in 1992, where he had made a half-century of league starts. Manager Willie Miller saw something that caught his attention while watching Duncan Shearer in action for the Lancashire side and eventually got his man. Miller classes Richardson and Shearer as his two best buys, with each mating spirit and talent in equal measure to provide a flashback to the type of characters who dominated during the glory days that their manager had been used to during his playing career.

Before landing in Aberdeen's lap, Richardson had served his apprenticeship with Halifax and Watford in England's lower leagues. It was in Scotland's top flight that he flourished.

The midfield general became a favourite for the Aberdeen support, an appreciation clearly not shared by the country's officials. In just 80 appearances he was booked 22 times and sent off twice, enduring suspension after suspension at a time when his team were desperately attempting to break the dominance of Rangers. The club finished runners-up in the league in each of Richardson's two seasons in Scotland's top flight and endured two cup final disappointments.

Rangers won the Scottish Cup and League Cup finals of the 1992/93 season 2-1, with Richardson's goal in the Scottish Cup showdown not enough to prevent the Ibrox men from lifting the trophy.

It was an enormous source of frustration for the player, along with the ongoing battle against the nation's referees, and in 1994 he chose to seek fresh pastures. He commanded a £325,000 fee when he joined Oldham Athletic to chase his dream of Premiership football.

Three years with the Latics did not bring the reward of top flight football and he went on to serve a loan stint with Stockport before switching permanently to Huddersfield. Loan moves to Bury in 1999 and Livingston in 2000 followed before hopping back over the border to link up with Chesterfield. He moved from player to manager with the club in 2007, spending two years in charge of the Spireites.

Tommy Ring

Debut: League, 6 April 1963 v Clyde (h) lost 2-0
Appearances: League 2
Also played for: Scotland (12 caps), Clyde, Everton, Barnsley, Fraserburgh, Stevenage Town

Scotland international left winger Tommy Ring, capped a dozen times in the 1950s, was a veteran when he checked in at Pittodrie in 1963 after his release by Barnsley.

The former Clyde man had also starred for Everton but made only two appearances for the Dons before being freed by Tommy Pearson and joining Fraserburgh in the Highland League and playing on with Stevenage Town. Ring died in 1997.

Steve Ritchie

Debut: League, 21 March 1978 v Clydebank (h) won 2-0
Appearances: League 10, Scottish Cup 2
Goals: Scottish Cup 1
Also played for: Morton, Hereford Town, Torquay

Billy McNeill snapped up the former Morton defender from Hereford for £10,000 in the spring of 1978, his final signing as Dons boss. The tall left-back took over from Chic McLelland for the title run-in as Aberdeen came within two points of matching champions Rangers. He also scored in the 2-1 Scottish Cup final defeat aganst the Ibrox men that term. He was released by Alex Ferguson and joined Torquay in 1980.

Willie Robb

Debut: League, 2 January 1950 v Dundee (a) drew 1-1
Appearances: League 4
Also played for: Leyton Orient, Albion Rovers, Bradford City

Wing-half Willie Robb made well over 100 appearances for Bradford City in the mid-1950s after finding a football home in Yorkshire. The Cambuslang-born player turned out four times for Aberdeen in the 1949/50 season after joining from the junior ranks in his native Glasgow. A spell at Leyton Orient followed by service with Albion Rovers preceded his time with Bradford, which ended in 1958 when he returned to Scotland with Rutherglen Glencairn.

Clark Robertson

Debut: League, 1 May 2010 v Hamilton (h) lost 3-1
Appearances (up to end of 2011/12): League 25, League Cup 1, Scottish Cup 3

Mark McGhee blooded the versatile Clark Robertson late in the 2009/10 season and continued to push the teenager forward the following term as injuries and a lack of form forced the manager to shuffle his pack. Robertson returned to the under-19 squad to continue his football education after Craig Brown was appointed.

Craig Robertson

Debut: League, 17 December 1988 v St Mirren (h) won 3-1
Appearances: League 34, Scottish Cup 3, League Cup 2, Europe 4
Goals: League 3, Europe 2
Also played for: Raith Rovers, Dunfermline Athletic

A stunning long range strike against Rapid Vienna at Pittodrie in a 2-1 Uefa Cup win in the 1989/90 season was Craig Robertson's most famous contribution to the Dons cause. The Austrians won 1-0 in the return leg on the continent to go through to the next round but Robertson had enjoyed his moment in the sun by then. Signed by Alex Smith from Dunfermline for £160,000 the previous year, the midfielder served as a squad man for three years before returning to the Pars. He was recruited by Aberdeen for a second time when he was appointed chief scout under director of football and former team-mate Willie Miller.

Hugh Robertson

Debut: League, 26 March 1994 v Dundee United (h) won 1-0
Appearances: League 22, Scottish Cup 3, League Cup 3, Europe 1
Goals: League 2
Also played for: Dundee, Brechin City (on loan), Ayr United (on loan), Caley Thistle (on loan), Ross County, Hartlepool United

A thunderous shot became the trademark of emerging youngster Hugh Robertson's game. The Aberdonian's hammer like left boot posed a genuine threat at set-pieces, whether going for goal or with dangerous dead ball deliveries, and he was a candidate to fill the troublesome left-back berth as he was eased into the first team by Willie Miller in the 1993/94 season. Robertson remained in the squad for the next three seasons before moving on to Dundee in 1997. Loan spells with Brechin, Ayr and Caley Thistle followed before he found his football home at Ross County. The powerfully built defender made more than 100 appearances for the Staggies and followed manager Neale Cooper to Hartlepool in 2004, returning for a second stint with County three years later.

Ian Robertson

Debut: League, 12 May 1984 v St Mirren (a) lost 3-2
Appearances: League 22, Scottish Cup 7
Also played for: Montrose

Between his first appearance and his last, Ian Robertson spent eight seasons as part of Aberdeen's first team squad. The defender was hot property as a schoolboy growing up in Inverness and was capped by Scotland at schoolboy level before pledging his football to Alex Ferguson and the Dons. He was introduced to the first team fray in the final game of the 1983/84 season and filled in at full-back before being released at the end of the 1990/91 campaign. Robertson was snapped up by Montrose and went on to skipper the Links Park side.

Jimmy Robertson

Debut: League Cup, 17 August 1960 v Raith Rovers (a) lost 4-1
Appearances: League 2, League Cup 1
Also played for: Newport County, Bath City, Motherwell

Small and pacy inside forward Jimmy Robertson was one of the teenage recruits discovered during one of manager Tommy Pearson's scouting trips. He joined as a teenager from juvenile side Edinburgh Thistle in 1960 and made three appearances before being released after a single season. Robertson went on to play for Newport County and Bath City before turning out for Motherwell and in South African football.

Ben Robson

Debut: League, 28 April 1947 v Queen of the South (a) won 5-1
Appearances: League 1
Also played for: Southport, Annfield Plain

Gateshead-born defender Ben Robson's single Aberdeen appearance came in a 5-1 win at Queen of the South late in the 1946/47 season when he turned out at left-back. Robson joined Southport in 1949, before moving on to Annfield Plain.

David Robertson

Debut: League, 18 August 1986 v Hamilton (h) won 2-0
Appearances: League 133+2, Scottish Cup 10, League Cup 20+1, Europe 9+1
Goals: League 2, League Cup 1
Also played for: Scotland (3 caps), Rangers, Leeds United, Montrose
Managed: Elgin City, Montrose.

At the end of his debut season David Robertson arrived at Pittodrie to find a new four year contract awaiting his signature. The teenage defender was one of the hottest properties in British football and the Dons were sending out a clear warning to the big guns who had set their sights on the speedy left back. The Aberdonian did not need time to think about his next move, agreeing to a deal which would see him spend his key developing years in the north-east.

Robertson was signed from local juvenile side Deeside by Alex Ferguson and launched his Aberdeen career as the legendary manager was winding down his days in Scotland. The teenager was introduced gently by Ferguson at the age of 17 in 1986. He made his first start less than two months later and by the end of the 1986/87 campaign had 42 appearances under his belt across all three domestic competitions and the European Cup Winners' Cup. He was also being fast-tracked at international level, a Scotland B cap at the tender age of 18 after less than a season in the club game.

In the 1989/90 season Robertson enjoyed his finest spell in the red of his home town team. The Dons completed an Old Firm cup double, with a 2-1 victory over Rangers in the League Cup final followed up with the dramatic penalty shoot-out win against Celtic in the Scottish Cup showpiece.

A Premier Division runners-up medal completed an impressive haul for the emerging talent and he was a key part of the 1991 side which ran Rangers even closer in the league, only missing out on the title on the final day of the season when a 2-0 defeat to Rangers kept the flag at Ibrox by virtue of two points.

That heartbreak proved to be the catalyst for Robertson's switch to the champions in a £970,000 deal in the summer of 1991. The defender was 22 when he switched to the Govan club and an established Scotland under-21 international. He went on to become a main man in the dominant Light Blues side of that period.

Between 1991 and 1997 he won the league championship every year and added Scottish Cup and the League Cup medals as well as playing European football year in and year out. With Rangers he also realised his Scotland ambitions but his tally of three caps did not do justice to his standing in the club game.

In 1997 he switched to the English Premiership with a £500,000 transfer to Leeds United, led by George Graham, at the age of 28. Injury restricted his appearances for the Elland Road side and he retired in March, 2000. Two years later he moved back to the north-east and joined the coaching staff at Montrose, combining his training ground duties with a brief playing comeback. He launched his management career with Elgin City in 2003 and returned to Montrose to take the top job at Links Park in 2006. He resigned the following year and emigrated to the USA to take up a youth coaching role with Arizona club Sereno.

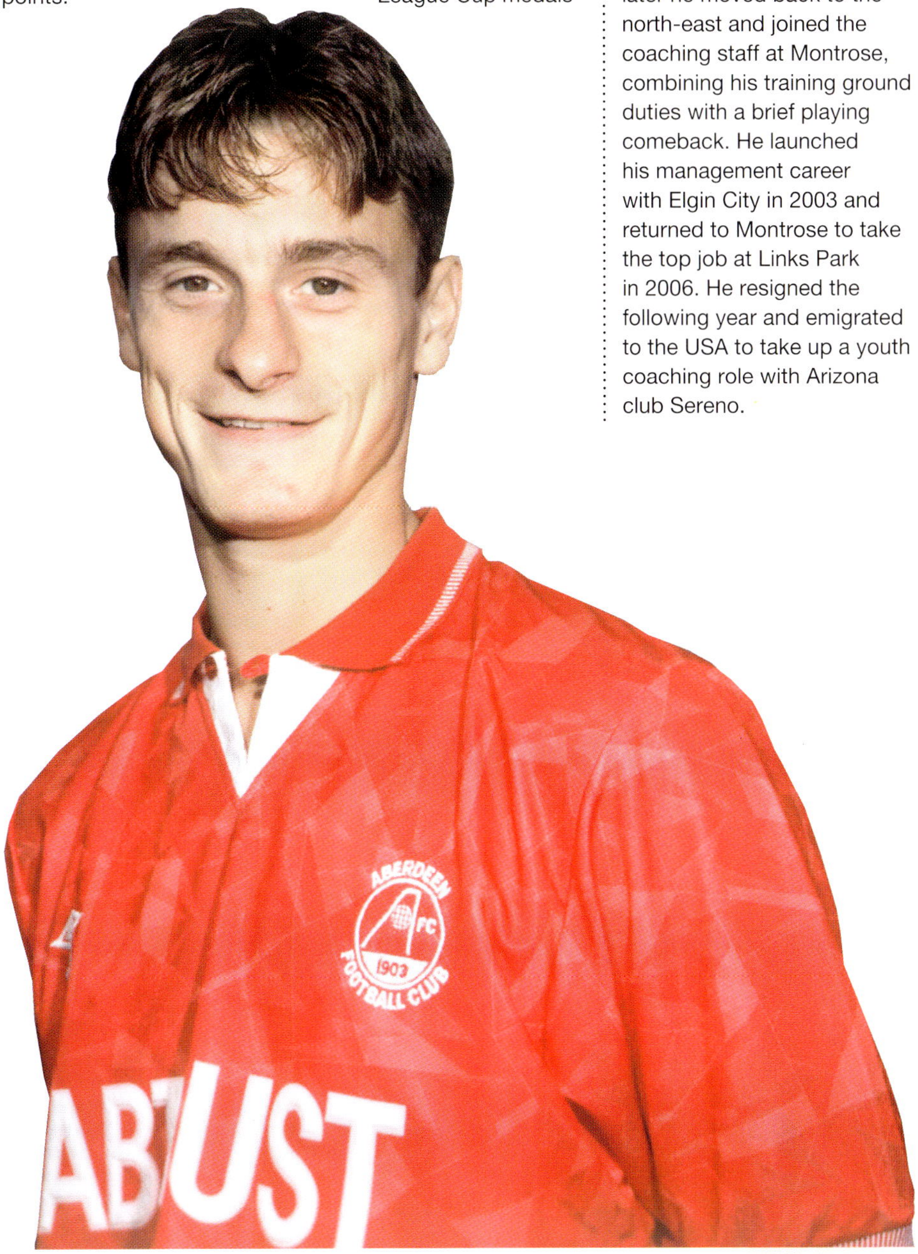

Davie Robb

Debut: Scottish Cup, 28 January 1967 v Dundee (a) won 5-0
Appearances: League 251+14, Scottish Cup 27+2, League Cup 51+4, Europe 16
Goals: League 78, Scottish Cup 10, League Cup 8, Europe 2
Also played for: Scotland (5 caps), Newburgh, Tampa Bay Rowdies, Norwich City, Dunfermline Athletic

In a split second inside extra-time in a Hampden cup final Davie Robb had the chance to make himself a legend and, as he did 98 times for the club in the space of twelve years, he hit the back of the net without a second thought. It was the most important goal in his career and came in the 93rd minute of the 1976 League Cup final as a match which had enthralled a crowd close to 70,000 moved into extra-time. Celtic were the opponents and it was the Hoops who drew first blood.

Kenny Dalglish was judged to have been fouled by Drew Jarvie inside the Dons box and the Celtic striker dusted himself down before converting the opener from the spot in the 11th minute. King Kenny may have been in green and white, but the reds had their own stars who were just as keen to make an impact on the big stage.

It was Jarvie who made it 1-1 just 13 minutes later with a header from a Joe Harper assist and the tie remained in the balance until Robb struck the killer blow with his first goal in eight appearances in that season's cup run. It was the ideal time to open his account and the player known affectionately as The Brush had successfully swept the Parkhead men aside.

It was the second winner's medal Robb had claimed with Aberdeen, having been at the beating heart of the team which had won the Scottish Cup in 1970. Again Celtic were the defeated finalists, falling to a 3-1 defeat on that occasion but Robb had played his part in the final and in the run to Hampden, having played in four of the five ties and scored a double in the 4-0 first round victory against Clyde to set the ball rolling. The Scottish Cup win had ended a long period without success, since the 1955 league triumph, and re-established the Dons as a significant force in the evolving Scottish game thanks to an emerging crop of young and energetic players.

When he first savoured that winning feeling Robb was in his fourth season as a Pittodrie player. The Dundonian signed in 1965 from junior side Newburgh spent a season and a half learning his trade in the Dons reserves, in five different positions, before being handed his senior debut by Eddie Turnbull in a 5-0 victory against Dundee in the first round of the Scottish Cup at Dens Park on January 28, 1967.

At 19 he had taken his bow as a right winger but his combative style and full blooded approach ensured he would have a more central role to play in the seasons ahead, both in midfield and attack. Robb was a robust and all action star who not surprisingly, given those qualities, had endeared himself to the Red Army and become a cult hero.

His goalscoring ability was demonstrated when he scored the first hat-trick of his Aberdeen career in a 6-0 mauling of Clyde at Pittodrie at the start of the 1969/70 season, by which time he was an established first team player having made 42 appearances the season before and 20 in 1967/68 as he built on his introduction to the first team the previous term. Between 1969 and 1972 he played in excess of 40 games a season for four consecutive campaigns, hinting at stamina to go with the power which was such a major part of his game.

The cup win in 1970 provided an early cup highlight and the following year there was cause for celebration on the international stage. Robb made his Scotland debut against Portugal in Lisbon in April, 1971, as Bobby Brown's side fell to a 2-0 defeat. Each of his five caps came in the same year as his debut was followed by defeats against England, Denmark and the USSR as well as a draw with Wales. It had been a whirlwind international experience for the east coast man, another box ticked as he piled up experience with club and country.

While his international career ended at the age of 24 his work with his club was far from over and Robb remained at Pittodrie until 1978, playing under Eddie Turnbull as well as Jimmy Bonthrone, Ally MacLeod and Billy McNeill. They were four very different managers but each of them had seen the merit of including Robb in their side in various positions.

In addition to two cup winner's medals Robb collected league runners-up badges in 1971, 1972 and 1977. He overcame a serious injury in 1974 and battled to reclaim his first team place. In his final campaign in 1977/78 he played 13 games and scored a hat-trick in a 4-1 win at home to Motherwell just over a month before his final outing in a 2-1 victory against Celtic in January, 1978. There was no chance of going out with a whimper.

When he left it was for the glitz and glamour of the North American Soccer League, signing a three year deal with the Tampa Bay Rowdies early in 1978 to join the army of Brits abroad. Scotland had provided a steady stream of stars for the NASL and Robb was far from the first ex-Aberdeen man to win a contract on the other side of the Atlantic, with Graham Leggat and Dave Smith among those to have sampled the US game years earlier.

The flame haired attacker combined his US commitments with a spell at Norwich City before a brief stint with Dunfermline in 1981. That year he retired from playing to take up a new career in the oil industry and has also been involved in the licensed trade in the north-east.

Admiral

Doug Rougvie

Debut: League Cup, 9 August 1975 v Celtic (a) lost 1-0
Appearances: League 181+19, Scottish Cup 26, League Cup 45+7, Europe 28+2
Goals: League 19, League Cup 2
Also played for: Scotland (1 cap), Keith, Chelsea, Brighton, Shrewsbury, Fulham, Dunfermline, Montrose, Huntly, Cove Rangers
Managed: Montrose, Huntly, Cove Rangers

In twelve years on the Aberdeen staff Doug Rougvie became a playing legend, feared opponent and cult hero during the glory days of the lates 1970s and early 1980s. On the pitch the Rougvie name went hand in hand with heart on the sleeve performances and a steely defensive resolve while off the park he was synonymous with some of the more bizarre incidents of the time, all of which endeared him to the Pittodrie faithful.

Tales of the European Cup Winners' Cup hero's exploits are the stuff of legend, including his dispute over his decision to swap the safety of four wheels for the high speed thrills of a motorbike during Alex Ferguson's reign. The manager was not amused, to put it mildly, but Rougvie's passion for bikes lives on to this day.

During the 1984 Scottish Cup victory parade the towering stopper lost his false teeth from the top deck of the open top bus as it made its way along Union Street, prompting a comical scramble among the adoring fans below. They were eventually launched back onto the bus to a grateful Rougvie but what price would those gnashers fetch in the world of internet auction sites today?

Rougvie's larger than life character in the dressing room did not disguise his fearsome reputation and formidable appearance once he crossed the white line, with the 6ft 2in defender no stranger to suspensions in a lengthy playing career.

The Fifer signed for the Dons from juvenile football in 1972 and was farmed out to Keith for an early introduction to the man's game and won a Highland League Cup winner's medal to whet his appetite for what was to follow with the Dons.

He made his breakthrough under Jimmy Bonthrone in 1975 in a 1-0 League Cup defeat against Celtic on August 9 but had a patient three year wait to truly establish himself in the first team as an Alex Ferguson player, sharing the duties of partnering Willie Miller at the heart of the defence with Alex McLeish and Willie Garner in the 1978/79 campaign.

That season he had his first taste of controversy, becoming the only player in the history of the League Cup to be red carded in a final after a penalty box incident involving Rangers striker Derek Johnstone. The Ibrox men won 2-1, with Rougvie and his team-mates furiously protesting his innocence. The two men at the centre of the clash later became team-mates at Chelsea but Rougvie refused to forgive and forget the striker for his part in one of his most disappointing afternoons in football.

The following term he was switched to left back and made 22 starts in the league championship winning team of 1980 to collect his first medal as a Dons player.

The Scottish Cup followed in 1982, when Rangers were beaten 4-1 in the final,

to pave the way for the European Cup Winners' Cup success in which Rougvie had a major part to play. He missed just two ties in that victorious run to Gothenburg glory, one leg of both the first and second rounds, and answered an SOS from Ferguson for the 2-1 final win against Real Madrid when he switched from left back to the right side of the defence to fill the place of the injured Stuart Kennedy.

With another Scottish Cup medal in the bag courtesy of a 1-0 win over Rangers in the 1983 final, Rougvie was an unmovable member of Ferguson's renowned side and added another Scottish Cup badge to his collection afer a 2-1 final win against Celtic in 1984 as well as a European Super Cup medal when he played in the first leg of the 1983 win against Hamburg.

In December, 1983, Rougvie was capped by Scotland manager Jock Stein against Northern Ireland in Belfast. It ended in a 2-0 defeat but completed his set of domestic honours, European success and international recognition by the time he was 27.

In the summer of 1984 Rougvie moved to Chelsea in a £250,000 deal. Former Dons player Ian McNeill was in charge of the Blues at that point, deputising for boss John Neal, and had been alerted to the big defender's unique talents. The lure of far improved wages and the challenge of pitting his wits against the household names in English football tempted the Fifer to move to Stamford Bridge, where he endeared himself to the London fans despite not settling particularly well in the surroundings of the league he found himself in. While his new life was south of the border, Rougvie's heart never truly left his football first love at Pittodrie. He became a regular at meetings of the Metropolitan and South England branch of the Aberdeen Supporters Club while based in the capital and would even travel north with the exiled Dons fans when there were breaks in playing commitments with Chelsea, who benefited from his familiar commitment whenever called upon.

McNeill was so impressed with his new man's heart and resilience he actually signed him twice, recruiting Rougvie for Shrewsbury after taking charge at the club. The defender also had spells with Brighton and Fulham before returning to his roots with Dunfermline in 1989.

He spent a season with the Pars before, at the age of 34, being appointed co-manager of Montrose with former Pittodrie team-mate Chic McLelland. He won promotion to the First Division with the Angus side before being replaced by Jim Leishman in 1992, continuing his career in the Highland League as a player for Steve Pateron's dominant Huntly side of the 1990s. Rougvie succeeded Paterson as manager at Christie Park in 1995 and enjoyed title success before parting company with the club. His last involvement in the senior game was as manager of Cove Rangers immediately after his Huntly tenure, now concentrating instead on a career in the oil industry which has taken him from Aberdeen to Dubai.

Andy Roddie

Debut: League, 9 November 1991 v Celtic (a) lost 2-1
Appearances: League 18, Scottish Cup 1
Goals: League 5
Also played for: Motherwell, St Mirren, Peterhead, Elgin City, Inverurie Locos

Andy Roddie was the man charged with bringing the dying art of wing wizardry back to the fore at Pittodrie. The former Glasgow United youngster was signed on an S-Form by Alex Ferguson in the early 1990s. Roddie, capped by Scotland at under-17, under-19 and under-21 level, spent three seasons under Alex Smith and then Willie Miller before being snapped up for £150,000 by former Dons team-mate Alex McLeish at Motherwell. He embarked on a whistle-stop tour taking in Hong Kong, Sweden and Iceland before returning to Britain. He played for St Mirren, amongst others, before settling back in the north-east with Peterhead, Elgin and Inverurie Locos. Roddie serves as chairman of Kintore United Boys' Club and co-manager of Colony Park Juniors.

Allan Rodger

Debut: League Cup, 25 August 1951 v Queen of the South (a) lost 2-0
Appearances: League 2, League Cup 3
Also played for: Ayr United

Defender Alan Rodger was spotted by Aberdeen while playing for Kello Rovers in Dumfries and Galloway. He made five appearances in the 1951/52 season. Rodger conceded defeat and moved on to Ayr United in 1952 and established himself as a regular with the Honest Men.

Ian Rodger

Debut: League, 8 April 1950 v Hearts (h) lost 5-0
Appearances: League 31, Scottish Cup 13, League Cup 5
Goals: League 13, Scottish Cup 4
Also played for: Forfar Athletic, St Johnstone

Versatile attacker Ian Rodger suffered the heartbreak of defeat in the 1953 Scottish Cup final against Rangers. He had been ever present on the right wing in the run to the Hampden showdown, which went to a replay before the Dons fell to a 1-0 defeat. Rodger also turned out at centre forward after joining from Forfar Athletic in 1950 and hit double figures in the 1951/52 campaign with 10 goals from 15 appearances. He spent three years at Pittodrie before switching to St Johnstone and then returning to Forfar in 1957 for a two year spell.

Ken Ronaldson

Debut: League Cup, 8 August 1964 v Rangers (a) lost 4-0
Appearances: League 1, League Cup 1
Also played for: Bristol Rovers, Gillingham

Teenage forward Ken Ronaldson went from starring for juvenile side Edinburgh Rangers to going head to head with Glasgow Rangers at Ibrox within the space of a year. He was introduced to the Dons first team in 1964 in a 4-0 reverse against the Govan side. Ronaldson joined Bristol Rovers in 1965. He turned out for Gillingham before joining the police force in Kent.

Maurice Ross

Debut: League, 24 October 2009 v Dundee United (h) lost 2-0
Appearances: League 6, Scottish Cup 1
Also played for: Scotland (13 caps), Rangers, Sheffield Wednesday, Millwall, Wolves, Viking Stavanger (Norway), Kocaelispor (Turkey), Guoan (China)

Anyone with a Rangers background faces a real challenge in winning over Aberdeen's fiercely partisan support, but circumstances dictated that former Scotland international Maurice Ross had to be welcomed and allegiances placed to one side at a time when it was all hands to the pumps to try and keep the Dons afloat in the SPL. The experienced defender, who had seen service with Sheffield Wednesday as well as Millwall, Wolves, Norwegian club Viking Stavanager and Turkish outfit Kocaelispor after leaving Ibrox in 2005, bolstered Mark McGhee's struggling squad during the 2009/10 campaign. McGhee had hoped to keep the 13 times capped player longer but Ross opted to join Chinese champions Guoan in Beijing early in 2010.

David Rowson

Debut: League, 2 March 1996 v Kilmarnock (h) won 3-0
Appearances: League 133, Scottish Cup 7, League Cup 9, Europe 7
Goals: League 10, Scottish Cup 1, Europe 1
Also played for: Livingston (on loan) Stoke City, Partick Thistle, Northampton Town, Darlington, Boston United (on loan)

Roy Aitken knew a thing or two about midfield play as one of the finest exponents of the art of his generation. When he plucked 19-year-old prospect David Rowson from the Aberdeen youth ranks to hand him his debut in 1996 it was a massive vote of confidence for the local youngster.

Rowson was the perfect modern midfielder thanks to his sharp tackling, tidy use of the ball and ability to effortlessly play from box to box. Aside from a brief loan spell with Livingston in 2000 he was a regular at the heart of the Dons team under Aitken, Alex Miller, Paul Hegarty and Ebbe Skovdahl before the lure of English football proved too strong to resist. With the promise of a bumper pay packet and prospect of new challenges, it was an appealing package. As so many have discovered, the grass is not always greener away from Pittodrie.

Rowson rejected the offer of a new contract from the Dons and instead opted to join Stoke City in the summer of 2001. He played only a handful of games and stayed less than two years, returning to home soil to join Partick Thistle in January 2003.

Rowson rebuilt his confidence with the Jags and earned a second crack at the English game with Northampton. A spell with Darlington and loan stint with Boston United came before he linked up with Partick again in 2007 to sail past the 100 appearance mark.

Willie Roy

Debut: League, 28 February 1947 v Airdrie (h) won 3-0
Appearances: League 25, League Cup 3
Also played for: St Mirren, Dundee, Elgin City, Inverness Thistle, Forres Mechanics

Dependable defender Willie Roy served a solid apprenticeship in football as a junior stopper in his native Glasgow and then in the senior game with St Mirren. He moved to Aberdeen during the 1947/48 season and took over from Frank Dunlop at the heart of the Dons backline. Roy proved to be a reliable centre-half who had a habit of rising to the big occasion against Scotland's big name forwards. He played out his career with Dundee, Elgin City, Inverness Thistle and Forres Mechanics before retiring due to a back injury.

Bobby Russell

Debut: League, 24 October 1959 v Rangers (h) lost 5-0
Appearances: League 1
Also played for: Stenhousemuir, Third Lanark, Morton

Former Cambuslang Rangers junior player Bobby Russell was one of seven goalkeepers used in the turbulent 1959/60 season. The 18-year-old made his one appearance in a 5-0 home defeat against Rangers before returning to Cambuslang. He returned to the senior game with Stenhousemuir, Third Lanark and Morton.

Kevin Rutkiewicz

Debut: League, 27 November 1999 v Hibs (a) lost 2-0
Appearances: League 53, Scottish Cup 6, League Cup 6, Europe 2
Goals: League 1
Also played for: St Johnstone, Dunfermline (on loan)

When Kevin Rutkiewicz released his debut album in August 2010 it represented the realisation of a dream for the rugged defender. The singer songwriter, who has supported Midge Ure amongst others while fitting in gigs alongside his playing commitments, has established a niche for himself as Scottish football's chart hopeful.

Music has been a major part of the Glaswegian's life since his schooldays and he has successfully juggled his two identities to forge careers in both fields, with his album Handwritten receiving critical acclaim.

Reviews do not pay the bills and football has been the main breadwinner since he made his first appearance for Aberdeen during Ebbe Skovdahl's first season in charge in 1999/2000.

He was one of a clutch of players fast-tracked from the youth ranks to the first team as the Dane looked for fresh impetus. David Lilley, Rachid Belabed, Phil McGuire, Darren Mackie and Jamie McAllister were also blooded within months of each other.

The central defender made more than half a century of appearances before joining St Johnstone in 2004, going on to captain the Saints and winning the First Division championship with the Perth side.

Two knee injuries pushed him down the pecking order at McDiarmid Park and he was loaned out to Dunfermline during the January transfer window in 2011 to help the Pars with their championship win in the First Division.

George Samuel

Debut: League, 3 November 1951 v Queen of the South (h) drew 1-1
Appearances: League 4, League Cup 1
Goals: League 1
Also played for: Dunfermline Athletic, Stenhousemuir

Wing-half George Samuels turned out five times as a part-time player over the course of two seasons in the early 1950s. The civil servant switched to Dunfermline in 1954 and also featured for junior side Peebles Rovers before stepping back up with Stenhousemuir in 1958.

George Sang

Debut: League, 21 November 1959 v Hearts (h) lost 3-1
Appearances: League 3
Also played for: Arbroath, Peterhead, Buckie Thistle

Teenage defender George Sang progressed from juvenile outfit King Street A to juniors Rosemount and then on to Aberdeen. He played just a handful of games before moving on to Arbroath and then playing in the Highland League with Peterhead and, as skipper, Buckie Thistle. Sang, renowned for a rocket shot, returned to the junior game with Rosemount and played on past his 35th birthday.

Charlie Scott

Debut: League, 13 March 1948 v Queen's Park (a) lost 3-1
Appearances: League 1
Also played for: Arbroath

Goalkeeper Charlie Scott was drafted in as cover for regular No.1 George Johnstone in the spring of 1948 and made his solitary first team appearance in a 3-1 defeat away to Queen's Park. The former Leslie Hearts player moved on to Arbroath the following year and after a handful of appearances for the Angus side dropped down to the junior ranks with Fife outfit Markinch Victoria.

George Scott

Debut: League Cup, 14 August 1965 v Clyde (a) won 2-1
Appearances: League 2, League Cup 5
Goals: League 1, League Cup 1
Also played for: Liverpool, Tranmere Rovers

George Scott was lured south by Liverpool after completing his studies at Aberdeen's Middle School. He returned as a 20-year-old to sign for the Dons in the summer of 1965 and, despite going straight into Eddie Turnbull's side on the right wing, drifted out of the reckoning during his first season. Scott was released after a year with his home town club and went on to play for Tranmere Rovers as well as sampling football in South Africa.

Joe Shaughnessy

Debut: League, 14 May 2011 v Hibs (a) won 3-1
Appearances (up to end of 2010/11): League 1

Defender Joe Shaughnessy was pitched into action in the final game of the 2010/11 season and emerged with a win bonus after playing 90 minutes in the 3-1 win against Hibs at Easter Road. His debut came on the back of a two-year contract award by Craig Brown as the manager planned for the future.

Ian Scanlon

Debut: League, 29 April 1978 v Hibs (a) drew 1-1
Appearances: League 92+13, Scottish Cup 10+2, League Cup 18+1, Europe 10+2
Goals: League 12, Scottish Cup 6, League Cup 2
Also played for: East Stirling, Notts County, St Mirren

Aberdeen had not won the Scottish title for quarter of a century when they travelled to Easter Road on May 3, 1980. The Dons needed a victory against struggling Hibs and for third-placed St Mirren to take a point against second-placed Celtic for the long wait to end and that afternoon in Edinburgh it all fell into place.

Steve Archibald broke the deadlock in the capital after 26 minutes and two minutes later Andy Watson doubled the advantage. After the interval a double from Ian Scanlon, with a Mark McGhee goal sandwiched in between, put them on easy street.

With a 5-0 win in the bag, a tense wait for the delayed final whistle at Love Street ended when news filtered through the Saints had held the Parkhead men to a 0-0 draw. The Premier Division prize was Aberdeen's and Scanlon was an unlikely hero.

Unlikely for two particular reasons. The first was that he had actually quit football years earlier, claiming he had become disenchanted with the game. The second was that he had told manager Alex Ferguson he wanted to leave his club 17 months before collecting his championship medal. Fortunately, on that occasion Ferguson was in forgiving mood and the wide man remained firmly in his plans.

Scanlon was an unpredictable talent but gave the 1980 title winning side a valuable outlet on the left wing. His tendency to beat his marker more than once before finally delivering a cross infuriated Ferguson and provoked the famous hair-dryer treatment more than once, but Scanlon kept his place on the team-sheet.

In that championship winning season he featured in all but seven of the league games, starting 25 games and making four appearances from the bench. He scored eight Premier Division goals, including that vital double against Hibs to clinch the flag. Scanlon got his first big break with Notts County, joining as a teenager from East Stirling in 1972 and became a Meadow Lane favourite. At the age of 21 he topped the County scoring chart for the first time and continued to be their main man in attack until his dramatic decision to retire in November, 1977, at the age of 25. He claimed to have fallen out of love with the game and planned to use an inheritance to open a pub in the Nottingham area.

His exile proved short and in March, 1978, he was back in the game and back at the top after Aberdeen manager Billy McNeill negotiated a £40,000 deal with Notts County to enable Scanlon to make his comeback with the Dons.

Ferguson replaced McNeill that summer and installed Scanlon as his first choice No.11. Just three months into the campaign he knocked on the manager's door to request a transfer after he and his wife failed to settle in the north-east. Despite that off-field unrest he still appeared in 45 games in the 1978/79 season and was back at his elegant best for the victorious league campaign the following season.

A league runners-up medal followed in 1981 before a switch to St Mirren as part of the deal which brought Peter Weir to Pittodrie. Scanlon finally realised his ambition to venture into the licensed trade when he opened a pub in Glasgow following his depature from the Buddies.

Jocky Scott

Debut: League Cup, 20 August 1975 v Dumbarton (a) won 1-0
Appearances: League 52+11, Scottish Cup 4, League Cup 11+1
Goals: League 17, Scottish Cup 1, League Cup 4
Aberdeen co-manager: August 1988 to September 1991
Also played for: Scotland (2 caps), Chelsea, Dundee, Seattle Sounders.
Also managed: Dundee, Dunfermline, Arbroath, Notts County, Raith Rovers, Stirling Albion.

Jocky Scott was a cup double winning co-manager with Aberdeen in his successful stint alongside Alex Smith in the late 1980s and early 1990s but he also tasted the sweet taste of victory as a Dons player. Scott's goals helped earn his home town club a place in the 1976 League Cup final and he was part of the side which defeated Celtic 2-1 to lift the trophy.

Drew Jarvie and Davie Robb were the players on target in that Hampden showdown but Scott's own contribution should not be underestimated. He put his name on the scoresheet in the 2-0 quarter-final replay against Stirling Albion and helped himself to a hat-trick in the memorable 5-1 demolition of Rangers in the semi-final.

That cup run, under Ally MacLeod, was the peak of Scott's time in a red jersey. He was recruited by Jimmy Bonthrone in the summer of 1975 when the Pittodrie manager parted with £15,000 and Ian Purdie to secure the versatile Dundee attacker as he prepared for life after Joe Harper.

Scott, who was 27 when he returned home to the north-east, had twice been capped by Scotland four years previously but failed to add to those appearances he notched up while playing for Dundee. He had also been capped by Scotland at schoolboy level while a pupil at Aberdeen Grammar School, traditionally a rugby hotbed, before moving to Chelsea on an apprenticeship in 1963 from Aberdeen Lads' Club Spurs.

Homesickness led him back to Scotland just a year later when his long relationship with Dundee began. With the Dens Park side he established himself as a powerful and potent striker, helping the Tayside men to the League Cup in 1974.

He was a regular in his first full season on the Pittodrie playing staff, following in the footsteps of his father Willie who had turned out for the Dons in the 1930s, but made more sporadic appearances in the next two. In November 1977, after a brief stint on loan to Seattle in the North American Soccer League, he returned to Dens Park in a £15,000 deal.

He soon became reserve team coach at Dundee before stepping up to take on first team duties in 1981 under Donald Mackay. The Aberdonian went on to serve under Archie Knox and had the Dons to thank for his promotion to the Dens Park manager's seat. When Knox returned to Pittodrie to link up with Alex Ferguson for a second spell in 1986 it was Scott who benefited, becoming a manager in his own right for the first time at the age of 38.

Within two years he followed the same route when he was appointed co-manager with Alex Smith in 1988 with the Dons, part of a three man management team completed by former team-mate Drew Jarvie. The League Cup and Scottish Cup double in the 1989-90 season vindicated the board's decision to go with safety in numbers but Scott was keen to branch out on his own again and got the chance with Dunfermline in September 1991.

He went on to serve as a coach under Alex Miller at Hibs, which included a spell as caretaker boss at Easter Road, before also leading Arbroath, Dundee on two further occasions, Notts County, Raith Rovers and Viborg. In 2011 Scott return to management with Stirling Albion for a brief spell.

Teddy Scott

Debut: League, 18 February 1956 v Stirling Albion (a) won 2-0
Appearances: League 1
Also played for: Sunnybank, Brechin City, Elgin City

It takes a special man to attract a sell out crowd to Pittodrie and in Teddy Scott the Dons found that big draw. Scott was not a superstar player or a prolific goalscorer in his playing heyday but went on to become as loyal a servant as Aberdeen Football Club has ever known.

In 1999 the ground he called home for more than half a century was packed to the rafters to honour him. On the pitch, Alex Ferguson had taken his Manchester United team north to pay his own tribute to the man who had been a valuable ally on the Dons backroom team during his own time on the staff. The Teddy Scott testimonial attracted the rarity of a capacity crowd, a measure of the esteem in which Scott was held at that time. In the years that have followed none of that affection has evaporated.

Richard Donald, another great club servant, had a stand named after him but Scott also had a part of Pittodrie which will forever be part of Dons folklore. What became known as 'Teddy's Room' was part of life at the club for generations of players, coaches and staff. Packed with a treasure trove of football mementos collected during a lifetime in the game and contributed to by the great and good from every club he ever crossed paths with, it became the equivalent of Liverpool's famous boot room at Anfield. Scott was a confidante and father figure to players, coaches, managers and staff for decade after decade until his emotional decision to retire at the age of 74.

The association with Aberdeen began in 1954 when he signed as a 22 year-old centre half from Sunnybank, the club he had won the coveted junior Scottish Cup with that year. Bank returned to the headlines in 2010 when they shocked opponents Albion Rovers in the senior Scottish Cup, but it is the class of 54 who won a special place in the hearts of all junior fans in the north-east with their heroics.

After making the leap from junior to senior football, Scott made his first team debut for Aberdeen in a 2-0 win at Stirling Albion on February 18, 1956. It proved to be his only appearance for Dave Shaw's side, moving to Brechin 10 months later to continue his playing career in Angus before switching to Elgin City in the Highland League. His exploits in the red shirt were far from spectacular, but Scott's commitment to the cause was never in question. It was that quality, amongst others, that ensured his short playing career was not his only opportunity at Pittodrie.

In September, 1958, he returned to the Pittodrie staff as assistant trainer under Shaw and his second stint proved longer than anyone could have imagined. What started as a one year trial turned into a 45 year marathon as manager after manager recognised his contribution to the cause with a plethora of roles at the heart of the operation.

He became a fully qualified coach and thrived in his place on the Dons staff, even finding time to lend his expertise to Elgin City and Forres Mechanics by training the north duo's Aberdeen

players in the 1970s. In 1975 he was in the unique position of having all three of his clubs involved in the Scottish Cup at the same time. He also trained the area's referees up until 1982, when he was appointed honorary president of the Aberdeen and District Referees' Association. That was just one of a trail of honours from a long list of clubs and societies, including the Scottish Football Association and Scottish Professional Footballers' Association as well as UEFA, amassed over his decades of service as a trainer, reserve team coach and, prior to his retirement, kit man. He also served on the Scotland back-room team at the 1986 World Cup in Mexico to add to his impressive collection of experiences that combined to make him Aberdeen's resident wise old owl.

When the curtain fell on his Aberdeen career, tributes flooded in from football's hierarchy, led by Sir Alex Ferguson. Looking back on his arrival in 1978, Ferguson said: 'It soon became clear that Teddy was the one man I couldn't do without. It makes me proud to be able to describe him as a friend.'

Aberdeen 1969/1970; Teddy Scott; Arthur Graham; Bobby Clark; Dave Robb; Derek McKay; Eddie Turnbull; George Buchan; George Murray; Henning Boel; Jim Forrest; Jim Hermiston; Jimmy Bonthrone; Joe Harper; Martin Buchan; Tommy McMillan.

As Ferguson is never shy to point out, it was Scott who first spotted the defensive potential of a reserve striker by the name of Willie Miller. And so another legend was born, one of the many young players to have been nurtured by a man who was renowned as a coach with a brilliant eye for potential and who had the ability to get the best out of those who fell under his charge. He was a scout and coach rolled into one indispensable package.

Scott is also the man credited with the instigation of the youth system which provided top quality, international class players. Alex McLeish and Jim Leighton were just two of the young players to fall under his wing. He worked under every manager from Dave Shaw to Steve Paterson and remained a point of reference and trusted ear for generations of players and managers who continued to keep in touch long after they had left the north-east behind.

With five grandchildren to keep him busy, Scott retired to his home town of Ellon in Aberdeenshire in 2003 with the best wishes of an entire industry ringing in his ears. He received a rousing send off during a pre-season friendly against Liverpool, was treated to lunch by the directors and was presented with a silver salver and other gifts by his appreciative employers. Scott died in 2012 but the legacy will live on through the memories created by the players he helped to produce during the glory days of Aberdeen's rich history and his link to the most successful years ever witnessed by Dons fans.

Scott Severin

Debut: League, 7 August 2004 v Rangers (h) drew 0-0
Appearances: League 166, Scottish Cup 13, League Cup 8, Europe 7
Goals: League 12
Also played for: Scotland (15 caps up to end 2010/11), Hearts, Watford, Kilmarnock (on loan), Dundee United.

When Scott Severin signed on the dotted line at Pittodrie in the summer of 2004 the club completed a hat-trick by recruiting a defender, midfielder and attacker rolled into one. Under Jimmy Calderwood the Stirling born player patrolled all three of those beats, albeit fleetingly up front, for Aberdeen and proved an accomplished performer in each department.

He also served as captain for the Dons but it is his achievements in earning Scotland caps while on the Aberdeen payroll that, in the fullness of time, will separate Severin from those who served around him.

International honours have been in short supply in modern times. Kevin McNaughton and Russell Anderson flitted in and out of the national squads but Severin succeeded in establishing himself for a prolonged period.

Severin's debut for the national side came as a Hearts player in a 2-1 win over Lithuania at Hampden in 2001, at the end of Craig Brown's tenure as Scotland coach.

He added a further 14 appearances at the game's top level under Berti Vogts and Walter Smith, with seven of those made after his switch from Tynecastle to Aberdeen.

Highlights in dark blue during his time with the Dons included a role in the 5-1 trouncing of Bulgaria in the 2006 Kirin Cup, a game in which he was at the heart of Smith's team, and an appearance in the 6-0 rout against the Faroes in the European Championship qualifiers later that year. While not blessed with blistering pace, he had the ability to dictate the tempo of a game.

The versatile Stirling-born player established himself as a mainstay of the Hearts team at the tail end of the 1998/99 season, aged just 19 at the time. He was a solid and dependable young player, performing with a maturity which belied his tender years, and settled quickly into the cut and thrust of the SPL.

The departure of manager Jim Jefferies in 2000 did not hinder his progress in Gorgie and as part of Craig Levein's side he continued to flourish, sampling European football for the first time in the 2000/2001 campaign to add to an impressive cv.

Hearts and Severin were back in the Uefa Cup in his final season at the club and by the time he left he had clocked up 175 appearances in just five full seasons.

Frustratingly European football proved rare with Aberdeen but his move to the north-east at the start of Calderwood's tenure did coincide with a revival in the club's fortunes, finishing fourth in the SPL in his debut season in 2004/05 compared to 11th the previous term. He got another crack at the Uefa Cup in 2007/08 when the brave Dandies battled their way through the group stages to set-up the memorable showdown with Bayern Munich in the last 16 of the competition.

Severin had to overcome niggling injury problems during his time on the Aberdeen staff but came through those strains and stresses to establish himself as a vital cog in the machine which emerged as a major player in the top half of the SPL.

His influence on and off the park was noted when Calderwood appointed him vice-captain to fellow Scotland squad man Anderson, with the armband passed on following the defender's move to Sunderland.

The ideal role was at the centre of the team but injuries to Dutch sweeper Karim Touzani following his arrival in 2006 forced the Dons boss to use Severin as a more than able deputy in that area.

Strong on the ball and an intelligent passer, Severin was the perfect modern midfielder. His tackling ability and reading of the game made him a well tuned defensive operator while a powerful shot and ability from dead ball situations ensured a clutch of spectacular and important goals. A viciout volley to seal a 2-1 win against Hibs in the 90th minute of the October 2006 meeting of the two sides was credited as one of the finest Pittodrie has ever seen.

In June 2009, after five years on the staff, Severin severed his Aberdeen ties. It was a changing of the guard on and off the pitch, with old gaffer Calderwood replaced by Mark McGhee. Under freedom of contract, Severin followed the path trodden by so many of his contemporaries and opted to secure a bumper pay day in the English Championship. Watford were the club who moved to secure the services of the experienced campaigner.

While the improved wages were a major attraction, the departing Dons skipper also fired what appeared to be a parting shot at the Scottish game when he claimed he had gone stale in the SPL due to the monotony of playing the same teams so often each season. Between Hearts and Aberdeen he had played for a decade in the top flight and was ready for a new challenge.

The only nagging fear among observers being whether the Scot would be able to keep pace at that level. Those fears perhaps proved well founded, with Severin making just a dozen appearances for the Hornets before being reunited with Jimmy Calderwood at Kilmarnock early in 2010. His guile and leadership qualities helped keep Killie in the SPL that season. Calderwood's stint in charge at Rugby Park was a temporary one and loan signing Severin also departed at the end of the 2009/10 season.

At the start of the 2010/11 campaign he was recruited by Dundee United to strengthen the Tannadice squad on the back of their success in the Scottish Cup.

The Arabs handed their new man a two year contract but injury disrupted his debut campaign in tangerine, requiring surgery on an ankle injury that kept him sidelined for several months in the first half of the term. He was eventually forced to retire.

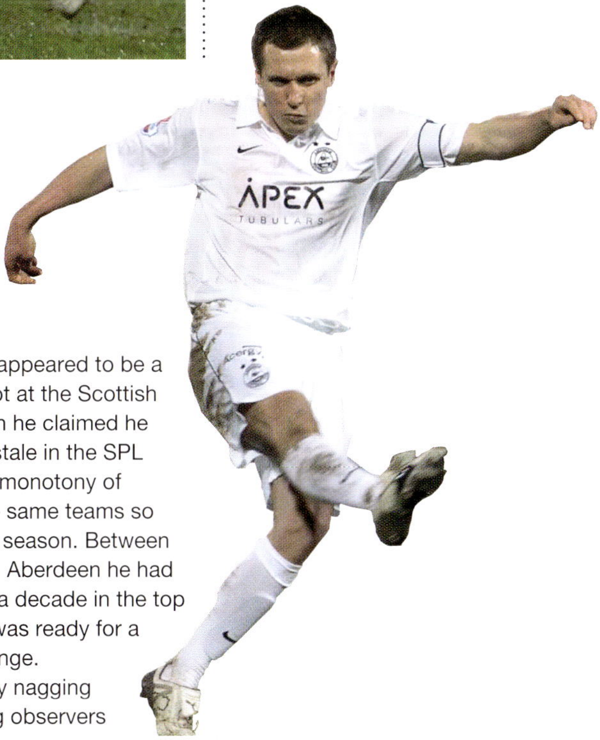

Davie Shaw

Debut: League Cup, 12 August 1950 v Clyde (h) won 4-3
Appearances: League 50, Scottish Cup 14, League Cup 17
Goals: League 1
Also played for: Scotland (9 caps), Hibs
Managed: Aberdeen

Davie Shaw will best be remembered as the manager who led Aberdeen to League Cup success in his first season in charge – but behind the coaching career lay a great playing pedigree. Shaw's triumph as boss, when his Dons men beat St Mirren 2-1 in the 1955/56 final, was the highlight of the five seasons he spent in the top job but he also had a hand in the 1955 league championship as trainer under manager Dave Halliday.

He had first arrived at Pittodrie in 1950 after a long and distinguished association with Hibs, during which time he had earned Scotland recognition and played alongside his brother Jock 'Tiger' Shaw, of Rangers fame, for the national team.

Shaw was in the twilight of his playing career when he was recruited by Halliday to add experience to the Dons squad and slotted in at left back for three seasons before making way for fresh blood and concentrating on coaching commitments, appointed trainer in 1953 before stepping up to the manager's role two years later after impressing as part of the backroom team.

When he was replaced by Tommy Pearson in 1959 there was still a place for the popular coach on the Pittodrie staff as he reverted to his trainer's role and served in that capacity until the arrival of Eddie Turnbull in 1966. Shaw died in Aberdeen in 1976 at the age of 60.

Paul Sheerin

Debut: Scottish Cup, 25 January 2003 v Queen of the South (a) drew 0-0
Appearances: League 47, Scottish Cup 6, League Cup 3
Goals: League 9, Scottish Cup 1
Also played for: Alloa, Southampton, Caley Thistle, Ayr United, St Johnstone
Managed: Arbroath

A criticism of Aberdeen in the modern era has been that the club has ignored Scotland's lower leagues when searching for talent. Paul Sheerin is a player who demonstrated that bargains can be found if you know where to look.

The cultured midfielder with the sweet left foot cost in the region of £12,000 when he was lured away from Ayr United in January 2003. It was not a blind purchase by manager Steve Paterson, who had worked with Sheerin at Caley Thistle previously.

For his modest investment he received a 28-year-old player who had been over the course before and who provided some much needed class to the Dons team of that time. With excellent passing ability, a healthy set-piece repertoire and dangerous array of crosses he was an excellent attacking option.

The Edinburgh-born midfielder, comfortable on the left wing or in a central role, started his career with Alloa before being picked up by Southampton in the early 1990s. He returned to Alloa briefly before finding a permanent home in Inverness with the Caley Jags in 1998. Ayr provided his next stop three and a half years later, leading to his big break with the Dons.

Sheerin spent 18-months at Pittodrie before a long and distinguished period of service with St Johnstone, lasting more than six years and bringing in excess of 200 appearances as he helped the Saints back to the SPL. He was appointed manager of Arbroath at the start of 2010/11 to open a new chapter in his life and led the Red Lichties to victory in the Third Division championship.

Ally Shewan

Debut: League, 20 March 1962 v Third Lanark (a) won 3-1
Appearances: League 221, Scottish Cup 26, League Cup 46, Europe 8
Goals: League 8, League Cup 1
Also played for: Elgin City, Ross County, Lossiemouth

The next time you consider the complaints of today's football professionals that the playing schedule is too hectic, think back to the exploits of the legendary Aberdeen defender Ally Shewan.

Between 1964 and 1969 the dependable Dons man made an incredible 314 consecutive appearances in league, cup, friendly and tour matches. The unbroken sequence marks a record that is unlikely to be broken and is testament to Shewan's commitment to the cause of the club he still follows as a supporter.

The left back began his career as a forward with Cuminestown in the Banff welfare league and then Formartine United during the club's amateur days.

Shewan was picked up by Aberdeen as a 19-year-old in the early 1960s, making his debut under Tommy Pearson in 1962. Having replaced Jimmy Hogg in the team, Shewan also inherited the captaincy from his predecessor in the No.3 shirt.

He came close to honours when he helped lead the side to the 1967 Scottish Cup final, when Celtic ran out winners. Two years later he departed Pittodrie to sample Australian football before returning to join Elgin City in the Highland League. He had two spells with Elgin and also featured for Ross County and Lossiemouth before dropping down to the junior ranks with Caberfeidh.

Billy Smith

Debut: League, 2 January 1952 v East Fife (h) won 2-1
Born: 1931, Aberdeen
Appearances: League 71, Scottish Cup 6, League Cup 16
Also played for: Sunnybank, Third Lanark, Deveronvale

You just don't get commitment like you used to in football. In August, 1953, Billy Smith broke off from his wedding celebrations to dash from his big day at Garthdee church in his striped morning suit to make the short journey to Pittodrie. Without time to catch his breath, he pulled on the No.3 shirt and helped the Dons to a 2-0 win over Airdrie in the group stage of the League Cup. After a quick post-match wash, he made it back to the Palace Restaurant in time to catch the rest of his own wedding reception as it got into full flow.

The following day he took his new bride on a one day honeymoon – making sure he was back in time for another League Cup tie, against East Fife, three days after he had stood at the altar. That's devotion.

Smith was a true unsung hero at Pittodrie, recruited from local junior side Sunnybank as a forward. He made his debut in a 2-1 win against East Fife on home turf on January 2, 1952, and became the man manager Dave Halliday utilised as a Mr Fixit.

In his first three seasons as a Dons player he played at left back, right half, centre half, inside right and inside left. He even stood in for injured goalkeeper Fred Martin twice.

Smith flitted in and out of the team but was always considered a dependable performer when required. His sole Scottish Cup final appearance of 1953/54 illustrated that point perfectly – called into the side for the final against Celtic, who won 2-1.

When the utility man finally found a settled position it led to a landmark campaign for Aberdeen. With Smith firmly planted at left back, the Dons won their first ever league championship in the 1954/55 campaign.

He played 25 of the 30 league games that term as well as every League Cup tie and five of the club's six Scottish Cup excursions. In all but one of those games he played at No.3 – when he switched sides, to play right back, it was with disastrous consequences.

In the Scottish Cup semi-final against Clyde in 1955, as Aberdeen gunned for a league and cup double, Smith deputised in the No.2 shirt after Jimmy Mitchell had fallen ill. He broke his leg shorly after the half-time interval, Clyde equalised in injury time and went on to clinch a place in the final with victory in the replay.

Smith attempted to come back from that blow just six months later but broke his leg again in a match against an Aberdeenshire junior select and, after eight appearances in the 1956/57 season, he was allowed to move on to Third Lanark.

Business commitments took him back north from Glasgow, combining his work in Banff with playing and coaching duties with Deveronvale in the Highland League.

Smith, who played 93 games for the Dons without scoring, spent nine years with Vale and was awarded a testimonial by the Banffers before emigrating to South Africa in 1967 to continue his work in the poultry industry.

MAGIC MOMENTS

16 March 1983
ABERDEEN 3, BAYERN MUNICH 2

Winning the European Cup Winners' Cup with victory against Real Madrid in the final was only part of the story in 1983. Reaching that showdown with the Spaniards was the chapter that brought just as much drama and excitement.

The quarter-final draw paired the Dons with the German megastars of Bayern Munich. The first leg trip to Bavaria saw the Scottish side earn a credible 0-0 draw to keep the dream alive for the return match at Pittodrie.

What followed was the most pulsating evening ever experienced in the old ground, with the stadium rocked to its foundations as a quite staggering spectacle unfolded in front of a capacity crowd of more than 24,000 lucky fans.

The hopes of progressing looked to be in tatters with just 10 minutes on the clock when Bayern took the lead.

Paul Breitner side-footed the free kick to Klaus Augenthaler and the legendary German international strode forward to send a shot arrowing into the net, beating a despairing effort from Jim Leighton to keep it out.

Aberdeen were down, but far from out. In the 38th minute they pulled themselves level when a wonderful cross from Mark McGhee fell perfectly for Eric Black to head towards goal – the effort was blocked, but the alert Neil Simpson was on hand to force the ball home. Game on.

It marked the start of an onslaught from the home side, but the men from Munich held firm through to the interval. After the break it was more of the same from the fired up Pittodrie heroes, with Simpson going close just minutes after the restart to signal their intentions.

However, there was another cruel blow when the Germans scored against the run of play to make it 2-1. Karl Del'Haye and Wolfgang Dremmler combined on the right and the full back's cross was nodded on by Uli Hoeness for Hans Pflugler so send a curling shot past Leighton.

Two goals in the space of a minute sent the Red Army into wonderland – and their team into the semi-finals.

In 76 minutes Gordon Strachan and John McMaster fooled the German defence with their now infamous free kick routine, with the well worked dummy resulting in Strachan's cross being headed home by Alex McLeish.

Before the celebrations had subsided it had moved from 2-2 to 3-2 in Aberdeen's favour. Eric Black had a header well saved but super sub John Hewitt volleyed home the winning goal.

The final whistle brought scenes never before seen at Pittodrie, with the jubilant players swamped by a sea of supporters desperate to savour the occasion. The Dons stars even returned to the pitch for an ovation as the party went on well after the end of the match. Mission accomplished.

ABERDEEN – Leighton, Kennedy (McMaster), Rougvie, Cooper, McLeish, Miller, Strachan, Simpson (Hewitt), McGhee, Black, Weir.

Duncan Shearer

Debut: League, 1 August 1992 v Hibs (h) won 3-0
Appearances: League 108+43, Scottish Cup 13+5, League Cup 11+4, Europe 4+4
Goals: League 54, Scottish Cup 8, League Cup 14, Europe 2
Also played for: Scotland (7 caps), Fort William, Chelsea, Huddersfield Town, Swindon Town, Blackburn Rovers, Inverness Caley Thistle
Managed: Buckie Thistle

In 1981 a young and raw striker from Fort William travelled down to Aberdeen and smashed home five goals in a single practice match for the Dons under the watchful eye of manager Alex Ferguson. The 19 year-old goal machine was Duncan Shearer and nobody would have predicted that afternoon that it would take him more than a decade to finally take his bow at Pittodrie.

Shearer, then starring for Clach in the Highland League, never won a coveted contract with the north-east side after deciding against returning for a second trial stint. Instead he ended up moving from Lochaber to the bright lights of London in 1983 to sign for Chelsea in a £22,000 deal. He feared his chance in the professional game had gone after trials at both Aberdeen and Partick had passed without developments but made up for lost time in England after finding his feet as a full-time player.

Shearer's route to Dons stardom was long and winding, forcing himself to the fringes of the Stamford Bridge first team and making a handful of appearances for the Blues, scoring three goals in two games in the absence of Kerry Dixon and David Speedie, before switching to Huddersfield in 1986.

He became a prolific scorer in the English leagues, continuing his progress with Swindon Town when he moved in a club record £250,000 deal in 1988. He worked under Lou Macari, Ossie Ardilles and Glenn Hoddle at the Wiltshire club and the influence of all three had a major impact on his career.

Four years later his penalty box exploits attracted the interest of Kenny Dalglish and a £700,000 move confirmed the pace at which the Highlander's stock was rising, joining a Blackburn outfit chasing promotion to the top flight. He was part of the Rovers squad that won a Premier League place, although he spent just four months at Ewood Park before Aberdeen finally moved in and got their man – incredibly at the fourth time of asking. In 1981 a combination of factors saw Shearer slip through the Pittodrie net as a teenager, in 1987 Ian Porterfield received a call from Huddersfield offering the striker at a cut price £250,000 but rejected the deal while in March, 1992, manager Willie Miller lost out to Blackburn when he initially made his move. Miller's persistence paid off in July that year when his £500,000 bid was accepted and Shearer travelled north to finally join the Aberdeen staff.

To say he was worth the wait is an understatement. Shearer finally introduced himself to the Pittodrie crowd on August 1, 1992, when he struck a double in a 3-0 win against Hibs. The account was open, but those two goals were far from the final deposits in that debut season.

Shearer was the runaway scoring king that term, putting 28 goals on the board with a collection which featured a league cup hat-trick against Falkirk which was followed in the Premier Division by consecutive trebles against Partick Thistle and Hearts in incredible games which the Dons won 7-0 and 6-2 respectively. His partnership with Mixu Paatelainen was formidable physically and technically, with the imposing Finnish international adding 20 goals himself as part of a freescoring side. Eoin Jess scored 19, Scott Booth grabbed 16 – Miller's team was not short of attacking options.

Those goals earned the runners-up spot in the league and took Aberdeen to both finals in the knock-out competitions, Shearer's goal in the League Cup not

enough to prevent his side slipping to a 2-1 defeat against Rangers after extra-time and the Ibrox men winning the Scottish Cup final by the same margin.

A haul of 26 goals made Shearer the leading scorer again in 1993/94 but again honours proved elusive, with Rangers pipping the Dons to the title by just three points.

It took until November, 1995, for Shearer to finally get his hands on silverware with Aberdeen. The striker did his bit to take the trophy back to Pittodrie, giving his side a comfortable 2-0 cushion with his goal to add to the opener from Billy Dodds in the first-half and etching his name into the history books as a cup winner as well as a goal scoring legend.

The League Cup medal was Shearer's only major honour from his Aberdeen playing days but the Dons also helped him realise his Scotland dream. At the age of 31 he made his international debut in a 2-1 win in Austria in 1994 and went on to make six further appearances in dark blue, scoring against Finland and Holland along the way.

In 1997, at the age of 35, the striker returned to his Highland roots when he signed for Steve Paterson at Caley Thistle. He helped the Inverness side gain promotion from the Second Division, earning a personal promotion to assistant manager in the process, and late in 2002 the duo were headhunted by Aberdeen to form a new coaching dream team.

Shearer's second stint at Pittodrie, as assistant manager, ended in May, 2004, when Jimmy Calderwood and Jimmy Nicholl were recruited to take charge after a disappointing season in which the club had finished 11th after a huge cost cutting exercise on the playing front and a turbulent period behind the scenes as Paterson battled his personal demons.

Shearer, now living and working in Inverness, returned to football as manager of Highland League title challengers Buckie Thistle in 2004 and led the Moray side to a trio of cup final successes before parting company with the club in 2008. The former Scotland star, who released his autobiography *Shearer Wonderland* in 2010, was quickly recruited by Caley Thistle to join the coaching team at the club's Inverness youth academy and currently serves full-time as under-19 coach.

Jim Shirra

Debut: League, 23 October 1976 v Celtic (h) won 2-1
Appearances: League 40, Scottish Cup 2, League Cup 5, Europe 2
Goals: League Cup 1
Also played for: Falkirk, Dundee, Stirling Albion

Assured performances in his early days with the club made midfielder Jim Shirra an instant hit with the Red Army. Signed from Falkirk by Ally MacLeod in a deal worth in excess of £20,000 in 1976, the left-sided player's fortunes changed when Billy McNeill took the helm and offered him as a makeweight in the deal to bring Gordon Strachan north from Dundee. Shirra moved to Dens as part of the Strachan swap deal late in 1977. The Dark Blues also pocketed £40,000 as well as gaining a player who went on to give four years of good service. Shirra also played in Australian football before returning to Scotland with Stirling Albion.

Gordon Sim

Debut: League, 7 November 1959 v Motherwell (a) lost 3-1
Appearances: League 21, Scottish Cup 2, League Cup 3
Also played for: Leeds United, Morton

With power and pace, Shettleston defender Gordon Sim had attributes which made the transition from junior to senior player painless. Sim was snapped up in 1959 after helping his Glasgow side to the Scottish Junior Cup final and challenged for the No.3 shirt over the course of two seasons at Pittodrie. After clocking up 26 appearances and winning Scotland under-23 recognition, he was signed by Don Revie for Leeds United in 1962. Sim, who had a spell with Morton after leaving English football behind, became one of a band of players who swapped Scotland for South Africa as he continued his playing career overseas.

Alex Smith

Debut: League Cup, 9 August 1969 v Dunfermline (h) drew 2-2
Appearances: League 2, League Cup 3
Goals: League Cup 1
Also played for: Dunfermline, Rangers

He joined Aberdeen in a £25,000 transfer in 1969 from Rangers and was appointed club captain in recognition of his experience and influence. When injury struck he settled into a role as a guiding light to the reserves.

Smith became Scottish football's most expensive player when he joined Rangers from Dunfermline Athletic for £55,000 in 1966. He finished leading scorer at Ibrox in his first season and helped them to the final of the European Cup Winners' Cup. The Fifer, who had starred in Dunfermline's Scottish Cup win in 1961, fell out of favour at Rangers before being handed the chance to shine by Aberdeen.

Cammy Smith

Debut: League, 21 April 2012 v Caley Thistle (a) won 2-0
Appearances (up to the end of 2011/12): League 2

Scotland youth international Cammy Smith was one of the youngsters who immediately caught the eye of Craig Brown when he took over at Pittodrie, but he had to wait to get his chance. He was too young under SPL rules for Brown to introduce him straight away. Smith, capable of playing in midfield or attack, had turned in a string of impressive displays for the national age group sides before making his Dons debut towards the end of the 2011/12 term.

Dan Smith

Debut: League, 19 August 2006 v St Mirren (a) drew 1-1
Appearances: League 9, Scottish Cup 2, League Cup 1
Also played for: Sunderland

A huge weight of expectation was on Dan Smith's shoulders when he took his bow in an Aberdeen shirt. The 19-year-old had travelled north from Sunderland in August 2006 after catching the eye of Jimmy Calderwood while in reserve team action and was heavily hyped by the Dons boss.

He was sent off for two bookable offences when making his Sunderland debut and made five appearances before being released.

He made his Aberdeen debut against St Mirren on the left wing but was also capable of playing on the left side of the defence and was expected to be a key man after penning a three year contract. Smith, who had made a Premiership appearance for Sunderland, struggled to adapt to the frenetic pace of the Scottish game and drifted out of the first team, eventually being released in 2008.

Aberdeen squad, 1993/1994.

Gary Smith

Debut: League, 20 November 1991 v Hearts (h) lost 2-0
Appearances: League 170+3, Scottish Cup 16+2, League Cup 19, Europe 3
Goals: League 2
Also played for: Rennes, Hibs, Cowdenbeath, Dundee

On December 15, 1995, football was rocked to its core when the European Court of Justice in Luxembourg passed the Bosman ruling. The reverberations of the decision that football players should be eligible for free transfers at the end of their contracts could be felt in the corridors of power at every club on the continent. The waves of fear were as strong at Pittodrie as anywhere else in Europe as the Aberdeen directors weighed up the potential implications of the new regulations. The player who hammered home the harsh new realities of football was Gary Smith. In November, 1995, he was an influential member of the Aberdeen team which ended a five year wait for silverware when they defeated Dundee 2-0 in the League Cup final.

Smith became the first Dons player to exploit the Bosman rule when he joined French club Rennes in August, 1996, and a player the Aberdeen management team rated at £1.5million left for nothing. It sparked a furious reaction within the club. The sour ending to the saga tarnished the memories of the outstanding service Smith had given in his four seasons at the club. Signed from Falkirk in a £200,000 deal in the summer of 1991 after helping the Bairns win the First Division championship, he recovered from a nightmare debut to become a versatile and reliable performer for the Reds.

Smith took his bow at Pittodrie in a midweek Premier Division game against Hearts on November 20, 1991, and was red carded as his new side slumped to a 2-0 defeat. The 20 year-old showed strength of character to come back stronger from that early blow and played sixteen games in a season in which he had not been expected to even get near to the first team due to the stiff competition for places in a defence which included Stewart McKimmie, Alex McLeish and Brian Irvine. Injuries to key players led to him filling in at centre-half and right-back and under Willie Miller in the 1992/93 season he became an automatic selection at the heart of the Pittodrie defence.

He was called up to the Scotland squad during that campaign, having impressed in the Scotland under-21 team, but a cap proved elusive for the composed and athletic defender who was promoted to the senior pool by Andy Roxburgh at the age of 21.

The League Cup success of 1995 proved to be his only honour as he suffered the pain of final defeats against Rangers in both the Scottish Cup and League Cup in the 1992/93 season. Smith spent just a year in France. Before the start of the 1997/98 season he was handed a shock reunion with Roy Aitken as Aberdeen invested £170,000 to bring him back from Rennes.

He spent a further three years with the Dons, playing under Aitken, Alex Miller, Paul Hegarty and Ebbe Skovdahl in that rollercoaster period in the club's history, before switching to Hibs in 2000.

Six seasons with the Easter Road side were followed by a brief stint as player coach at Cowdenbeath in 2006 before Smith joined Dundee in the First Division for a six month stint.

Neil Simpson

Debut: League, 20 December 1980 v Partick Thistle (a) drew 1-1
Appearances: League 200+19, Scottish Cup 34, League Cup 33+4, Europe 37+5
Goals: League 19, Scottish Cup 5, League Cup 1, Europe 6
Also played for: Scotland (5 caps), Newcastle United, Motherwell, Cove Rangers

Neil Simpson is one of the four men who were with Aberdeen every step of the way on the road to glory in Gothenburg in 1983, playing in each of the 11 European Cup Winners' Cup ties and starring throughout.

The midfielder was part of the unbreakable spine which ran through Alex Ferguson's side on that run and joined goalkeeper Jim Leighton, defender Willie Miller and striker Mark McGhee on the list of ever presents.

Simpson was among the group of six players who scored in the opening game against Sion as Aberdeen cruised to a 7-0 win but it was far from his most important strike of the campaign.

In the breathtaking, nerve shredding quarter-final second leg against Bayern Munich at Pittodrie it was Simpson who cancelled out Klaus Augenthaler's early opener for the Germans, forcing the ball home in the 38th minute from an Eric Black header in typical never say die spirit.

That goal helped the Dons to the famous 3-2 win against Bayern and set up the semi-final against Waterschei and Simpson was on form and on target again, rampaging through the Belgian side's defence in the fourth minute to score. It was not the first goal, that honour went to Eric Black two minutes earlier, and the 5-1 home leg triumph made the return match on the continent academic. Aberdeen were on their way to Gothenburg.

Simpson was a main man for the Dons yet he had only celebrated his 21st birthday six months before he savoured his finest moment on a football pitch. He was a player who had been tipped for greatness from an early age. Born in London but brought up in Newmachar in Aberdeenshire, he linked up with the Dons as a teenager after learning the game with Middlefield Boys Club in Aberdeen and was part of Andy Roxburgh's Scotland under-17 and under-18 sides before he had made his breakthrough at club level.

He was introduced to first team football by Ferguson on December 20, 1980, as a substitute in a 1-1 draw at Partick Thistle. By the end of the season he was emerging as a key player, starting each of the final 10 league games as Aberdeen lost the title race to Celtic.

Honours soon followed thick and fast as Simpson collected a Scottish Cup winner's medal after the 4-1 win against Rangers in 1982 and a matching badge the following year after a 1-0 victory against the same side, both finals going to extra-time.

The European Cup Winners' Cup success in 1983 had propelled the young midfielder to the forefront of European football and he stepped up to the international stage just months later, making his Scotland debut under Jock Stein in a 0-0 draw against Northern Ireland at Hampden.

Simpson, a Scotland under-21 captain, won a total of five full caps, the first three awarded by Stein before a three year absence from the national team between the summers of 1984 and 1987, when Simpson was

recalled by Andy Roxburgh for an Auld Enemy clash. He patrolled the midfield as Scotland drew 0-0 with England, playing again in the return match the following year at Wembley when the hosts ran out 1-0 winners.

Having added Premier Division championship winning medals to his collection in 1984 and 1985 as well as yet another Scottish Cup winner's badge in 1984 when he played in the 2-1 extra-time victory over Celtic, Simpson also earned a second continental prize when he scored the opener in the 2-0 European Super Cup final second leg at Pittodrie against Hamburg.

In 1990, after 331 appearances and 31 goals, he left his first club behind on the back of 12 years' service in the first team and moved to Newcastle United in a £180,000 transfer. He joined Mark McGhee and Roy Aitken on Tyneside but left a year later to join Motherwell, spending two years at Fir Park before retiring through injury after a brief stint back in Aberdeen with Cove Rangers.

Simpson's expertise was put to good use by the SFA, who appointed him as the north's community development officer, and that post led to a return to Aberdeen as the club's senior community coach before his appointment as assistant director of the Dons youth academy in 2006.

It is in that role that he now thrives, aiming to give the current generation of young north-east hopefuls the same start he enjoyed at Pittodrie. Simpson said: "We used to come in and train on the Pittodrie car park but the quality of training with Bobby Clark and Lenny Taylor was first class. More than anything they taught us so much about the commitment and work ethic that every player needs. If you look at the best players in the world, they haven't got where they are with talent alone - they all have the desire to be the best and the right attitude.

"I've been through the system myself and we want to recreate a modern equivalent of what the club had then, when so many good young players were coming through the system. In the Gothenburg team alone Jim Leighton, Doug Rougvie, Alex McLeish, Willie Miller, Neale Cooper, Eric Black, John Hewitt and I had all joined as kids hoping to make the grade."

Simpson concedes the game has changed since the glory days of the 1980s and not all of the developments have been positive. He added: "Where it is different now is that we have to show kids some of the basic skills that people used to pick up in the playground or playing on the streets. There has to be an emphasis on coaching to compensate for the fact kids are spending less time playing in those environments but at the same time we have to strike a balance of allowing young players to express themselves and develop the ability to do things off the cuff. I never played organised football at primary school, with maybe the exception of one game for the school at Newmachar, and everything I did was small sided with friends in the park or playground. Now our kids are involved in organised teams from an earlier age and we have to make sure they can thrive in that environment."

Fred Smith

Debut: League Cup, 9 October 1948 v Third Lanark (h) lost 4-2
Appearances: League 2, League Cup 3
Also played for: Hull City, Sheffield United, Millwall, Chesterfield, Montrose

Aberdonian Fred Smith had to travel to make his name in the game that he launched himself into with the Dons in the 1948/49 season. The former Hall Russell forward made two league appearances before joining Hull City in October 1949. Successful spells with Sheffield United and Millwall followed before a brief stop at Chesterfield on his way back to the north-east with Montrose during the 1956/57 campaign.

Ivor Smith

Debut: League, 19 April 1954 v Hibs (a) lost 3-0
Appearances: League 1
Also played for: Dundee, Buckie Thistle, Keith

Forward Ivor Smith was given one chance to impress in the first team at Pittodrie. He played in the final game of the 1953/54 season, a 3-0 defeat at Hibs, under Dave Halliday. In 1955 the former Scotland junior international, who had cut his teeth with St Clement's in the Granite City, was released to join Dundee and the attacker went on to play in the Highland League with Buckie Thistle and Keith.

Jamie Smith

Debut: League, 30 July 2005 v Dundee United (a) drew 1-1
Appearances: League 85, Scottish Cup 7, League Cup 6, Europe 4
Goals: League 12, Scottish Cup 3, League Cup 1, Europe 2
Also played for: Celtic, Den Haag, Colorado Rapids (USA)

Pittodrie was bouncing, the adrenalin was coursing through the veins of the players and once again the Dons were bossing European ties. For a fleeting moment it could have been the 1980s all over again as Danish cracks Copenhagen were torn apart.

The year was not 1983. Instead it was 2007 and it was Jamie Smith and his attacking colleagues who were conducting proceedings as they drove their side to a 4-0 Uefa Cup win. It was a season that would end in the knock-out stages of the competition with gallant defeat against Bayern Munich and Jamie Smith was at the heart of it. His two goal salvo against Copenhagen clinched the passage from the group stages to the last 32 and demonstrated his class.

Smith's talent was never in any doubt. He was a skilled and perceptive forward, comfortable playing wide or through the middle of the midfield or attack, with a catalogue of deft touches. On top of those qualities he also posed a genuine goal threat. The only drawback was a series of frustrating injuries which limited his contribution for the Dons.

Smith was a man to Calderwood's own heart after expanding his football horizons with a spell in the Dutch league with Den Haag, whom he had joined after leaving Celtic in 2004. He spent a season overseas before Calderwood made his move and took the former Hoops starlet to Pittodrie in the summer of 2005. He spent four years in the north-east before joining the Colorado Rapids in America.

Jonathan Smith

Debut: League, 5 January 2008 v Falkirk (a) drew 0-0
Appearances: League 1, Scottish Cup 1
Also played for: Accrington Stanley, Peterhead

Teenage striker Jonathan Smith had learnt his trade with Liverpool and Wigan Athletic before being tempted north by Jimmy Calderwood in the summer of 2007.

The Englishman had impressed during Pittodrie trials but after two fleeting appearances from the bench was released after a single season.

He went on to play for Accrington Stanley and had a brief spell with Peterhead in the 2009/10 campaign.

Steven Smith

Debut: League, 1 February 2011 v Celtic (h) lost 3-0
Appearances: League 16, Scottish Cup 4
Also played for: Rangers, Norwich City

The former Rangers star, who made more than 70 first team appearances for the Ibrox side between his debut in 2004 and joining Norwich City in 2010, was loaned to the Dons at the turn of 2011. Smith, who overcame a serious pelvic injury while with the Light Blues, was keen to return to Scotland to be closer to he and his wife's family as he slotted into Craig Brown's side at left-back.

Ferne Snoyl

Debut: League, 4 February 2006 v Hearts (a) lost 3-0
Appearances: League 12, Scottish Cup 1
Goals: League 1
Also played for: Feyenoord, NEC Nijmegen, RKC Waalwijk, NAC Breda (all Netherlands)

The old boys network worked overtime to smooth Ferne Snoyl's passage to the SPL. He was striving to make his mark with Feyenoord when Jimmy Calderwood's son, who remains based in the Netherlands after growing up on the continent when his father played in the Dutch league, tipped off his dad about the young prospect's ability. Snoyl arrived on loan in 2006, at the age of 20, and impressed during the second half of the 2005/06 campaign. Calderwood attempted to keep the Dutch youth international left-back in Scotland but could not match his financial demands and he returned to his homeland to play for NEC Nijmegen, RKC Waalwijk and NAC Breda.

Joe Smith

Debut: League, 16 December 1972 v Rangers (a) drew 0-0
Appearances: League 142+8, Scottish Cup 12+3, League Cup 34, Europe 3+1
Goals: League 7, Scottish Cup 1, League Cup 3
Also played for: Motherwell, Peterhead, Dunfermline

Big brother Jimmy got the Scotland cap as a Dons player but it was Joe Smith who collected a coveted winner's medal as an Aberdeen player. It took him the best part of a decade, but in 1976 he did it. Joe Smith was an integral part of Ally MacLeod's side in the 1976/77 season as the Pittodrie side marched into the final of the League Cup and defeated Celtic 2-1 in front of almost 70,000 at Hampden. Smith played in every game in that run and was on target in the quarter-final against Stirling Albion, rifling home a low shot to make it 2-0 and take the Dons through.

It was the midfielder's finest season in the red of his first club, sitting out just a single league game as MacLeod steered the club to third in the Premier Division. When the manager left Pittodrie at the end of the campaign to take over as Scotland boss he did not forget Smith, a player who built his reputation on the type of skilful running and clever passing his brother was famed for. MacLeod immediately called him up to his squad for the home international series and a South American tour in the summer of 1977. He was on the bench for games against Argentina and Brazil but never made it on to the pitch to win a cap to join the Smith collection started by his big brother.

The 6ft tall Scotland youth cap would undoubtedly have been in the running to be part of the senior squad for the 1978 World Cup in Argentina but was cruelly robbed of the chance to continue to impress the national team coach by a knee injury suffered in a league game against Ayr just months into the 1977/78 season.

The game against Ayr proved to be his final start for Aberdeen. On his recovery from the knee injury at the start of the 1978/79 season he was sent on loan to Arbroath by new manager Alex Ferguson and made just two appearances from the bench before being reunited with MacLeod, by that time in charge at Motherwell, two days before Christmas in 1978.

The £40,000 deal resulted in a three year stay at Fir Park before he returned to the north-east to play briefly under former Pittodrie team-mate Joe Harper with Peterhead in the Highland League. He returned to the senior ranks with Dunfermline soon after but retired from the senior game in 1983.

The Glaswegian midfielder spent fourteen years as a professional, joining the Dons as a 15 year-old in 1969 and turning out for Banks o' Dee A in the juvenile leagues before stepping up to the Dons reserve team a year later.

By 1973/74 he was a regular in the Aberdeen side and he began to attract the attention of the international under-23 and Scottish Football League selectors, turning out for both sides in 1976 to cap a year in which he savoured his finest moment in football with glory at Hampden for his club.

MAGIC MOMENTS

20 December 1983
ABERDEEN 2, SV HAMBURG 0

The dandy Dons were crowned kings of the continent as they added the European Super Cup to the roll of honour. The two-legged tie against European Cup winners SV Hamburg proved once and for all that Aberdeen could live in exalted company.

A 0-0 draw in Germany set the scene for a winner takes all encounter back on Scottish soil and, as had become the custom, Alex Ferguson's side did not let their manager down.

The first half had been a cagey affair, with a capacity crowd not treated to the feast they may have expected. But an enthralling second half display ensured the home support were sent home happy with another cup win to savour.

The visitors had enjoyed the better of the opening 45 minutes, displaying typically efficient and patient build-up play without a cutting edge, but were left chasing shadows after the break as the Reds hit top gear, inspired by the midfield driving force of Neil Simpson.

It was Simpson who opened the account just a minute into the second period, although it was Peter Weir who was chief engineer with a 60-yard run down the wing that left his marker trailing behind gasping for breath. John Hewitt was the target of Weir's cross and although he could not convert the chance, the striker did enough to push the ball into the path of Simpson for him to steady himself before shooting home to ease the tension.

Within minutes there were further opportunities, with Mark McGhee seeing a shot pushed over the bar and Hewitt sending a volley over the bar after the Dons had sprung Hamburg's offside trap.

It became one-way traffic after the first goal and in 64 minutes the lead was doubled. A Weir corner, aimed initially at recently introduced substitute Eric Black, swerved away from its intended target and landed for Willie Miller. The captain had the presence of mind to lay the ball off for McGhee to convert from close range and clinch the match, the trophy and the kudos for his club.

The goal knocked the stuffing out of a German team which had been on an energy sapping tour of the Far East in the weeks leading up to their trip to Scotland. That was no excuse though, with Hamburg outplayed by an Aberdeen team who were full of confidence after their earlier heroics in Gothenburg.

Miller was singled out as one of the top performers on the night, with Weir also earning praise for his dashing display on the wing. Once again, it was a team performance by a special group of individuals that left the opposition without an answer as the pace, precision and poise of the Scottish stars had their highly fancied continental rivals on the ropes for the bulk of the 90 minutes.

ABERDEEN – Leighton, McKimmie, McMaster, Simpson, McLeish, Miller, Strachan, Hewitt (Black), McGhee, Bell, Weir.

David Smith

Debut: League, 10 January 1962 v St Johnstone (h) drew 1-1
Appearances: League 133, Scottish Cup 14, League Cup 19
Goals: League 8, Scottish Cup 1, League Cup 4
Also played for: Scotland (2 caps), Rangers, Arbroath, Arcadia Shepherds (South Africa), Los Angeles Aztecs (USA), Berwick Rangers, Huntly, Peterhead
Managed: Berwick Rangers, Huntly, Peterhead

Aberdeen's involvement in the Scottish national side has become a given as season by season and decade by decade the list of Dons in dark blue grows. It has not always been that way. From George Mulhall's appearance against Northern Irealnd in October, 1959, there was an astonishing international drought at Pittodrie which lasted 79 months.

It was fitting that a homegrown player ended what was by far the most barren spell in the post-war history of the club. On May 11, 1966, it was David Smith who ran out at Hampden to drag his home town club back out of the international wilderness.

Smith's promptings did not prevent Scotland from slipping to a 3-0 defeat against the Dutch masters of Holland but the long wait for the north-east's legion of Tartan Army members to cheer on one of their own was over.

It proved to be one of the Aberdonian's final acts as a Pittodrie player as just months later he was on his way to join new Scotland colleagues John Greig, Davie Provan, Ronnie McKinnon, Willie Henderson and Willie Johnston at Rangers.

His sale pulled in a club record fee of £45,000 to boost the Pittodrie coffers and substantially aid the rebuilding exercise Eddie Turnbull was in the process of carrying out.

Smith was just 22 when he became Pittodrie's biggest football asset but by that time he was already an established first team player with a wealth of experience in the top flight as well as Scotland under-23 honours.

The former Middlefield primary and Hilton academy pupil had caught the eye of the Dons while playing junior football for Aberdeen Lads' Club. He signed for the Dons at the age of 17 and made his debut on January 10, 1962, in a 1-1 draw against St Johnstone at Pittodrie.

He kept his place in the side for the next game, a 1-1 home draw against Airdrie, before returning the No.6 shirt to Doug Fraser and

biding his time. It took just one game on the sidelines at the start of the 1962/63 First Division season for Smith to get the call from Tommy Pearson and the 18 year-old never looked back, making 35 appearances in his first full term in the first team.

The lack of international recognition in the early 1960s was not an indication of west coast bias, more a reflection on the difficulties the Dons were experiencing at the time.

In the season Smith made his fleeting introduction Pearson's charges finished 12th in the 18 team top flight. His full introduction coincided with a mini-revival in fortunes as the Dons clambered to sixth place but throughout his time finishing in the top half of the table was the main aim rather than a chase for major honours.

The bright spots of the era were the emergence of young talents such as Smith, Charlie Cooke and Martin Buchan. All would be sold at a major profit within years and it was that conveyor belt which ensured the club's finances thrived.

Smith said: "I think it is a fallacy to say players from Aberdeen were or are ignored when it comes to Scotland selection. At that time we were a team in transition and I don't think people were being overlooked during that period. Scotland had some good players in that era and they were in the national team on merit. It was difficult to get into the Scotland team but that is the way it should be. In recent years it has been easy for average players to get 50 caps because there's been such a dearth of talent.

"Charlie Cooke went on to play international football but, like me, he was still a young player when he was at Pittodrie. The fact Dundee were able to buy Charlie, one of Aberdeen's best players, maybe puts into context Aberdeen's standing at that stage – Dundee wouldn't be able to buy any of the Pittodrie first team players now, but back then the roles were reversed."

Smith was thrust into an international team packed full of household names but was not daunted by the experience, insisting he took it in his stride. He said: "Stepping up is never a problem because you are surrounded by quality players. Good players never find it difficult to play in good teams because everyone is on the same wavelength. I actually found it far more difficult dropping down a level. When I played and managed in the Highland League at the tail end of my career, I had to wait to see what the other players were going to do before playing the ball whereas players at a higher level would read your passes and naturally find the areas you wanted to hit."

Smith's switch to Ibrox in the summer of 1966 brought further recognition, with his second and final cap coming in 1968 in a rematch against Holland which ended 0-0, and his first taste of continental football at club level.

With Rangers he was a losing finalist in the European Cup Winners' Cup final of 1967, when Bayern Munich triumphed, but he collected a winner's medal in 1972 after a man of the match performance in the final against Moscow Dynamo in Barcelona.

His performance that season also earned the Scottish football writers' player of the year award, his name carved next to the 1971 winner Martin Buchan on the roll of honour. The two Dons of the 1960s remain the only Aberdonians ever to be crowned as the country's player of the year.

Smith remained with the Light Blues for eight years, overcoming two leg breaks along the way, before becoming player coach at Arbroath. Playing spells in South Africa and America, alongside George Best in the LA Aztecs team, followed before his return to Scotland as player-manager of Berwick Rangers in 1976. He led what had been Scotland's worst team to the Second Division championship in 1979, the only honour in the history of the Borders club, before returning to his north-east roots with spells in charge at Huntly and Peterhead in the Highland League in the early 1980s. Smith is retired from the licensed trade and now lives in Fife.

Jimmy Smith

Debut: League, 4 April 1966 v Morton (h) won 5-3
Appearances: League 103, Scottish Cup 14, League Cup 15, Europe 8
Goals: League 21, Scottish Cup 5, League Cup 8, Europe 3
Also played for: Scotland (4 caps), Benburb, Newcastle United, Celtic

He came, he thrilled crowds, won international honours and left with a substantial financial legacy trailing in his wake. Jimmy Smith was a flamboyant winger who stood out like a beacon during the transitional early days of Eddie Turnbull's reign at Pittodrie. Spotted by renowned scout Bobby Calder while playing for Benburb in his home city of Glasgow, Smith's close control combined with ability to beat defenders and incisive distribution made him a stand out as a youngster playing in only his first season in the junior ranks.

Turnbull made his move in the summer of 1965, beating Aston Villa and Wolves to the punch, to recruit the promising 18 year-old winger and by the end of the season the new boy had been fast tracked into the first team.

Jinky made his debut in a 5-3 home win against Morton on April 4, 1966, and opened his goalscoring account in his fifth start to help the Dons to a 2-1 win over Dundee. It was the first of 37 goals he would score in just three and a quarter seasons at Pittodrie.

In 1966/67 he marked his first full season as a senior player by finishing joint leading scorer for Aberdeen with 20 strikes in 43 games in all competitions. It was an eventful campaign for Smith, who was called into the Scotland under-23 team and took part in his first cup final as Celtic ran out 2-0 winners in the 1967 Scottish Cup showdown.

That proved to be the final opportunity to compete

for a domestic honour with Aberdeen during a short but eventful career with the club but he did win international recognition. To catapult himself from a provincial club's team-sheet to the international stage was a momentous effort, overcoming a perceived bias in favour of Old Firm stars and proving that there are few barriers to stand in the way of genuine talent.

The national dream came true in 1968 when he and team-mate Bobby Clark lined-up together as Scotland faced Holland at the Olympic Stadium in Amsterdam. The game ended 0-0 but Smith did help the national side to victory against Wales in 1974, also picking up caps in a defeat against Northern Ireland in the same year and a 1-1 draw with West Germany in 1974.

Those final three caps came as a Newcastle United player. Smith, after 140 appearances for the Dons, was sold to the English side for £100,000 in the summer of 1969.

The timing of his departure ensured he left Pittodrie empty handed, at least in terms of precious metal. In place of medals, he moved south with only precious memories to treasure from his time with his first professional club. Although he returned to Scottish football briefly on loan with Celtic in the mid-1970s, it transpired that the Dons were to be Jinky's one and only permanent football home north of the border.

Few of the supporters at Pittodrie could grudge him his move. Aside from the financial benefits of becoming a £100,000 star, he was being afforded the opportunity to join a club very much in the ascendancy. Just months earlier the Magpies had triumphed in Europe when they clinched the Inter-Cities Fairs Cup with a two-legged victory over Hungarian outfit Ujpest. They had won 6-2 on aggregate to underline their credentials as one of the continent's finest teams.

By securing the talents of the talented Scot, Newcastle were bolstering a squad tipped to add domestic honours to the European prize already in the bag. The six-figure fee represented a new record for the Magpies and represented a gamble by manager John Harvey on a player who was no stranger to suspensions at Pittodrie, mainly after retaliating to meaty treatment dished out by defenders in Scotland. He could also give as good as he got, sent off for a heavy challenge inside the first minute of a cup tie while playing for Newcastle against Birmingham in 1973.

Manchester City and Celtic, the team Smith had supported as a boy, had both shown an interest in 1969 but were blown out of the water by the fee tabled by Newcastle. The fanfare surrounding the Scotsman's arrival on Tyneside quadrupled the reserve attendance for his debut, with an 8,000 attendance for his match-winning performance in a second string encounter against Aston Villa.

Smith was seen as the ideal foil for star striker Malcolm Macdonald but injury wrecked his chances of making a lasting impression, undergoing two knee operations in 1971 alone as years of heavy challenges began to tell. In between enforced spells on the sidelines, Smith had enough time on the pitch to earn cult status among the Toon Army. Like their Dons counterparts, the Newcastle faithful were wowed by his close control and the confidence that oozed from every pore.

Jinky returned to fitness and form to reclaim his international place in 1973 and remained in the Newcastle side to take his place on the Wembley turf for the 1974 FA Cup final against Liverpool in front of more than 100,000 people. There was no fairytale ending, with a Kevin Keegan double and another goal from Steve Heighway giving the Reds a 3-0 victory.

It was to be one of the final highs of Smith's career as the injuries continued to take their toll. A brief loan spell with Celtic in 1976 ended prematurely when another knee injury began to cause concern and forced his retirement from the senior game at the age of 1979. He remained on Tyneside, working as a taxi driver in Newcastle until heart problems and arthritis forced his retirement.

Theo Snelders

Debut: League, 13 August 1988 v Dundee (a) drew 1-1
Appearances: League 228+1, Scottish Cup 23, League Cup 31, Europe 14
Also played for: Netherlands (1 cap), Twente Enschede, Rangers, MVV Maastricht

It was always going to take a big man to fill the No.1 shirt vacated by Scotland star and Gothenburg hero Jim Leighton and when that onerous task fell to Alex Smith in 1988 he was forced to look far and wide for a replacement.

Leighton's switch to Manchester United left a huge void at Pittodrie and presented a goalkeeping headache the club had not had to contemplate since he had first broken into the team in 1980.

Theo Snelders had in fact been a target of Alex Ferguson and Manchester United before they switched their attention to luring Leighton from Aberdeen.

Signing a new goalkeeper was the first task presented to Smith following his appointment as a successor to Ian Porterfield and he wasted no time in singling out Snelders, watching the Dutchman in action.

Snelders was out of contract with Twente Enschede but, in the pre-Bosman days, still commanded a fee of £300,000. He proved to be worth every single penny and much more.

He had launched his career in Holland's top flight at the age of just 17 and had been voted the best goalkeeper in the country three years prior to his arrival in Scotland.

At the age of 24 he made his Dons debut in a 1-1 draw away to Dundee on August 13, 1988 and that season he conceded just 25 goals in 36 Premier Division games to give his new club the best defensive record in the league. It was still not enough to prevent Rangers from winning the league and the Ibrox men inflicted a 3-2 defeat on the Dons in the League Cup final to compound their misery.

That disappointment was tempered by personal joy for one of Scotland's most successful imports, who after playing in every single one of the 48 games the club took part in, was named as the national players' player of the year winner at the end of his first season. He stunned the audience at the awards night in Glasgow by opening his acceptance speech with the line 'fit like' but that would have been no surprise to anyone who had sat in the Pittodrie stands and listened to the 6ft 2in keeper roar at his defenders to get 'oot' of their own half.

Snelders was a favourite among his peers and an even bigger favourite among the Aberdeen supporters. The

appreciation was mutual.

Snelders, relaxing at his home in the Netherlands, said: "I have very happy memories from Aberdeen. I spent 11 years in Scotland and it was a big part of my life - I have kept all the newspaper cuttings and we took lots of photographs to remind us of the happy times we had. Our two children, Ryan and Kayleigh, were both born in Aberdeen so we will always have a link to the city.

"My wife and I were not married when we moved across. For her it was the first time she had left her parents so it was a big adventure. We sometimes struggled with the accent to begin with but we got the hang of it - I remember when we stayed in a semi-detached house and noticed smoke pouring from the chimney. It was coming from next door but the lady was a true Aberdonian and it was difficult for us to get her to realise. There was a lot of waving of arms and shouting before we got the message across!

"It was a big step into the dark for us. We knew very little about Scotland, let alone Aberdeen. The combination of the city and the club made it for us. I joined at a good time for the club. There were a lot of full Scotland internationals in the side and we were challenging for honours."

In 1989/90 he completed the process of winning over the Dons support when he helped his side to a cup double, first with a 2-1 victory over Rangers in the League Cup and then with his central role in the Scottish Cup win against Celtic. After shutting out the Hoops over 90 minutes and extra-time, Snelders blocked Anton Rogan's penalty in the shoot-out to present Brian Irvine with the opportunity to convert the cup winning spot kick and take the trophy north.

Snelders, who made his debut for the Dutch national team in a friendly in 1989, was continually frustrated in his quest for further trophy success at Pittodrie but amassed 292 games over the course of more than seven years along the way.

He was an imposing figure behind the defence he marshalled so well and an athletic shot stopper who was never afraid to throw himself into dangerous situations, as he found to his cost in November, 1995, when he dived to collect the ball on a wet surface and had his cheekbone shattered by a sliding challenge by Rangers striker Ally McCoist.

Snelders was stretchered off, replaced by Scott Thomson, and never played for the Dons again. By the time he recovered from that injury in 1996 a £300,000 bid by Rangers tempted him to Ibrox, where he played 13 games as a back-up keeper for the Light Blues.

In 1999 he returned to Holland to wind down his playing career with MVV Maastricht before moving into goalkeeping coaching with Twente Enschede and played his part in the provincial club's fairytale win the Dutch championship in 2010, working under English coach Steve McClaren as Twente shocked the Netherlands establishment of Ajax, PSV and Feyenoord by storming to the title.

Snelders added: "I'm enjoying coaching with Twente - but I still get the time to keep in touch with what is happening in Scotland and look out for the Aberdeen results."

Thomas Solberg

Debut: League, 29 August 1999 v St Johnstone (h) lost 3-0
Appearances: League 63, Scottish Cup 10, League Cup 2
Goals: League 5
Also played for: Viking Stavanger (Norway), Moss (Norway)

When club captain Derek Whyte was relegated to the sidelines with a knee injury in the early days of Ebbe Skovdahl's reign at Pittodrie there was only one market the new coach was likely to turn to. The Dane looked east to Scandinavia and came up with experienced Norwegian defender Thomas Solberg, a player galloping towards his 30th birthday.

Solberg did not come cheap and the Dons were forced to pay Viking Stavanger in the region of £300,000 to land their target. He had been captain of his club in Norway and arrived in Scotland with a reputation as a strong and athletic stopper, standing 6ft 2in tall and providing a substantial presence in the back four.

He played in both the League Cup and Scottish Cup finals in his first season as an Aberdeen player but left without a winner's medal on each occasion. Whyte had returned to action by the time those competitions were concluded and Skovdahl was not averse to playing the two men side by side in the defence, as he did in the Scottish Cup final defeat against Rangers that term.

Despite being assured of a place in the Pittodrie team, Solberg soon decided the grass was not greener on the Scottish side of the North Sea. Instead he made an early decision to return to his hometown team Moss in Norway when his two-year Dons contract expired. He was eventually released early, making the switch in March 2002.

Derek Soutar

Debut: League Cup, 22 August 2006 v Queen's Park (a) drew 0-0 (lost 5-3 on penalties after extra time)
Appearances: League 13, Scottish Cup 3, League Cup 1
Also played for: Dundee, Alloa Athletic (on loan), Brechin City (on loan), Ross County, APEP Pitsilia (Cyprus), Formartine United

Have gloves, will travel. Goalkeeper Derek Soutar has gone far and wide to stay in the game. The Scotland under-21 player was a star man for Dundee as a rookie, sent out to Alloa and Brechin on loan to gain experience, and was snapped up as cover for former Dens colleague Jamie Langfield by Jimmy Calderwood in 2006. He was promoted to first choice at Aberdeen after Langfield's stag night misdemeanours saw him bombed out of the team, but eventually had to settle back into a support role.

Soutar played for Ross County and Dundee after leaving Pittodrie before a short spell with Cypriot club APEP Pitsilia. He returned to Scotland in January 2011 to sign a three year contract with Highland League side Formartine United.

Kevin Souter

Debut: League, 24 May 2003 v Dundee United (a) won 2-0
Appearances: League 4
Also played for: Buckie Thistle, Kansas City Wizards (USA)

Kevin Souter bounced back in style when he was released by Steve Paterson in 2004 after just four appearances for the Dons. Souter regrouped in the Highland League with Buckie before pursuing the American dream and landing a college scholarship in Iowa. From there he beat 200 hopefuls in an open trial to win a contract with Major League Soccer franchise Kansas City Wizards in 2008.

Arild Stavrum

Debut: League, 21 November 1999 v St Johnstone (a) drew 1-1
Appearances: League 54, Scottish Cup 10, League Cup 3, Europe 1
Goals: League 26, Scottish Cup 2, League Cup 1
Also played for: Helsingborgs (Sweden), Besiktas (Turkey)
Managed: Molde (Norway), Skeid (Sweden)

Norwegian striker Arild Stavrum's controversial departure from Aberdeen in 2001 left a sour taste in the mouth of supporters and directors alike. What that anger could not overshadow was the impressive contribution the Scandinavian goal getter made during his brief time in the north-east of Scotland.

Stavrum used a clause in his Pittodrie contract to join Turkish outfit Besiktas in the summer of 2001. The Turks landed the player for a cut price £120,000 fee because of the get out figure inserted in the small print. Aberdeen were understandably upset at losing their main goal threat for such a paltry return but were powerless to stand in his way, having agreed to the trigger fee before realizing the impact their import would have in the Premier Division.

Stavrum signed from Swedish side Helsingborgs in 1999. Despite arriving four months into the season he

quickly made up for lost time, scoring 12 times to finish leading scorer.

He retained the club's golden boot the following term with an improved return of 17 goals in 36 games and not surprisingly attracted interest from elsewhere. He was a true poacher, a player who came alive in the box and could look uninterested outside of the penalty area.

His colourful character made Stavrum a fans' favourite, helped by his frequent appearances on the score sheet. In 2000/01, his first full season in a red shirt, he bagged hat-tricks against St Mirren and Dundee United to underline his predatory instincts.

After a season in Turkey he returned to Norway, where he cut his coaching teeth with Baerum SK before being appointed manager of Molde. He has also managed Swedish side Skeid.

Jimmy Stenhouse

Debut: Scottish Cup, 7 February 1948 v Nithsdale (a) won 5-0
Appearances: League 31, Scottish Cup 7, League Cup 6
Goals: League 1, Scottish Cup 2, League Cup 1
Also played for: St Mirren, Kettering Town

Impressive performances with St Mirren brought wing-half Jimmy Stenhouse to Aberdeen's attention as he won a Scotland cap during the war years. He went on to spend four seasons as a squad man at Pittodrie after joining in 1947, most notably as a regular in the 1948/49 campaign under Dave Halliday. Kettering Town was the next stop before coaching roles with Corby Town and Ross County in the 1950s and 60s.

Hugh Stewart

Debut: League, 28 December 1963 v Partick Thistle (h) lost 5-0
Appearances: League 10
Also played for: Third Lanark

Defender Hugh Stewart was a 19-year-old rookie when he made his debut in Tommy Pearson's side in 1963. A product of Glasgow junior side St Roch's, he was released by Aberdeen in 1966 after failing to cement a first team place and returned to the central belt to sign for Third Lanark.

John Stewart

Debut: League, 9 March 2004 v Partick Thistle (h) drew 0-0
Appearances: League 51, Scottish Cup 4, League Cup 4
Goals: League 5
Also played for: Falkirk, St Johnstone (on loan), Queen of the South (on loan), Ross County, Peterhead, Clyde

Pace was always John Stewart's major weapon. The forward, who was utilised on the wing and through the centre of the attack, emerged during the closing weeks of Steve Paterson's reign and continued to knock on the door of the first team under Jimmy Calderwood. He made more than half a century of appearances for the Dons, mainly from the bench, before joining Falkirk in a £50,000 deal in September 2006. Despite a flying start with the Bairns he struggled to make an impact and had loan spells with St Johnstone and Queen of the South before joining Ross County in 2009. After less than a year in Dingwall the Glaswegian switched to Peterhead and then Clyde at the start of 2010.

Sammy Stewart

Debut: League, 24 May 2009 v Hibs (h) won 2-1
Appearances: League 1
Also played for: Glenavon

Big things were expected of skilful Ulsterman Sammy Stewart when he pitched up in Aberdeen in 2008 from Glenavon. The speedy teenage midfielder shone in early appearances for the second string but, after a single appearance from the bench, returned to Glenavon in 2010 after being released.

Derek Stillie

Debut: League, 5 March 1994 v Hearts (h) lost 1-0
Appearances: League 22, Scottish Cup 3, League Cup 2
Also played for: Wigan Athletic, Dunfermline, Dundee United, Gillingham

Dutch star Theo Snelders, Gothenburg hero Jim Leighton and Scotland international Nicky Walker were three of the reasons goalkeeper Derek Stillie never made the Aberdeen No.1 shirt his own. The Irvine-born shot stopper was a regular for the national under-21 team during his time at Pittodrie but the youth product was restricted to bit parts as support for a string of big names. Stillie went on to have a sterling career as a first choice for Wigan, after joining from the Dons in 1999, as well as Dunfermline and Dundee United. After gaining a legal degree while at Tannadice he moved to Gillingham in 2007.

Jim Storrie

Debut: League, 4 March 1967 v Hearts (a) won 3-0
Appearances: League 12, Scottish Cup 4, League Cup 6, Europe 2
Goals: League 3, Scottish Cup 1, League Cup 3, Europe 4
Also played for: Airdrie, Leeds United, Rotherham United, Portsmouth
Managed: St Johnstone

Leeds United's Jim Storrie was a big name signing for Aberdeen when he checked in at Pittodrie early in 1967. The former Airdrie forward had cost Leeds £15,000 when he moved to Don Revie's side in 1962 and the Dons were thought to have gone close to matching that fee to take the 26-year-old back to Scotland. The new boy did not have the impact manager Eddie Turnbull hoped for and within a year he had been moved on to Rotherham United under Tommy Docherty for £7,000 after 24 appearances and 11 goals. Storrie then moved to Portsmouth before cutting his teeth in management on the south coast with Waterlooville. He returned north to take charge of St Johnstone in 1976.

Billy Stark

Debut: League, 20 August 1983 v Dundee (h) won 3-0
Appearances: League 112+12, Scottish Cup 12+4, League Cup 14+3, Europe 11+1
Goals: League 41, Scottish Cup 11, League Cup 7, Europe 1
Also played for: St Mirren, Celtic, Kilmarnock, Hamilton
Managed: Morton, St Johnstone, Queen's Park, Scotland Under-21s

Billy Stark, the hero of some of Aberdeen's finest moments in cup football, was the mastermind behind one of the darkest night's in the history of the Dons in knock-out competition.

In his role as manager, it was Stark's plucky amateur Queen's Park players who dumped the highly paid Pittodrie side out of the League Cup in 2006 in a penalty shoot-out in Glasgow.

Stark, who was in charge at St Johnstone for three years before taking charge of the Hampden side, worked wonders with his unpaid team and the result against the Dons confirmed his progress. But then, the manager did know a thing or two about cup finals.

In 1985/85 he helped Alex Ferguson's team to a double and scored in both finals. The League Cup was first on the agenda and Hibs were the opponents as Ferguson aimed for his first triumph in the competition with the Dons.

After nine minutes Eric Black opened the scoring and three minutes later Stark settled any lingering nerves, tucking away a John Hewitt cross to make it 2-0. A second from Black after the break wrapped up the tie.

In the Scottish Cup Stark was relegated to the bench for the final showdown with Hearts but he still had a starring role, heading home a 75th minute goal to add to John Hewitt's double and make it a season to remember.

Stark was a player who often divided opinion among the supporters in the Pittodrie stands. Many appreciated his cultured promptings going forward and ability to chip in with vital goals, others mistook his languid style for laziness.

Scotland managers clearly fell into the latter camp, with Stark surprisingly never earning a Scotland cap despite the frequency his colleagues in the Aberdeen team appeared on the international stage. Even at under-21 level he was denied the chance of playing for his country despite being involved in the young national squad.

Alex Ferguson did not need to be persuaded about Stark's potential despite his failure to break into the under-21 side and tried twice to sign him from St Mirren before making it third time lucky in the summer of 1983 with a £75,000 bid.

Stark was joining a club high on the European success of the previous year but was not daunted by the illustrious company he was in,

forcing his way into the side for the opening day of the Premier Division campaign as the Dons got off and running on August 20 with a 3-0 win against Dundee at Pittodrie. He signalled his prowess in front of goal with a hat-trick against Raith Rovers in the League Cup just four days later and went on to net 11 times in just 14 starts and six appearances from the bench in his introductory season as he helped his new club to win the championship and the Scottish Cup, coming on as a substitute in the 2-1 win against Celtic in the final.

If Stark had played a supporting role in the 1984 Premier Division title win, with 11 starts, that claim could not be levelled at him when the Dons defended their crown in 1985. The Glaswegian made the No.4 shirt his own and was absent from the starting line-up just six times as the league was won with seven points to spare.

The cup double the following season proved to be his final honours in an Aberdeen shirt and, after 169 appearances and 60 goals, he switched to Celtic in a £75,000 deal having jointly led the Dons scoring chart in his final season at the club despite playing in midfield. He tied on 14 goals with John Hewitt.

He won a league winner's medal in 1988 with the Parkhead side, the third of his career, and capped off a fine season when he appeared in the Scottish Cup final win against Dundee United – marking a milestone of winning three badges in the competition without ever starting in a final. When he did get a starting place, in the 1990 final against Aberdeen, he ended up on the losing side as the Dons won on penalties.

After that defeat against Aberdeen he linked up with former Hoops team-mate Tommy Burns at Kilmarnock, signed for £50,000. In 1991 he moved to Hamilton to combine playing with duties as assistant manager and added a Scottish Football League Challenge Cup winner's medal to his collection with Accies before returning to Killie to become right hand man to Burns and help steer the club back into the Premier League.

The Burns and Stark partnership was recruited by Celtic in 1994 and the duo spent three years in charge. Following their departure from Parkhead the former Dons midfielder became a manager in his own right with Morton in 1997, leading to appointments at St Johnstone and then Queen's Park.

In 2008 he was headhunted by the SFA to become full-time coach to the Scotland under-21 team, making up in part for the disappointment of missing out on international recognition as a player. It confirmed that the former Dons man's stock as a coach was rising and in the position at Hampden he has enhanced his credentials with his solid stewardship of the country's young guns.

The departure of Mark McGhee from the Aberdeen manager's office in 2010 led to speculation that Stark would be his replacement at Pittodrie, with confirmed support from within the club for the studious coach. In the end it was the wise old head Craig Brown who got the vote from the Dons directors – but Stark has time on his side as he bids to earn a return to the club he served so well as a player.

Gordon Strachan

Debut: League, 5 November 1977 v Dundee United (a) won 1-0
Appearances: League 183+8, Scottish Cup 29, League Cup 46+3, Europe 34+4
Goals: League 54, Scottish Cup 7, League Cup 20, Europe 8
Also played for: Scotland (50 caps), Dundee, Manchester United, Leeds United, Coventry City
Managed: Coventry City, Southampton, Celtic, Middlesbrough.

All hail football's king of the put down. On the pitch the legend of Gordon Strachan was born when he starred in the European Cup Winners' Cup victory in Gothenburg, off the park a new reason for infamy was created in the form of cutting sarcasm the moment he was asked for a quick word by a reporter and responded with 'velocity', before striding off.

As a manager Strachan has perfected a talent for body swerving media questions with his own brand of humour. The journalists so often on the receiving end can't help but come back for more.

While in charge of Southampton he was asked in which area he felt Middlesbrough had outplayed his side, responding with 'the big green area out there.'

Confidence was never an area Strachan struggled in as a player and in management that trait continued. Take the time he was asked if he was the right man for the job after one of his English appointments, when he hit back with 'No, I think they should have got George Graham because I'm useless'. There's really no answer to that.

When asked if he could take the fact an unbeaten run had ground to a halt Strachan hit back with 'no, I'm just going to crumble like a wreck. I'll go home, become an alcoholic and maybe jump off a bridge'.

One particular one liner summed up his approach to the media spotlight he has found himself under since branching out into management. When a reporter asked 'You don't take losing lightly do you Gordon?' he was hit with a typically curt comeback of 'I don't take stupid questions lightly either'.

His love-hate relationship with the media could not detract from his record in Celtic's top job, leading the club to the championship in his first season in charge and then into the last 16 of the Champions League in 2006. It was the first time in Celtic's history they had reached that stage and the progress came courtesy of a 1-0 win over a certain Alex Ferguson. Football's a funny old game, as another media savvy football favourite would tesify to.

Strachan's career has been nothing short of extraordinary. Born in Edinburgh, he launched his senior career with Dundee as a teenager and made an immediate impact as he rose to become captain at Dens Park.

In 1977 he made the switch to Pittodrie in a deal which took Jim Shirra and £40,000 to Dundee. It was an inspired piece of business by Aberdeen manager Billy McNeill.

The inspirational midfielder was just 20 when he signed, already an under-21 international, and his best days were certainly in front of him.

He had a poor first season by his own high standards and was a target for flak from the Pittodrie fans but by the time he left the Dons to join Ron Atkinson's Manchester United in 1984 he was laden with honours. The first success came when Alex Ferguson and his Dons side won the Premier Division championship in 1980, the season in which Strachan's majestic performances won him the Scottish player of the year award.

He scored in the 1982 Scottish Cup final on his way to the first of three winner's medals in that competition in addition to adding another top flight title in 1983/84 with Aberdeen.

Add the European Cup Winners' Cup and European Super Cup into the equation and the considerable sum total of an amazing Pittodrie career is complete. In less than seven years Strachan played 307 games and scored 89 goals after making his debut in a 1-0 win at Dundee United on November 5, 1977.

When he parted company he claimed he was going stale in the Scottish game. He came close to moving to Germany with Cologne but had a late change of heart and signed at Old Trafford in a £600,000 transfer.

He was an FA Cup winner with United in his first season before Alex Ferguson followed him to Manchester. The pair's relationship had always been stormy and that intensified in England, to the point Strachan was offloaded to Leeds for £200,000 in 1989.

He became captain at Elland Road, leading them to the Second Division title and earning the English player of the year title on their return to the top flight in 1991. The following year the fairytale was complete as Leeds won the First Division ahead of United.

An incredible club career was matched at international level, with Strachan making it into Scotland's hall of fame with his 50 cap tally from his debut in 1980 to his final appearance in 1992. He played in the World Cup finals in both 1982 and 1986.

He rounded off his playing career with Coventry, the club where he launched his managerial career in 1996. Five years in charge of Coventry were followed by three at Southampton before his appointment to Celtic's top job in 2005 to succeed Martin O'Neill, bringing the title back to Parkhead at the first attempt and going on to enjoy tremendous success with the Hoops as the title was clinched three years in succession.

He also won the League Cup twice and the Scottish Cup before stepping down in May 2009 after being pipped to the title by Rangers.

Strachan bounced back when he was appointed manager of Middlesbrough just months after leaving Parkhead as the ambitious north-east side looked for a lift in the wake of Gareth Southgate's sacking. The new boss returned north of the border to sign a succession of players, including former Celtic charges Barry Robson and Scott McDonald as well as Old Firm adversary Kris Boyd, but did not get the response he had hoped for on Teesside. His stint at the Riverside lasted just under a year as results in the Championship proved disappointing and the team slipped into the relegation zone. He was replaced at Boro by Tony Mowbray, the man who had stepped into his shoes at Celtic.

Dom Sullivan

Debut: League Cup, 14 August 1976 v Kilmarnock (h) won 2-0
Appearances: League 98+11, Scottish Cup 12, League Cup 21+2, Europe 7+2
Goals: League 11, League Cup 3
Also played for: Clyde, Celtic, Manchester City, Morton
Managed: Alloa, East Stirling

Within three months of his first appearance as an Aberdeen player Dom Sullivan had a winner's medal safely tucked away in his pocket. The Glaswegian midfielder could have been forgiven for thinking the streets of Aberdeen were paved with gold but the League Cup victory in 1976 proved to be his only reward for four years of service under three managers at Pittodrie.

He was a promising Scotland under-23 international when Ally MacLeod signed him in 1976. Sullivan had spent seven years on the Clyde books, winning a Second Division championship medal, and was being courted by a string of English clubs alerted by rave reports about the potential of the rising midfield star. He was playing part-time football with the Glasgow outfit but would soon be earning a living from the game he loved.

It was Aberdeen who won the race for his signature with a £25,000 deal and he made the No.7 shirt his own after arriving in the north-east, one of five ever presents in the 11 game run to the League Cup final against Celtic and a key man in the 2-1 win against the Hoops.

Sullivan continued to prove a big hit with MacLeod's successor Billy McNeill and was part of the team which came within two points of pipping Celtic to the league title in 1978, when he was also on the losing side in the Scottish Cup final against Rangers.

Alex Ferguson became his third boss in as many years when he breezed into Pittodrie in 1978 and he stuck by Sullivan for one term before relegating him to the periphery of the side for the 1979-80 title win, when he made just five appearances.

Before the half-way point in that campaign his desire from a move away from Pittodrie, after a series of rejected transfer requests, was met in October 1979. He had become frustrated by the lack of first team opportunities but there was no shortage of interest in the player.

Sullivan was reunited with McNeill at boyhood heroes Celtic in a £92,000 transfer having rejected an approach from Jim McLean at Dundee United. Celtic went on to win the top flight in his first two full seasons at Parkhead but in 1983 Sullivan was freed and switched to Morton after a month's trial with old mentor McNeill at Manchester City.

He completed his full set of Scottish league winner's medals with the Cappielow outfit when he helped them to the First Division flag in 1984 to add to his Second Division win with Clyde and Premier Division success with Celtic.

In 1985 he continued his playing career with Alloa and it was the Wasps who handed Sullivan his managerial break the following year, with former Dons team-mate Stuart Kennedy recruited to bolster the backroom team. He went on to take the helm at East Stirling before stepping down in 1992 to concentrate on his career in the licensed trade in the central belt.

Bobby Street

Debut: League, 10 March 1973 v Partick Thistle (h) drew 0-0
Appearances: League 11
Also played for: Montrose, Kilmarnock, Keith, Huntly, Cove Rangers

Serious injuries wrecked striker Bobby Street's chances of making a major impact in a red shirt. The young recruit from Port Glasgow made his breakthrough in the 1972/73 season but fractured his right leg after just one further appearance. He returned to the fray in the following campaign but suffered another leg break and another frustrating spell on the treatment table.

Street was released in 1976 and joined Montrose for a two year stint. He joined Kilmarnock in 1978 and finished the following season as leading scorer for the Rugby Park side on their return to the Premier Division. He returned to the north-east to play Highland League football with Keith and also had a second stint at Montrose as well as playing for Huntly, Cove Rangers and coaching with Buckie Thistle.

Tommy Sutherland

Debut: League, 5 November 1969 v St Mirren (a) lost 2-0
Appearances: League 5
Also played for: Hamilton Academical, Crystal Palace

An impressive debut at right-back against St Mirren at Love Street in 1969 marked out teenage defender Tommy Sutherland as one for the future. The teenager had been signed from Shotts Bon Accord the previous year but, after making five appearances in his maiden campaign, drifted out of the first team picture and was released in 1970.

Sutherland had short stints with Hamilton and Crystal Palace before returning to the junior ranks.

Bobby Tait

Debut: League, 4 March 1961 v Airdrie (a) lost 3-1
Appearances: League 2
Also played for: Elgin City, Notts County

Left winger Bobby Tait proved there can be life after Aberdeen when he bounced back from the disappointment of being released in 1961 by rebuilding his career with Elgin City and then earning a full-time deal with Notts County. Tait had arrived from Loanhead Mayflower in 1960 but made just two appearances for the first team.

Stephen Tarditi

Debut: League, 15 May 2004 v Dundee (h) lost 2-1
Appearances: League 1
Also played for: East Fife

Stephen Tarditi stood out from the crowd in more ways than one. The 6ft 2in forward's height made him a handful for defences and he was a regular scorer for the under-19 and under-21 sides at Pittodrie. The Airdrie-born youth product made just a single substitute's appearance for the first team. He was released in 2004 and joined East Fife before dropping into the junior ranks.

Ian Taylor

Debut: League, 22 October 1966 v Airdrie (a) won 2-1
Appearances: League 122, Scottish Cup 12, League Cup 30, Europe 13
Goals: League 22, Scottish Cup 1, League Cup 3, Europe 2
Also played for: Motherwell, St Johnstone, Fraserburgh, Elgin City, Peterhead.
Managed: Peterhead

Ian Taylor gave eight years of dedicated service to Aberdeen during the 1960s and 70s. As football evolved to become a squad game, he proved to be a valuable attacking asset for both Eddie Turnbull and Jimmy Bonthrone.

The Aberdonian played his juvenile football for Banks o' Dee A and had been on Aberdeen's radar since he was a 12-year-old pupil at Aberdeen Academy, the school later renamed Hazlehead Academy.

He turned full-time with the Dons in 1967, turning his back on a fledgling career in the insurance industry, after making his first team debut under Eddie Turnbull in the 1966/67 season. He was on the bench for the Scottish Cup final defeat that term and part of the squad for the victory in the same competition three years later.

With searing pace, Taylor was used as a left winger and centre forward in those early days as the club exploited his attacking qualities. He spent eight seasons as a valuable squad man before clinching a £10,000 transfer to Motherwell at the tail end of the 1973/74 season. Ian St John was the man who recruited him for the Steelmen, tempted by Taylor's promising displays in a variety of midfield and forward positions.

After two years with Well he moved on to St Johnstone and then branched out into Highland League football with Fraserburgh, Elgin City and Peterhead in the late 1970s. He was appointed Peterhead manager in 1980 before stepping aside to let Joe Harper take charge the following year due to business commitments. He remained heavily involved with north football in the Highland League and junior scene, most recently managing Banks o' Dee up until 2010.

Theo Ten Caat

Debut: League, 10 August 1991 v Airdrie (a) won 2-1
Appearances: League 48, Scottish Cup 3, League Cup 1, Europe 2
Goals: League 5
Also played for: Groningen, Vitesse Arnhem

Cultured midfielder Theo Ten Caat was far removed from the stereotype of the modern footballer. The Dutchman was a keen artist, a committed conservationist and loved nothing more than a spot of political debate. Ten Caat was also a talented player, tempting Alex Smith to spend £260,000 to sign him from Groningen in time for the 1991/92 season. Ten Caat spent three seasons in and around the first team, showing flashes of class during a consistent maiden campaign before falling out of the picture during Willie Miller's tenure. He joined Vitesse Arnhem in his homeland in a £100,000 deal in 1994.

MAGIC MOMENTS

20 December 2007
ABERDEEN 4, COPENHAGEN 0

The Danes of Copenhagen arrived in Scotland needing only a draw against Aberdeen to secure their passage to the lucrative round of 32 in the 2007/2008 Uefa Cup. They left with their tails between their legs, on the receiving end of a vintage European performance reminiscent of the good old days of the 1980s.

It was Jimmy Calderwood, not Alex Ferguson, who master-minded the triumph and his troops did him proud – not least Jamie Smith, a player who tantalised and frustrated in equal measure during his injury-hit stay in the North-east.

The former Celtic man had just returned from a hamstring strain when he took his place in the team to face the men from Denmark. Smith proved to be central to the four-star show from the Dons in what would be his finest display in Aberdeen colours. The hosts had it all to do when they ran out at Pittodrie. While their Scandinavian opponents could settle for a point from the group game, Calderwood knew nothing less than victory would take his team through to the knock-out stages of the competition.

With former Premiership stars Jesper Gronkjaer and Marcus Allback to call upon, there was no doubting Copenhagen had class at their disposal.

It was the Danes who threatened first, with Rasmus Wurtz going close, but it was far from one way traffic. Lee Miller, latching onto a pass from Michael Hart, spurned a glorious opportunity to put his side in front before Copenhagen roared back with opportunities of their own. Gronkjaer, rolling back the years to his Chelsea heyday, was tormentor in chief to a wary Dons defence – with Andrew Considine and Richie Byrne tasked with taming him.

Calderwood rallied his men at half-time and within two minutes of the restart he had his reward. A capacity crowd was brought to its feet when Smith cutely killed a long clearance from goalkeeper Jamie Langfield and produced an astonishing lob from 30 yards to make it 1-0.

In the 55th minute Smith made it a double when he collected a long pass from Miller and blasted a 20-yard stunner into the back of the net. It was a magical period of play and a dream game for Smith. The game was wrapped up in the 71st minute, with a helping hand from the visitors. A Miller free-kick from the right was deflected past the helpless keeper to put hopes of an all-important draw out of reach for Copenhagen.

With nine minutes left on the clock the humiliation was complete for the highly fancied continental outfit when substitute Chris Maguire, who had replaced goal hero Smith, raced away to send over a cross that fell perfectly for Richard Foster to tuck the ball home at the far post.

It was a seminal performance and result for Calderwood, a night on which all of his hopes and dreams for the side he had assembled aligned perfectly to show the Granite City's football public the potential being harnessed at Pittodrie. Ultimately the cast could not be retained, with several key performers drifting away over time, but the future was not a concern for the fans who partied long into the night on the back of a stellar display from the team they followed with such passion.

ABERDEEN: Langfield, Hart, Byrne, Diamond, Considine, Nicholson, Severin, Clark, Aluko (Foster 59), Miller, Jamie Smith (Maguire 74).

George Taylor

Debut: League, 26 March 1938 v Hamilton (h) won 1-0
Died: 1982, Plymouth
Appearances: League 63, Scottish Cup 8, League Cup 11
Goals: League 6, League Cup 1
Also played for: Hall Russells, Plymouth Argyle

On May 11, 1946, a wait of more than four decades ended for the hordes of Aberdeen fans who had trekked south to watch their heroes tackle Rangers in the Southern League Cup final. For the Dons fans in the crowd of 135,000 at Hampden it was their first taste of success in a national competition, with the Southern League Cup acting as the precursor to the League Cup.

The man who ended a trophy famine stemming from Aberdeen's formation in 1903 was George Taylor, the only north-east player in the starting line-up on that momentous day.

The score was poised at 2-2 going into the final minute of an end to end final. Right winger Alec Kiddie broke clear and when his cross was only half cleared it was Taylor who stepped forward to crack home the winning goal off the post. It was 3-2 on the day but the magic number was 1 – the first of many trophies to be inked on the club's honours list.

Taylor started out as a centre forward with junior side Hall Russell but with Aberdeen he made his name as a left-half. He signed in 1938 and made his debut in a 1-0 win on March 26 at home to Hamilton that year.

After the war he remained in the thick of the action at Pittodrie and was Dave Halliday's first choice No.6 in the successful 1945/46 season. In addition to the Southern League Cup win the team claimed third spot in the reformed post-war top flight.

In the following campaign he made it two cups in the space of two terms when he played in all but one of the seven ties on Aberdeen's run to the Scottish Cup final against Hibs. For the game against the Easter Road side he switched to left-back and had a key if unwanted involvement – watching his back pass slip past goalkeeper George Johnstone in the early stages to give Hibs the lead. His team bounced back to win 2-1 and confirm their rising status in the game, reinforced by another third place finish in the league.

The chance to add a League Cup winner's medal passed the King Edward born player by when he was part of the team which lost 4-0 to Rangers in the inaugural final in 1947.

His final season in the north-east saw Taylor sit out just a single game as he continued to thrive in Halliday's team.

He notched up 82 appearances for the Dons and scored six goals before his form tempted Plymouth Argyle to step in and take him south in 1948 and it proved a long and fruitful relationship with the English outfit.

By 1955 he had progressed from playing to become Plymouth's head trainer, looking after six teams at the peak of his powers. He spent more than a decade in that post before becoming chief scout for Argyle in 1966.

Taylor, who moved into the licensed trade following his retirement from football, died in Plymouth in 1982 at the age of 67.

Lewis Thom

Debut: League, 16 September 1961 v Dundee (h) won 3-1
Appearances: League 35, Scottish Cup 4
Goals: League 5
Also played for: Dundee United, Shrewsbury Town, Lincoln City, Altrincham, Bradford Park Avenue, Elgin City, Clach, Huntly

Starlet Lewis Thom was one of a small band of players in the 1960s who bypassed junior football and went straight in at the top level. Thom, a product of the renowned Banks o' Dee A juvenile side, made his Dons debut as a 17-year-old early in the 1961/62 season. The left winger was a regular the following term as part of an Aberdeen team pushing for a top five finish. Thom was released in 1964 after losing his first team place and rejected an approach from Charlton in favour of signing for Dundee United. The Aberdonian went on to play for Shrewsbury, Lincoln, Altrincham and Bradford Park Avenue before settling back in the north-east to play in the Highland League with Elgin City, Clach and then Huntly.

Eddie Thomson

Debut: League, 24 March 1973 v Kilmarnock (a) won 2-0
Appearances: League 99, Scottish Cup 7, League Cup 23, Europe 3
Goals: League 1, League Cup 1
Also played for: Hearts, San Antonio Thunder (USA)

Have boots, will travel. Central defender Eddie Thomson developed a wanderlust after leaving the Dons behind in 1976 and established a glowing worldwide reputation both as a player and coach.

Thomson, who died from cancer in his adopted homeland of Australia in 2003, made his first short haul move in 1973 when his first club Hearts sold him to Aberdeen in 1973. The Edinburgh-born stopper, who played more than 150 games for the Jambos over the course of seven years, spent three years as the pivot in the Pittodrie defence, sailing past a century of appearances, before turning his attentions long haul.

In 1976 he switched to the North American Soccer League with San Antonio Thunder and spent a season in the US as part of a flood of British talent travelling to sample the glamour and glitz of sport stateside.

He went on to find a new and permanent home in Australia with Sydney City. He won the championship three times as a player, using his experience and ability to tremendous effect, and then four times in six years as coach as well as guiding his charges to the Philips Cup. Those achievements earned the Scot promotion to the assistant coach role with the Australia national team in 1984 and six years later he took over in the top job, both with the international and Olympic sides.

Thomson also served as a coach in the burgeoning Japanese league and became a hugely respected figure throughout world football.

Scott Thomson

Debut: League Cup, 12 August 1992 v Arbroath (a) won 4-0
Appearances: League 20, Scottish Cup 1, League Cup 4
Goals: League 1
Also played for: Shrewsbury Town, Brechin City, Raith Rovers, Dunfermline Athletic, East Fife

Aberdeen's £100,000 move for Brechin City's 19-year-old prospect Scott Thomson handed the Aberdonian a lifeline in the full-time game. Having trained with the Dons as a schoolboy, Thomson chose to join Shrewsbury Town on an apprenticeship. He returned north after failing to settle in England and linked up with Brechin before winning his dream switch to Pittodrie. Thomson, capable of playing wide or through the centre of the attack, made sporadic appearances before moving to Raith early in 1996 in search of regular football. Thomson moved across Fife to Dunfermline in 1998 and in 11 years with the Pars made more than 300 appearances, mainly in defence. He also featured for East Fife after leaving Dunfermline in 2009.

Kenny Thomson

Debut: League Cup, 11 September 1948 v St Mirren (h) won 3-1
Appearances: League 29, Scottish Cup 5, League Cup 18
Also played for: Stoke City, Middlesbrough, Hartlepools United

Central defender Kenny Thomson was another Banks o' Dee player who made the leap to the senior game with Aberdeen. He joined in the late 1940s and eventually succeeded Alec Young at the heart of Dave Halliday's defence, with his performances earning a place on the Scotland reserve list and attention from clubs on both sides of the border. Stoke City spent £22,000 on the Aberdeen stopper, still only 22, in 1952 and he also turned out for Middlesbrough and Hartlepools United before retiring from the game to train as a teacher.

Thomson died in 1969 at the age of 39.

Ben Thornley

Debut: League, 4 August 2001 v Hearts (a) lost 1-0
Appearances: League 30, Scottish Cup 2, League Cup 3
Goals: League 3, Scottish Cup 1, League Cup 1
Also played for: Manchester United, Huddersfield Town, Blackpool, Bury, Halifax Town

Any player who can list Manchester United on their cv has a headstart when it comes to winning over the Red Army. After all, if you are good enough for Sir Alex Ferguson then you are good enough for the Dons.

Winger Ben Thornley had three England under-21 caps to his credit, after breaking through at Old Trafford alongside David Beckham and Paul Scholes, but had to go out on the road to earn a living. He was sold by Ferguson to Huddersfield in 1998 for £175,000 but three years later was released. That was when Ebbe Skovdahl entered the equation, recruiting him after a trial spell. Thornley dazzled in his early days as a Dons player but could not maintain that form and joined Blackpool 18 months later. Spells with Bury and Halifax Town followed.

Steve Tosh

Debut: Scottish Cup, 25 January 2003 v Queen of the South (a) drew 0-0
Appearances: League 57, Scottish Cup 8, League Cup 5
Goals: League 6, League Cup 3
Also played for: Arbroath, St Johnstone, Raith Rovers, Livingston, Falkirk, Gretna, Queen of the South, Cove Rangers

If Steve Paterson had been able to find 11 players with the determination of Steve Tosh there is every chance he would have been able to prolong his tenure as Aberdeen manager.

Tosh, a proud Fifer from Kirkcaldy, cost just £30,000 when he joined from Falkirk in January 2003 and repaid that fee with ease during two years on the staff. His all action midfield performances and passion for the cause made him a hit with the Red Army, although even his promptings could not rouse those around him during difficult times for Paterson and his team.

He was the archetypal journeyman and a solid professional. His playing credits listed Arbroath, St Johnstone, Raith Rovers, Livingston and Falkirk before he inked his Dons deal and since leaving in January 2005 he has seen service with Gretna and Queen of the South as well as having a second spell with Livingston.

Tosh was central to Jimmy Calderwood's team when he made his surprise departure to join big spending Gretna in the Third Division. He was offered a financial package that offered the type of long term security the Dons simply could not match.

In 2010/11 he returned to the north-east to sign for Cove Rangers in the Highland League and proved there is life in the veteran schemer yet with some inspirational performances after earlier bouncing back from a broken leg suffered while playing for Queens, a low to counter the high of scoring for the Dumfries minnows in the Scottish Cup final defeat against Rangers in 2008.

Karim Touzani

Debut: League, 29 July 2006 v Hibs (a) drew 1-1
Appearances: League 24, Scottish Cup 2, Europe 2
Goals: League 1
Also played for: Twente Enschede, Sparta Rotterdam (both Netherlands)

It is unusual for any player to be remembered for his part in a Dons defeat but that is exactly what Karim Touzani's legacy is at Pittodrie. Touzani's exemplary performance on Uefa Cup duty in Spain as the Dons went down to a brace 2-0 against Atletico Madrid was a reminder of just what the Dutchman was capable of as he kept the millionaires of the continental giants at bay with a sterling performance anchoring Jimmy Calderwood's midfield. Touzani often featured in central defence during two seasons in Scotland, never looking as comfortable in that position as he did in the middle of the park. Having joined from Twente Enschede in July 2006 he returned to the Netherlands with Sparta Rotterdam in 2008.

Fergus Tiernan

Debut: League, 28 April 2001 v St Johnstone (a) won 3-0
Appearances: League 52, Scottish Cup 1, League Cup 6, Europe 1
Goals: League 1
Also played for: Ross County, Dumbarton, Queen's Park

Scott Michie's reward for scoring in the Scottish Youth Cup final against Celtic was his first team debut. Fergus Tiernan, who had scored the opener in the 2-0 victory at Hampden, gained a new two-year contract as the Dons moved quickly to tie the talented midfield playmaker to the club. He had already played for Ebbe Skovdahl's senior side when he lifted the youth cup, showing maturity during his top team outings, with an excellent range of passing and a neat touch, but fell out of favour after Jimmy Calderwood's arrival in 2004. He joined Ross County before the year was out, spending two and a half years in the Highlands before heading south to Dumbarton. In 2009 he briefly linked up with his former Pittodrie mentor Gardner Speirs at Queen's Park.

Tzanko Tzvetanov

Debut: League, 10 August 1996 v Celtic (h) drew 2-2
Appearances: League 39, League Cup 7, Europe 4
Also played for: Bulgaria, SV Waldhof Mannheim (Germany), Cottbus (Germany), Levski Sofia (Germany)

The arrival of Bulgarian international star Tzanko Tzvetanov in the wake of his role in his country's Euro 96 exploits was a statement of intent from the Dons board as they backed manager Roy Aitken to the hilt. The £600,000 investment proved not to be entirely successful, with the import suffering a hamstring injury months into his first season and then drifting out of the side when Alex Miller took the helm. Tzvetanov had 39 caps when he moved to Pittodrie from German side SV Waldhof Mannheim and returned to the country when he joined Cottbus in a cut price £100,000 deal in the summer of 1998. He also went on to represent Levski Sofia in his home country before retiring.

Daniel Uchechi

Debut: Scottish Cup, 14 February 2012 v Queen of the South (a) won 2-1
Appearances (up to the end of 2011/12): League 1, Scottish Cup 1
Also played for: FC Dender (Nigeria)

Nigerian trickster Daniel Uchechi joined the Dons cause in the January transfer window in 2012 after impressing while on trial. It was his latest attempt to make a breakthrough in the British game. The striker, with his repertoire of ball skills, had been taken on by Charlton and West Ham in his youth without progressing to either first team. He had appeared for Sheffield Wednesday prior to arriving at Aberdeen but struggled to make an impression in the SPL and was released just months after moving north after just two appearances.

Willem van der Ark

Debut: League, 21 January 1989 v Motherwell (a) won 2-0
Appearances: League 64, Scottish Cup 4, League Cup 5, Europe 4
Goals: League 11, Scottish Cup 3, League Cup 1
Also played for: Cambur, Willem II, Utrecht

At 6ft 5in tall there was no hiding place for Dutch striker Willem van der Ark on the football pitch. The towering import is one of the most distinctive players ever to have pulled on the red shirt of Aberdeen, far from the most technically gifted but always ready and willing to give his all for the cause.

Van der Ark arrived mid-way through the 1988/89 campaign. Alex Smith, a keen follower of the market in the Netherlands, was persuaded to part with £280,000 from the Pittodrie coffers to recruit the big man from Willem II, the top flight side he had joined from Cambur just a season earlier. His height belied his preference to have the ball played to feet, with aerial ability not one of the former basketball player's strongest attributes.

Over the course of two years in Scotland, which included a lengthy spell on the sidelines due to injury, he made over 70 appearances and became a cult figure for Dons fans after scoring on his debut at Motherwell.

In January 1992 the Scottish adventure drew to a close when Utrecht weighed in with a £200,000 bid that was reluctantly accepted by Smith, who had fought hard to retain the services of his unique striker when earlier talk of a Pittodrie exit had surfaced. Van der Ark later returned to Cambur before retiring due to a groin injury and concentrating on a new career as an estate agent.

Peter Van De Ven

Debut: League Cup, 21 August 1990 v Queen's Park (a) won 2-1
Appearances: League 32, Scottish Cup 1, League Cup 4 Europe 4
Goals: League 2
Also played for: Fortuna Sittard, Roda, Charleroi (Belgium), Willem II, Hearts, Racing Genk (Belgium)

Moustachioed midfielder Peter van de Ven looked to be another shrewd piece of business by Alex Smith when he was recruited from Willem II in the summer of 1990. The 29-year-old Dutchman had a reputation as an accomplished player who was comfortable anywhere in the midfield or defence and quickly adapted his talents to the Scottish game, slotting straight into Smith's side and rarely putting a foot wrong during an impressive run of early performances.

He was a typically proficient continental professional, a regular for the Netherlands under-21 side while emerging with Fortuna Sittard and picked four times for his country's senior squad while with Roda in the mid-1980s. A spell in Belgium with Charleroi ended his international ambitions but when he returned to the Dutch league with Willem II he caught the attention of Smith during one of his scouting missions on foreign shores.

A combination of injury and the emergence of a clutch of young players in the positions the utility man covered contrived to cut short his Pittodrie stay, with the appointment of Willie Miller as manager seeing him edged out of the first team picture once and for all.

Hearts, managed by Joe Jordan, moved in with a £90,000 bid in time for the 1992/93 season and van de Ven made the hop down the east coast to Tynecastle to continue his Scottish sojourn. Jordan had earmarked him as the ideal replacement for Rangers-bound defender Dave McPherson. The Dutchman left the Edinburgh side in 1994 for a second spell in Belgium, this time with Racing Genk.

Zoltan Varga

Debut: League, 14 October 1972 v Falkirk (h) drew 2-2
Appearances: League 26, Scottish Cup 3, League Cup 2.
Goals: League 10.
Also played for: Hungary (14 caps), Ferencvaros, Hertha Berlin, Ajax, Borussia Dortmund
Managed: Ferencvaros

Zoltan Varga won nothing in his brief dalliance with Scottish football except the undivided attention of a generation of Dons fans. He spent less than a full season at Pittodrie and competes with Scotland international Alex Jackson for the title of the club's ultimate one-hit wonder. In 1924-25 Jackson racked up 40 appearances to Varga's 31 before his wing wizardry took him to Huddersfield.

While those who saw Jackson in action are few and far between, the Varga fan club lives on and his bespoke performances at the heart of the Aberdeen team for that one season stay with the paid up members.

Can a man who played so few games, with no return in terms of silverware, be categorised as a legend? Perhaps not, but the circumstances of his Scottish sojourn are most certainly the stuff of legend.

Varga, an Olympic gold medal winner with Hungary's football team in 1964, was a leading light in German football when scandal struck. The Hertha Berlin playmaker was caught up in a bribery row in the Bundesliga and found himself banned for two years.

He had played in two European finals, the Fairs Cup in both 1965 and 1968 against Juventus and Leeds United, for first club Ferencvaros after making his debut as a 16 year-old.

Yet, at the age of 27 and hitting his prime, he found himself out of the club game. Step forward Jimmy Bonthrone, who spent £40,000 of Aberdeen's money to bring the continental master to Scottish shores.

The intriguing tale began in August 1972. At the beginning of that month Hertha Berlin had visited Pittodrie to play a friendly match and it would seem conversation in the boardroom soon turned to the 14 members of the German club's squad who did not feature. They were the group who had been banned from plying their trade by the German football federation for two years, a punishment meted out the previous year after a probe into bribery allegations.

The players had been left in limbo and the club in the unenviable position of having an entire staff sitting twiddling their thumbs during that lengthy period of forced inactivity. There was a loophole though, with the ban only applicable in the German game. In a flash of inspiration, Hertha and the Dons latched onto that gap in the red tape and struck a deal to allow a 27-year-old Hungarian by the name of Varga to spend a week on trial in Scotland with a view to a permanent move. Few, if any, of the Aberdeen supporters had even heard the name before but the mere possibility of attracting the mysterious international put the Dons back on top of the news agenda.

His introduction to the rough and tumble of the game in this country was a harsh one and the slightly built Varga required stitches in a head wound after his first training session with his new team-mates. It did not put him off, nor did the fact his pre-match routine of stretching rather than running or ball striking drew frowns or that his desire to return after training for extra practice was a novelty.

If the Dons fans had questioned their manager's judgement, they had to wait just a matter of weeks for reassurance. Varga, in only his third game for the club, scored one of the most memorable goals Pittodrie has witnessed with a sublime lob against Celtic in a 3-2 defeat in October 1972. Varga scored both goals that day, two of the 10 strikes on his Scottish record.

His close control, passing ability and eye for goal endeared him to the Dons supporters. The continental import became a familiar sight on the roads of the city and its suburbs during a spell of rehabilitation from injury, when as part of the recovery plan he was prescribed plenty of cycling and swimming. He took to his bike to make the run from his home in Milltimber to Pittodrie each day, greeted with cheery waves and beeping horns along the route.

The relationship proved short-lived. A knee injury sidelined Varga after that first season and in November 1973 Varga returned to Europe, citing poor wages at Pittodrie as the reason.

Hertha Berlin repaid the £40,000 the Dons had splashed out and took him back to Germany but, not for the first time, controversy followed Varga. Just four days after touching down in Berlin there was another transfer – this time Ajax paid £70,000 to take Varga to Holland and Hertha celebrated a swift £30,000 profit. Not bad for less than one week's work and clearly part of the plan when they moved to end Varga's career with the Dons.

He was recruited as a replacement for Johan Cruyff and lived the life of a superstar, with fame and fortune, but failed to sparkle in the Netherlands. Instead he played out his career back in Germany with Borussia Dortmund. Then a Second Division side, his first training session attracted 2,000 to Dortmund's base in the city and the gate for Varga's debut in 1974 leapt by 30,000 to 45,000.

After retiring in the early 1980s he turned to coaching in the amateur ranks in his adopted homeland before returning to take charge of Hungarian champions Ferencvaros in 1996 for a short period. He also served with Kispest Honved, Diosgyor and Gyor. He continued to coach in his homeland into his 60s and when Varga died in 2010 he did so on the football pitch, collapsing during a veterans match in Budapest.

Andrius Velicka

Debut: League, 16 October 2010 v Hearts (h) lost 1-0
Appearances: League 6
Goals: League 1
Also played for: Kaunus, Hearts, Viking, Rangers, Bristol City (on loan)

Former Hearts strker Andrius Velicka was the player Mark McGhee snapped up when a player-swap deal was struck with Rangers to loan Richard Foster to the Ibrox side. The Glasgow club got the better end of the deal, with Velicka never fully fit during his days with the Dons and managing just a single goal in half a dozen appearances before being released by the club to return to Rangers early in 2011.

Scott Vernon

Debut: League, 21 August 2010 v St Johnstone (a) won 1-0
Appearances (up to end of 2011/12): League 68, Scottish Cup 10, League Cup 5
Goals (up to the end of 2011/12): League 21, Scottish Cup 5, League Cup 2
Also played for: Oldham Athletic, Blackpool, Colchester, Northampton (on loan), Gillingham (on loan), Southend (on loan)

When Scott Vernon was hailed as the 'new' Duncan Shearer the hopes of the Aberdeen faithful began to rise. Had the Dons finally found a 20-goal-a-season striker to join the ranks of the attacking greats? A run of five goals in four games early in the 2010/11 season suggested the Englishman could indeed be the real deal and his purposeful style enhanced his growing reputation as well as sparking the comparisons with Shearer.

Vernon travelled a long and winding road to earn his chance to shine in Scotland's top flight. His stops along the way were at various lower league outposts in England, although he did enjoy 15 minutes of fame at the top level south of the border when he scored the only goal of the game as Oldham Athletic dumped Kevin Keegan and Manchester City out of the FA Cup in 2005. It was the high point of his time at Boundary Park and earned him national recognition for his part in a major cup upset.

The Manchester-born striker rose through the ranks at Oldham to the first team. A brief loan spell at Blackpool was followed by a permanent switch to the Seasiders. He was loaned out by Blackpool to Colchester in 2006 and again went on to make a permanent switch to the club. While with Colchester he was sent out for temporary service with Northampton, Gillingham and Southend to take his running total to seven clubs in eight years by the time he signed for Mark McGhee at Aberdeen in July 2010.

Etienne Verveer

Debut: League Cup, 19 August 1995 v St Mirren (h) won 3-1
Appearances: League Cup 1
Also played for: FC Chur (Switzerland), Millwall, Bradford City (on loan), Ischia (Italy)

Dutch national Etienne Verveer arrived at Pittodrie in the summer of 1995 after a four year stint with Millwall. The Surinam-born midfielder, who had been part of the Ajax youth set-up, made just a single appearance from the bench before being shown the door by manager Roy Aitken. He went on to kick-start his career in the Italian lower leagues with Ischia.

Javan Vidal

Debut: League, 24 January 2009 v Rangers (h) 0-0
Appearances: League 13, Scottish Cup 1
Goals: Scottish Cup 1
Also played for: Manchester City, Grimsby (on loan), Derby County (on loan), Chesterfield (on loan)

Manchester City prospect Javan Vidal was brought to Aberdeen in January 2009 as a replacement for fellow loan recruit Jared Hodgkiss. He had a reputation as a talented attacking right-back and had represented England at under-17, under-18, under-19 and under-20 level. Vidal, who had been a team-mate of Sone Aluko in those international squads, quickly pushed his way into Jimmy Calderwood's team and made ten starts for Aberdeen before returning to Eastlands after four months in Scotland. Vidal was also loaned to Derby County in 2010 and then Chesterfield in 2011 as he waited patiently for a break with the big spending Manchester club.

Nikola Vujadinovic

Debut: League, 11 September 2010 v Dundee United (a) lost 3-1
Appearances: League 18, Scottish Cup 5, League Cup 2
Goals: League 1
Also played for: CSKA Sofia, Udinese

Montenegro under-21 international Nikola Vujadinovic became the first player to make the switch from the glamour of Italy's Serie A to Pittodrie when he signed on loan from Udinese in 2010. He had become a 1million Euro star when he had joined the Italians from CSKA Sofia in 2008 and it was considered a signing coup when Mark McGhee succeeded in luring him to the SPL. The versatile defender's contribution was limited by injury in the first half of the season but he established himself under Craig Brown as a regular in a back line that had become the cornerstone on which the move away from the relegation trap door was built upon.

Willie Waddell

Debut: League, 1 October 1938 v Falkirk (h) won 4-1
Appearances: League 71, Scottish Cup 4, League Cup 20
Also played for: Kettering Town

Some players spend their entire career battling to get their hands on a winner's medal. When Willie Waddell succeeded in doing so, he attempted to give his prize away. The popular left-half won his place in the Aberdeen team for the 1947 Scottish Cup showdown with Hibs after Willie Cooper had suffered an injury in the semi-final success against Arbroath.

The rest is history. The reshuffled Dons side, with Waddell included, went on to beat the men from Leith and take the famous trophy back up the road to the Granite City. Waddell made the sporting move of offering his medal to stricken team-mate Cooper, a measure of the man extending the gesture and also of the esteem that Cooper was held in. In the end it was not necessary for Waddell to make the sacrifice, with the SFA agreeing to allow an extra medal to be struck. The cup triumph was the highlight of Waddell's career. He had joined the Pittodrie staff from Renfrew juniors in 1938 as a teenager. War interrupted his time with the club, during which time he turned out for Celtic, but he returned to the fold in peacetime and became a key man. By the time he departed in 1949 he had become captain of the side and he also served as skipper with Kettering Town after joining the English side following his Pittodrie swansong.

Waddell, who built a successful business in England after retiring from the game in 1958, died at the age of 60 after suffering a heart attack in 1979.

Ernie Waldron

Debut: League, 23 November 1946 v Hearts (h) won 2-1
Appearances: League 8
Goals: League 3
Also played for: Crystal Palace

Birmingham-born forward Ernie Waldron was in the twilight of his career when he plugged a gap in Dave Halliday's Aberdeen side in the 1946/47 season. Aged 33 when he made a scoring debut against Hearts in a 2-1 win at Pittodrie that term, the Englishman notched three goals in seven appearances. He had previously turned out for Crystal Palace.

Andy Walker

Debut: League, 12 October 1957 v Airdrie (a) won 6-2
Appearances: League 2
Also played for: Bristol Rovers

Birmingham City and Celtic were among the clubs tracking Andy Walker when he signed for Aberdeen in 1957. A Scottish Junior Cup winner with Banks o' Dee in the year he moved to Pittodrie, Walker progressed to the first team two years later after being converted from an inside forward to a wing half. After two appearances he was released in 1959 and joined Bristol Rovers.

Jimmy Walker

Debut: League, 12 October 1957 v Airdrie (a) won 6-2
Appearances: League 18, Scottish Cup 4, League Cup 2
Also played for: Bradford Park Avenue, Corby Town, Keith

Strong and athletic right back Jimmy Walker arrived from Inverurie Locos in 1953. The 19-year-old had attracted strong interest from Dundee and several English sides after starring in the junior game but opted to join the Dons and, after two years of national service, eventually made his debut in 1957. He served as an able deputy to Dave Caldwell and then Willie Clydesdale over the course of two seasons.

The Aberdonian departed in 1959 to join Bradford Park Avenue on a free transfer and also played for Corby Town before joining Highland League outfit Keith in 1965.

Josh Walker

Debut: Scottish Cup, 2 February 2008 v Hamilton (h) won 1-0
Appearances: League 8, Scottish Cup 2, League Cup 1, Europe 2
Goals: Europe 1
Also played for: Middlesbrough, Bournemouth (on loan), Rotherham (on loan), Watford, Stevenage (on loan), Northampton (on loan)

With an assured flash of his right boot, Josh Walker won a place in the rich European history of Aberdeen FC. Signed on loan from Middlesbrough just a fortnight earlier, the confident English teenager fired the Dons ahead against Bayern Munich in February 2008. The Uefa Cup tie ended in a 2-2 draw and Walker looked to have confirmed his place as a player with the world at his feet. He returned to Boro the following term and began to establish himself in the top team before being sent out on loan to Rotherham. A permanent move to Watford followed in 2010 before further loan stops with Stevenage and Northampton.

Nicky Walker

Debut: League, 25 August 1996 v Hearts (h) won 4-0
Appearances: League 19, League Cup 2, Europe 4
Also played for: Scotland, Leicester City, Motherwell, Rangers, Hearts, Partick Thistle, Ross County, Caley Thistle

Man of many clubs Nicky Walker had collected two Scotland caps by the time he landed in Aberdeen in 1996 after playing against the USA just weeks earlier and Germany in 1993. He had first savoured representative honours as a schoolboy international while growing up in Moray, turning out for Elgin City as a teenager

before joining Leicester City. Walker went on to star for Motherwell, Rangers, Hearts and Partick before landing at Pittodrie under Roy Aitken in the 1996/97 season. He moved on to Ross County the following term and became a key man for the Dingwall side as well as going on to play for Caley Thistle.

Walker retired to concentrate on his business commitments with his prominent family firm Walkers Shortbread.

Jim Wallace

Debut: League Cup, 23 August 1952 v Motherwell (h) lost 1-0
Appearances: League 9, League Cup 2
Goals: League 1
Also played for: Northampton Town

Teenage stopper Jimmy Wallace looked destined for a long and prosperous Pittodrie career when he was introduced to the Dons team in 1952. The defender, who had been plucked from the junior ranks where he had been playing for his hometown team Kirkintilloch Rob Roy, was in and around the Aberdeen first team for three seasons and set the ball rolling at the start of the glorious 1954/55 championship winning season.

The defender was in Dave Halliday's team for the opening game of the season and scored in the 5-0 win at home to Stirling Albion that day. After four further games he was replaced by Jack Allister in the side during one of six seasons as part of the first team squad. Wallace joined Northampton Town in May 1955. He returned to Glasgow with juniors Ashfield after a season in the English game.

Jimmy Wallace

Debut: League, 29 September 1956 v Hibs (h) won 3-1
Appearances: League 11
Goals: League 1
Also played for: Dundee United, Inverness Caledonian, Buckie Thistle

Defender Jimmy Wallace was another player to roll off the Banks o' Dee conveyor belt, moving on to Dundee United in 1958 before he saw service with Inverness Caledonian and Buckie Thistle. Wallace retired from football in the early 1960s to concentrate on a career in teaching, rising to become assistant head at Linksfield Academy in Aberdeen.

John Ward

Debut: League, 30 March 1956 v Queen of the South (a) drew 2-2
Appearances: League 12
Goals: League 1
Also played for: Raith Rovers

Forward John Ward was brought north by Dave Shaw early in his tenure. The Baillieston juniors player was given big boots to fill, replacing Harry Yorston at the tail end of the 1956/57 campaign. He played half a dozen consecutive matches and dipped in and out of the side the following term before moving on to Raith Rovers on a free transfer.

Noel Ward

Debut: League, 15 March 1975 v Partick Thistle (a) lost 1-0
Appearances: League 8
Also played for: Portadown, Wigan Athletic

Centre forward, central defender, goalkeeper. That was the sequence Northern Irish player Noel Ward followed after signing for Aberdeen from Portadown in 1973. The 6ft 2in Ulsterman was quickly converted from an attacker and made his Dons debut in defence as a deputy for Willie Young in 1975. He struggled to hold down a first team place and was pressed into action as a keeper in the reserves before moving to Wigan in 1976 and starred as a centre-half. His career was brought to a premature end in 1980 when he suffered a broken leg while on duty for the English side.

Tony Warner

Debut: League, 17 April 1999 v Dundee United (h) lost 4-0
Appearances: League 6
Also played for: Trinidad and Tobago, Liverpool, Swindon (on loan), Celtic (on loan), Millwall, Cardiff, Fulham, Leeds (on loan), Norwich (on loan), Barnsley (on loan), Hull City, Leicester City (on loan), Charlton Athletic (on loan), Scunthorpe, Tranmere Rovers

Liverpudlian goalkeeper Tony Warner became one of football's greatest late starters. He was a loyal reserve for Liverpool during five years in the first team squad in the 1990s and it was during that period that he arrived in Aberdeen on loan, signing for the final weeks of the 1998/99 campaign under Paul Hegarty but ending up on the losing side in five of the six matches he played for the Dons. Warner bounced back by establishing himself as Millwall's No.1 and eventually earned his top flight break with Fulham in 2005 before being rewarded with his international debut for Trinidad and Tobago the following year. He has since featured for Hull City, Scunthorpe and Tranmere Rovers as well as serving a number of clubs on loan.

Andy Watson

Debut: League, 7 January 1978 v Ayr United (a) drew 1-1
Appearances: League 131, Scottish Cup 17, League Cup 16, Europe 13
Goals: League 13, Scottish Cup 1, League Cup 2, Europe 1
Also played for: Leeds United, Hearts, Hibs

Andy Watson has enjoyed a glittering coaching career as right hand man to Alex McLeish at Motherwell, Hibs, Rangers, Scotland and Birmingham. It was a relationship that has been built on granite foundations as the two men forged their friendship as emerging young players at Aberdeen.

While McLeish boasts the more illustrious playing cv, Watson can be proud of his achievements on the park. He made 179 appearances for the Dons between 1977 and 1983 and was a consistent and reliable performer.

The Hilton Academy pupil attracted interest from a string of clubs, including QPR and Aston Villa, before pledging his future to Aberdeen. He had been

a standout performer with juvenile side Sunnyside and toughened up with a spell in the junior ranks with Rosemount before being given his big break in the Dons first team.

Watson went on to win a Premier Division winner's medal as part of Alex Ferguson's triumphant side in 1980, also collecting Scotland under-21 caps along the way. He was part of the squad that went on to enjoy European success in 1983, making two appearances but missing out on the Gothenburg glory.

Weeks later he switched to Leeds United in a £60,000 deal after a determined pursuit by the English side. The Aberdonian later turned out for Hearts and Hibs before retiring in 1989, at the age of 29, due to a knee injury and embarking on a coaching career at the very highest level.

Frank Watson

Debut: League, 2 January 1947 v Celtic (a) won 5-1
Appearances: League 33, Scottish Cup 6, League Cup 1

Goalkeeper Frank Watson's death in 1952 cast a long shadow over Pittodrie. The popular Dons player was just 23 when polio claimed his life. Watson had joined from Peebles Rovers in his native East Lothian in 1946 and was called upon regularly during his time with the club and, despite his young age, was elevated to first choice shot stopper during the 1949/50 season before dropping back to the reserves following Fred Martin's emergence. Watson combined his playing commitments with his studies at Aberdeen University and was in the third year of a geography degree when he died.

Graham Watson

Debut: League, 18 April 1990 v Dundee United (h) won 1-0
Appearances: League 15, Scottish Cup 2, League Cup 1, Europe 2
Goals: League 1
Also played for: Clyde

Midfielder Graham Watson was making only his sixth appearance in the Aberdeen first team when he faced the most important moment in his whole career. After being introduced from the bench in the 1990 Scottish Cup final against Celtic, the Fifer was one of the Dons men to hit the net from the spot as the trophy was won in a nerve wracking penalty shoot-out. Watson looked to have a bright future ahead of him but three leg breaks in as many years hampered his attempts to establish himself as a regular. The St Andrews-born player was reunited with his Aberdeen mentor Alex Smith when he joined the veteran coach at Clyde in 1994.

Gregg Watson

Debut: League, 25 February 1989 v Hearts (h) won 3-0
Appearances: League 23, League Cup 1, Europe 1
Also played for: Partick Thistle, Livington, Stenhousemuir

Glaswegian Gregg Watson was one of a string of youngsters introduced to the first team by Alex Smith. He came through the ranks alongside the likes of Scott Booth and Eoin Jess in the late 1980s. After being struck by injuries he fell out of the first team picture under Willie Miller and was sold to Partick Thistle for £50,000 in 1993. He made close to 150 appearances for the Jags in five years and also turned out for Livingston and Stenhousemuir in the late 1990s.

Willie Watt

Debut: League, 24 September 1966 v Rangers (a) lost 3-0
Appearances: League 19
Goals: League 8
Also played for: Preston North End, Raith Rovers, Rothes, Ross County

An incredible start to his career with Aberdeen was not enough to secure a permanent place in Eddie Turnbull's starting team. Watt had served his apprenticeship with Preston North End after being lured south when spotted starring for Aberdeen's school select side. He landed back in the north-east in 1966 after seeking a return to familiar surroundings and found a welcoming football home at Pittodrie. After being eased into the team by Turnbull early in the 1966/67 season he went on an impressive run of goal scoring – netting in a 2-1 win against Hibs in only his second game and then grabbing doubles in matching 3-1 wins against Hearts and St Mirren in his next two outings. Watt faced competition from Jimmy Wilson and then Dave Johnston for the No.11 shirt and moved on to Raith Rovers in 1968. Spells with Rothes and Ross County followed.

Noel Whelan

Debut: League, 7 August 2004 v Rangers (h) drew 0-0
Appearances: League 20, Scottish Cup 3
Goals: League 5
Also played for: Leeds United, Coventry City, Middlesbrough, Crystal Palace (on loan), Millwall, Derby County, Boston, Livingston, Dunfermline, Darlington

Man of many clubs Noel Whelan made a major impact in a short but eventful stop in the north-east. The big and bustling centre forward added height and muscle to Jimmy Calderwood's side in the 2004/05 season, scoring winning goals against Dunfermline and Caley Thistle along the way but ultimately collecting more bookings than goals. The Englishman arrived from Derby when his career was in a lull, having been a £2million striker when signed by both Coventry and Middlesbrough just a few seasons earlier. The former Leeds star had also served with Millwall and on loan at Crystal Palace before landing in the SPL. He went on to play for Boston, Livingston, Dunfermline and Darlington after being freed by Calderwood in 2005.

Michael Watt

Debut: League, 26 December 1989 v Hibs (h) lost 2-1
Appearances: League 78+2, Scottish Cup 7, League Cup 5, Europe 4
Also played for: Blackburn Rovers, Norwich City, Kilmarnock

If anyone can testify to the slings and arrows of outrageous fortune, and misfortune, in life as a professional footballer it must surely be Michael Watt. In 1996 the Aberdonian goalkeeper was revelling in his status as one of the country's top rated shot stoppers and pushing for inclusion in Craig Brown's Scotland squad for Euro 96 in England.

It came on the back of his long awaited promotion to the No.1 jersey at Pittodrie and a string of impressive displays on his way to helping the Dons to their first trophy in five seasons. Watt shut out Dundee in the final of the 1995 League Cup final to become only the fifth keeper in the club's history to earn a winner's medal. He was 25 when he held the League Cup aloft and had to be patient before getting his chance.

He had taken over the keeper's jersey from Theo Snelders earlier that season and at last held the position he had coveted since joining the club in 1988 upon leaving Robert Gordon's College, where he had gained the qualifications needed to win a university place. Instead of university he chose to study football with the Dons, having caught his home town club's eye while starring for Cove in the juvenile leagues.

His talent as an emerging player was never in doubt and Watt collected twelve caps for the Scotland under-21 team while serving as understudy to Snelders. After holding down a place in the Dons team in the 1995/96 season, following the Dutchman's move to Rangers, he was propelled into the Scotland B squad and was pushing for a place in the senior squad for the Euro 96 adventure as third choice keeper. In the end it was Nicky Walker who got the call and ultimately the same man led to Watt calling time on his Dons career.

By the end of 1996 he was seeking a transfer away from Pittodrie. That request came after he found himself relegated to third choice behind new recruit Walker and young gun Derek Stillie. It was hard to take for a player who made his debut seven years earlier when he deputised for Snelders in a 2-1 defeat at home to Hibs on December 26, 1989.

Watt went on to make 96 appearances for the club, notably when he was thrown in at the deep end for the Premier Division decider at Ibrox in 1991. Rangers needed a victory to prevent the Dons from winning the title and set about trying to intimidate the young opposition keeper, with Mark Hateley using his power to knock Watt's confidence at every opportunity. A 2-0 win for the home side ensured the championship remained in Glasgow.

Watt had a loan spell at Blackburn Rovers in 1997, which was cut short by injury, before a permanent switch to Norwich City in 1998. The following year, after a handful of top team appearances for the Canaries, he returned north to sign for Kilmarnock. After just four games for Killie, at the age of 29, he walked away from the game and concentrated on a career in financial services. His interest in the game was revived when he began coaching with the Rangers youth teams in 2005.

Derek Whyte

Debut: League, 20 December 1997 v Kilmarnock (a) lost 1-0
Appearances: League 131+2, Scottish Cup 11, League Cup 8, Europe 1
Also played for: Scotland (12 caps), Celtic, Middlesbrough, Partick Thistle
Managed: Partick Thistle

On a cold December morning in 1997 there was a moment of realisation for new Aberdeen manager Alex Miller. Less than a month into the job, Miller trudged off the training field knowing he desperately needed to bolster his defensive options. Within hours the ink on a cheque for £200,000 was drying and Derek Whyte was packing his bags to leave Middlesbrough behind for a new life with the Dons. Miller, assistant manager to Scotland boss Craig Brown, was convinced he had bagged a bargain having worked with Whyte during national squad gatherings. The defender went on to win the final two of his twelve caps while with the Dons. Whyte's international career began just weeks after his 19th birthday when the promising young Celtic defender appeared from the bench in a 2-0 victory over Bulgaria at Hampden under Andy Roxburgh.

By that stage Whyte was an experienced club campaigner, having made his Hoops debut as a 17 year-old when he was part of the Premier Division winning squad of 1986 and an established first team player when the title was won again in 1988. He collected Scottish Cup winner's medals with the Bhoys in both 1988 and 1989.

In 1992 he was lured away from Parkhead and joined Middlesbrough, becoming the Teeside club's record signing when he made his £950,000 switch in 1992. He had made 216 appearances for Celtic and went on to add 196 Boro appearances to his record before returning north to Aberdeen.

Whyte served as skipper at Pittodrie until 2002, when it became clear he would not be renewing his Aberdeen contract and Ebbe Skovdahl handed the armband to Darren Young. He had joined the club during a difficult period, embroiled in a succession of battles against the drop and only avoiding a relegation play-off in 2000 by virtue of the fact that First Division runners-up Falkirk did not have a ground which met SPL regulations.

The high spots came in the cup, with the Dons reaching both domestic cup finals in the 1999/2000 season. Whyte missed the League Cup showdown with Celtic due to injury but was at the heart of the defence as Rangers ran out 4-0 winners in the Scottish Cup equivalent later that term, a game marred by the facial injury to Jim Leighton which forced the Dons to play with striker Robbie Winter in goals for 88 minutes of the match.

Whyte's final contribution as a Pittodrie employee was to lead his side back into European football courtesy of a fourth place finish in the SPL in 2002. By the time the Dons embarked on their Uefa Cup campaign they had lost their captain to Partick Thistle. He captained the Jags before being appointed player co-manager, along with Gerry Britton, in the final month of 2003.

The duo lasted 13 months before being shown the exit door at Firhill and it signalled the end of Whyte's involvement on the frontline of the game. He went on to lead a property company in Dubai, utilising his football contacts to source potential investors, and also works as a television football pundit in his new home country.

Peter Weir

Debut: League Cup, 8 August 1981 v Kilmarnock (h) won 3-0
Appearances: League 160+11, Scottish Cup 19+2, League Cup 28+1, Europe 29+3
Goals: League 23, Scottish Cup 7, League Cup 2, Europe 6
Also played for: Scotland (6 caps), St Mirren, Leicester City, Ayr United

Peter Weir has been tasked with becoming a legend all over again. The Gothenburg Great breezed back into Pittodrie in 2006 to confirm his appointment as the new man in charge of the club's west coast scouting and coaching network.

His job description, put simply, is to fill the shoes of the late Bobby Calder. It was Calder who unearthed gem after gem after gem for the Pittodrie side decade after decade. His finds included Willie Miller, Alex McLeish, Jim Leighton, Arthur Graham, Archie Glen ... the list goes on and the value of the talent runs into millions.

Now Weir, who had earned his stripes scouting opposition teams for Tommy Burns at both Kilmarnock and Celtic as well as during a stint as assistant manager to Billy Stark at Morton before joining the Rangers youth set-up, is back working for the club which means more to him than any other.

Weir, speaking as he approached his first anniversary in his scouting and coaching role, said: "I've been an Aberdeen supporter since I was a boy. It started when my dad got tickets for the 1970 cup final, when Celtic were beaten 3-1, and we stood in the Dons end. After that I started travelling to games on the supporters bus and on the train right through the 1970s. To be back working with the club now is fantastic, it's crazy how these things work out.

"We're beginning to make good headway with attracting good young players to the club and hopefully in time for the 2007/08 season we will have three or four turning full-time. None of the boys we have approached have turned us down, quite the opposite – we have recently had one turning down a good offer from Rangers to join us instead.

"Rangers and Celtic are trying to nip in and sign many of the same players and there are scouts from so many other clubs watching them too. What we try to do is treat the kids right and treat the parents right and demonstrate that they have a chance to progress with Aberdeen."

The Glaswegian, recruited by director and former team-mate Willie Miller, will have a huge part to play in the future of the Dons but will struggle to match his past achievements with the Pittodrie side.

It was Weir's pass which fed Mark McGhee to cross for John Hewitt's famous winner in the European Cup Winners' Cup final against Real Madrid in 1983.

Up to that point he had missed just the opening tie of the European campaign when Sion had been hammered 7-0. From that point on Weir held the No.11 shirt and a goal in the 2-0 second round victory against Lech Poznan and the 5-1 semi-final victory against Waterschei helped the Dons on their march to Gothenburg. By that stage he was already a seasoned performer on the European stage, upstaging highly fancied Ipswich with a stunning double in the 3-1 Uefa Cup victory against the holders in 1981.

Weir believes the legacy of those glory days can help him recruit the next generation of Pittodrie stars. He added: "Of course we can't say Aberdeen will win a European trophy again but we also can't believe it is impossible. The Gothenburg team was packed full of young players who had come through the ranks at the club and formed a tremendous team and we are striving to return to the days when the club was producing so many quality players."

Weir's professional association stretches back more than quarter of a century. He had joined the Pittodrie staff in 1981 when Alex Ferguson, who had the player under his wing during his time in charge at St Mirren, tempted the Buddies with a player plus cash offer. Ian Scanlon moved to Love Street along with around £200,000 in cash while the 23 year-old winger travelled north to begin his Aberdeen career. It was a substantial package, a record at the time, but the club was investing in an international player. Weir had made his Scotland debut in 1980 and had four caps to his credit by the time he left the Paisley side. Despite domestic and European honours he added just two further international appearances as a Dons player, the last in a 2-0 defeat in Northern Ireland at the end of 1983.

The European Cup Winners' Cup was Weir's first trophy success but far from his last. Just 10 days after glory in Gothenburg he added a Scottish Cup medal after helping his team to a 1-0 win against Rangers and another followed in 1983/84 when Celtic were beaten 2-1. That season Weir also starred in both legs of the European Super Cup final victory against Hamburg, supplying both goals in the crucial 2-0 home win, and played in 27 of the 36 Premier Division games as Aberdeen stormed to the championship title.

Another league winner's medal followed in 1985 before Weir collected his third Scottish Cup badge when the Dons defeated Hearts 3-0 in 1986. The winger was a key man in the final, crossing for John Hewitt to score the second goal of the afternoon, but had an even more important role on the road to Hampden. In the quarter-final replay against Dundee at Pittodrie he scored a sublime goal in the 101st minute of the game, floating the ball over the helpless Bobby Geddes, to put Aberdeen through after the game had finished 1-1 at the end of 90 minutes. Ferguson loved having Weir in his side to give him the width and balance he craved, doing on the left wing what Gordon Strachan and then Joe Miller did on the right.

His successor Ian Porterfield was less of a fan and allowed Weir to move on to Leicester City in an £80,000 transfer at the beginning of 1988 after 253 games and 38 goals for the club. Aged 29 at the time, his offer of committing himself to Aberdeen for the rest of his career was rejected by the management team and Leicester took advantage.

After less than a year in England he returned to Scotland with the option of joining either Aberdeen, under Alex Smith, or St Mirren. He opted for the Saints, but later admitted it was his one regret from a tremendous playing career. In 1990 Weir switched to Ayr United before being forced out of the game by an ankle injury at the age of 34.

MAGIC MOMENTS

14 February, 2008
ABERDEEN 2, BAYERN MUNICH 2

Love was very much in the air as the Red Army showed their appreciation to their team at the end of a pulsating Valentine's Day encounter with Bayern Munich in 2008.

The stunning victory against Copenhagen had won the right to face the Bundesliga stars in the final 32 of the Uefa Cup and, far from being overawed by the prospect, Jimmy Calderwood's team gave as good as they got against the German favourites.

Bayern were tipped not only to win the match but to win the tournament, but found stubborn opposition when they checked in for the first leg encounter in Scotland.

Aberdeen were on song from the start of the match and within 24 minutes had taken a shock lead through loan player Josh Walker. The English youngster's curling shot was worthy of a game of such magnitude and it was the highlight of an accomplished performance by the Middlesbrough midfielder.

However, he would not be the match winning hero – Miroslav Klose made sure of that when he levelled the tie at 1-1 in the 29th minute after capitalising on good work by Lucio found Luca Toni in the build-up.

A frenetic atmosphere only served to heighten the sense of anticipation among the Dons fans packed into the ground for a big European night under the lights and the remainder of the game did not disappoint.

With half-time looming, it was another loan find who did the damage. Sone Aluko, sent north to gain experience by Birmingham City, chased down a through ball by Lee Miller and skipped past the Bayern defence to beat the keeper with a low left foot shot. The England under-19 international was a livewire the Germans struggled to cope with and his goal was well deserved.

Clearly stung by the situation they found themselves in, Bayern responded with a new vigour and determination after the break. It took just eight minutes to make it 2-2 and prevent an embarrassing defeat.

Again it was one of Calderwood's temporary recruits who was at the centre of the action, this time inside the Dons box. Experienced defender Alan Maybury's luck deserted him as he conceded a penalty by handling the ball in the box as a cross flew in, with Hamit Altintop stepping up to score from the rebound after his spot kick had been saved by Jamie Langfield.

With the prospect of a tricky second leg in Germany to follow, Calderwood was desperate to restore the advantage his team had twice held. He threw on Steve Lovell to add to the attacking options but there was no way through a visiting team galvanised by their fightback.

Unexpectedly it was the Munich side who were on the back foot, holding on to take a 2-2 draw away with them. Ultimately that was plenty for Bayern, who blew Aberdeen away with a 4-1 blast in the return fixture to halt an impressive European run in its tracks. Dons fans, with memories of Copenhagen, Madrid, Moscow and others, were left to reflect on a satisfying return to continental football's top table – beaten, but far from disgraced after an enjoyable adventure that had lasted well past the more usual Christmas hiatus.

Aberdeen: Langfield, Maybury, Diamond, Considine, Mair, Nicholson, Walker (Touzani 87), Severin, Aluko, Mackie (Lovell 68), Miller.

Stan Williams

Debut: League, 26 March 1938 v Hamilton (h) won 1-0
Appearances: League 72, Scottish Cup 10, League Cup 17
Goals: League 20, Scottish Cup 6, League Cup 8
Also played for: Plymouth Argyle, Dundee, Floriana
Managed: Floriana

Of all the imports to have landed on Aberdeen soil, few can claim to match South African star Stan Williams in terms of impact. It was the overseas striker who grabbed a dramatic winner for the Dons in the club's first ever Scottish Cup victory.

On April 19, 1947, the Pittodrie players were on duty in the Hampden final against Hibs and it was the Easter Road club who drew first blood inside the first minute. After 36 minutes Williams took a grip on proceedings, crossing for George Hamilton to head home the equaliser. Six minutes later the South African went one better, chasing a Tony Harris through ball and just managing to keep it in play before darting towards the touchline and hammering home what turned out to be the winner from the narrowest of angles. The red army in the crowd of 82,100 were sent into raptures and Williams was the undoubted star of the show.

The occasion vindicated his decision to travel half way around the globe to pursue his dream of making it big in football. Williams had been taken to Scotland by Dons manager Pat Travers in 1938 and made his debut in a 1-0 win at home to Hamilton that year on March 26.

The outbreak of war stalled his Pittodrie career. When football returned in the 1945/46 season he was in the thick of the action. In the 1946 Southern League Cup, as the club claimed its first national honour with a 3-2 victory over Rangers, he set up Archie Baird for the opening goal in the opening minutes and tucked home the second himself 18 minutes later. Despite a spirited comeback by the Light Blues it was the Dons who emerged triumphant.

Williams was the goal scoring hero again in the 1947 Scottish Cup final but his contribution to help get Aberdeen onto the big stage should not be overlooked. In the quarter-final his side tackled Dundee at Dens Park and trailed 1-0 at the break before Williams levelled the tie on the hour mark and volleyed home a spectacular winner after an incredible 39 minutes of extra-time. The SFA had ruled the game would be played to a finish to compensate for a fixture backlog.

The semi-final brought a return to Dens, this time to tackle Arbroath, and once again it was the diminutive but lethal Williams who hit the headlines with a double to clinch a 2-0 win and confirm Aberdeen's place in the final.

The prolific No.9 ended his time in the north-east with a record of 34 goals in just 99 games, moving on to Plymouth Argyle in 1949 before returning to Scotland with Dundee in the early 1950s. He was appointed coach of Floriana in Malta in 1952 and spent two years on the continent before moving back to South Africa to begin life outside of football in the engineering industry.

In 2005 the latest generation of the Williams football dynasty made an emotional return to the north-east. Keven Williams starred for the Old Benonians youth team at the Aberdeen International Youth Festival.

Billy Williamson

Debut: League, 10 April 1971 v Cowdenbeath (a) won 2-1
Appearances: League 93+7, Scottish Cup 10, League Cup 22+6
Goals: League 18, League Cup 5
Also played for: Kirkconnel Amateurs, Dundee United, Dundee

Billy Williamson managed to do two things during his Aberdeen career that every aspiring Dons player dreams of doing. First he performed a one man demolition act against one half of the Old Firm in front of a jubilant home support and secondly he walked out at a packed Hampden Park to play his part in a memorable cup triumph. On both occasions it was Celtic who were on the receiving end in the two most memorable matches in Williamson's steady spell of service with the club between 1969 and 1977.

At the age of 22 the Dumfries born player single handedly inflicted Celtic's first defeat at Pittodrie in nine years when he scored his first senior hat-trick in 1975. Amazingly Williamson was on the transfer list at the time but he did not let the uncertainty put him off his game, helping the Dons to a 3-2 win in the pulsating league fixture.

On November 6, 1977, Williamson enjoyed another defining moment against Celtic when the Dons clinched a 2-1 win in the League Cup final against the Hoops. This time the versatile borderer claimed the left back berth, having come into the team in place of Chic McLelland in time for the 5-1 semi-final victory against Rangers.

By the following season Ally MacLeod had departed, replaced by Billy McNeill, and Williamson's days were numbered. He moved to Dundee United in a £14,000 deal late in 1977 and moved across the city to join Dundee the following year for a three year spell at Dens Park.

The football adventure had started in the final few days of 1969 when a series of trial matches for Eddie Turnbull at Aberdeen won the 17 year-old Kirkconnel Amateurs striker his first professional contract.

He was an instant hit with the Dons reserves and a regular scorer but Turnbull and his backroom staff spotted potential in a different area of the park and in his second season at Pittodrie he was given a taster of first team action as a right back in a 2-1 win at Cowdenbeath on April 10.

He had a frustrating wait for regular first team action, not truly establishing himself as a regular in the top team until Jimmy Bonthrone put his faith in the versatile squad man in the 1974/75 campaign. Williamson was utilised in defence and attack and missed just three league games, with his appearances including that hat-trick against Celtic.

He went even better the following term, starting 35 of 36 Premier Division games and featuring in the remaining fixture as a substitute as he played in every department for both Bonthrone and new manager MacLeod.

His elevation to a first team regular vindicated his persistence but the League Cup success of 1977, during a season in which he had drifted back to the periphery of the first team, added him to the elite list of Dons players to have winner's medals under lock and key. Williamson emigrated to Australia after retiring from the game.

Tommy White

Debut: League Cup, 14 August 1965 v Clyde (a) won 2-1
Appearances: League 14, League Cup 4
Goals: League 4, League Cup 1
Also played for: Raith Rovers, St Mirren, Hearts, Crystal Palace, Blackpool, Bury

Bustling Hearts striker Tommy White was exchanged for Dons player Don Kerrigan in the summer of 1965. The former Raith Rovers and St Mirren star had been a frequent scorer for the Jambos, despite struggling to hold down a regular place in the Tynecastle team. White, the younger brother of the late Spurs and Scotland star John White, was handed the No.9 shirt by Turnbull during an extended run in the Dons side but could not rediscover his goal touch. He joined Crystal Palace after just a year on the staff. He went on to play for Blackpool and Bury, later returning to the Seasiders to serve on the board.

Jim Whyte

Debut: League, 11 September 1965 v St Johnstone (a) drew 2-2
Appearances: League 105, Scottish Cup 20, League Cup 24, Europe 4
Goals: League 6, Scottish Cup 1, League Cup 2
Also played for: Kilmarnock

When Jim Whyte walked out of Pittodrie to join Kilmarnock in 1970 he relinquished his place as the longest serving member of the Aberdeen playing staff. The left-back was a loyal servant to the Dons over the course of eight years but, at the age of 25, decided to seek a fresh start as he looked for the regular first team football that had not been available under Eddie Turnbull.

Whyte had been snapped up from junior side Kilsyth Rangers and went on to win Scotland under-23 caps after bursting into the Aberdeen side in 1965/66, when he emerged as the first choice for the No.3 shirt.

It was Turnbull who handed Chalky, as he was known throughout football, his debut and he relied upon the full-back for four seasons before Henning Boel, Jim Hermiston and George Murray moved ahead in the queue for the two wide places in the back line after Whyte ruptured his Achilles tendon and was forced to spend an extended period on the sidelines. The strong and determined defender moved on to Kilmarnock in the closing weeks of 1970 and went on to skipper the Rugby Park side. He moved into junior football with Kirkintilloch Rob Roy in 1975 and began to turn his attention to life outside of the game as a sales representative with whisky firm Bells. After hanging up his boots, Whyte retained his interest in football by joining Aberdeen's scouting team and in 1992 he returned to Pittodrie full-time as part of the club's commercial team.

Alex Willoughby

Debut: League Cup, 9 August 1969 v Dunfermline (h) drew 2-2
Appearances: League 124, Scottish Cup 12, League Cup 31, Europe 11
Goals: League 10, Scottish Cup 1, League Cup 3, Europe 1
Also played for: Rangers, Hong Kong Rangers

There was no questioning the pedigree of Alex Willoughby when he walked through the front door at Pittodrie in the summer of 1969. Not only did the Glaswegian have the benefit of six years in and around the Rangers first team, he also boasted a family link that ensured he would be welcomed by Aberdeen fans.

Willoughby, the younger cousin of Jim Forrest who played alongside Forrest in the Rangers team that won the League Cup in the 1963/64 season, cost the Dons £20,000. He was a man comfortable playing in attack or on the right wing, a confident passer of the ball and a real threat in front of goal. He was a Scotland schoolboy international when he joined Rangers as a 15-year-old in 1960 and had a strong reputation as a talent for the future.

By the time he pitched up in the north-east he was a seasoned campaigner and spent three terms with Aberdeen, eventually joining the Pittodrie coaching staff. A two year stint abroad with Hong Kong Rangers in the early 1970s followed and he also served in South Africa, Australia and Iceland before retiring from the game in 1984.

Alec Wilson

Debut: League, 20 April 1963 v Partick Thistle (a) won 3-2
Appearances: League 11
Also played for: Albion Rovers

Scotland junior international Alec Wilson was spotted by Aberdeen while playing for Shotts Bon Accord. The inside-left spent two seasons in the first team squad, although his progress was hampered by surgery to repair cartilage damage. He joined Albion Rovers in the summer of 1965.

Bob Wilson

Debut: League Cup, 3 September 1955 v Clyde (a) won 2-1
Appearances: League 20, Scottish Cup 2, League Cup 7
Goals: League 1
Also played for: Norwich City, Accrington Stanley, Chester

After just six weeks as a first team player, right-half Bob Wilson collected a coveted winner's medal as part of the triumphant Dons team for the 1955/56 League Cup final against St Mirren. It was one of just 29 appearances Wilson made over the course of two seasons – but ensured he left Pittodrie with a prize that many long serving stars never got their hands on. He joined as a 20-year-old from Musselburgh juniors in 1954 and left for Norwich City three years later. Gillingham and Accrington Stanley, as captain, were added to his list of playing credits, joining Chester in 1962 when Stanley folded.

Jimmy Wilson

Debut: League Cup, 14 August 1965 v Clyde (a) won 2-1
Appearances: League 75, Scottish Cup 11, League Cup 20, Europe 4
Goals: League 24, Scottish Cup 3, League Cup 7
Also played for: Newcastle United, Morton, Motherwell, Dundee, Falkirk, Hamilton, Elgin City

Winger Jimmy Wilson's longevity on Aberdeen's sporting scene owed much to his post-football career as a publican in the Granite City. Wilson's Sports Bar on Market Street was home to the former Dons player until he retired from the licensed trade, having first set out in the bar business in the 1970s.

Wilson, who cut his teeth with junior side Shotts Bon Accord, had been brought to the north-east by Eddie Turnbull in 1965, signing from Morton in a five-figure transfer as the Dons manager aimed to inject pace to the flanks. The left-winger, who had a spell in England with Newcastle prior to landing at Cappielow and helping Morton to the Second Division title in 1964, spent two and a half years at Pittodrie before moving to Motherwell as part of the deal which brought George Murray to Aberdeen.

In his first campaign he was an ever-present, in his second he topped the club's scoring chart with Jimmy Smith on 20 goals and in his third he was shipped out. It was an eventful period which included an appearance in the Scottish Cup defeat against Celtic in 1967.

Stints with Dundee, Falkirk and Hamilton as well as a brief period in South African football followed his move to Well. In 1976 he was appointed player-coach of Elgin City but left to concentrate on his pub commitments before reappearing on the Highland League scene as coach, assistant manager and then manager with Keith. He enjoyed league and cup success with the Kynoch Park club and also had short spells in charge of Cove Rangers and Bon Accord.

Pat Wilson

Debut: League, 10 September 1966 v Dundee (a) lost 2-1
Appearances: League 7, League Cup 5
Also played for: Dunfermline Athletic, Raith Rovers, Berwick Rangers, Cowdenbeath
Managed: Cowdenbeath

Dunfermline gave winger Pat Wilson his debut at the tender age of 16. Aberdeen recruited the versatile player, who was comfortable playing at inside forward or on either flank, in 1966 on the recommendation of Dons striker Harry Melrose. Wilson was released to join Raith in 1969 and also had spells with Berwick and Cowdenbeath, serving as manager with the Blue Brazil until resigning in 1980.

Ernie Winchester

Debut: League, 25 April 1962 v Rangers (h) won 1-0
Appearances: League 126, Scottish Cup 15, League Cup 30
Goals: League 72, Scottish Cup 10, League Cup 12
Also played for: Chicago Spurs, Kansas City Spurs, Hearts, Arbroath

Powerhouse forward Ernie Winchester was head and shoulders above his school football peers, quite literally. The powerfully built youngster had physical prowess from a young age and was a schoolboy international by the time he was signed up by Aberdeen in the late 1950s.

The Torry teenager made his debut in the man's world of reserve team football at the age of 15 and appeared destined for big things. Winchester was promoted to the first team for the final two games of the 1961/62 season and from then until his departure in 1967 was a regular in the side. In his first full campaign he bagged 20 goals, including his first senior hat-trick in a 10-0 mauling of Raith Rovers at Pittodrie, and from 1963/64 was leading scorer for the Dons for three consecutive seasons with tallies of 27, 15 and 21 goals. His bustling style and physical stature made Winchester a nightmare for opposition defenders and for a young man he handled the responsibility of leading the forward line with ease.

In 1967 the Aberdonian tried his luck on foreign soil with the Chicago Spurs and Kansas City Spurs, causing consternation back in the north-east by turning his back on his home town club.

After a brief American adventure he was tempted back to Scotland by Hearts. He played out his senior career with Arbroath, where he had been converted to play as a central defender, and retired in 1973 at the age of 29 to concentrate on a career in the motor trade.

Tommy Wilson

Debut: League Cup, 9 August 1969 v Dunfermline (h) drew 2-2
Appearances: League 29, Scottish Cup 4, League Cup 8
Goals: League 1, League Cup 3
Also played for: Elgin City, Buckie Thistle

The versatile Tommy Wilson bagged a hat-trick inside his first month as an Aberdeen first teamer. He moved north from Glasgow side Sandyhills as a 16-year-old and was rated one of the finest prospects on the books in the late 1960s.

Wilson made his debut at the start of the 1969/70 season and grabbed his treble against Clyde in the League Cup during a run of first team games. Fierce competition for places restricted Wilson's appearances, although his ability to play in midfield or as sweeper added to his value, and in 1973 he was released. Seven years with Elgin City followed as well as a stint with Buckie Thistle. Wilson also coached with Keith and Huntly.

Dean Windass

Debut: League, 2 December 1995 v Partick Thistle (a) lost 1-0
Appearances: League 72, Scottish Cup 7, League Cup 7, Europe 6
Goals: League 20, Scottish Cup 3, League Cup 6, Europe 1
Also played for: Hull City, Oxford United, Bradford City, Middlesbrough, Sheffield Wednesday (on loan), Sheffield United, Darlington

He came, he saw, he won the hearts of the Red Army and he left again. Dean Windass bulldozed his way through life in Scotland with a vigour and enthusiasm that proved to be infectious for the fans who worshipped him from the Pittodrie stands.

The Yorkshireman cost £700,000 when he was signed from Hull in December 1995 – but he proved to be worth every penny, and more. Windass, capable of playing in midfield or attack, was as strong as an ox but had subtlety to go with his power. Add to the package a fierce shot and deadly accuracy, not to mention a will to win that at times led the English star into hot water with the authorities, and a picture of a formidable package begins to emerge. He was the perfect foil to the out and out strikers in the squad, playing alongside Duncan Shearer and then Billy Dodds to great effect.

Windass, who spent two and a half years with Aberdeen, was sold to Oxford United for £475,000 in advance of the 1998/99 campaign. A spell with Bradford led to a move to Middlesbrough, where he was subsequently sent out on loan to both Sheffield clubs. A permanent move to Sheffield United came before he returned to Bradford in 2003, spending four years with the Bantams and becoming a hero all over again before taking his career full circle by rejoining Hull in 2007 and helping them to the promised land of the Premier League. Windass, by then 40, was released to join Darlington in July 2009.

David Winnie

Debut: League, 10 August 1991 v Airdrie (a) won 2-1
Appearances: League 63, Scottish Cup 3, League Cup 10, Europe 4
Goals: League 1
Also played for: St Mirren, Middlesbrough (on loan), Hearts, Dundee, St Mirren, Ayr United

He was far from a fashionable signing, but defender David Winnie clocked up 80 appearances for the Reds over the course of four seasons at Pittodrie under three different managers. The Scotland under-21 international and St Mirren captain left the Paisley side in 1991 to link up with his former Love Street boss Alex Smith at Aberdeen in a £250,000 deal. The tall defender featured mainly at left-back but also filled in at the centre of the back line. He was loaned to Middlesbrough during the 1993/94 season and moved permanently to Hearts in the summer of 1995. He went on to play for Dundee, St Mirren and Ayr United before switching to Icelandic football in 1999.

Colin Woodthorpe

Debut: Uefa Cup, 9 August 1994 v Skonto Riga (a) drew 0-0
Appearances: League 48, Scottish Cup 4, League Cup 6, Europe 7
Goals: League 1, League Cup 1
Also played for: Chester City, Norwich City, Stockport County, Bury

Injuries ensured the Pittodrie faithful did not see the best of big money signing Colin Woodthorpe. Recruited from Norwich City during the summer of 1994 for £400,000 by Willie Miller, the English left-back suffered a back injury which required surgery and broke bones in his foot during his first two seasons in Scotland. He battled back to full fitness but fell out of favour when Roy Aitken took charge and was sold to Stockport County in 1997 for £120,000. Woodthorpe, who had launched his career at Chester, went on to make more than a century of appearances for County before six seasons with Bury up to his playing retirement in 2008. He then joined the coaching staff of Colwyn Bay.

Paul Wright

Debut: League, 2 April 1984 v Hearts (h) drew 1-1
Appearances: League 67, Scottish Cup 9, League Cup 3, Europe 5
Goals: League 16, Scottish Cup 2, Europe 1
Also played for: Queens Park Rangers, Hibs, St Johnstone, Kilmarnock, Falkirk, Morton

Paul Wright had the potential to be one of Aberdeen's all-time striking greats. The history books show the compact forward never scaled those heights but in flashes he displayed all the attributes required to make it to the very top. He had pace, power and the ability to sniff out a chance in the blink of an eye.

Wright joined as a teenager during Alex Ferguson's tenure and was rapidly pushed into the first team by his new boss. The East Kilbride born attacker made his debut as a 16-year-old in April 1984 in a 1-1 draw against Hearts at Pittodrie. He was eased into the team by Ferguson over the course of three seasons and was part of the Scotland youth and under-21 teams as he continued his progress. Under Ian Porterfield and Alex Smith he continued to provide a genuine goal threat but it was not always an easy relationship between club and player, with the striker himself admitting he was over-confident after making his breakthrough and Alex Smith losing patience when the protégé refused to commit to a new contract. The protracted will he, won't he signing saga drew to a close in July 1989 when he joined the Trevor Francis inspired Queen's Park Rangers in a deal set at £250,000 by a transfer tribunal. He returned to Scotland with Hibs for the same fee less than a year later and moved on to St Johnstone in a club record £285,000 transfer in July 1991. Wright moved on to Kilmarnock four years later and scored the Scottish Cup winning goal for the Rugby Park club in 1997 before winding down with Falkirk and then Morton in the 2001/02 season.

Jamie Winter

Debut: League, 16 January 2005 v Celtic (h) lost 1-0
Appearances: League 19, Scottish Cup 2, League Cup 2
Goals: League 1, League Cup 1
Also played for: Leeds United, St Johnstone (on loan), Chesterfield, Formartine United

Dundonian midfielder Jamie Winter signed for Jimmy Calderwood in January 2005 after serving an apprenticeship with Leeds United which saw him become a Scotland under-19 cap. With a cultured left foot and excellent passing ability, he joined the first team squad immediately but struggled to adjust to the pace of the SPL and was sent out on loan to St Johnstone in his second season as a Dons player. Released in 2007, he spent two years with Chesterfield before returning to the north-east and turning out in the Highland League alongside a number of former senior players with the ambitious Formartine United.

Robbie Winters

Debut: League, 23 September 1998 v Rangers (h) drew 1-1
Appearances: League 124+8, Scottish Cup 9+2, League Cup 6+1, Europe 1
Goals: League 41, Scottish Cup 2, League Cup 1, Europe 1
Also played for: Scotland (1 cap), Dundee United, Luton Town, Brann Bergen.

The date was 26 May 2000 and the venue Hampden Park. Robbie Winters was making Scottish Cup history but he cut a lonely figure as he patrolled the Dons penalty box in unfamiliar goalkeeper's kit.

He had arrived at the national stadium for the cup final against Rangers with dreams of becoming an Aberdeen goalscoring hero but within minutes the script had been torn up.

When Jim Leighton crumpled to the turf in the the 2nd minute it was clear the veteran was in trouble. A horrific facial injury forced him out of the game and eccentric Dons manager Ebbe Skovdahl had a problem.

The Dane had opted not to name a back-up goalkeeper among his substitutes and Aberdeen faced playing the remainder of the tie against the Premier League champions with an outfield player between the sticks. Winters was the man who shouldered the burden and despite his valiant efforts the Dons tumbled to a 4-0 defeat. It was a season of cup final heartache for the striker, who had come on from the bench in the League Cup final earlier that season against Celtic but was unable to prevent a 2-0 defeat.

Winters left Pittodrie in 2002 empty handed, save for the precious Scotland cap he collected after joining Pittodrie colleagues Eoin Jess and Derek Whyte in the international side which defeated Germany 1-0 in Bremen in 1999. That appearance for the national side was his only experience at the top level.

Winters arrived at Pittodrie in September 1998 in the most difficult of circumstances. Manager Alex Miller had paid £500,000 to Dundee United and thrown in fans' favourite Billy Dodds to clinch the deal for a striker who was still only 24.

He had made his debut as a winger under United manager Ivan Golac in 1994 and quickly established himself as a livewire performer with pace to burn. A back injury stalled his progress but in 1997 Winters was named Scotland's young player of the year as his stock continued to rise.

That type of form tempted Miller to gamble on the Dodds deal but Winters had a hard act to follow and the reasonable return of 12 goals in 28 games in his first season did not convince the majority that it had been a good piece of business.

The west coast player persevered and in his final season with the club finished at the top of the scoring charts with 14 strikes as the Dons rallied from the relegation haunted form of previous years to climb to the comparatively heady heights of fourth in the SPL.

Winters played through difficult times during Skovdahl's tenure, with the dubious honour of scoring his single European goal in the embarrassing 2-1 Uefa Cup defeat against Irish outfit Bohemian at Pittodrie in the first leg of the tie which saw the club crash out of the competition at the hands of the underdogs.

Winters switched to Norway with Brann Bergen in 2002 and spent six years in Scandinavia. A short spell with Clyde was followed by a move to Livingston in 2009, helping the side to promotion from the Third Division in his first campaign.

Bobby Wishart

Debut: League, 5 December 1953 v Raith Rovers (h) won 2-0
Appearances: League 178, Scottish Cup 22, League Cup 36
Goals: League 45, Scottish Cup 7, League Cup 10
Also played for: Merchiston Thistle, Dundee, Airdrie, Raith Rovers

The usual suspects have dominated league football in Scotland for as long as most people can remember. Rangers, Celtic, Hearts and Hibs won 32 of the first 35 top flight campaigns to confirm their place at the head of the football food chain.

One man loved breaking that monopoly so much he did it twice with two of the only three provincial clubs who upset the establishment between the resumption of football in 1945 and the emergence of Alex Ferguson's dominant Dons in 1980.

Bobby Wishart's first championship medal against the odds was with Aberdeen's legendary title winning side of 1955. His second came with Dundee in 1962, when he won a place in Dens Park folklore with his contribution to the only league triumph the club has ever savoured.

The Edinburgh born player was recruited by Aberdeen from juvenile side Merchiston Thistle in 1952. It was proof that even in that era there was no complacency at Pittodrie, with the club prepared to look well beyond its own doorstep to find the best young talent Scotland had to offer.

A skilful and creative inside forward, the new recruit made his first start on December 5 the year after he signed as Aberdeen carved out a 2-0 win against Raith Rovers at Pittodrie.

By the following season he had taken Joe O'Neil's place at inside left on a permanent basis, coinciding with Aberdeen's title winning campaign. He contributed seven league goals in 23 starts but it was the ammunition he supplied for Paddy Buckley and Harry Yorston that made him such a vital piece in Dave Halliday's jigsaw.

His second Dons winner's medal came in the 1955/56 League Cup final following a 2-1 win against St Mirren in the Hampden final. Wishart was an ever present in the competition and he came to the fore in the semi-final against old foes Rangers when he scored with a 22-yard rocket after a quick break upfield to add to Graham Leggat's opener. The Light Blues pulled a goal back in the second half but could not stop the Dons bandwagon rolling on to the final.

Wishart's performances won recognition at Scotland under-23 level and for the Scottish Football League select as he embarked on a long and distinguished career in the red of his first senior club.

He missed out on the chance to complete a domestic clean sweep in 1959 when he was part of the Aberdeen side which fell to a 3-1 defeat against St Mirren in the Scottish Cup final and at the beginning of 1961, with first team opportunities proving limited at Pittodrie, he was snapped up by Dundee for the bargain price of £3,500 after 236 appearances and 62 goals for the Dons.

At the age of 27 he became a wing-half with Dundee and helped the Tayside outfit pip Rangers to the 1962 First Division prize by just three points. It was an inspired move by Wishart, with the Aberdeen team he left behind languishing in 12th spot. He went on to play in the European Cup as the Dens Park side progressed to the semi-final of the competition the following term and is as fondly remembered by the Dundee fans who watched him ply his trade as he is by Dons supporters of a certain vintage.

Wishart wound down his playing days with Airdrie and Raith Rovers before returning to the Edinburgh area, becoming a building society manager. He is now enjoying his retirement in Currie and is able to reflect on the momentous achievements of his life in football.

Wishart said: "The league success with Aberdeen was significant because it gave the club a chance to believe in itself. That was a big thing.

"I didn't think we would win the league that year because the team had been put together fairly quickly. When I left to my national service in 1951 it was an ageing team, with players like Tommy Pearson, George Hamilton and Tony Harris. There were good players at the club but the team struggled to get any consistency.

"I came back two years later and the likes of Jack Allister, Fred Martin and Paddy Buckley were breaking through. The team had changed very quickly and we won the league on the back of that."

Wishart believes Aberdeen were the masters of their own downfall when it came to their failure to add to the initial championship success.

He said: "We slipped up by transferring some of the best reserves to English clubs. That included Ian MacFarlane, Ian McNeill, George Taylor and Bobby Wilson. We left ourselves short.

"When Tommy Pearson came in he instigated a youth policy and, given I had been around the club for a number of years, I didn't fit in with that. I never had any intention of leaving until then. I always got on well with Dick Donald and I'm pretty sure I would have stayed on at the club either in a coaching or even managerial capacity if I had played out my career at Pittodrie."

Instead of a long term career with the Dons he embarked on a new playing chapter on Tayside and those days at Dens provide as many happy memories as his Dons adventure.

Wishart added: "What happened with Dundee was quite amazing. I never expected to win another league championship but I had joined a very good side. Dundee played total football, whereas Aberdeen played good football with a hard hitting edge.

"I think that Dundee side was as good a team as I had seen in Scotland. Bob Crampsey, a man steeped in the Glasgow game, said that Dundee team played the finest football Scotland had ever produced and that was high praise indeed."

THE MANAGERS: PART TWO

ALLY MACLEOD

Pittodrie needed a lift after the toil of Jimmy Bonthrone's final few months in charge and in Ally MacLeod the board of directors found the perfect personality to do just that. The effervescent MacLeod, who had cut his teeth with Ayr United, swept into Aberdeen with energy and ambition and did not disappoint. He landed the League Cup in 1976 and with his captivating personality was very much a managerial star on the rise. He was plucked away from the Granite City in 1977 to take charge of Scotland on the back of his impressive early results with the Dons.

BILLY MCNEILL

It would take a big name to fill the sizeable void left by Ally MacLeod and they came no bigger than Billy McNeill. The Celtic and Scotland legend accepted his first managerial challenge with Clyde just months before being lured to Pittodrie and, having enjoyed such success as Hoops skipper in his playing heyday, was a man who commanded respect from his players.

McNeill, a defensive stalwart as a player, spent just a season in charge before he returned home to Parkhead to lead his old team and attempt to carry on where Jock Stein had left off.

ALEX FERGUSON

Alex Ferguson represented the biggest managerial gamble ever taken by the custodians of Aberdeen Football Club. At just 35 years of age, the former East Stirling and St Mirren boss was an inexperienced rookie who had demonstrated considerable promise in his first coaching jobs.

With the Dons he turned potential and promise into tangible success as he inspired the greatest period in the club's proud history and catapulted the Reds into the football stratosphere.

The former Rangers and Falkirk striker had initially been linked with the Dons job in 1977 but pledged his future to the Buddies at that juncture, leaving the path clear for Billy McNeill to take the reins.

A year later Ferguson was finally installed and he used his now celebrated eye for a player to assemble an all-star cast on a relatively modest budget. By the end of the 1979/80 season he had driven Aberdeen to the head of Scotland's league ladder as Premier Division champions and it proved to be only the beginning.

The Scottish Cup in 1982 followed before the glory of 1983, with the European Cup Winners' Cup and European Super Cup triumphs on the back of a second Scottish Cup victory, highlighted the quality of the team he had created.

He had rebuffed serious approaches from Wolves and Rangers to remain in charge at Aberdeen and his decision was vindicated when the Dons regained the league crown in 1983/84. Another approach, this time from Spurs, was rejected by the determined young coach as he put finances to one side to concentrate on the business of winning trophies.

A hat-trick of championship successes was completed in 1984/85 and the following term saw the Pittodrie chief elevated to the position of Scotland manager in the most tragic of circumstances as he filled in following the shock death of Jock Stein.

As with everything he did, Ferguson coped admirably with the situation he found himself in and it was no surprise when clubs continued to beat a path to the North-east to try and lure him away.

In November 1986 the news broke that, after so many failed attempts by English sides, a team had finally managed to turn Ferguson's head. That team was Manchester United and the rest is history. An amazing new chapter was about to open in the incredible story of Alex Ferguson, arguably the greatest manager the game has ever seen.

IAN PORTERFIELD

His was an impossible job – to try and replicate the phenomenal success enjoyed by Alex Ferguson. In reality, Ian Porterfield's task was always likely to be a thankless one and his reign from 1986 to 1988 was unspectacular. The former Sunderland star, who came closest to silverware when his side was beaten on penalties in the 1987 League Cup final, attempted to raid the English leagues for talent capable of maintaining the standards set by Ferguson. When the new recruitment policy failed to reap rewards, Porterfield walked away from Pittodrie and left the directors to return to the drawing board.

ALEX SMITH

After the left-field decision to appoint Ian Porterfield came the more calculated decision to install Alex Smith into high office alongside former Reds favourite Jocky Scott. A Scottish Cup winner with unfancied St Mirren, Smith had the experience and contacts to steady the ship. He did so with notable success, winning the Scottish Cup in dramatic circumstances in 1989/90 when his Dons side beat Celtic on penalties and also claiming the League Cup earlier that same season as well as running Rangers close in the league throughout his tenure. It was not enough to spare Smith the ignominy of being sacked early in 1992.

WILLIE MILLER

Fan power had a huge part to play in removing Alex Smith from office and the appointment of Pittodrie hero Willie Miller as his successor was a hugely popular move by the Dons board. It proved to be the start and finish of Miller's managerial career as his three year stint in charge provided hope and frustration in almost equal measure. After initial bright signs, Miller's radical overhaul of Smith's successful but ageing squad brought a slump in form and, as a relegation battle ensued, his departure was announced in February 1995 as he and the board admitted the experiment had failed.

ROY AITKEN

When Willie Miller needed an assistant manager, he looked no further than former Scotland colleague Roy Aitken. When the Aberdeen board needed a replacement for Miller, they too turned to the former Celtic captain. Aitken's short tenure, running from 1995 to 1997, was punctuated by what would transpire to be a rare trophy win when he led his men to the League Cup prize with victory against Dundee in the 1995/96 campaign. His other key achievement was saving the Dons from relegation from the top flight after taking charge of a beleaguered squad in the second half of the 1994/95 season.

Stephen Wright

Debut: League, 28 April 1990 v St Mirren (h) won 2-0
Appearances: League 142+7, Scottish Cup 13, League Cup 11+1, Europe 5+1
Goals: League 2
Also played for: Scotland (2 caps), Rangers, Wolverhampton Wanderers, Bradford City, Dundee United, Scunthorpe United

In the summer of 1995 Stephen Wright became the most valuable defender in the history of Aberdeen Football Club when Rangers signed a cheque for £1.5million to add one of Scottish football's most promising players to the Ibrox squad. Wright made the move in search of the prizes which had eluded him during his time with the Dons. Less than four months later he watched his old Aberdeen team-mates lift the League Cup while he faced up to the prospect of months on the Ibrox treatment table nursing an injured knee and suffering from a massive dose of bad luck.

The dream move turned into a nightmare for Wright, who damaged his ligaments in a 4-0 European Cup defeat against Juventus at Ibrox just three months into his career with the club. His comeback in 1996 lasted just one game before another knee injury in training led to another frustrating spell on the sidelines and by 1998 he was sent out on loan to Wolves to mark the end of his Rangers days.

It was the Light Blues who made the big investment but the team in red most certainly got the best days out of a defender who was rated as one of the finest of his generation. The Bellshill born player was signed as a schoolboy by Alex Ferguson and joined the Pittodrie groundstaff under Ian Porterfield but got his big break when Alex Smith took charge of the Dons.

Wright was 18 when he appeared as a substitute in a 2-0 home win against St Mirren on April 28, 1990. In the second half of the 1990/91 campaign he stepped in to deputise for Stewart McKimmie at right back and played 15 consecutive games in the nail biting conclusion to the season in which the league was lost on the final day of the season. By that time McKimmie had been switched into the centre of defence to team up with Alex McLeish, with the right back berth safe in the hands of his teenage deputy.

His club form earned almost instant recognition at Scotland under-21 level, breaking into the team in 1990 and going on to skipper the young Scots. Having already won youth international caps during his school days in Hamilton, Wright completed a full set when he made his senior debut in a 1-0 defeat against Germany at Ibrox in March, 1993. Two months later his second and final cap came when Andy Roxburgh's team beat Estonia 3-0 in Tallinn.

He was still only 21 when he burst onto the big stage with Scotland but injuries ultimately put paid to his hopes of carving out a long international career. The first knee problems actually came at Aberdeen, with a minor operation in 1991 solving an early recurring injury. The subsequent damage with Rangers proved much more serious and Wright never regained the form which made him a stand out player for the Dons.

His temporary switch to Wolves was followed by a permanent switch to Bradford in the summer of 1998. He joined Alex Smith's Dundee United in 2000 for an injury hit spell, joining Scunthorpe in 2002 before retiring from the game.

Tommy Wright

Debut: League, 16 August 2008 v Motherwell (a) won 1-0
Appearances: League 18, Scottish Cup 3, League Cup 1
Goals: League 1, Scottish Cup 1
Also played for: Leicester City, Brentford (on loan), Blackpool (on loan), Walsall (on loan), Barnsley, Darlington

Bruising attacker Tommy Wright was a young player Jimmy Calderwood hoped to tame after staking a £100,000 transfer fee on the Leicester-born player in August 2008. He had been the leading scorer with Darlington in his previous campaign but was recovering from a knee injury when recruited and struggled with injury throughout his time in Scotland, making only a handful of starts and falling foul of referees on a number of occasions as his yellow card count stacked up. Wright, who had played for Leicester as well as Barnsley and Grimsby amongst others before heading for Scotland, was released in January 2010. He returned to Grimsby and has since gone back to Darlington for a second spell.

Dennis Wyness

Debut: League, 28 September 1996 v Dundee United (a) lost 1-0
Appearances: League 24
Goals: League 1
Also played for: Caley Thistle, Hearts, St Mirren, Queen of the South (on loan), Dumbarton, Peterhead

Aberdonian striker Dennis Wyness confirmed his place as a Caley Thistle legend when he became the Inverness club's all time record goal scorer. He had joined Aberdeen from school and made his Dons debut in 1996 and made over 20 appearances, primarily from the bench, before being loaned out to the Caley Jags in 1999 to begin a fruitful relationship with Scotland's newest senior team. He made the move permanent and his form won a return to the SPL with Hearts in 2003 before returning on loan to Inverness in 2005 and then making the switch permanent. Two years with St Mirren from 2008 to 2010 incorporated a loan spell with Queen of the South while Wyness has also served with Dumbarton and Peterhead since then.

Darren Young

Debut: League Cup, 13 August 1996 v Queen of the South (a) won 2-0
Appearances: League 133, Scottish Cup 9, League Cup 7, Europe 10
Goals: League 3, Scottish Cup 1, Europe 2
Also played for: Dunfermline, Dundee, Morton

Midfielder Darren Young was just 17-years-old when he was blooded by Roy Aitken at the start of the 1996/97 season. What he lacked in height he made up for in energy and aggression, with Young proving capable of living in Premier Division company despite his tender years.

It was after Ebbe Skovdahl's appointment as manager that he finally emerged as a mainstay of the team and the Glaswegian was elevated to the position of captain by the Dane as a mark of the faith he had in the player. Having progressed through the youth ranks, he knew exactly what it meant to be a Dons player and had the confidence to cope with the expectations at the club.

When Skovdahl departed Pittodrie at the tail end of 2002, his skipper was not far behind. Young ignored attempts by new boss Steve Paterson to keep him at the club and instead chose to link up with Jimmy Calderwood at Dunfermline.

The Pars were prepared to pay top dollar to attract the players to fit Calderwood's masterplan and Young, who was joined by brother and Dons team-mate Derek Young at East End Park at the same time, fitted the bill.

He spent five years with the Fifers, playing well over 100 games, before moving on to Dundee in 2008 for a two year spell that was hampered by injury. Young turned out for both Queen of the South and Morton as he attempted to kick-start his career.

Harry Yorston

Debut: League, 25 December 1947 v Third Lanark (a) lost 3-2
Appearances: League 201, Scottish Cup 29, League Cup 47
Goals: League 98, Scottish Cup 21, League Cup 22
Also played for: Scotland (1 cap), Lossiemouth

Some players take months, some take years and some never succeed but for Harry Yorston it took all of 300 seconds to show the Aberdeen supporters that he knew how to score goals.

Christmas Day in 1947 was a day to remember. Bizarrely his new club was on league duty at Third Lanark on December 25 and Yorston converted the first corner kick of the match, in the fifth minute, to announce his arrival in style. It was not all smiles though, with his new side falling to a 3-2 defeat.

Yorston was a bustling striker who did his best to endear himself to the Pittodrie faithful over the course of a decade, banging in 141 goals in 277 games after signing from Aberdeen juvenile side St Clement's in 1946 to become one of the most prolific forwards ever to pull on the jersey. He had obviously inherited the goalscoring gene from his father's side of the family, with second cousin Benny Yorston already a legend at Aberdeen long before he even set foot inside the ground.

In six starts he had six matching goals in 1948 but it was in the 1949/50 season that the striker really made his mark as he deposed George Hamilton as the club's leading scorer thanks to a 17 goal haul.

He was impossible to shift from Dave Halliday's side and remained in possession of the No.8 shirt right through to his finest year in football. It began on September 11, 1954, when the Dons launched their championship campaign with a 5-0 win at home to Stirling Albion.

Yorston scored the fifth and final goal and went on to net 11 further times in 27 additional league games on the way to the historic title triumph in 1955. He was the lynchpin in the lauded championship winning team, a hero to a generation who watched their team humble Scottish football's big two with their dashing displays.

Along the way he collected a coveted Scotland cap when he helped his international colleagues to a 1-0 win against Wales in Cardiff. Paddy Buckley, one of Yorston's team-mates at club level, scored the winner. He had previously played for Scotland against Ireland at Dalymount Park in 1951.

With a championship medal safely secured, the influential inside forward set about adding a League Cup badge the following season. He scored in the group stages and the quarter-final of the 1955/56 competition and was part of the winning team in the 2-1 final victory against St Mirren.

Then came the bombshell. On June 8, 1957, Aberdeen fans were left spluttering over their cornflakes when the morning's *Press and Journal* proclaimed in bold type: 'Harry Yorston is quitting football for fish'.

It was the type of story it is impossible to comprehend in the current football climate. Yorston, a player at the peak of his powers as a 28 year-old international who had collected two medals in the space of two seasons, turned his back on the game which had made him a household name and became a porter at Aberdeen's fish market.

Manager Dave Shaw was stunned, the supporters were shocked but Yorston was unmoved. His father had worked in the same job and he knew the rewards were decent, offering a £16.50 weekly wage in comparison to his £16 pay packet as a football player, while the long term security was assured. The fact he had played in the face of almost constant criticism from his own club's supporters also played a part in his decision.

Yorston stressed at the time that the Pittodrie crowd's failure to embrace him universally was one of the key factors in his decision to leave: He said: "I never had any regrets. I was as happy as Larry when I packed it in. Every time Aberdeen lost, I took it personally – or my family and friends got it in the neck. That had a big bearing on my decision."

The striker was tagged the Golden Boy by the media during his playing days but sections of the crowd would barrack his every move, perhaps motivated by jealousy as the dashing young Aberdonian set about making his mark in the Dons history books. His impact was dramatic and for a limited time only, as he made the career move that proved his head ruled his heart.

The job of a porter was highly sought after and a new intake of rookies was welcomed only every two or three years. With an age limit of 30 set by the market, it was a case of now or never for Yorston when his application was accepted sooner than expected. He had grown up in the east end of the city, around the bustling harbour and fish market, and it was as much a part of his life as the football club was.

Despite his clean break from the game at the top level, Yorston was back in the headlines in 1972 and again football was at the root of his fame – when a 25p stake on the pools netted him a £170,000 windfall.

Despite his new found wealth he returned to work as a driver, a role he combined with a place on Ally MacLeod's backroom team when he returned to Pittodrie to launch a new youth programme in 1976. He also scouted for Manchester United following his playing retirement.

Yorston, who briefly played in the Highland League with Lossiemouth after his split from the Dons, died at the age of 62 in Aberdeen in 1992.

THE MANAGERS: PART THREE

ALEX MILLER

He had experience, extensive contacts and a reputation as a steady pair of hands. On paper Alex Miller had all the makings of a successful Aberdeen manager but the former Hibs boss endured a torrid time after arriving in 1997. Miller, who infuriated supporters by swapping fans' favourite Billy Dodds for the inconsistent Robbie Winters as well as paying a premium to Dundee United to smooth the deal, lasted just a single year before being sacked. Having worked under Gordon Strachan at Coventry before arriving in the Granite City, Miller went on to become an integral member of Liverpool's scouting and coaching team.

PAUL HEGARTY

The brief was simple when Dundee United stalwart Paul Hegarty took charge of team affairs late in 1998 – save Aberdeen's Premier Division status. Alex Miller had left with the club rooted to the foot of the table and Hegarty, who was given funds to sign players including German midfielder Andreas Mayer, succeeded in dragging the Dons clear of relegation after presiding over a mini-revival that brought three wins in three games. A run of three defeats in the final three league matches hampered Hegarty's hopes of landing the job permanently and he parted company with the club in the summer of 1999.

EBBE SKOVDAHL

Eccentric Danish coach Ebbe Skovdahl brought a colourful turn of phrase to the Pittodrie press room after landing on Scottish soil in 1999 but struggled to translate that entertainment into performances on the pitch, despite leading the Dons to the League Cup and Scottish Cup finals in the eventful 1999/2000 season. Those cup runs were rare highlights as the Scandinavian set about following orders to slash the wage bill and blood young players with mixed results.

After finishing fourth in the SPL in 2002/03 the results took a turn for the worse and Skovdahl agreed to step down in December 2002.

STEVE PATERSON

The rise and rise of Steve 'Pele' Paterson continued in the winter of 2002 when he was paraded as the new manager of Aberdeen. Having been successful in the Highland League with Huntly and in the Scottish Football League with Caley Thistle, the big break with the Dons was the logical next step. Personal problems plagued the new man and his attempts to bolster the squad with inexpensive recruits from the lower leagues failed to bear fruit, having been tasked with further reducing the playing budget. Paterson was dismissed in the summer of 2004 after Willie Miller returned as director of football.

JIMMY CALDERWOOD

Hindsight can be a glorious thing in football. When Jimmy Calderwood and his coaching team of Jimmy Nicholl and Sandy Clark were ushered through the exit door in May 2009 there were only murmurs of discontent from some sections of the Dons support. What the Red Army could not have predicted was the massive dip in fortunes that would follow the departure of the Glaswegian, who had been in charge since 2004 and had brought steady progression throughout his time in the North-east.

Calderwood had been appointed by Willie Miller after impressing as boss of Dunfermline, putting to good use the knowledge and experience gained during a playing and coaching career in the Netherlands after being recruited by the Pars. He would ultimately be sacked by the same man.

In the good times the manager was heavily backed by Miller and the rest of the Dons board and was able to bring in quality players including Barry Nicholson, Scott Severin and Lee Miller. Transfer fees and wages were no barrier during that rebuilding process, although in the latter stages of his tenure there were significant losses as Nicholson, Chris Clark and skipper Russell Anderson departed.

The dividend for directors after the initial cash injection was a welcome return to consistent league performances which saw the team become a fixture in the all-important top six of the SPL and brought European qualification.

Calderwood's greatest legacy as Aberdeen manager is the memory of the enthralling and exhilarating run in the Uefa Cup in the 2007/08 season, bringing qualification for the knock-out stages of the competition after a series of impressive performances on the continental stage.

The following term it was the bread and butter of the domestic game that became the focus of attention and, despite some horrendous cup results which included humiliating defeats against Queen's Park and Queen of the South under Calderwood, there was an air of respectability surrounding Aberdeen as they clinched fourth spot on the final day of the 2008/09 term.

Just minutes after the final whistle the whispers began to spread around the ground – Calderwood's time in charge was at an end. Official confirmation followed that the manager had been told to clear his desk as a new direction was sought to try and take the team to the next level. It represented a massive gamble – the big question was whether it would pay off.

MARK MCGHEE

The old adage about never returning was one that proved apt in the case of Mark McGhee. The Gothenburg Great was the man chosen to follow on from Jimmy Calderwood and move the club forward. What transpired was a reversal in form that few could have predicted after McGhee's good work at previous club Motherwell. He failed to repeat that at Pittodrie and the good work of the heroics of his playing days in Dons colours faded into the background as he struggled to carve out results as manager. He served from June 2009 to December 2010 and faced a constant struggle at the wrong end of the SPL.

CRAIG BROWN

For the second time in a row, Aberdeen turned to Motherwell when searching for a new manager. Veteran campaigner Craig Brown was the candidate chosen to succeed Mark McGhee, bringing with him former Dons assistant manager Archie Knox as his right hand man. The wise old owl of Scottish football succeeded in shoring up the leaky Dons defence to ensure relegation was not an issue in 2010/11, although his first full season saw his side continue to toil in the lower reaches of the SPL as wins proved to be in short supply for the long suffering Pittodrie faithful.

MAGIC MOMENTS

26 November, 1995
ABERDEEN 2, DUNDEE 0

When captain Stewart McKimmie lifted the League Cup in 1995, nobody could have predicted how long the subsequent trophy drought would last. The Aberdeen support who travelled to Hampden celebrated in style, savouring the type of occasion they had once been accustomed to.

Roy Aitken's team had been overwhelming favourites to leave the national stadium with the silverware as they tackled First Division opponents Dundee. Not that the Dens side were expected to be pushovers, with plenty of experience to call upon in their wily squad as well as some emerging young players who would soon make their mark at the highest level.

Neil McCann was among those in the Dundee team, on his way to becoming a Scotland international and star with Hearts and Rangers, while future Celtic star Morten Wieghorst was also in the team for the showdown.

It was the last cup final to take place at 'old' Hampden Park, with the ground closing for redevelopment after the match as the South Stand was demolished to make way for the impressive new design. It ensured Aberdeen could claim a slice of history as their own as they became the last club to triumph in the traditional arena.

Semi-final success against Rangers had paved the way to square up to the Tayside hopefuls and there was a belief that the hard work had been done. Dundee found it difficult to match the Dons, who produced an assured display to clinch the prize.

With Scott Booth out through injury, the partnership of Billy Dodds and Duncan Shearer was given a chance to shine. They seized the opportunity with both hands, playing central parts in the story that unfolded.

Stephen Glass was the provider in the 33rd minute when his left wing cross was deflected towards goal before being pushed out by Dee keeper Michel Pageaud – straight into the path of Dodds, who wasted no time in forcing home the opener.

Just seconds later, Aberdeen were 2-0 ahead and cruising. Glass, who won the man of the match award for his tenacious efforts, was again the architect as he picked out Shearer with a high looping cross – and the Scotland striker made no mistake with his powerful header.

There were opportunities for the Dons to increase the lead but luck escaped them as Eoin Jess, Shearer and Joe Miller all went close to beating Pageaud on what was a busy shift for the Dundee shot stopper.

The First Division underdogs did rally in the last 20 minutes of the match but Michael Watt in the Dons goal was rarely troubled as his defence stood firm to see out the match and claim a welcome clean sheet and complete a good day's work.

That left McKimmie, playing against the club at which he had launched his professional career, free to step forward and pick up the glittering League Cup as well as accepting the vital Uefa Cup qualification that went hand in hand with his team's success in the final.

ABERDEEN: Watt; Grant, Inglis, Smith, McKimmie; Miller (Robertson, 79), Jess (Hetherston, 85), Bernard, Glass; Shearer, Dodds.

Benny Yorston

Debut: League, 20 August 1927 v Raith Rovers (a) won 3-2
Appearances: League 143, Scottish Cup 13
Goals: League 101, Scottish Cup 24
Also played for: Scotland (1 cap), Mugiemoss, Richmond, Montrose, Sunderland, Middlesbrough

Every striker is judged on black and white statistics and Benny Yorston is the only player in the history of Aberdeen to have a perfect season marked on his Pittodrie report card. In 38 league games in 1929/30 the pocket sized attacker scored 38 goals.

It does not get much better than that. Or does it? In four Scottish Cup ties in the same season he bagged eight goals to take his total to 46 and that too has never been beaten by any other Dons striker. His breathtaking haul included four hat-tricks and 10 doubles. Standing at 5ft 4in tall, what the Aberdonian star lacked in height he made up for in killer instinct.

He topped the scoring charts in his first four seasons at Pittodrie and was on course to make it five in a row before he dropped out of the side in 1931 to end a torrid time for Scotland's defenders.

Yorston had scored 10 hat-tricks in three full seasons up against the elite of the domestic game. Hamilton, Partick, Queen's Park twice, Clyde twice, Dundee twice and Raith all felt the force of the fearsome No.9's triple salvos while he reserved four of his best for Falkirk.

The striker, who had cut his teeth with Sunnybank's juvenile teams and then Mugiemoss and Richmond in the Aberdeen juniors ranks before stepping up to the senior game with Montrose, was signed by Pat Travers in 1927. One of the greatest goalscorers the club has ever had cost £30, just three times his bonus for a single goal at Montrose. He went on to score 125 goals in just 156 games yet amazingly Yorston's form in front of goal was not enough to bring silverware to Aberdeen.

Even for Scotland he gained scant recognition for his ability, with just one senior cap in a 0-0 draw against Northern Ireland at Windsor Park. He was just 25 at the time, and already a youth and junior international, but his performance in dark blue was deemed not good enough and the Nigg born player was cast aside by the international selectors.

Not surprisingly he came in for heavy treatment from opposition defenders and was known to take to the field with his legs heavily bandaged from top to bottom as the result of the previous week's battles. He would even persuade trainers to treat decoy injuries rather than the one which had really brought him to the turf to ensure his temporary weaknesses were not exposed to the defenders he outfoxed with such regularity.

Yorston's copy book was blotted in 1931 when he and four fellow Dons players were caught up in match fixing allegations. The group were dumped from the team and a £2,000 move to Sunderland was the striker's escape route in 1932. Two seasons at Roker Park led to a spell with neighbours Middlesbrough before the outbreak of war effectively ended Yorston's career. He moved into the property business in London, where he remained until his death in 1977.

Alec Young

Debut: League Cup, 16 August 1950 v Rangers (a) won 2-1
Appearances: League 168, Scottish Cup 23, League Cup 30
Goals: League 1
Also played for: Strathclyde, Kilsyth Rangers, Blantyre Victoria, Ross County
Managed: Ross County

In seven full seasons at Pittodrie Alec Young battled back from three career threatening knee injuries, a broken ankle and an emergency appendix operation. He kept coming back for more and his persistence was rewarded with the greatest domestic prize of all in 1955 when he helped the Dons to the league title.

His influence on that title winning team was substantial. Young, Archie Glen and Jackie Hather were the three men who played in each of the 30 league games in that glorious campaign, when Celtic were relegated to the runners-up spot by Aberdeen's maiden championship success.

The centre-half was already a proven winner when he signed at Pittodrie in 1950, having collected the Scottish Junior Cup with Blantyre Victoria earlier that year.

He went straight into the Dons team in the early stages of the 1950/51 season and, barring injuries, was a defensive rock until he left in 1958. Young racked up 221 appearances in that time, including two unsuccessful Scottish Cup finals.

Those cup occasions were the major disappointments of Young's time in the north-east as he came desperately close to adding a senior medal to the junior one he had claimed in his native Glasgow, where he had turned out for Strathclyde and Kilsyth Rangers before settling with Blantyre.

In 1953 the Dons took Rangers to a replay before falling to a 1-0 defeat at the hands of the Ibrox men. The following year they were back at Hampden to face Celtic but it was an afternoon to forget for Young, who scored an own goal in the 2-1 loss to the Hoops.

His League Cup hopes were dashed by injury, with Young sidelined in the 1955/56 season when his team-mates lifted the trophy.

Despite captaining Scotland's junior international side he never made the transition to the senior team despite a string of dominant and impressive performances at the heart of the Aberdeen defence. He became renowned for split second timing in the tackle, although his talents had slipped through the net at Parkhead where he had an unsuccessful trial spell with Celtic before linking up with Aberdeen.

Despite spending his youth as a centre forward, Young's forte was certainly in defence.

He was offered the chance to stay on the staff in 1958 but opted instead to join Ross County as player-coach and played on for a further six years before finally calling time. He changed the mindset at County, ditching a long ball style for a passing game and importing the fitness regime he had thrived under at Pittodrie as well as the high standards of discipline he had experienced under Dave Shaw.

After leaving County in 1964, on the advice of doctors, he remained in the north to continue running the grocery business he had built up in Fortrose.

MAGIC MOMENTS

12 May 1990
CELTIC 0, ABERDEEN 0

Brian Irvine, that most dependable of central defenders, was a man who could be relied on in most situations. But could the big defender, more adept at preventing than scoring goals, shoulder the burden of taking a crucial penalty when all hopes rested on him hitting the target? The answer was a resounding 'yes'. Irvine, that most unlikely of striking heroes, did not flinch as he fired in the spot kick that won the Scottish Cup for Aberdeen in the most tense of circumstances – giving the Dons a 9-8 victory in the first ever penalty shoot out in the national competition's showpiece final.

The shoot-out brought a dramatic end to what had been a cagey 120 minutes of football, with two teams desperate to avoid mistakes and keep their hopes of lifting the prize alive.

The pressure was all on Celtic, who had struggled in the league under Billy McNeill and needed victory in the Scottish Cup to secure a place in Europe for the following season. The circumstances only added to the sense of nervousness surrounding the game.

Aberdeen had worries of their own, with veteran skipper Willie Miller ruled out through injury. In stepped Irvine to take his place, little realising how the afternoon would unfold for him.

Charlie Nicholas, playing his final game for the Dons before switching back to Celtic, came close to putting the Hoops to the sword but saw his shot blocked by Paul Elliott. Celtic substitute Mike Galloway's heavy tackles were one of the few other notable points in a game that stumbled into extra-time, at which point the shackles were tightened and the fear of losing a goal intensified.

With the SFA's new rule of settling the game on the day, both teams appeared content to play for penalties and sure enough that was how the tie ended. The game had failed to sparkle, but the resulting shoot-out provided enough entertainment to last a season.

There was an early glimmer for the Dons when Dariusz Wdowczyk blasted high and wide. Brian Grant's miss levelled things though, with tit for tat goals taking the contest way past the prescribed five penalty takers on each side.

It ran all the way to Celtic's 10th penalty, when Anton Rogan had his effort brilliantly saved by Theo Snelders to hand the initiative back to Aberdeen. Snelders celebated, Irvine contemplated as he prepared to take what could be the match winning kick. After a deep breath and pause for thought, the stopper strode forward to hammer past Pat Bonner in the Celtic goal and make it 9-8.

Alex Smith and his Aberdeen team had won the cup and with it had claimed that piece of history as the first team to claim the Scottish Cup by virtue of a penalty contest. High drama, high stakes and a highlight for Irvine as he emerged once and for all from the shadow of Miller.

ABERDEEN: Snelders, McKimmie, Robertson D, Grant, McLeish, Irvine, Nicholas, Bett, Mason (Graham Watson), Connor, Gillhaus

Derek Young

Debut: League Cup, 8 August 1998 v Caley Thistle (a) won 3-0
Appearances: League 207, Scottish Cup 22, League Cup 15, Europe 11
Goals: League 19, Scottish Cup 1, League Cup 2
Also played for: Dunfermline, St Johnstone, Partick Thistle

The phrase 'dream move' is bandied around all too often in football – but Derek Young is proof positive that dreams can come true. In the summer of 2007 he was a player without employment, having been deemed surplus to requirements by lowly Partick Thistle. By the time the new season kicked-off he was an SPL star once again after being thrown a surprise lifeline by Jimmy Calderwood and Aberdeen.

Young, like his big brother Darren, was a product of the Pittodrie youth system. He broke into the team in 1998, at the age of 18, during Alex Miller's tenure and was a livewire forward who displayed tenacity in abundance. He became a regular under Ebbe Skovdahl in the 2000/01 season but followed his sibling to Dunfermline, where Calderwood was then in charge, in time for the 2003/04 campaign.

Three years with the Pars proved unspectacular and short spells with St Johnstone and then Partick were also frustrating. Then came the homecoming, with Young added to the Dons squad to add depth and experience.

Supporters could have been forgiven for expecting Young to play a back-up role, but he ended up taking centre stage in a string of important games during his first season back in the north-east as Calderwood led his team into the last 32 of the Uefa Cup. His versatility, with the ability to play across the front line and midfield as well as providing cover at full-back on occasion, ensured Young became a key man in his second spell in the red shirt of his first club before being released by Craig Brown in 2011. He was promoted to serve as captain in the closing weeks of his Dons career in recognition of his sterling service, going on to join Morton.

JOHN YULE

Debut: League, 31 October 1959 v Clyde (a) lost 7-2
Appearances: League 1
Also played for: Lossiemouth

Goalkeeper John Yule packed a lot into his one and only appearance for Aberdeen. The former East End junior played in a 7-2 defeat at Clyde in the 1959/60 season and suffered a chipped knuckle. Yule joined Lossiemouth at the end of the campaign and also played for Sunnybank before concentrating on his career as a policeman.

DAVID ZDRILIC

Debut: League, 9 August 2003 v Hearts (a) lost 2-0
Appearances: League 31, Scottish Cup 5, League Cup 2
Goals: League 4, Scottish Cup 2, League Cup 2
Also played for: Australia, Sydney United (Australia), Aarau (Switzerland), SSV Ulm (Germany), Unterhaching (Germany), Walsall

When Australian striker David Zdrilic netted 80 seconds into his debut in 2003 it looked as though a new shooting star had been born. The powerful forward's goal against Liverpool in that pre-season friendly proved to be something of a collector's item as he toiled in a struggling Dons team during his one and only season in Scottish football. The Australia cap, who scored eight times in one international fixture against American Samoa, had been plying his trade with Walsall before being recruited by Steve Paterson. He also had a spell in German football on his cv. Zdrilic returned to domestic football in his homeland after leaving Pittodrie in 2004.

Willie Young

Debut: League, 5 September 1970 v Dundee (a) won 2-1
Appearances: League 133, Scottish Cup 12, League Cup 31, Europe 11
Goals: League 10, Scottish Cup 1, League Cup 3
Also played for: Tottenham, Arsenal, Nottingham Forest, Norwich City, Brighton (on loan), Chesterfield, Darlington

What makes the ideal Aberdeen Football Club captain? Maturity and experience, a level-headed attitude and deep sense of responsibility are some of the qualities that would be on the check-list for most managers. In the case of 1970s boss Jimmy Bonthrone the rule book went out the window when he looked for a new skipper in February 1973 and instead opted for a fiery red-headed 6ft 3in bundle of youthful exuberance when he bestowed the honour upon Willie Young.

Young was selected to take over from Steve Murray, who had relinquished the captaincy in the wake of submitting a transfer request to the Pittodrie board. He had been a first team player for less than three years – but in that short time the towering centre-half had made a big impact in the Scottish top flight.

The Edinburgh-born stopper, a Hibs fan in his youth, was spotted playing for juvenile outfit Seton Athletic in his home city and was spirited north in 1969 with the promise of getting his big break with the Dons. He did not have long to wait, making his debut at Dundee in September 1970 and quickly establishing himself as a cornerstone of the side with his powerful tackles and ability in the air.

Young's physical presence made him a standout player, although subtlety was not one of his strong points. He was booked on his first appearance, red carded inside his first four months as a senior professional and had a habit of attracting headlines when it came to discipline on and off the field.

Young, a Scotland under-21 star who was called into the full international squad in the same year he was appointed captain by his club, was one of the Copenhagen five who were banned for life by the SFA after a nightclub fracas in Denmark in 1975. Billy Bremner, Pat McCluskey, Arthur Graham and Joe Harper were the other members of the infamous group.

By that stage the towering defender had already had brushes with controversy while at Pittodrie. He was stripped of the captaincy in 1974 after a bout of verbal sparring with manager Bonthrone on the team bus after a fixture in Dunfermline and during the 1974/75 campaign hurled his jersey at Bonthrone in the Aberdeen dugout after being substituted.

That incident hastened Young's exit, with Tottenham Hotspur succeeding with a £150,000 bid in September 1975. He spent less than two years with the White Hart Lane club before joining bitter North London rivals Arsenal toward the tail end of the 1976/77 season. Young was sold to Nottingham Forest for £170,000 in 1981 after more than 200 appearances for the Gunners, becoming a cult hero at Highbury and an FA Cup winner in 1979. He also went on to represent Norwich City and Brighton, on loan, before winding down with Chesterfield and Darlington in the mid-1980s.

Hicham Zerouali

Debut: League, 8 December 1999 v Hearts (h) won 3-1
Appearances: League 37, Scottish Cup 5, League Cup 4, Europe 2
Goals: League 11, Scottish Cup 2
Also played for: Morocco, Fus Rabat, Al Nasr

Hicham Zerouali was the sparkling diamond in the rough period around the new Millennium. As the Dons toiled at the wrong end of the table, the brief introduction of the Moroccan provided a welcome distraction for a group of supporters suffering through the pain of watching their team struggle.

As Zoltan Varga had done decades earlier, Zerouali proved that an import policy can be successful. He brought tricks, flicks and a clutch of impressive goals – as well as a broad smile and carefree style of play that was at odds with the mood at the time.

His SPL career spanned just fourteen starts and 31 months, but in that time he was taken to the hearts of the Dons fans. His death in 2004 in a car crash in his homeland at the age of 27 was greeted with a genuine sense of mourning in the north-east, where he was gone but far from forgotten.

It was director of football Keith Burkenshaw who first spotted the potential after taking delivery of one of the many tapes touting overseas players for a move to the British game. Burkenshaw persuaded manager Ebbe Skovdahl to take a closer look and both men agreed they had watched a player who they desperately wanted to bring to Aberdeen.

He had started his professional career with Fus Rabat in his homeland and became a Moroccan international before he moved to Aberdeen. Zerouali went on to make seventeen appearances for the Atlas Lions and scored three goals.

He signed late in 1999, making his debut in a 3-1 win over Hearts on December 8. The first goal came seventeen days later in a 3-1 victory against Dundee United and it was the first of a series of important and spectacular strikes in league and cup.

It brought cult status for the African attacker, with the fez becoming the headwear of choice at Dons games and the novel idea of giving Zero the shirt number zero to wear on his back. It led to a boom in sales, although the player was not convinced and later reverted to No.11 after just a year.

He felt wearing zero brought bad luck and he certainly had his share of that during his time in the north-east. In the 2000/2001 season an ankle break in a game against Motherwell kept him sidelined for the bulk of the campaign, requiring two operations to repair the damage.

He battled back to full fitness, although his fiery temperament caused brushes with both referees and the management team. The single minded approach to the game manifested itself off the park too, with Zerouali rejecting a contract offer from the Dons in March 2002 and moving on to the United Arab Emirates club Al Nasr that summer.

He saw out his contract in Dubai but in December 2004 the Dons supporters were rocked by the news their idol had been killed in a car accident. The tributes flowed thick and fast but there were no empty sentiments or tired clichés. The despair was genuine for a much loved former player and the pavements outside Pittodrie quickly developed into a shrine to Zerouali. On the anniversary of his death the floral tributes can still be found.

Pre-war appearance records

Hugh Adam
Seasons: 1931-35
Appearances: League 16, Scottish Cup 1
Goals: League 3

Wilfred Adey
Seasons: 1938-39
Appearances: League 26, Scottish Cup 6

Fred Alexander
Seasons: 1921-22
Appearances: League 9

Harry Ambler
Seasons: 1916-17
Appearances: League 32
Goals: League 9

Douglas Anderson
Seasons: 1934-35
Appearances: League 1

George Anderson
Seasons: 1914-22
Appearances: League 205, Scottish Cup 8

William Armstrong
Seasons: 1923-25
Appearances: League 6

Simpson Bainbridge
Seasons: 1921-22
Appearances: League 22, Scottish Cup 7
Goals: League 1, Scottish Cup 1

Robert Ballantyne
Seasons: 1931-32
Appearances: League 11

Ron Barclay
Seasons: 1913-14
Appearances: League 2

Frank Barrett
Seasons: 1903-05
Appearances: League 20, Scottish Cup 1

John Barron
Seasons: 1903-04
Appearances: League 5, Scottish Cup 1
Goals: League 2

Jack Beattie
Seasons: 1931-34
Appearances: League 60, Scottish Cup 3
Goals: League 12, Scottish Cup 1

Jack Benyon
Seasons: 1932-37
Appearances: League 126, Scottish Cup 14
Goals: League 34, Scottish Cup 3

Arthur Biggs
Seasons: 1938-39
Appearances: League 23, Scottish Cup 5
Goals: League 8, Scottish Cup 2

Jimmy Black
Seasons: 1927-32
Appearances: League 155, Scottish Cup 15
Goals: League 4

Robert Blackburn
Seasons: 1908-09
Appearances: League 22, Scottish Cup 2
Goals: League 10, Scottish Cup 1

Harry Blackwell
Seasons: 1921-30
Appearances: League 216, Scottish Cup 36

John Bonnar
Seasons: 1903-04
Appearances: League 4, Scottish Cup 1

Alec Bowie
Seasons: 1924-25
Appearances: League 6
Goals: League 2

Patrick Boyle
Seasons: 1905-07
Appearances: League 52, Scottish Cup 3
Goals: League 2

Tom Brady
Seasons: 1937-39
Appearances: League 27, Scottish Cup 2
Goals: League 9, Scottish Cup 2

Willie Brebner
Seasons: 1904-08
Appearances: League 11, Scottish Cup 4

George Brewster
Seasons: 1912-20
Appearances: League 119
Goals: League 9

Jim Bridges
Seasons: 1905-06
Appearances: League 1

Joe Brown
Seasons: 1935-36
Appearances: League 3, Scottish Cup 1

Duff Bruce
Seasons: 1922-28
Appearances: League 94, Scottish Cup 15

Robert Bruce
Seasons: 1924-28
Appearances: League 94, Scottish Cup 16
Goals: League 36, Scottish Cup 9

Sam Cail
Seasons: 1914-20
Appearances: League 90
Goals: League 18

Charles Calder
Seasons: 1915-17
Appearances: League 37

Edward Carroll
Seasons: 1925-26
Appearances: League 5
Goals: League 1

Charlie Chatwin
Seasons: 1913-16
Appearances: League 45
Goals: League 1

Jacky Connon
Seasons: 1919-24
Appearances: League 93, Scottish Cup 13
Goals: League 22, Scottish Cup 3

Laurie Conwell
Seasons: 1934-35
Appearances: League 6, Scottish Cup 1
Goals: League 1

Mike Cosgrove
Seasons: 1924-28
Appearances: League 65, Scottish Cup 7
Goals: League 5

William Cruickshank
Seasons: 1916-17
Appearances: League 13
Goals: League 1

J. F. Cumming
Seasons: 1915-17
Appearances: League 26
Goals: League 4

Dave Cummings
Seasons: 1930-34
Appearances: League 13

Joe Cunningham
Seasons: 1924-25
Appearances: League 1

Jimmy Dalgarno
Seasons: 1908-09
Appearances: League 5
Goals: League 2

James Daly
Seasons: 1932-33
Appearances: League 4

Norman David
Seasons: 1930-32
Appearances: League 13
Goals: League 7

Joe Devine
Seasons: 1935-38
Appearances: League 14
Goals: League 3

Tommy Devers
Seasons: 1934-36
Appearances: League 11
Goals: League 5

Andrew Dick
Seasons: 1922-24
Appearances: League 11, Scottish Cup 1

Percy Dickie
Seasons: 1929-33
Appearances: League 33, Scottish Cup 4
Goals: League 3

William Dickson
Seasons: 1911-12
Appearances: League 1

Dick Donald
Seasons: 1930-39
Appearances: League 18, Scottish Cup 1
Goals: League 6

Pat Doolan
Seasons: 1925-26
Appearances: League 3, Scottish Cup 1
Goals: League 1, Scottish Cup 1

Martin Dorward
Seasons: 1903-04
Appearances: League 1

Sam Douglas
Seasons: 1911-12
Appearances: League 3

Thomas Drain
Seasons: 1907-08
Appearances: League 7

Tom Dryden
Seasons: 1930-31
Appearances: League 1

Thomas Duff
Seasons: 1916-17
Appearances: League 3

Alf Duggins
Seasons: 1922-23
Appearances: League 2

Johnny Edgar
Seasons: 1904-12
Appearances: League 55, Scottish Cup 5
Goals: League 9, Scottish Cup 1

Jock Edward
Seasons: 1924-28
Appearances: League 87, Scottish Cup 16
Goals: League 3

John Ellis
Seasons: 1904-05
Appearances: League 3
Goals: League 1

George Erskine
Seasons: 1937-38
Appearances: League 3

Eddie Falloon
Seasons: 1927-38
Appearances: League 223, Scottish Cup 26
Goals: League 5

Bert Ferguson
Seasons: 1915-16
Appearances: League 1

Peter Fisher
Seasons: 1920-22
Appearances: League 23
Goals: League 14

Harry Flanaghan
Seasons: 1920-22
Appearances: League 29, Scottish Cup 4
Goals: League 5

Charles Forbes
Seasons: 1923-26
Appearances: League 6

John Ford
Seasons: 1906-07
Appearances: League 6

Matt Forsyth
Seasons: 1920-26
Appearances: League 161, Scottish Cup 24

Bob Fraser
Seasons: 1931-38
Appearances: League 194, Scottish Cup 21
Goals: League 4

Willie Gall
Seasons: 1933-34
Appearances: League 22
Goals: League 3

Tom Gallacher
Seasons: 1915-16
Appearances: League 9

David Galloway
Seasons: 1931-32
Appearances: League 14
Goals: League 1

James Gault
Seasons: 1905-07
Appearances: League 50, Scottish Cup 3

Charlie Gavin
Seasons: 1933-36
Appearances: League 14, Scottish Cup 3

Willie Godfrey
Seasons: 1932-33
Appearances: League 15, Scottish Cup 3

Robert Graham
Seasons: 1938-39
Appearances: League 10

Donald Grant
Seasons: 1938-39
Appearances: League 4
Goals: League 1

Walter Grant
Seasons: 1915-25
Appearances: League 91, Scottish Cup 9
Goals: League 7, Scottish Cup 5

William Green
Seasons: 1913-14
Appearances: League 6

Andy Greig
Seasons: 1911-17
Appearances: League 80, Scottish Cup 7

Sandy Grosert
Seasons: 1920-23
Appearances: League 67, Scottish Cup 8
Goals: League 1

Alex Halkett
Seasons:
Appearances: League 116, Scottish Cup 13
Goals: League 2

Andrew Hamilton
Seasons: 1905-06
Appearances: League 1

John Hannah
Seasons: 1903-04
Appearances: League 1

Bobby Hannah
Seasons: 1910-22
Appearances: League 115, Scottish Cup 11
Goals: League 1

Archie Harper
Seasons: 1909-12
Appearances: League 6

John Harvey
Seasons: 1904-06
Appearances: League 8
Goals: League 2

James Haxton
Seasons: 1906-07
Appearances: League 7
Goals: League 1

Peem Henderson
Seasons: 1905-06
Appearances: League 8

Jimmy Hickie
Seasons: 1929-30
Appearances: League 14
Goals: League 1

Sid Hilton
Seasons: 1905-06
Appearances: League 1

Jock Hume
Seasons: 1907-20
Appearances: League 282, Scottish Cup 23
Goals: League 3

Alex Jackson
Seasons: 1924-25
Appearances: League 34, Scottish Cup 6
Goals: League 8

Jimmy Jackson
Seasons: 1923-25
Appearances: League 67, Scottish Cup 9
Goals: League 2, Scottish Cup 4

T. S. Jackson
Seasons: 1916-17
Appearances: League 10
Goals: League 2

Walter Jackson
Seasons: 1924-26
Appearances: League 47, Scottish Cup 6
Goals: League 18

W. K. Jackson
Seasons: 1924-32
Appearances: League 183, Scottish Cup 23
Goals: League 7, Scottish Cup 1

William Jaffrey
Seasons: 1904-05
Appearances: League 1

Stewart Jamieson
Seasons: 1915-16
Appearances: League 6
Goals: League 2

Bert Johnson
Seasons: 1932-35
Appearances: League 15, Scottish Cup 4
Goals: League 2

W. G. Johnston
Seasons: 1903-05
Appearances: League 22, Scottish Cup 1
Goals: League 6

Pat Kelly
Seasons: 1938-39
Appearances: League 4

Arthur King
Seasons: 1908-13
Appearances: League 71, Scottish Cup

John Knowles
Seasons: 1904-05
Appearances: League 2
Goals: League 1

Johnny Lang
Seasons: 1935-38
Appearances: League 47, Scottish Cup 7
Goals: League 16, Scottish Cup 3

Allan Lawrie
Seasons: 1906-07
Appearances: League 1

Hector Lawson
Seasons: 1926-28
Appearances: League 24, Scottish Cup 1
Goals: League 1

Andy Lees
Seasons: 1920-21
Appearances: League 3

Ned Legge
Seasons: 1928-32
Appearances: League 46, Scottish Cup 4

Duggie Livingstone
Seasons: 1927-30
Appearances: League 76, Scottish Cup 5

Henry Low
Seasons: 1903-07
Appearances: League 95, Scottish Cup 8
Goals: League 19, Scottish Cup 3

Wilfred Low
Seasons: 1904-09
Appearances: League 107, Scottish Cup 12
Goals: League 3

Willie Low
Seasons: 1909-17
Appearances: League 45, Scottish Cup 2

Augustus Lowe
Seasons: 1904-05
Appearances: League 3
Goals: League 6

Willie MacAulay
Seasons: 1903-06
Appearances: League 63, Scottish Cup 6
Goals: League 20, Scottish Cup 1

James McBoyle
Seasons: 1921-24
Appearances: League 12

Alec McCombie
Seasons: 1920-21
Appearances: League 2

John McConnell
Seasons: 1912-13
Appearances: League 19, Scottish Cup 1

Bob McDermid
Seasons: 1925-33
Appearances: League 247, Scottish Cup 27
Goals: League 45, Scottish Cup 4

John McDonald
Seasons: 1906-08
Appearances: League 44, Scottish Cup 7
Goals: League 9, Scottish Cup 1

Kenneth McDonald
Seasons: 1919-21
Appearances: League 23, Scottish Cup 5
Goals: League 5, Scottish Cup 1

Victor McEchern
Seasons: 1907-10
Appearances: League 19
Goals: League 3

George MacFarlane
Seasons: 1908-11
Appearances: League 10, Scottish Cup 3

John MacFarlane
Seasons: 1926-29
Appearances: League 7

Rab MacFarlane
Seasons: 1904-08
Appearances: League 111, Scottish Cup 12

Charlie McGill
Seasons: 1931-38
Appearances: League 218, Scottish Cup 22
Goals: League 1

Frank McGregor
Seasons: 1903-04
Appearances: League 14

Jock McHale
Seasons: 1925-30
Appearances: League 64, Scottish Cup 5
Goals: League 3, Scottish Cup 1

Angus McIntosh
Seasons: 1910-14
Appearances: League 65, Scottish Cup 5
Goals: League 22, Scottish Cup 1

James McIntosh
Seasons: 1907-09
Appearances: League 63, Scottish Cup 8
Goals: League 1

David McKay
Seasons: 1903-04
Appearances: League 15
Goals: League 9

George McKay
Seasons: 1915-17
Appearances: League 12

Hector McKay
Seasons: 1909-10
Appearances: League 2
Goals: League 2

Roddy McKay
Seasons: 1903-05
Appearances: League 2

Daniel MacKenzie
Seasons: 1928-31
Appearances: League 3

George MacKenzie
Seasons: 1909-10
Appearances: League 1

Charlie Mackie
Seasons: 1903-06
Appearances: League 27, Scottish Cup 3
Goals: League 10, Scottish Cup 4

James Mackie
Seasons: 1920-22
Appearances: League 4
Goals: League 2

Jim Mackie
Seasons: 1903-05
Appearances: League 14, Scottish Cup 1
Goals: League 1

Dave McKinlay
Seasons: 1906-08
Appearances: League 18, Scottish Cup 2
Goals: League 5

Bert MacLachlan
Seasons: 1914-27
Appearances: League 315, Scottish Cup 43
Goals: League 16

Fred MacLachlan
Seasons: 1921-22
Appearances: League 6

Hugh McLaren
Seasons: 1928-32
Appearances: League 105, Scottish Cup 10
Goals: League 4, Scottish Cup 1

James McLaughlin
Seasons: 1919-21
Appearances: League 13
Goals: League 2

Adam McLean
Seasons: 1930-33
Appearances: League 74, Scottish Cup 10
Goals: League 24, Scottish Cup 2

Angus McLeod
Seasons: 1913-16
Appearances: League 22
Goals: League 6

Tommy McLeod
Seasons: 1925-31
Appearances: League 44, Scottish Cup 4
Goals: League 4

Willie McLeod
Seasons: 1922-23
Appearances: League 1

Joe McMeekin
Seasons: 1931-32
Appearances: League 5

Lachie McMillan
Seasons: 1930-31
Appearances: League 1, Scottish Cup 2
Goals: League 1, Scottish Cup 1

William McNair
Seasons: 1908-09
Appearances: League 15
Goals: League 3

John McNair
Seasons: 1915-16
Appearances: League 2

Duncan McNicol
Seasons: 1903-05
Appearances: League 34, Scottish Cup 4

George McNicol
Seasons: 1904-06
Appearances: League 26, Scottish Cup 1
Goals: League 14

Allan McRobbie
Seasons: 1915-20
Appearances: League 8

Peter McSevich
Seasons: 1925-28
Appearances: League 34, Scottish Cup 2

Willie McWhinnie
Seasons: 1906-07
Appearances: League 1

Dave Main
Seasons: 1911-17
Appearances: League 150, Scottish Cup 8
Goals: League 54, Scottish Cup 4

Robert Main
Seasons: 1924-25
Appearances: League 2

John Markey
Seasons: 1913-14
Appearances: League 4

James Massie
Seasons: 1919-20
Appearances: League 4

Alex Merrie
Seasons: 1927-31
Appearances: League 32
Goals: League 26

Billy Middleton
Seasons: 1920-23
Appearances: League 110, Scottish Cup 16
Goals: League 7, Scottish Cup 1

James Miller
Seasons: 1909-12
Appearances: League 77, Scottish Cup 7
Goals: League 2

Johnny Miller
Seasons: 1921-27
Appearances: League 109, Scottish Cup 14
Goals: League 54, Scottish Cup 7

Vic Milne
Seasons: 1919-23
Appearances: League 110, Scottish Cup 12
Goals: League 3, Scottish Cup 4

William Milne
Seasons: 1912-13
Appearances: League 18, Scottish Cup 1
Goals: League 9

Rab Mitchell
Seasons: 1916-17
Appearances: League 1

Joseph Moffatt
Seasons: 1909-10
Appearances: League 14
Goals: League 1

Alec Moir
Seasons: 1921-24
Appearances: League 31
Goals: League 2

James Moir
Seasons: 1916-17
Appearances: League 16

Hugh Mooney
Seasons: 1931-33
Appearances: League 15

John Moore
Seasons: 1925-26
Appearances: League 5

Paddy Moore
Seasons: 1932-35
Appearances: League 66, Scottish Cup 8
Goals: League 45, Scottish Cup 2

James Muir
Seasons: 1907-14
Appearances: League 30, Scottish Cup 6
Goals: League 7, Scottish Cup 2

Malcolm Muir
Seasons: 1925-29
Appearances: League 14

Jock Munro
Seasons: 1914-16
Appearances: League 14

Jack Murphy
Seasons: 1903-04
Appearances: League 1

Alex Murray
Seasons: 1916-17
Appearances: League 1

Herbert Murray
Seasons: 1908-14
Appearances: League 47, Scottish Cup 4
Goals: League 5, Scottish Cup 1

Robert Murray
Seasons: 1904-06
Appearances: League 27, Scottish Cup 3

Tom Murray
Seasons: 1907-11
Appearances: League 76, Scottish Cup 7
Goals: League 29, Scottish Cup 6

Allan Mutch
Seasons: 1923-24
Appearances: League 6
Goals: League 1

Cody Mutch
Seasons: 1906-10
Appearances: League 75, Scottish Cup 7

Charlie Neilson
Seasons: 1910-12
Appearances: League 8

John Neilson
Seasons: 1911-12
Appearances: League 1
Goals: League 1

Jack Newlands
Seasons: 1906-07
Appearances: League 1

John Newton
Seasons: 1937-38
Appearances: League 8

Tom Niblo
Seasons: 1908-09
Appearances: League 14, Scottish Cup 2
Goals: League 2, Scottish Cup 1

Sid Nicholson
Seasons: 1937-39
Appearances: League 50, Scottish Cup 10
Goals: League 4, Scottish Cup 1

W. D. Nicol
Seasons: 1909-11
Appearances: League 9, Scottish Cup 2
Goals: League 2, Scottish Cup 5

Charlie O'Hagan
Seasons: 1906-10
Appearances: League 99, Scottish Cup 13
Goals: League 22, Scottish Cup 2

Joe O'Reilly
Seasons: 1932-34
Appearances: League 38, Scottish Cup 3

Tom Owen
Seasons: 1903-04
Appearances: League 2

S. Paterson
Seasons: 1916-17
Appearances: League 1

Willie Paterson
Seasons: 1930-32
Appearances: League 2

John Paton
Seasons: 1915-17
Appearances: League 31
Goals: League 2

John Paton
Seasons: 1923-25
Appearances: League 33, Scottish Cup 7
Goals: League 5, Scottish Cup 1

Jock Pattillo
Seasons: 1938-39
Appearances: League 9, Scottish Cup 5, League Cup 1
Goals: League 11, Scottish Cup 4

Alex Perry
Seasons: 1915-17
Appearances: League 22

Tom Pirie
Seasons: 1924-26
Appearances: League 37, Scottish Cup 15
Goals: League 6, Scottish Cup 11

John Polland
Seasons: 1928-29
Appearances: League 1

Andy Rankine
Seasons: 1920-25
Appearances: League 136, Scottish Cup 22
Goals: League 33, Scottish Cup 5

Alec Reid
Seasons: 1925-27
Appearances: League 68, Scottish Cup 12
Goals: League 21, Scottish Cup 1

Dick Ritchie
Seasons: 1934-38
Appearances: League 9, Scottish Cup 1

George Ritchie
Seasons: 1923-28
Appearances: League 17, Scottish Cup 3

George Ritchie
Seasons: 1904-05
Appearances: League 13, Scottish Cup 4
Goals: League 2, Scottish Cup 1

Jim Ritchie
Seasons: 1920-21
Appearances: League 7

Robert Ritchie
Seasons: 1903-04
Appearances: League 12

Willie Ritchie
Seasons: 1903-04
Appearances: League 3

Alex Robertson
Seasons: 1932-34
Appearances: League 5
Goals: League 1

Arthur Robertson
Seasons: 1913-23
Appearances: League 96, Scottish Cup 7
Goals: League 6

Gowie Robertson
Seasons: 1903-07
Appearances: League 11, Scottish Cup 1

Jack Robertson
Seasons: 1916-17
Appearances: League 1

Jimmy Robertson
Seasons: 1904-07
Appearances: League 54, Scottish Cup 6
Goals: League 3, Scottish Cup 3

Jimmy Robertson
Seasons: 1910-11
Appearances: League 1

James Robey
Seasons: 1937-38
Appearances: League 2, Scottish Cup 2

Ken Ross
Seasons: 1907-08
Appearances: League 1

Willie Ross
Seasons: 1926-28
Appearances: League 18, Scottish Cup 1

Tom Ruddiman
Seasons: 1904-05
Appearances: League 11, Scottish Cup 4
Goals: League 7, Scottish Cup 3

John Sangster
Seasons: 1903-05
Appearances: League 13, Scottish Cup 1
Goals: League 1

John Scorgie
Seasons: 1912-15
Appearances: League 24, Scottish Cup 2
Goals: League 3, Scottish Cup 2

George Scott
Seasons: 1936-39
Appearances: League 23, Scottish Cup 2
Goals: League 2, Scottish Cup 1

Stewart Scott
Seasons: 1909-10
Appearances: League 1

Willie Scott
Seasons: 1935-38
Appearances: League 23, Scottish Cup 1
Goals: League 8

Claud Sharp
Seasons: 1931-32
Appearances: League 3

Alex Shiach
Seasons: 1903-04
Appearances: League 3
Goals: League 1

Bert Shinner
Seasons: 1903-04
Appearances: League 14
Goals: League 6

Bobbie Simpson
Seasons: 1906-10
Appearances: League 86, Scottish Cup 4
Goals: League 29, Scottish Cup 2

J. J. Simpson
Seasons: 1907-08
Appearances: League 1

Peter Sloan
Seasons: 1915-16
Appearances: League 2

Charlie Smith
Seasons: 1937-39
Appearances: League 21, Scottish Cup 3
Goals: League 5, Scottish Cup 2

Jimmy Smith
Seasons: 1922-31
Appearances: League 297, Scottish Cup 39
Goals: League 54, Scottish Cup 10

Richie Smith
Seasons: 1934-38
Appearances: League 50, Scottish Cup 7
Goals: League 16, Scottish Cup 1

Steve Smith
Seasons: 1930-37
Appearances: League 233, Scottish Cup 24

Jimmy Soye
Seasons: 1909-15
Appearances: League 187, Scottish Cup 14
Goals: League 20, Scottish Cup 5

Tom Spalding
Seasons: 1923-24
Appearances: League 1

Sam Spencer
Seasons: 1925-28
Appearances: League 9, Scottish Cup 3

John Spittal
Seasons: 1934-35
Appearances: League 8
Goals: League 1

James Stevenson
Seasons: 1921-22
Appearances: League 2

Tom Strang
Seasons: 1903-07
Appearances: League 91, Scottish Cup 9
Goals: League 2, Scottish Cup 1

Billy Strauss
Seasons: 1936-39
Appearances: League 80, Scottish Cup 14
Goals: League 42, Scottish Cup 11

Colin Strathearn
Seasons: 1916-17
Appearances: League 1

George Sutherland
Seasons: 1920-21
Appearances: League 4

Kenneth Sutherland
Seasons: 1923-25
Appearances: League 3

Eddie Swan
Seasons: 1922-23
Appearances: League 7

Bob Temple
Seasons: 1936-38
Appearances: League 20, Scottish Cup 4

Alex Thomson
Seasons: 1916-17
Appearances: League 11

Daniel Thomson
Seasons: 1923-24
Appearances: League 11
Goals: League 1

Douglas Thomson
Seasons: 1920-23
Appearances: League 95, Scottish Cup 12
Goals: League 27, Scottish Cup 5

George Thomson
Seasons: 1932-39
Appearances: League 213, Scottish Cup 31
Goals: League 16, Scottish Cup 4

Paddy Travers
Seasons: 1910-14
Appearances: League 97, Scottish Cup 7
Goals: League 21, Scottish Cup 3

Duncan Urquhart
Seasons: 1935-37
Appearances: League 5

John Urquhart
Seasons: 1906-07
Appearances: League 3

Joseph Walker
Seasons: 1911-17
Appearances: League 132, Scottish Cup 6
Goals: League 24, Scottish Cup 1

Alf Ward
Seasons: 1905-07
Appearances: League 26, Scottish Cup 1
Goals: League 10

Dave Warnock
Seasons: 1931-39
Appearances: League 133, Scottish Cup 17
Goals: League 39, Scottish Cup 1

Colin Watson
Seasons: 1919-20
Appearances: League 1

Charlie Watt
Seasons: 1920-21
Appearances: League 1

Doug Westland
Seasons: 1934-36
Appearances: League 10, Scottish Cup 2

Jim Westland
Seasons: 1933-35
Appearances: League 3
Goals: League 2

Sam Willox
Seasons: 1903-07
Appearances: League 14

Andrew Wilson
Seasons: 1919-21
Appearances: League 24, Scottish Cup 1
Goals: League 2

George Wilson
Seasons: 1906-14
Appearances: League 182, Scottish Cup 15
Goals: League 12, Scottish Cup 2

John Wilson
Seasons: 1927-29
Appearances: League 14
Goals: League 2

John Wishart
Seasons: 1903-04
Appearances: League 2
Goals: League 1

John Wood
Seasons: 1911-14
Appearances: League 54, Scottish Cup 5
Goals: League 13, Scottish Cup 3

Alex Wright
Seasons: 1913-22
Appearances: League 126, Scottish Cup 17
Goals: League 9, Scottish Cup 2

Jacky Wright
Seasons: 1919-20
Appearances: League 2

Willie Wylie
Seasons: 1913-20
Appearances: League 119, Scottish Cup 3
Goals: League 12

Jock Wyllie
Seasons: 1910-20
Appearances: League 170, Scottish Cup 13
Goals: League 26, Scottish Cup 2

Duncan Yuill
Seasons: 1928-30
Appearances: League 70, Scottish Cup 8

Robert Yule
Seasons: 1919-22
Appearances: League 27, Scottish Cup 2
Goals: League 1